A BASIC GUIDE TO EXPORTING
3rd Edition

World Trade Press

General References

Global Road Warrior
World Trade Almanac
Importers Manual USA
Exporting to the USA
Dictionary of International Trade
Services: The Export of the 21st Century

Country Business Guides

ARGENTINA Business
AUSTRALIA Business
CANADA Business
CHINA Business
HONG KONG Business
JAPAN Business
KOREA Business
MEXICO Business
PHILIPPINES Business
SINGAPORE Business
TAIWAN Business
USA Business

Short Course in International Trade Series

A Short Course in International Negotiating
A Short Course in International Marketing
A Short Course in International Payments
A Short Course in International Contracts
A Short Course in International Trade Documentation
A Short Course in International Business Culture
A Short Course in International Economics
A Short Course in International Marketing Blunders

Passport to the World Series

Passport Hong Kong
Passport China
Passport Japan
Passport Mexico
Passport United Kingdom
Passport Vietnam
Passport Israel
Passport France
Passport USA
Passport Italy
Passport Thailand
Passport India
Passport Germany
Passport Philippines
Passport Spain
Passport Singapore
Passport Taiwan
Passport Korea
Passport Brazil
Passport South Africa
Passport Argentina
Passport Russia
Passport Poland
Passport Indonesia

CD-ROM

Global Road Warrior CD-ROM
World Trade Almanac CD
Importers Manual USA CD
Exporting to the USA CD

A BASIC GUIDE TO EXPORTING
3rd Edition

Alexandra Woznick
U.S. Department of Commerce
World Trade Press

WORLD TRADE PRESS®
Professional Books for International Trade

A Basic Guide to Exporting, 3rd Edition

World Trade Press
1450 Grant Avenue, Suite 204
Novato, California 94945 USA
Tel: +1 (415) 898-1124
Fax: +1 (415) 898-1080
USA Toll-free Order Line: +1 (800) 833-8586
E-mail: worldpress@aol.com
www.worldtradepress.com
wwwglobalroadwarrior.com

Disclaimer

This publication is designed to provide general information concerning exporting from the United States and other issues related to international trade. It is sold with the understanding that the publisher is not engaged in rendering legal or any other professional services. If legal advice or other expert assistance is required, the services of a competent professional should be sought.

Library of Congress Cataloging-in-Publication Data:

Printed in the United States of America

Table of Contents

Introduction

Ten Keys to Export Success

Exports have become an engine of growth for the U.S. economy. U.S. merchandise and service exports account for an increasingly large percentage of the Gross National Product (GNP). Today, many firms export occasionally but want exporting fully integrated into their marketing plans. Others export regularly to one or two markets and want to expand into additional countries.

There is tremendous potential for U.S. business to become more active in exporting. Just 15 percent of U.S. exporters account for 85 percent of the value of U.S.-manufactured exports. The majority of exporters sell in only one foreign market. Only about 20 percent of exporters—less than 3 percent of U.S. companies overall—export to more than five markets.

There is profit to be made by U.S. firms in exports. The international market is more than four times larger than the U.S. market. Growth rates in many overseas markets far outpace domestic market growth. And meeting and beating innovative competitors abroad can help companies keep the edge they need at home.

There are also real costs and risks associated with exporting. It is up to each company to weigh the necessary commitment against the potential benefit.

Ten important recommendations for successful exporting should be kept in mind:

1. Obtain qualified export counseling and develop a master international marketing plan before starting an export business. The plan should clearly define goals, objectives, and problems encountered.
2. Secure a commitment from top management to overcome the initial difficulties and financial requirements of exporting. Although the early delays and costs involved in exporting may seem difficult to justify in comparison with established domestic sales, the exporter should take a long-range view of thi process and carefully monitor international marketing efforts.
3. Take sufficient care in selecting overseas distributors. The complications involved in overseas communications and transportation require international distributors to act more independently than their domestic counterparts.
4. Establish a basis for profitable operations and orderly growth. Although no overseas inquiry should be ignored, the firm that acts mainly in response to unsolicited trade leads is trusting success to the element of chance.
5. Devote continuing attention to export business when the U.S. market booms. Too many companies turn to exporting when business falls off in the United States. When domestic business starts to boom again, they neglect their export trade or relegate it to a secondary position.
6. Treat international distributors on an equal basis with domestic counterparts. Companies often carry out institutional advertising campaigns, special discount offers, sales incentive programs, special credit term programs, warranty offers, and so on in the U.S. market but fail to make similar offers to their international distributors.
7. Do not assume that a given market technique and product will automatically be successful in all countries. What works in Japan may fall flat in Saudi Arabia. Each market has to be treated separately to ensure maximum success.
8. Be willing to modify products to meet regulations or cultural preferences of other countries. Local safety and security codes as well as import restrictions cannot be ignored by foreign distributors.
9. Print service, sale, and warranty messages in locally understood languages. Although a distributor's top management may speak English, it is unlikely that all sales and service personnel have this capability.
10. Provide readily available servicing for the product. A productwithout the necessary service support can acquire a bad reputation quickly.

Using A Basic Guide to Exporting

A Basic Guide to Exporting is designed to help U.S. firms learn the costs and risks associated with exporting and develop a strategy for exporting. The 10 keys to export success that have been mentioned will be explored, along with ways to avoid the pitfalls and roadblocks that may be encountered. Five appendixes are provided for reference: I, Export Glossary; II, Directory of Federal Export Assistance; III, State and Local Sources of Assistance; IV, U.S. and Overseas Contacts for Major Foreign Markets; and V, Selected Bibliography.

This guide discusses what decisions need to be made and where to get the knowledge to make those decisions. You will be directed to sources of assistance throughout the federal and state governments as well as the private sector.

Chapter 1

Export Strategy

Assessing a Product's Export Potential

There are several ways to gauge the overseas market potential of products and services. (For ease of reading, products are mentioned more than services in this guide, but much of the discussion applies to both.) One of the most important ways is to assess the product's success in domestic markets. If a company succeeds at selling in the U.S. market, there is a good chance that it will also be successful in markets abroad, wherever similar needs and conditions exist.

In markets that differ significantly from the U.S. market, some products may have limited potential. Those differences may be climate and environmental factors, social and cultural factors, local availability of raw materials or product alternatives, lower wage costs, lower purchasing power, the availability of foreign exchange (hard currencies like the dollar, the British pound, and the Japanese yen), government import controls, and many other factors. If a product is successful in the United States, one strategy for export success may be a careful analysis of why it sells here, followed by a selection of similar markets abroad. In this way, little or no product modification is required.

If a product is not new or unique, low-cost market research may already be available to help assess its overseas market potential (*refer to* Chapter 3, "Market Research," beginning on page 17 for more information on market research techniques and resources). In addition, international trade statistics, available in many local libraries, can give a preliminary indication of overseas markets for a particular product by showing where similar or related products are already being sold in significant quantities. One of the best sources for U.S. export-import statistics is the National Trade Data Bank (NTDB), which can be accessed at many libraries and U.S. Department of Commerce district offices across the country. The NTDB is also available on CD-ROM or on the Stat-USA web site for a very reasonable price.

If a product is unique or has important features that are hard to duplicate abroad, chances are good for finding an export market. For a unique product, competition may be nonexistent or very slight, while demand may be quite high.

Finally, even if U.S. sales of a product are now declining, sizeable export markets may exist, especially if the product once did well in the United States but is now losing market share to more technically advanced products. Countries that are less developed than the United States may not need state-of-the-art technology and may be unable to afford the most sophisticated and expensive products. Such markets may instead have a surprisingly healthy demand for U.S. products that are older or that are considered obsolete by U.S. market standards.

Making the Export Decision

Once a company determines it has exportable products, it must still consider other factors, such as the following:

- What does the company want to gain from exporting?
- Is exporting consistent with other company goals?
- What demands will exporting place on the company's key resources—management and personnel, production capacity, and finance—and how will these demands be met?
- Are the expected benefits worth the costs, or would company resources be better used for developing new domestic business?

A more detailed list of questions is shown in the table on page 4. Answers to these questions can help a company not only decide whether or not to export but also determine what methods of exporting should be initially used.

The Value of Planning

Many companies begin export activities haphazardly, without carefully screening markets or options for market entry. While these companies may or may not have a measure of success, they may overlook better export opportunities. In the event that early export efforts are unsuccessful because of poor planning, the company may even be misled into abandoning exporting altogether. Formulating an export strategy based on good information and proper assessment increases the chances that the best options will be chosen, that resources will be used effectively, and that efforts will consequently be carried through to completion.

The purposes of the export plan are, first, to assemble facts, constraints, and goals and, second, to create an action statement that takes all of these into account. The statement includes specific objectives; it sets forth time schedules for implementation; and it marks milestones so that the degree of success can be measured and help motivate personnel.

The first draft of the export plan may be quite short and simple, but it should become more detailed and complete as the planners learn more about exporting and their company's competitive position. At least the following ten questions should ultimately be addressed:

1. What products are selected for export development? What modifications, if any, must be made to adapt them for overseas markets?
2. What countries are targeted for sales development?
3. In each country, what is the basic customer profile? What marketing and distribution channels should be used to reach customers?
4. What special challenges pertain to each market (competition, cultural differences, import controls, etc.), and what strategy will be used to address them?
5. How will the product's export sales price be determined?
6. What specific operational steps must be taken and when?
7. What will be the time frame for implementing each element of the plan?
8. What personnel and company resources will be dedicated to exporting?
9. What will be the cost in time and money for each element?
10. How will results be evaluated and used to modify the plan?

One key to developing a successful plan is the participation of all personnel who will be involved in the exporting process. All aspects of an export plan should be agreed upon by those who will ultimately execute them.

A clearly written marketing strategy offers six immediate benefits:

1. Because written plans display their strengths and weaknesses more readily, they are of great help in formulating and polishing an export strategy.
2. Written plans are not as easily forgotten, overlooked, or ignored by those charged with executing them. If deviation from the original plan occurs, it is likely to be due to a deliberate choice to do so.
3. Written plans are easier to communicate to others and are less likely to be misunderstood.
4. Written plans allocate responsibilities and provide for an evaluation of results.
5. Written plans can be of help in seeking financing. They indicate to lenders a serious approach to the export venture.
6. Written plans give management a clear understanding of what will be required and thus help to ensure a commitment to exporting. In fact, a written plan signals that the decision to export has already been made.

This last advantage is especially noteworthy. Building an international business takes time; it is usually months, sometimes even several years, before an exporting company begins to see a return on its investment of time and money. By committing to the specifics of a written plan, top management can make sure that the firm will finish what it begins and that the hopes that prompted its export efforts will be fulfilled.

The Planning Process and the Result

A crucial first step in planning is to develop broad consensus among key management on the company's goals, objectives, capabilities, and constraints. Answering the questions listed in the table on page 4 is one way to start.

The first time an export plan is developed, it should be kept simple. It need be only a few pages long, since important market data and planning elements may not yet be available. The initial planning effort itself gradually generates more information and insight that can be incorporated into more sophisticated planning documents later.

From the start, the plan should be viewed and written as a management tool, not as a static document. For instance, objectives in the plan should be compared with actual results as a measure of the success of different strategies. Furthermore, the company should not hesitate to modify the plan and make it more specific as new information and experience are gained.

A detailed plan is recommended for companies that intend to export directly. Companies choosing indirect export methods may require much simpler plans. An outline of an export plan is presented in the table on page 5.

Approaches to Exporting

The way a company chooses to export its products can have a significant effect on its export plan and specific marketing strategies. The basic distinction among approaches to exporting relates to a company's level of involvement in the export process. There are at least four approaches, which may be used alone or in combination:

1. **Passively filling orders from domestic buyers who then export the product.**
   These sales are indistinguishable from other domestic sales as far as the original seller is concerned. Someone else has decided that the product in question meets foreign demand. That party takes all the risk and handles all of the exporting details, in some cases without even the awareness of the original seller. (Many companies take a stronger interest in exporting when they discover that their product is already being sold overseas.)
2. **Seeking out domestic buyers who represent foreign end users or customers.**
   Many U.S. and foreign corporations, general contractors, foreign trading companies, foreign government agencies, foreign distributors and retailers, and others in the United States purchase for export. These buyers are a large market for a wide variety of goods and services. In this case a company may know its product is being exported, but it is still the buyer who assumes the risk and handles the details of exporting.
3. **Exporting indirectly through intermediaries.**
   With this approach, a company engages the services of an intermediary firm capable of finding foreign markets and buyers for its products. Export management companies (EMCs), export trading companies (ETCs), international trade consultants, and other intermediaries can give the exporter access to well-established expertise and trade contacts. Yet, the exporter can still retain considerable control over the process and can realize some of the other benefits of exporting, such as learning more about foreign competitors, new technologies, and other market opportunities.
4. **Exporting directly.**
   This approach is the most ambitious and difficult, since the exporter personally handles every aspect of the exporting process from market research and planning to foreign distribution and collections. Consequently, a significant commitment of management time and attention is required to achieve good results. However, this approach may also be the best way to achieve maximum profits and long-term growth. With appropriate help and guidance from the Department of Commerce, state trade offices, freight forwarders, international banks, and other service groups, even small or medium-sized firms, can export directly if they are able to commit enough staff time to the effort. For those who cannot make that commitment, the services of an EMC, ETC, trade consultant, or other qualified intermediary are indispensable.

Approaches number 1 and 2 represent a substantial proportion of total U.S. sales, perhaps as much as 30 percent of U.S. exports. They do not, however, involve the firm in the export process. Consequently, this guide concentrates on approaches three and 4. There is no single source or special channel for identifying domestic buyers for overseas markets. In general, they may be found through the same means that U.S. buyers are found, for example, trade shows, mailing lists, industry directories, and trade associations.

If the nature of the company's goals and resources makes an indirect method of exporting the best choice, little further planning may be needed. In such a case, the main task is to find a suitable intermediary firm that can then handle most export details. Firms that are new to exporting or are unable to commit staff and funds to more complex export activities may find indirect methods of exporting more appropriate.

Using an EMC or other intermediary, however, does not exclude all possibility of direct exporting for the firm. For example, a U.S. company may try exporting directly to such "easy" nearby markets as Canada, Mexico, or the Bahamas while letting its EMC handle more ambitious sales to Egypt or Japan. An exporter may also choose to gradually increase its level of direct exporting later, after experience has been gained and sales volume appears to justify added investment.

For more information on different approaches to exporting and their advantages and disadvantages, *refer to* Chapter 4, "Methods of Exporting and Channels of Distribution," beginning on page 25. Consulting advisers before making these decisions can be helpful. The next chapter presents information on a variety of organizations that can provide this type of help—in many cases, at no cost.

Table 1-1: Management Issues Involved in the Export Decision

Management objectives

- What are the company's reasons for pursuing export markets? Are they solid objectives (e.g., increasing sales volume or developing a broader, more stable customer base) or are they frivolous (e.g., the owner wants an excuse to travel)?
- How committed is top management to an export effort? Is exporting viewed as a quick fix for a slump in domestic sales? Will the company neglect its export customers if domestic sales pick up?
- What are management's expectations for the export effort? How quickly does management expect export operations to become self-sustaining? What level of return on investment is expected from the export program?

Experience

- With what countries has business already been conducted, or from what countries have inquiries already been received?
- Which product lines are mentioned most often?
- Are any domestic customers buying the product for sale or shipment overseas? If so, to what countries?
- Is the trend of sales and inquiries up or down?
- Who are the main domestic and foreign competitors?
- What general and specific lessons have been learned from past export attempts or experiences?

Management and personnel

- What in-house international expertise does the firm have (international sales experience, language capabilities, etc.)?
- Who will be responsible for the export department's organization and staff?
- How much senior management time (a) should be allocated and (b) could be allocated?
- What organizational structure is required to ensure that export sales are adequately serviced?
- Who will follow through after the planning is done?

Production capacity

- How is the present capacity being used?
- Will filling export orders hurt domestic sales?
- What will be the cost of additional production?
- Are there fluctuations in the annual work load? When? Why?
- What minimum order quantity is required?
- What would be required to design and package products specifically for export?

Financial capacity

- What amount of capital can be committed to export production and marketing?
- What level of export department operating costs can be supported?
- How are the initial expenses of export efforts to be allocated?
- What other new development plans are in the works that may compete with export plans?
- By what date must an export effort pay for itself?

Table 1-2: Sample Outline for an Export Plan

Table of Contents

Executive Summary (one or two pages maximum)

Introduction: Why This Company Should Export

Part I—Export Policy Commitment Statement

Part II—Situation/Background Analysis

- Product or Service
- Operations
- Personnel and Export Organization
- Resources of the Firm
- Industry Structure, Competition, and Demand

Part III—Marketing Component

- Identifying, Evaluating, and Selecting Target Markets
- Product Selection and Pricing
- Distribution Methods
- Terms and Conditions
- Internal Organization and Procedures
- Sales Goals: Profit and Loss Forecasts

Part IV—Tactics: Action Steps

- Primary Target Countries
- Secondary Target Countries
- Indirect Marketing Efforts

Part V—Export Budget

- Pro Forma Financial Statements

Part VI—Implementation Schedule

- Follow-up
- Periodic Operational and Management Review (Measuring Results Against Plan)

Addenda: Background Data on Target Countries and Market

- Basic Market Statistics: Historical and Projected
- Background Facts
- Competitive Environment

Chapter 2

Export Advice

For companies making initial plans to export or to export in new areas, considerable advice and assistance are available at little or no cost. It is easy, through lack of experience, to overestimate the problems involved in exporting or to get embroiled in difficulties that can be avoided. For these and other good reasons, it is important to get expert counseling and assistance from the beginning.

This chapter gives a brief overview of sources of assistance available through federal, state, and local government agencies and in the private sector. Other chapters in this guide give more information on the specialized services of these organizations and how to use them. Information on where to find these organizations can be found in the appendices.

Some readers may feel overwhelmed at first by the number of sources of advice available. Although it is not necessary to go to all of these resources, it is valuable to know at least a little about each of them and to get to know several personally. Each individual or organization contacted can contribute different perspectives based on different experience and skills.

While having many sources to choose from can be advantageous, deciding where to begin can also be difficult. Some advice from experienced exporters may be helpful in this regard. Recognizing this point, President George Bush created the Trade Promotion Coordinating Committee (TPCC) and charged it with harnessing all the resources of the federal government to serve American exporting business. The TPCC conducts export conferences, coordinates trade events and missions that cross-cut federal agencies, and operates an export information center that can help exporters find the right federal program to suit their needs. For more information, call the Trade Information Center at (800) USA-TRADE).

In general, however, the best place to start is the nearest U.S. Department of Commerce Export Assistance Center or district office, which can not only provide export counseling in its own right but also direct companies toward other government and private sector export services.

Department of Commerce

The scope of services provided by the Department of Commerce (DOC) to exporters is vast, but it is often overlooked by many companies. Most of the information and programs of interest to U.S. exporters are concentrated in the department's International Trade Administration (ITA), of which the subdivision called the U.S. and Foreign Commercial Service (US&FCS) maintains a network of international trade specialists in the United States and commercial officers in foreign cities to help American companies do business abroad. By contacting the nearest DOC Export Assistance Center or district office, the U.S. exporter can tap into all assistance programs available from ITA and all trade information gathered by U.S. embassies and consulates worldwide. Addresses and phone numbers for all Export Assistance Centers and district offices, listed by state, are given in Appendix III, "State and Local Sources of Assistance," beginning on page 130. The following sections detail the kinds of assistance offered.

Export Assistance Available in the United States

Department of Commerce Offices

The Commerce Department has undergone some reorganization in recent years, most notably through its U.S. Export Assistance Centers. USEACs offer a full range of federal export programs and services under one roof. Clients receive assistance by professionals from the SBA, the Department of Commerce, the Export-Import Bank, and other public and private organizations. Each USEAC provides export marketing and trade finance assistance, customized counseling, and customer service. Fifteen USEACs opened in 1994 and 1995; they are located in Atlanta, Baltimore, Boston, Chicago, Cleveland, Dallas, Denver, Detroit, Miami, Los Angeles (Long Beach), Seattle, St. Louis, New Orleans, New York, and Philadelphia.

Other Department of Commerce Export Assistance Centers, district, and branch offices in cities throughout the United States and Puerto Rico can also provide information and professional export counseling to business people. Each district office is headed by a director and supported by trade specialists and other staff. Branch offices usually consist of one trade specialist. These professionals can counsel companies on the steps involved in exporting, help them assess the export potential of their products, target markets, and locate and check out potential overseas partners. In fact, because Commerce has a worldwide network of international business experts, district offices can answer almost any question exporters are likely to ask—or put them in touch with someone who can.

Each district office can offer information about

- international trade opportunities abroad,
- foreign markets for U.S. products and services,
- services to locate and evaluate overseas buyers and representatives,
- financial aid to exporters,
- international trade exhibitions,
- export documentation requirements,
- foreign economic statistics,
- U.S. export licensing and foreign nation import requirements, and
- export seminars and conferences.

Most DOC offices also maintain business libraries containing Commerce's latest reports as well as other publications of interest to U.S. exporters. Important data bases that provide trade leads, foreign business contacts, in-depth country market research, export-import trade statistics, and other valuable information, are often available at these offices. The National Trade Data Bank (NTDB) is the best-known of these data bases.

District Export Councils

Besides the immediate services of its own offices, the Department of Commerce gives the exporter direct contact with seasoned exporters experienced in all phases of export trade. Commerce Department offices work closely with district export councils (DECs) in every state, comprising hundreds of business and trade experts who volunteer to help U.S. firms develop solid export strategies.

These DECs assist in many of the workshops and seminars on exporting arranged by the district offices or they may sponsor their own. DEC members may also provide direct, personal counseling to less experienced exporters, suggesting marketing strategies, trade contacts, and ways to maximize success in overseas markets.

Assistance from DECs may be obtained through the local Department of Commerce offices with which they are affiliated.

Export Seminars and Educational Programming

In addition to individual counseling sessions, an effective method of informing local business communities of the various aspects of international trade is through the conference and seminar program. Each year, Commerce district offices conduct several thousand conferences, seminars, and workshops on topics such as export documentation and licensing procedures, country-specific market opportunities, export trading companies, and U.S. trade promotion and trade policy initiatives. The seminars are usually held in conjunction with DECs, local chambers of commerce, state agencies, and world trade clubs. For information on scheduled seminars across the country, or for educational programming assistance, contact the nearest district office.

Assistance Available From DOC Specialists in Washington, D.C.

Among the most valuable resources available to U.S. exporters are the hundreds of trade specialists, expert in various areas of international business, that the Department of Commerce has assembled in its Washington headquarters.

Country counseling. Every country in the world is assigned to an individual country desk officer or a regional office, such as the Asia Business Center. These desk officers and regional offices in Commerce's International Economic Policy (IEP) area look at the needs of an individual U.S. firm wishing to sell in a particular country, taking into account that country's overall economy, trade policies, political situation, and other relevant factors. Each desk officer and regional office collects up-to-date information on the country's trade regulations, tariffs and value-added taxes, business practices, economic and political developments, trade data and trends, market size and growth, and so on. Desk officers also participate in preparing Commerce's country-specific market research reports, available from the U.S. Government Printing Office, through the NTDB, and on the World Wide Web. The value of IEP's market data may be gauged from the fact that this agency develops much of the country-specific background for negotiating positions of the U.S. Trade Representative.

Individual country desk information questions should go to the Trade Information Center, Tel: (800) USA-TRADE; Fax: (202) 482-4473. For a complete list of country desk officers and regional offices, *see* "Department of Commerce International Economic Policy Division" on page 125. A partial list follows:

Africa
Tel: (202) 482-4925; Fax: (202) 482-6083

Office of Near East
Tel: (202) 482-1860; Fax: (202) 482-0878
Web site: www.mac.doc.gov/tcc

Asia and Pacific
Tel: (202) 482-0543; Fax: (202) 482-4473

Asia Business Center (ABC)
Asia Business Center (ABC) has been absorbed by the Trade Information Center, Tel: (800) USA-Trade; Fax: (202) 482-4473

Europe
Tel: (202) 482-5638; Fax: (202) 482-4098

Business Information Service for the Newly Independent States (BISNIS)
Tel: (202) 482-4655; Fax: (202) 482-2293
Web site: www.mac.doc.gov/bisnis.html

Central and Eastern Europe Business Information Center (CEEBIC)
Tel: (202) 482-2645; Fax: (202) 501-0787
Email: ceebic@usita.gov
Web site: www.mac.doc.gov/eebic/ceebic.html

Japan
Tel: (202) 482-2427; Fax: (202) 482-0469

Western Hemisphere
Tel: (202) 482-5324; Fax: (202) 482-4736

Office of NAFTA
Tel: (202) 482-0305; Fax: (202) 482-4473; Email: tic@ita.doc.gov
Web site: www.itaiep.doc.gov

Product and service sector counseling. Complementing IEP's country desks are the industry desk officers of Commerce's Trade Development area. They are grouped in units:

Technology and Aerospace Industries
Tel: (202)482-1872; Fax: (202) 482-0856; Web site: www.ita.doc.gov

Office of Aerospace
Tel: (202) 482-1228; Fax: (202) 482-3113; Web site: www.ita.doc.gov/aerospace

Office of Computers and Business Equipment
Tel: (202) 482-0571; Fax: (202) 482-0952; Web site: http://infoserv2.ita.doc.gov/ocbe/ocbehome.nsf

Office of Microelectronics, Medical Equipment and Instrumentation
Tel: (202) 482-2470; Fax: (202) 482-0975; Web site: www.ita.doc.gov/ommi

Office of Telecommunications
Tel: (202) 482-4466; Fax: (202) 482-5834
Web site: http://infoserv2.ita.doc.gov

Basic Industries
Tel: (202) 482-0614; Fax: (202) 482-5666; Web site: www.ita.doc.gov/bi

Office of Automotive Affairs
Tel: (202) 482-0554; Fax: (202) 482-0674; Web site: www.ita.doc.gov/auto

Office of Metals, Materials, and Chemicals
Tel: (202) 482-0575; Fax: (202) 482-0378; Web site: www.ita.doc.gov/ommc

Office of Energy and Infrastructure
Tel: (202) 482-1466; Fax: (202) 482-0170; Web site: www.ita.doc.gov/oeim

Environmental Technologies Exports
Tel: (202) 482-5225; Fax: (202) 482-5665; Web site: http://infoserv2.ita.doc.gov/ete

Services Industries and Finance
Tel: (202) 482-5261; Fax: (202) 482-4775; Web site: www.ita.doc.gov/sif/

Office of Export Trading Company Affairs
Tel: (202) 482-5131; Fax: (202) 482-4654; Web site: www.ita.doc.gov/oetca

Office of Finance
Tel: (202) 482-3277; Fax: (202) 482-5702; Web site: www.ita.doc.gov

Office of Service Industries
Tel: (202) 482-3575; Fax: (202) 482-2669; Web site: www.ita.doc.gov/sif

Textiles, Apparel and Consumer Goods Industries
Tel: (202) 482-3737; Fax: (202) 482-2331; Web site: http://otexa.ita.doc.gov

Office of Textiles and Apparel
Tel: (202) 482-5078; Fax: (202) 482-2331; Web site: http://otexa.ita.doc.gov

Office of Consumer Goods
Tel: (202) 482-0337; Fax: (202) 482-3981; Web site: www.ita.doc.gov/ocg

The industry desk officers participate in preparing reports on the competitive strength of selected U.S. industries in domestic and international markets. They also promote exports for their industry sectors through marketing seminars, trade fairs, foreign buyer groups, business counseling, and information on market opportunities.

If you are interested in exporting agricultural products, contact the Foreign Agricultural Service, Trade Assistance and Promotion Office (TAPO); Tel: (202) 720-7420; Fax: (202) 205-9728; Web site: www.gas.usda.gov. *See* "Department of Agriculture" on page 12 for more information on USDA assistance.

Other assistance. Rounding out the Trade Development area is a unit that cuts across industry sector issues. The Office of Trade and Economic Analysis in the International Trade Administration gathers, analyzes, and disseminates trade and investment data for use in trade promotion and policy formulation. It also includes specialists in technical areas of international trade finance, such as countertrade and barter, foreign sales corporations, export financing, and the activities of multilateral development banks. For more information, contact the nearest Department of Commerce office or call

Office of Trade and Economic Analysis
Tel: (202) 482-5145; Fax: (202) 482-4614
Web site: www.ita.doc.gov/tradestats

Export Marketing Information and Assistance Available Overseas

US&FCS Overseas Posts

Much of the information about trends and actual trade leads in foreign countries is gathered on site by the commercial officers of the US&FCS. About half of the US&FCS American officers working in nearly 70 countries have been hired from the private sector, many with international trade experience. All understand firsthand the problems encountered by U.S. companies in their efforts to trade abroad.

In addition, a valued asset of the US&FCS is a group of about 500 foreign nationals, usually natives of the foreign country, who are employed in the U.S. embassy or consulate and bring with them a wealth of personal understanding of local market conditions and business practices. The US&FCS staff overseas provides a range of services to help companies sell abroad: background information on foreign companies, agency-finding services, market research, business counselling, assistance in making appointments with key buyers and government officials, and representations on behalf of companies adversely affected by trade barriers. (Some of the more important services are described fully in Chapter 7, "Making Contacts," beginning on page 39.)

U.S. exporters usually tap into these services by contacting their local Department of Commerce office. While exporters are strongly urged to contact their district office before going overseas, U.S. business travelers abroad may also contact U.S. embassies and consulates directly for help during their trips. District offices can provide business travel facilitation assistance before departure by arranging advance appointments with embassy personnel, market briefings, and other assistance in cities to be visited.

US&FCS posts also cooperate with overseas representatives of individual states. Many states have such representation in some overseas markets, and their efforts are closely coordinated with the resources of the US&FCS.

Other Commerce Export Services

Besides ITA, a number of other Department of Commerce agencies offer export services.

Bureau of Export Administration

The under secretary for export administration is responsible for U.S. export controls. (*Refer to* Chapter 11, "Export Regulations, Customs Benefits, and Tax Incentives," beginning on page 60, for more information.) Assistance in complying with export controls can be obtained directly from local district offices or from the Exporter Counseling Division, Bureau of Export Administration (BXA) Office of Exporter Services. BXA also has two field offices that specialize in counseling on export controls and regulations: the Western Regional Office, and the Northern California Branch Office.

Some Bureau of Export Administration contacts follow. For a more complete list of BXA offices, *see* "Bureau of Export Administration" on page 121.

BXA, Office of Exporter Services
Tel: (202) 482-0436; Fax: (202) 482-3322; Web site: www.bxa.doc.gov

Exporter Counseling Division
Tel: (202) 482-4811; Fax: (202) 482-3617

Export Seminar Division
Tel: (202) 482-6031; Fax: (202) 482-2927

Regulatory Policy Division
Tel: (202) 482-2240; Fax: (202) 482-3355

Compliance & Special Licenses Division
Tel. (202) 482-0062; Fax: (202) 501-6750

BXA Western Regional Office, Orange County, CA
Tel: (949) 660-0144; Fax: (949) 660-9347; Web site: www.primenet.com/~bxawest

BXA N. Calif. Branch Office, Santa Clara County, CA
Tel: (408) 998-7402

Trade Adjustment Assistance

Trade Adjustment Assistance, part of Commerce's Economic Development Administration, helps firms that have been adversely affected by imported products to adjust to international competition. Companies eligible for trade adjustment assistance may receive technical consulting to upgrade operations such as product engineering, marketing, information systems, export promotion, and energy management. The federal government may assume up to 75 percent of the cost of these services. For more information, contact Trade Adjustment Assistance at (202) 482-2127; Fax: (202) 482-0466; Web site: www.doc.gov/eda/

Foreign Requirements for U.S. Products and Services

The National Center for Standards and Certification Information (NCSCI), established in 1965, provides information on U.S., foreign, and international voluntary standards; government regulations; and rules of conformity assessment for non-agricultural products. The Center serves as a referral service and focal point in the United States for information about standards and standards-related information.

NCSCI staff respond to inquiries, maintain a reference collection of standards and standards-related documents, and serve as the U.S. inquiry point for information to and from foreign countries.

For information about foreign standards and certification systems, contact

NCSCI
National Institute of Standards and Technology (NIST)
100 Bureau Dr., Stop 2150
Gaithersburg, MD 20899-2150
Tel: (301) 975-4040, 975-4038, 975-4036, 975-5155
Technical assistance: Tel: (301) 975-4033
Fax: (301) 926-1559; Web site: www.nist.gov/ts

NIST maintains a GATT/WTO (General Agreement on Tariffs and Trade/World Trade Organization) hotline at Tel: (301) 975-4041 with a recording that reports on the latest notifications of proposed foreign regulations that may affect trade. A second hotline for EU (European Union) standards is Tel: (301) 921-4164. Exporters can also get information from the nongovernmental American National Standards Institute (ANSI) at Tel: (212) 642-4900; Fax: (212) 302-1286; Email: info@ansi.org; Web site: www.ansi.org.

Foreign Metric Regulations

The Metric Program at NIST provides exporters with guidance and assistance on matters relating to U.S. transition to the metric system. It can also give referrals to metric contacts in state governments. For more information, contact

The Metric Program
Tel: (301) 975-3690; Fax: (301) 948-1416
Email: metric_prg@nist.gov
Web site: www.nist.gov/metric.

Minority Business Development Agency (MBDA)

The MBDA identifies minority business enterprises (MBEs) in selected industries to increase their awareness of their relative size and product advantages and to aggressively take them through the advanced stages of market development.

Through an interagency agreement with the ITA, MBDA provides information on market and product needs worldwide. MBDA and ITA coordinate MBE participation in Matchmaker and other trade delegations.

MBDA provides counseling through the Minority Business Development Center network to help MBEs prepare international marketing plans and promotional materials and to identify financial resources.

For general export information, the field organizations of both MBDA and ITA provide information kits and information on local seminars.

Minority Business Development Agency
Office of Program Development
U.S. Department of Commerce
Washington, DC 20230
Tel: (202) 482-5061; Fax: (202) 501-4698; Web site: www.mbda.gov

Fishery Products Exports

The National Oceanic and Atmospheric Administration (NOAA) assists seafood exporters by facilitating access to foreign markets. NOAA's National Marine Fisheries Service (NFMS) provides inspection services for fishery exports and issues official U.S. government certification attesting to the findings.

Office of Industry and Trade
National Marine Fisheries Service
1315 East-West Highway, Building 3, Room 3670
Silver Spring, MD 20910
Tel: (301) 713-2379; Fax: (301) 713-2384; Web site: www.nmfs.gov

Inspection Services Division
Tel: (301) 713-2355; Fax: (301) 713-1081.

Bureau of the Census

The Bureau of the Census is the primary source of trade statistics that break down the quantity and dollar value of U.S. exports and imports by commodity (product) and country. Commerce district offices can help retrieve Census export statistics for exporters who want to identify potential export markets for their products. Firms interested in more extensive statistical data can contact the Bureau of the Census at the numbers given below.

Census Customer Services
Tel: (301) 457-4100; Fax: (301) 457-4714 (General info), (301) 457-3842 (Orders only); Web site: www. census. gov

Foreign Trade Information
Tel: (301) 457-3041; Fax: (301) 457-1158; Web site: www.census.gov/foreign-trade/www/

Bureau of Export Administration
Tel: (202) 482-2721; Web site: www.bxa.doc.gov

Shippers' export declarations assistance
Tel: (301) 457-2238; Fax: (301) 457-3765

Department of State

The Department of State has a diverse staff capable of providing U.S. exporters with trade contacts. These staff members include bureau commercial coordinators, country desk officers, policy officers in the functional bureaus (such as the Bureau of Economic and Business Affairs), and all U.S. embassies and consular posts abroad. The Department of State provides commercial services in some countries and regions without US&FCS offices. Their addresses and telephone numbers are published in the directory titled *Key Officers of Foreign Service Posts,* available from the U.S. Government Printing Office (Tel: (202) 512-1800; Fax: (202) 512-2250; Web site: www.access.gpo.gov/su_docs; Price: $5.50).

The ambassador takes the lead in promoting U.S. trade and investment interests in every U.S. embassy. All members of U.S. diplomatic missions abroad have the following continuing obligations:

- To ascertain the views of the American business sector on foreign policy issues that affect its interests, in order to ensure that those views are fully considered in the development of policy.
- To seek to ensure that the ground rules for conducting international trade are fair and nondiscriminatory.
- To be responsive when U.S. firms seek assistance, providing them with professional advice and analysis as well as assistance in making and developing contacts abroad.
- To vigorously encourage and promote the export of U.S. goods, services, and agricultural commodities and represent the interests of U.S. business to foreign governments where appropriate.
- To assist U.S. business in settling investment disputes with foreign governments amicably and, in cases of expropriation or similar action, to obtain prompt, adequate, and effective compensation.

The State Department can be reached at Tel: (202) 647-4000 or on the internet at www.state.gov.

Publications. The State Department has a number of publications which may be of interest to exporters. *Country Commercial Guides*, which offer a wealth of practical information on over 100 countries. The State Department also publishes *Background Notes,* pamphlets on nearly every country in the world. These are updated irregularly. Both are available on the NTDB, on the State Department's web site (in the DOSFAN archives) and through NTIS or the Government Printing Office.

Bureau of Economic and Business Affairs

The Bureau of Economic and Business Affairs has primary responsibility within the Department of State for (1) formulating and implementing policies regarding foreign economic matters, trade promotion, and business services of an international nature and (2) coordinating regional economic policy with other bureaus. The bureau is divided into five units or deputates: communications; energy, resources and sanctions; finance and investment; trade; and transportation (aviation and maritime). The five deputy assistant secretaries who lead these units develop U.S. policy, administer programs, negotiate, and represent the Department before Congress, U.S. business and industry, and international organizations.

Office of the Coordinator for Business Affairs
Bureau of Economic and Business Affairs
Tel: (202) 647-1625; Fax (202) 643-3953

Regional bureaus

Regional bureaus, each under the direction of an assistant secretary of state, are responsible for U.S. foreign affairs activities in specific major regions of the world. Bureau economic policy staff can be reached at the following numbers:

Bureau of African Affairs
Tel: (202) 647-7371; Fax: (202) 736-4872

Bureau of East Asian and Pacific Affairs
Tel: (202) 647-9596; Fax: (202) 647-0136

Bureau of European Regional Affairs
Tel: (202) 647-9826; Fax: (202) 647-9959

Bureau of Near East Affairs
Tel: (202) 647-3487; Fax: (202) 736-4465

Bureau of Western Hemisphere Affairs
Tel: (202) 647-1232; Fax: (202) 736-7618

Bureau of South Asian Affairs
Tel: (202) 736-4255; Fax: (202) 736-4259

Country desk officers within the bureaus maintain day-to-day contact with overseas diplomatic posts and provide country-specific economic and political analysis and commercial counseling to U.S. business.

Cooperation between State and Commerce

The Departments of State and Commerce provide many services to U.S. business jointly. Firms interested in establishing a market for their products or expanding sales abroad should first seek assistance from their nearest Department of Commerce Export Assistance Center or district office, which can tap into the worldwide network of State and Commerce officials serving in U.S. missions abroad and in Washington.

Small Business Administration

The Small Business Administration (SBA) coordinates its international trade programs and services with other federal agencies through the Trade Promotion Coordinating Committee (TPCC). SBA's Office of International Trade (OIT) encourages small business exports and assists small businesses seeking to export. SBA/OIT helps small firms finance their export sales through the Export Working Capital Program, through which SBA provides a 75 percent guarantee on private-sector loans. SBA/OIT also works with SBA's resource partners to provide individual counseling to small business concerns to assess the feasibility of their export marketing plans and to determine and obtain necessary data to help package loan applications. Training and technical assistance is often available to new-to-export small companies.

These programs are provided through more than 100 field offices in cities throughout the United States. (*Refer to* Appendix III, "State and Local Sources of Assistance," beginning on page 130, for addresses and telephone numbers.) The no-cost development assistance services include the following:

- ***Export Legal Assistance Network (ELAN).*** Through an arrangement with the Federal Bar Association (FBA), exporters may receive initial export legal assistance. Under this program, qualified attorneys from the International Law Council of the FBA, working through SBA field offices, provide free initial consultations to small companies on the legal aspects of exporting.
- ***Export training.*** SBA field offices cosponsor export training programs with the Department of Commerce, other federal agencies, and various private sector international trade organizations. These programs are conducted by experienced international traders.
- ***Counseling.*** Counseling is available through the Small Business Institutes (SBIs), Small Business Development Centers (SBDCs) and through the Service Corps of Retired Executives (SCORE). The SBIs and SBDCs can provide services such as financial guidance, marketing, production, organizational development, engineering and feasibility studies. Some SBDCs have designated international trade centers, although all provide export counselling, referrals, and/or training. Members of SCORE with practical experience in international trade help small firms evaluate their export potential and strengthen their domestic operations by identifying financial, managerial, or technical problems. These advisers also can help small firms develop and implement basic export marketing plans, which show where and how to sell goods abroad.
- ***SBAtlas.*** SBA's Automated Trade Locator Assistance System (SBAtlas) can help you select the best markets for your product or service through either product-specific or country-specific reports.
- ***Research Strategic Venture Partners (RSVP)*** is an online system for matching U.S. small businesses with potential international joint venture partners. It is available through SBA Online at www.sbaonline.sba.gov.

A description of SBA loan programs may be found in Chapter 14, under "Small Business Administration Assistance" on page 104. For information on any of the programs funded by SBA, contact the nearest SBA district office, call the SBA Answer Desk at Tel: (800) 8-ASK-SBA, or go to the SBA web site on the Internet at www.sba.gov. For a list of SBA offices, *refer to* Appendix III, "State and Local Sources of Assistance," beginning on page 130.

Department of Agriculture

The U.S. Department of Agriculture (USDA) export promotion efforts are centered in the Foreign Agricultural Service (FAS), whose marketing programs are discussed in Chapter 7 in "Department of Agriculture Foreign Agricultural Service" on page 43. However, other USDA agencies also offer services to U.S. exporters of agricultural products: the Economic Research Service, the Animal and Plant Health Inspection Service, the Food Safety and Inspection Service, and the Federal Grain Inspection Service. A wide variety of other valuable programs is offered, such as promotion of U.S. farm products in foreign markets; services of commodity and marketing specialists in Washington, D.C.; trade fair exhibits; publications and information services; and financing programs. For more information on programs contact the director of

AgExport Services Division
Foreign Agricultural Service
U.S. Department of Agriculture
Washington, DC 20250
Tel: (202) 720-6343; Fax: (202) 690-0193; Web site: www.fas.usda.gov

To contact other USDA offices mentioned above:

Animal and Plant Health Inspection Service (APHIS)

Animal Exports
Tel: (301) 734-3277; Fax: (301)734-8226

Animal Products Exports
Tel: (301) 734-8364; Fax: (301) 734-6402

Plant Exports (Phytosanitary Certificates)
Tel: (301) 734-8537; Fax: (301) 734-5007

Federal Grain Inspection Service
Tel: (202) 720-5091 (Public Affairs and Information); Fax: (202) 205-9237

Economic Research Service
Tel: (202) 694-5000; Fax: (202) 694-5103

Food Safety and Inspection Service (FSIS)
Tel: (202) 720-7025; Fax: (202) 690-0550

Foreign Agricultural Service (FAS)
Tel: (202) 720-7115; Fax: (202) 720-1727
Web site: www.fas.usda.gov

U.S. Trade Assistance and Promotion Office (TAPO)

The Trade Assistance and Promotion Office of the Foreign Agricultural Service (FAS) serves as the first point of contact for persons who need information on foreign markets for agricultural products. The TAPO staff can provide basic export counseling and direct you to the appropriate USDA offices to answer your specific technical questions on exporting. In addition, the staff can provide country and commodity specific *Foreign Market Information Reports*, which focus on best market prospects and contain contact information on distributors and importers. Extensive information on the Foreign Agricultural Service is also available through the FAS home page on Internet (http://ffas.usda.gov/ffas).

Trade Assistance and Promotion Office (TAPO)
Tel: (202) 720-7420; Fax (202) 205-9728; Web site: www.fas.usda.gov

Agriculture Trade and Marketing Information Center

The Agriculture Trade and Marketing Information Center has ceased operations.

Economic Research Service (ERS)

ERS provides in-depth economic analysis on agricultural economies, trade policies of foreign countries, world agricultural trade and development issues, and on their linkages with the U.S. food and fiber economy. ERS analyses show how factors influencing demand (population, income, and tastes), production variables (inputs and technology), foreign governments' domestic and trade policies and programs (price controls, environmental and food safety laws, and tariffs), macroeconomic conditions (exchange rates and debt), and major events (breakup of the former USSR), affect countries' agricultural production, consumption, and trade; international food and fiber prices; and U.S. food and fiber competitiveness. ERS widely disseminates information and analyses on international agricultural trade and food aid and development through regional and commodity reports, bulletins and updates, periodicals, and electronic databases.

Economic Research Service (ERS)
Tel: (202) 694-5000; Fax: (202) 694-5103

The Foreign Market Development Program

The Foreign Market Development Program, also known as the cooperator program, is administered by the Foreign Agricultural Service of the U.S. Department of Agriculture. The goal of the program is to develop, maintain, and expand long-term export markets for U.S. agricultural products.

Created 40 years ago, the program fosters a trade promotion partnership between USDA and U.S. agricultural producers and processors who are represented by nonprofit commodity or trade associations called cooperators. Under this partnership, USDA and the cooperators pool their technical and financial resources to conduct market development activities outside the United States.

Participants in the program include approximately 40 groups representing specific U.S. commodity sectors, such as feed grains, wheat, soybeans, rice, tallow, dairy cattle, red meats, poultry, and forest products. These nonprofit groups are funded by their members, including individual farmers and ranchers, specialized producers or breeders, farmer cooperatives, and processors and handlers. Other cooperators in the USDA program include the National Association of State Departments of Agriculture and four State Regional Trade Groups representing the agricultural interests of the eastern, western, southern, and mid-American states. For more information about the cooperator program, contact

Marketing Operations Staff
1400 Independence Ave. SW
Ag Box 1042
Washington, DC 20250-1042
Tel: (202) 720-4327; Fax: (202) 720-9361; Web site: www.fas.usda.gov

The U.S. International Trade Commission (USITC)

The USITC is an independent, nonpartisan, quasi-judicial federal agency. Established by Congress in 1916 as the U.S. Tariff Commission (the Trade Act of 1974 changed its name to the U.S. International Trade Commission), the agency has broad investigative powers on matters of trade. The USITC is a national resource where trade data are gathered and analyzed. The data are provided to the President and Congress as part of the information on which U.S. trade policy is based.

The Office of External Relations is the USITC's primary liaison with the public and the news media. External Relations issues all USITC news releases, responds to inquiries, produces the agency's annual report, and offers a variety of brochures, pamphlets, and other materials to enhance public understanding of the ITC, its mission, and its role in U.S. international trade matters.

The Trade Remedy Assistance Office assists the public and small businesses seeking benefits or relief under U.S. trade laws. The office offers general information concerning remedies and benefits available under the trade laws of the United States, and it provides technical and legal assistance and advice to small businesses seeking those remedies and benefits.

The Office of the Secretary maintains a public reading room, open during agency hours, where researchers, journalists, and other interested parties may review public files containing non-confidential information for each USITC investigation. Photocopies of documents contained in the public files may be ordered for a fee from an outside duplicating firm. No on-site photocopying is available.

The USITC also maintains the National Library of International Trade, one of the most extensive libraries in the United States specializing in international trade. The library is located on the third floor of the USITC Building. The ITC Law Library is located on the sixth floor of the USITC Building. Both are open to the public during agency hours.

U.S. International Trade Commission
500 E Street, SW
Washington, DC 20436
Tel: (202) 205-1819; Fax: (202) 205-2798
Web site: www.usitc.gov/

State Governments

State economic development agencies, departments of commerce, and other departments of state governments often provide valuable assistance to exporters. State export development programs are growing rapidly. In many areas, county and city economic development agencies also have export assistance programs. The aid offered by these groups typically includes the following:

- ***Export education***—helping exporters analyze export potential and orienting them to export techniques and strategies. This help may take the form of group seminars or individual counseling sessions.
- ***Trade missions***—organizing trips abroad enabling exporters to call on potential foreign customers. (For more information on trade missions, *refer to* Chapter 7, "Making Contacts," beginning on page 39.)
- ***Trade shows***—organizing and sponsoring exhibitions of state-produced goods and services in overseas markets.

Appendix III, "State and Local Sources of Assistance," beginning on page 130, lists the agencies in each state responsible for export assistance to local firms. Also included are the names of other government and private organizations, with their telephone numbers and addresses. Readers interested in the role played by state development agencies in promoting and supporting exports may also wish to contact

National Association of State Development Agencies
750 First St. NE, Suite 710
Washington, DC 20002
Tel: (202) 898-1302; Fax: (202) 898-1312; Web site: www.nasda.com

To determine if a particular county or city has local export assistance programs, contact the appropriate economic development agency. Appendix III, "State and Local Sources of Assistance," beginning on page 130, includes contact information for some major cities.

Commercial Banks

More than 300 U.S. banks have international banking departments with specialists familiar with specific foreign countries and various types of commodities and transactions. These large banks, located in major U.S. cities, maintain correspondent relationships with smaller banks throughout the country. Larger banks also maintain correspondent relationships with banks in most foreign countries or operate their own overseas branches, providing a direct channel to foreign customers. International banking specialists are generally well informed about export matters, even in areas that fall outside the usual limits of international banking. If they are unable to provide direct guidance or assistance, they may be able to refer inquirers to other specialists who can. Banks frequently provide consultation and guidance free of charge to their clients, since they derive income primarily from loans to the exporter and from fees for special services.

A good source of information on international banks is the *Thomson Polk World Directory.* This annual publication lists banks located around the world. It is available from Thomson Financial Publishing, 4709 W. Golf Road, 6th Floor, Skokie, IL 60076; Tel: (800) 321-3373; Price: $309 for the annual edition; $345 for a one time purchase.

Many banks also have publications available to help exporters. These materials often cover particular countries and their business practices and can be a valuable tool for initial familiarization with foreign industry. Finally, large banks frequently conduct seminars and workshops on letters of credit, documentary collections, and other banking subjects of concern to exporters. Among the many services a commercial bank may perform for its clients are the following:

- Exchange of currencies
- Assistance in financing exports

- Collection of foreign invoices, drafts, letters of credit, and other foreign receivables
- Transfer of funds to other countries
- Letters of introduction and letters of credit for travelers
- Credit information on potential representatives or buyers overseas
- Credit assistance to the exporter's foreign buyers

Export Intermediaries

Export intermediaries are of many different types, ranging from giant international companies, many foreign owned, to highly specialized, small operations. They provide a multitude of services, such as performing market research, appointing overseas distributors or commission representatives, exhibiting a client's products at international trade shows, advertising, shipping, and arranging documentation. In short, the intermediary can often take full responsibility for the export end of the business, relieving the manufacturer of all the details except filling orders.

Intermediaries may work simultaneously for a number of exporters on the basis of commissions, salary, or retainer plus commission. Some take title to the goods they handle, buying and selling in their own right. Products of a trading company's clients are often related, although the items usually are noncompetitive. One advantage of using an intermediary is that it can immediately make available marketing resources that a smaller firm would need years to develop on its own. Many export intermediaries also finance sales and extend credit, facilitating prompt payment to the exporter. For more information on using export intermediaries *refer to* Chapter 4, "Methods of Exporting and Channels of Distribution," beginning on page 25.

World Trade Centers and International Trade Clubs

Local or regional world trade centers and international trade clubs are composed of area business people who represent firms engaged in international trade and shipping, banks, forwarders, customs brokers, government agencies, and other service organizations involved in world trade. These organizations conduct educational programs on international business and organize promotional events to stimulate interest in world trade. World trade centers (WTCs) or affiliated associations are located in major trading cities throughout the world.

By participating in a local association, a company can receive valuable and timely advice on world markets and opportunities from business people who are already knowledgeable on virtually any facet of international business. Another important advantage of membership in a local world trade club is the availability of benefits—such as services, discounts, and contacts—in affiliated clubs from foreign countries.

The World Trade Centers Association now has nearly 200 active member associations worldwide and more than 100 planned for the near future. *Refer to* Appendix III, "State and Local Sources of Assistance," beginning on page 130 for a WTC near you or check the World Trade Centers Association Web site at www.wtca.org/ for listings of WTCs and their services.

Chambers of Commerce and Trade Associations

Many local chambers of commerce and major trade associations in the United States provide sophisticated and extensive services for members interested in exporting. Among these services are the following:

- Conducting export seminars, workshops, and roundtables.
- Providing certificates of origin.
- Developing trade promotion programs, including overseas missions, mailings, and event planning.
- Organizing U.S. pavilions in foreign trade shows.
- Providing contacts with foreign companies and distributors.
- Relaying export sales leads and other opportunities to members.
- Organizing transportation routings and shipment consolidations.
- Hosting visiting trade missions from other countries.
- Conducting international activities at domestic trade shows.

In addition, some industry associations can supply detailed information on market demand for products in selected countries or refer members to export management companies. Most trade associations play an active role in lobbying for U.S. trade policies beneficial to their industries.

Industry trade associations typically collect and maintain files on international trade news and trends affecting manufacturers. Often they publish articles and newsletters that include government research.

American Chambers of Commerce Abroad

A valuable and reliable source of market information in any foreign country is the local chapter of the American chamber of commerce. These organizations are knowledgeable about local trade opportunities, actual and potential competition, periods of maximum trade activity, and similar considerations.

American chambers of commerce abroad usually handle inquiries from any U.S. business. Detailed service, however, is ordinarily provided free of charge only for members of affiliated organizations. Some chambers have a set schedule of charges for services rendered to nonmembers. For contact information on American chambers in major foreign markets, *refer to* Appendix IV, "U.S. and Overseas Contacts for Major Foreign Markets," beginning on page 157.

International Trade Consultants and Other Advisers

International trade consultants can advise and assist a manufacturer on all aspects of foreign marketing. Trade consultants do not normally deal specifically with one product, although they may advise on product adaptation to a foreign market. They research domestic and foreign regulations and also assess commercial and political risk. They conduct foreign market research and establish contacts with foreign government agencies and other necessary resources, such as advertising companies, product service facilities, and local attorneys.

These consultants can locate and qualify foreign joint venture partners as well as conduct feasibility studies for the sale of manufacturing rights, the location and construction of manufacturing facilities, and the establishment of foreign branches. After sales agreements are completed, trade consultants can also ensure that follow-through is smooth and that any problems that arise are dealt with effectively.

Trade consultants usually specialize by subject matter and by global area or country. For example, firms may specialize in high-technology exports to the Far East. Their consultants can advise on which agents or distributors are likely to be successful, what kinds of promotion are needed, who the competitors are, and how to deal with them. They are also knowledgeable about foreign government regulations, contract laws, and taxation. Some firms may be more specialized than others; for example, some may be thoroughly knowledgeable on legal aspects and taxation and less knowledgeable on marketing strategies.

Many large accounting firms, law firms, and specialized marketing firms provide international trade consulting services. When selecting a consulting firm, the exporter should pay particular attention to the experience and knowledge of the consultant who is in charge of its project. To find an appropriate firm, advice should be sought from other exporters and some of the other resources listed in this chapter, such as the Department of Commerce district office or local chamber of commerce.

Consultants are of greatest value to a firm that knows exactly what it wants. For this reason, and because private consultants are expensive, it pays to take full advantage of publicly funded sources of advice before hiring a consultant.

Chapter 3

Market Research

To be successful, exporters must assess their markets through market research. Exporters engage in market research primarily to identify their marketing opportunities and constraints within individual foreign markets and also to identify and find prospective buyers and customers.

Market research includes all methods that a company uses to determine which foreign markets have the best potential for its products. Results of this research inform the firm of

- the largest markets for its product,
- the fastest growing markets,
- market trends and outlook,
- market conditions and practices, and
- competitive firms and products.

A firm may begin to export without conducting any market research if it receives unsolicited orders from abroad. Although this type of selling is valuable, the firm may discover even more promising markets by conducting a systematic search. A firm that opts to export indirectly (*see* "Indirect Exporting" on page 25) by using an intermediary such as an export management company (EMC) or an export trading company (ETC) may wish to select markets to enter before selecting the intermediary, since many EMCs and ETCs have strengths in some markets but not in others.

A firm may research a market by using either primary or secondary data resources. In conducting primary market research, a company collects data directly from the foreign marketplace through interviews, surveys, and other direct contact with representatives and potential buyers. Primary market research has the advantage of being tailored to the company's needs and provides answers to specific questions, but the collection of such data is time-consuming and expensive.

When conducting secondary market research, a company collects data from compiled sources, such as trade statistics for a country or a product. Working with secondary sources is less expensive and helps the company focus its marketing efforts. Although secondary data sources are critical to market research, they do have limitations. The most recent statistics for some countries may be more than two years old. Product breakdowns may be too broad to be of much value to a company. Statistics on services are often unavailable. Finally, statistics may be distorted by incomplete data-gathering techniques. Yet, even with these limitations, secondary research is a valuable and relatively easy first step for a company to take. It may be the only step needed if the company decides to export indirectly through an intermediary, since the other firm may have advanced research capabilities.

Methods of Market Research

Because of the expense of primary market research, most firms rely on secondary data sources. Secondary market research is conducted in three basic ways:

1. By keeping abreast of world events that influence the international marketplace, watching for announcements of specific projects, or simply visiting likely markets. For example, a thawing of political hostilities often leads to the opening of economic channels between countries.
2. By analyzing trade and economic statistics. Trade statistics are generally compiled by product category and by country. These statistics provide the U.S. firm with information concerning shipments of products over specified periods of time. Demographic and general economic statistics such as population size and makeup, per capita income, and production levels by industry can be important indicators of the market potential for a company's products.
3. By obtaining the advice of experts. There are several ways of obtaining expert advice:
   - Contacting experts at the U.S. Department of Commerce and other government agencies.
   - Attending seminars, workshops, and international trade shows.
   - Hiring an international trade and marketing consultant.

- Talking with successful exporters of similar products.
- Contacting trade and industry association staff.

Gathering and evaluating secondary market research can be complex and tedious. However, several publications are available that can help simplify the process. The following approach to market research refers to these publications and resources described later in this chapter.

A Step-by-Step Approach to Market Research

The U.S. company may find the following approach useful.

1. Screen potential markets.

- ***Step 1.*** Obtain export statistics that indicate product exports to various countries. Contact the Bureau of the Census at the Commerce Department or the Office of Trade and Economic Analysis for statistics on U.S. exports and imports. The NTDB, available through many libraries and Commerce Department offices, is another good source of statistical information on U.S. trade.
- ***Step 2.*** Identify five to ten large and fast-growing markets for the firm's product. Look at them over the past three to five years. Has market growth been consistent year to year? Did import growth occur even during periods of economic recession? If not, did growth resume with economic recovery? See "Top Export Targets" on page 23 for some ideas.
- ***Step 3.*** Identify some smaller but fast-emerging markets that may provide ground-floor opportunities. If the market is just beginning to open up, there may be fewer competitors than in established markets. Growth rates should be substantially higher in these countries to qualify as up-and-coming markets, given the lower starting point.
- ***Step 4.*** Target three to five of the most statistically promising markets for further assessment. Consult with Commerce district offices, business associates, freight forwarders, and others to help refine targeted markets.

2. Assess targeted markets.

- ***Step 1.*** Examine trends for company products as well as related products that could influence demand. Calculate overall consumption of the product and the amount accounted for by imports. Various reports available from the Commerce Department and from the State Department give economic backgrounds and market trends for each country. The State Department's *Country Commercial Guides* are particularly useful. Demographic information (population, age, etc.) can be obtained from *The Statistical Yearbook* (United Nations).
- ***Step 2.*** Ascertain the sources of competition, including the extent of domestic industry production and the major foreign countries the firm is competing against in each targeted market, by using *Industry Sector Analyses* (ISAs) and *International Market Insights* (IMIs). Both are available from the Commerce Department via the NTDB and the EBB. Look at each competitor's U.S. market share.
- ***Step 3.*** Analyze factors affecting marketing and use of the product in each market, such as end user sectors, channels of distribution, cultural idiosyncrasies, and business practices. Again, ISAs are useful, as is the Customized Market Analysis (CMA) service offered by Commerce.
- ***Step 4.*** Identify any foreign barriers (tariff or nontariff) for the product being imported into the country. Identify any U.S. barriers (such as export controls) affecting exports to the country.
- ***Step 5.*** Identify any U.S. or foreign government incentives to promote exporting of the product or service.

3. Draw conclusions.

After analyzing the data, the company may conclude that its marketing resources would be applied more effectively to a few countries. In general, efforts should be directed to fewer than 10 markets if the company is new to exporting; one or two countries may be enough to start with. The company's internal resources should help determine its level of effort.

The following section describes the publications that have been mentioned and includes additional sources. Because there are many research sources, the firm may wish to seek advice from a Department of Commerce Export Assistance Center or district office (*refer to* Appendix III, "State and Local Sources of Assistance," beginning on page 130).

Sources of Market Research

There are many domestic, foreign, and international sources of information concerning foreign markets. Several of these sources are given here, and others may be found in the bibliography (Appendix V, "Selected Bibliography," beginning on page 182). Available information ranges from simple trade statistics to in-depth market surveys.

Trade statistics indicate total exports or imports by country and by product and allow an exporter to compare the size of the market for a product among various countries. Some statistics also reflect the U.S. share of the total country market in order to gauge the overall competitiveness of U.S. producers. By looking at statistics over several years, an exporter can determine which markets are growing and which are shrinking.

Market surveys provide a narrative description and assessment of particular markets along with relevant statistics. The reports are often based on original research conducted in the countries studied and may include specific information on both buyers and competitors.

Potential exporters may find many of the reports referred to in this section at a Department of Commerce district office (*refer to* Appendix III, "State and Local Sources of Assistance," beginning on page 130) or at a business or university library. In addition, the Foreign Trade Reference Room in the Department of Commerce offers extensive trade statistics. The Foreign Trade Reference Room is in Room 2233 of the main Commerce Department Building. Contact the staff there at Tel: (202) 482-2185; Fax: (202) 482-4614. The NTDB is a source for much of the following information. Call Stat-USA at (202) 482-1986 for more information on the NTDB; Fax: (202) 482-2164; Email: stat-usa@doc.gov; Web site: www.stat-usa.gov.

The following sources fall into two broad categories—general information resources and industry- or country-specific information resources. Each category is divided into several subgroups.

General Information Sources

One of the best sources of information is personal interviews with private and government officials and experts. A surprisingly large number of people in both the public and private sectors are available to assist exporters interested in any aspect of international market research. Either in face-to-face interviews or by telephone, these individuals can provide a wealth of market research information.

In the private sector, sources of market research expertise include local chambers of commerce, world trade centers or clubs, and trade associations. In the federal government, industry and commodity experts are available through the Department of Commerce, USDA, and SBA. In addition, these agencies provide the following publications, many of which can be found in local libraries.

Sources of General Information

- ***Business America: The Magazine of International Trade.*** This monthly publication of the Department of Commerce contains country-by-country marketing reports, incisive economic analyses, worldwide trade leads, advance notice of planned exhibitions of U.S. products worldwide, and success stories of export marketing. A typical issue includes an analytical piece on current U.S. trade policy, a "how to" article for the novice exporter, a picture of the nation's economic health, news of Congressional and government actions affecting trade, economic and market reports gathered by the Foreign Commercial Service, and other trade news generated by the International Trade Administration and other United States Government agencies as well as foreign governments. Annual subscriptions cost $47. (S/N 703-011-00000-4). Contact Superintendent of Documents, U.S. Government Printing Office, Washington, DC 20402; Tel: (202) 512-1800; Web site: www.access.gpo.gov/su_docs.
- ***Commerce Business Daily (CBD).*** Published daily, Monday through Friday (except holidays), by the Department of Commerce, CBD lists government procurement invitations, contract awards, subcontracting leads, sales of surplus property, and foreign business opportunities as well as certain foreign government procurements. A first-class mail subscription is $324 per year or $162 for six months; second-class, $275 per year or $137.50 for six months (GPO S/N 703-013-00000-7.) Contact Superintendent of Documents, U.S. Government Printing Office, Washington, DC 20402; Tel: (202) 512-1800; Web site: www.access.gpo.gov/su_docs. It is also available through the Internet for $95 to $195 per year. Contact Loren Data Corp., 4640 Admiralty Way, Suite 430, Marina del Rey, CA 90292; Tel: (310) 827-7400; Email: info@ld.com; Web site: www.ld.com.
- ***Trade Information Center.*** This information center was established as a comprehensive source for U.S. companies seeking information on federal programs and activities that support U.S. exports, including information on overseas markets and industry trends. It is an excellent starting point and referral center for new exporters. Tel: (800) USA-TRADE; Fax: (202) 482-4473; Web site: www.ita.doc.gov/how_to_export/.
- ***Economic Bulletin Board (EBB).*** The PC-based EBB is an on-line source for trade leads as well as the latest statistical releases from the Bureau of the Census, the Bureau of Economic Analysis, the Bureau of Labor Statistics, the Federal Reserve Board, the Department of the Treasury, and other federal agencies. It has been divided into two separate components: *State of the Nation* and *GLOBUS*.

  Internet connection charges are $50 per quarter or $150 per year for unlimited access to the STAT-USA site (NTDB and EBB).

  - Modem: (202) 482-3870 (300/1200/2400 bps)
  - Modem: (202) 482-2584 (9600 bps)
  - Modem: (202) 482-2167 (14.4. kbps)
  - Web site: www.stat-usa.gov

Set your communications software to no parity, 8 data bits, and 1 stop bit.

- ***National Trade Data Bank.*** The NTDB contains export promotion and international trade data collected by 15 U.S. government agencies. Updated each month and released on two CD-ROM discs, the data bank enables access to more than 200,000 documents. The NTDB contains the latest Census data on U.S. imports and exports by commodity and country; the complete set of *Country Commercial Guides;* current market research reports compiled by the Commercial Service; the complete Commercial Service International Contacts (CSIS), which contains over 80,000 names and addresses of individuals and firms abroad interested in importing U.S. products; State Department country reports on economic policy and trade practices; the publications *Export Yellow Pages* and the *National Trade Estimates Report on Foreign Trade Barriers*; the *Export Promotion Calendar*; and many other data series.

  The NTDB can be purchased in the form of CD-ROM discs (for $59 per monthly issue or $575 for a 12-month subscription) or it may be accessed on the Internet through Stat-USA. The NTDB is also available at over 1,100 federal depository libraries nationwide. Call the Trade Information Center at (800) USA-TRADE for a list of these libraries.

  For more information, or to order, contact Stat-USA at Tel: (800) STAT-USA or (202) 482-1986; Fax: (202) 482-2164; Email: stat-usa@doc.gov; Web site: www.stat-usa.gov.

- ***Selected SBA market research-related general resources.*** *Breaking into the Trade Game: A Small Business Guide to Exporting* and *Resource Directory for Small Business Management* are free from your local SBA office, or call Small Business Answer Desk, (800) 8-ASK-SBA or (202) 205-7333. The SBA also publishes and sells *Marketing for Small Business: An Overview* (MT02, $2); *Researching Your Market* (MT08, $3); and the video *Marketing: Winning Customers with a Workable Plan* (VT01, $27). Order these publications and video from SBA Publications, P.O. Box 46521, Denver, CO 80201-46521.

- ***U.S. Global Outlook, 1995-2000*** Focuses on seven export growth sectors, including medical equipment, computer software and information services, whose exports are projected to grow at double digit rates between 1995 and 2000. The Global Outlook also assesses U.S. export prospects in 18 key markets among the industrialized nations; the Big Emerging Markets of Asia, Africa and Latin America; and the Economies in Transition of Russia and Eastern Europe. Stock number: 003-009-00650-3. Price: $20. To order, contact the U.S. Government Printing Office, PO Box 371954, Pittsburgh, PA 15250-7954; Tel: (202) 512-1800; Fax: (202) 512-2250; Web site: www.access.gpo.gov/su_docs.

Worldwide General Information

- ***International Financial Statistics (IFS).*** Published monthly by the International Monetary Fund, IFS presents statistics on exchange rates, money and banking, production, government finance, interest rates, and other subjects. It is available by annual subscription for $246, which includes 12 issues plus the yearbook. Single copies are $30, or $65 for the yearbook only. Contact the International Monetary Fund, Publication Services, 700 19th Street NW, Washington, DC 20431; Tel: (202) 623-7430; Fax: (202) 623-7201; Email: publications@imf.org; Web site: www.imf.org.

- ***UN Statistical Yearbook.*** Published by the United Nations, this yearbook contains data for 220 countries and territories on economic and social subjects including population, agriculture, manufacturing, commodity, export-import trade, and many other areas. It is updated annually and costs $120. Contact United Nations Publications, Room DC2-0853, New York, NY 10017; Tel: (212) 963-8302; Fax: (212) 963-3489; Web site: www.un.org/publications.

- ***World Bank Atlas.*** The World Bank Atlas provides demographics, gross domestic product, and average growth rates for over 200 countries. It is updated annually and costs $20. Contact World Bank Publications, P.O. Box 960, Herndon, VA 20172-0960; Tel: (202) 473-1155; Fax: (703) 661-1501; Web site: www.worldbank.org.

- ***World Factbook.*** Produced annually in July by the CIA, this publication provides country-by-country data on demographics, economy, communications, and defense. The cost is $59. To order, contact U.S. Government Printing Office, PO Box 371954, Pittsburgh, PA 15250-7954; Tel: (202) 512-1800; Fax: (202) 512-2250; Web site: www.access.gpo.gov/su_docs.

- ***Worldcasts.*** The Worldcasts annual series has been discontinued.

General Industry and Agriculture Information

Foreign Agricultural Service Publications

- ***FAS Attache Country Reports.*** FAS overseas offices regularly prepare food and agricultural market and trade reports on more than 150 products. These reports include such topics as: production, supply and distribution situation; trade trends and forecasts; foreign government legislation and regulations; and trade policies affecting U.S. trade. Reports for the current month, current year and select reports for the previous year are available on the FAS Home Page (www.fas.usda.gov). Some reports can also be accessed through the Department of Commerce's EBB or the NTDB.

The following FAS publications may be ordered from the National Technical Information Service (NTIS), 5285 Port Royal Road, Springfield, VA 22161; Tel: (703) 605-6060; Fax: (703) 605-6900; Email: info@ntis.fedworld.gov; Web site: www.fedworld.gov.

- ***AgExporter.*** A monthly magazine for businesses selling farm products overseas; provides tips on exporting, descriptions of markets with the greatest sales potential, and information on export assistance available from the U.S. Department of Agriculture. The audience is U.S. agricultural producers, exporters, trade organizations, state departments of agriculture and any other export-oriented organization. Price: $59 domestic; $68 international.
- ***World Horticultural Trade and U.S. Export Opportunities.*** This monthly publication provides timely information on the world situation and outlook for horticultural products. It covers export competition, foreign market import potential and export opportunities for U.S. horticultural products. The circular also discuses trade policy developments that affect U.S. export potential. Price: $99 domestic; $199 international.
- ***U.S. Export Sales.*** This weekly report is based on reports submitted by private exporters. Outstanding export sales as reported and compiled with other data give a snapshot view of the current contracting scene. All countries with outstanding sales or accumulated exports are included for each class of wheat, all wheat, wheat products, corn, soybeans, soybean cake and meal, American pima cotton, all upland cotton, whole cattle hides, and wet blues. Price: $196 domestic; $358 international.

Country and Area Information

- ***Background Notes.*** This series surveys a country's people, geography, economy, government, and foreign policy. Prepared by the Department of State, it includes important national economic and trade information, including major trading partners. Available by subscription. Annual subscription cost is $23 (GPO S/N 844-002-00000-9). Individual *Background Notes* pamphlets are also available individually for $1-$2.50 each. Contact the U.S. Government Printing Office, PO Box 371954, Pittsburgh, PA 15250-7954; Tel: (202) 512-1800; Fax: (202) 512-2250; Web site: www.access.gpo.gov/su_docs.
- ***U.S. Agency for International Development (AID) Congressional Presentations .*** Published by AID's Office of Small and Disadvantaged Business Utilization, this document provides country-by-country data on nations to which AID will provide funds in the coming year, as well as detailed information on past funding activities in each country. It also lists projects the agency desires to fund in the upcoming year, for example, a hydroelectrical project in Egypt. Since these projects require U.S. goods and services, these presentations give U.S. exporters an early look at potential projects and, therefore, an opportunity to plan ahead. (*See* "Agency for International Development (AID)" on page 45 for more details on AID's programs.) Available through the National Technical Information Service (NTIS); Tel: (703) 605-6060; Fax: (703) 605-6900; Email: info@ntis.fedworld.gov; Web site: http://www.fedworld.gov.
- ***Country Commercial Guides.*** Prepared overseas by the Commerce Department and the State Department and other agencies of the U.S. Trade Promotion Coordinating Committee. Each Guide presents information on one country's commercial environment including market conditions, economic situations, political environment, best export sectors, trade regulations, investment incentives, finance techniques, upcoming trade events, marketing strategies, services for exporters, business travel tips, listings of contacts, and more. More than 100 CCGs are now available. They can be accessed through the NTDB, the EBB, or the State Department's Web site at http://www.state.gov/. To purchase separate CCGs, contact NTIS; Tel: (703) 605-6060; Fax: (703) 605-6000; Email. info@ntis.fedworld.gov; Web site: http://www.fedworld.gov.
- ***Exporters' Encyclopedia.*** This extensive handbook on exporting is updated annually and contains exhaustive, in-depth shipping and marketing information. More than 220 world markets are covered country by country. Topics include country profile, communications, trade regulations, documentation, marketing data, health and safety regulations, transportation, and business travel. The annual price is $520. Contact Dun's Marketing Services, Business Reference Solutions Department, 3 Sylvan Way, Parsippany, NJ 07054-3896; Tel: (800) 526-0651 or (973) 605-6000; Fax: (973) 605-6911; Web site: www.dnb.com/mdd/brsmenu.htm.
- ***Foreign Agriculture.*** This annual factbook is no longer published.
- ***Organization for Economic Cooperation and Development (OECD) Economic Surveys.*** These economic development surveys produced by OECD cover each of the 27-member OECD countries individually. Each survey presents a detailed analysis of recent developments in market demand, production, employment, and prices and wages. Short-term forecasts and analyses of medium-term problems relevant to economic policies are provided. An annual subscription costs $395; a single copy, $26. Contact OECD Washington Center, 2001 L Street

NW, Suite 650, Washington, DC 20036; Tel: (202) 785-6323; Fax: (202) 785-0350; Web site: www.oecdwash.org.

- **OECD publications.** OECD publishes widely on a broad range of social and economic issues, concerns, and developments, including reports on international market information country by country, such as import data useful in assessing import competition. The chartered mission of OECD is to promote within and among its 27-member countries policies designed to support high economic growth, employment, and standard of living and to contribute to sound economic expansion in development and in trade. For information and prices on these publications, contact OECD Washington Center, 2001 L Street NW, Suite 650, Washington, DC 20036; Tel: (202) 785-6323; Fax: (202) 785-0350; Web site: www.oecdwash.org.

Detailed Product- and Industry-Specific Data Resources

U.S. Government Product and Industry Resources

- ***Customized Market Analyses.*** A CMA report will give you an assessment of how your product or service will sell in a given market. Once you order your Customized Market Analysis, commercial research specialists in your target country will conduct interviews with knowledgeable local sources, such as importers, distributors, end-users, and manufacturers of products comparable to yours. Your report will be sent to you approximately 60 days after you place your order. Contact the Export Assistance Center nearest you for more information.
- ***Industry Sector Analyses.*** Prepared by the commercial sections of the U.S. embassies for US&FCS, ISAs provide the basis for quickly sizing up one particular commercial or industrial market in a particular country. ISAs present market demand, market size, competitive analysis, end user analysis, and market access criteria as well as marketing opportunities. Available on the NTDB and the EBB.
- ***International Market Insights.*** IMIs are short profiles of specific foreign market conditions or opportunities prepared in overseas markets and at multilateral development banks. These non-formatted reports include information on dynamic sectors of a particular country. *International Market Insights* are available on the NTDB and the EBB.
- ***Agricultural Trade Highlights.*** This monthly report has been discontinued.
- **Staff papers on best prospects.** These reports, produced by FAS, offer the best overall prospects for expansion of U.S. agricultural products over the next three to five years. They cover about 15 countries and are available on the Foreign Agricultural Service Web site: www.fas.usda.gov.

Private Sector Product and Industry Resources

- ***American Export Register.*** This two-volume directory of nearly 50,000 U.S. exporters and the materials, products, or services they sell internationally is published annually. Advertising is accepted. The cost is $100 for print, $125 for cd rom. Contact Thomas Publishing Company, Inc., Five Penn Plaza, New York, NY 10001; Tel: (212) 290-7355; Fax: (212) 290-8878; Email: info@aernet.com.
- ***Export Reference Manual.*** Published annually and updated biweekly, the manual is a two-volume looseleaf reference service containing up-to-date, country-by-country shipping and market research information. Social, political, economic, and commercial conditions of each country are profiled. Detail is given to policies, regulations, issues, development, and laws pertaining to commerce, especially foreign trade. The cost for a print subscription is $740 annually, updated biweekly; cd rom is $799 annually, updated monthly; via the web is $799, updated biweekly. Contact Bureau of National Affairs, Inc., 9435 Key West Ave., Rockville MD 20850; Tel: (800) 372-1033; Fax: (800) 253-0332.
- ***FINDEX: The Worldwide Directory of Market Research Reports, Studies and Surveys.*** This reference guide to commercially available market and business research, including international market research, contains listings of thousands of reports, studies, and surveys. Prices vary depending on whether customers order print, CD-ROM, or online verions. Contact Kalorama Information, 7200 Wisconsin Avenue, Bethesda, MD 20814; Tel: (800) 298-5699; Email: order @findexonline.com; Web site: http://www.marketresearch.com.
- ***Inside Washington: Government Resources for International Business*** and ***Power Money: The International Executive's Guide to Government Resources.*** These publications are complete source books on government assistance programs and services. The cost for *Inside Washington* is $49.95. The cost for *Power Money* is $35.00. For more information, contact Delphos International, 1101 30th St. NW, Suite 200, Washington, DC 20007; Tel: (202) 337-6300; Fax: (202) 333-1158.
- **Electronic data bases.** A number of private sector data bases are available to provide specific marketing information for firms interested in doing business internationally, such as Dow Jones News/Retrieval, DataTimes, service of the Journal of Commerce and DIALOG. Many of these data bases are accessible both at local public libraries and universities and directly by personal computer.

Top Export Targets

The lists below show the top markets for these U.S. commodities in 1996. It may give you some ideas about where to start your market research. The countries are listed alphabetically within each category.

Air Conditioning & Refrigeration Equipment

- Israel
- Italy
- Kuwait
- Saudi Arabia
- Singapore
- South Korea
- Taiwan
- United Arab Emirates

Aircraft and Parts

- China
- Germany
- Israel
- Italy
- Japan
- Malaysia
- South Korea
- Taiwan
- Saudi Arabia
- Singapore
- South Africa
- United Kingdom

Automotive Parts and Accessories

- Belgium
- Brazil
- China
- Indonesia
- Italy
- Japan
- Mexico
- Netherlands
- Saudi Arabia
- Singapore
- Thailand
- United Kingdom

Building Products

- Argentina
- India
- Indonesia
- Japan
- Philippines
- Singapore
- South Korea
- Taiwan
- United Arab Emirates

Computer Software

- Brazil
- Germany
- Hong Kong
- India
- Japan
- Malaysia
- Netherlands
- South Korea
- Spain
- Switzerland
- Taiwan
- United Kingdom

Computers and Peripherals

- Brazil
- China
- Germany
- Italy
- Japan
- Malaysia
- Singapore
- South Korea
- Spain
- Taiwan
- Thailand
- United Kingdom

Drugs and Pharmaceuticals

- Germany
- Hong Kong
- Japan
- Singapore
- South Africa
- Switzerland
- South Korea
- United Kingdom

Electrical Power Systems

- Argentina
- China
- Hong Kong
- India
- Indonesia

- Italy
- Japan
- Malaysia
- Philippines
- Saudi Arabia
- Singapore
- Taiwan

Electronics

- Brazil
- China
- France
- Germany
- Hong Kong
- India
- Japan
- Malaysia
- Netherlands
- Singapore
- Taiwan
- Italy

Environmental Technologies

- Belgium
- Chile
- China
- France
- Germany
- Hong Kong
- Italy
- Singapore
- South Korea
- Spain
- Taiwan
- United Kingdom

Instrumentation

- Belgium
- China
- Germany
- Indonesia
- Israel
- Italy
- Japan
- Malaysia
- Singapore
- Taiwan
- Thailand
- United Kingdom

Medical Instruments and Equipment

- Argentina
- Brazil
- China
- France
- Hong Kong
- Japan
- Netherlands
- Singapore
- South Korea
- Spain
- Taiwan
- United Kingdom

Telecommunications Equipment

- Argentina
- Brazil
- China
- Germany
- Hong Kong
- Japan
- Malaysia
- Philippines
- Singapore
- South Korea
- Thailand
- United Kingdom

Sporting Goods & Recreational Equipment

- Brazil
- Chile
- Germany
- Israel
- Japan
- Malaysia
- Netherlands
- Singapore
- South Korea
- Taiwan
- Turkey
- United Kingdom

Chapter 4

Methods of Exporting and Channels of Distribution

The most common methods of exporting are indirect selling and direct selling (*refer to* Chapter 1, "Export Strategy," beginning on page 1). In indirect selling, an export intermediary such as an EMC or an ETC normally assumes responsibility for finding overseas buyers, shipping products, and getting paid. In direct selling, the U.S. producer deals directly with a foreign buyer.

The paramount consideration in determining whether to market indirectly or directly is the level of resources a company is willing to devote to its international marketing effort. These are some other factors to consider when deciding whether to market indirectly or directly:

- The size of the firm
- The nature of its products
- Previous export experience and expertise
- Business conditions in the selected overseas markets

Distribution Considerations

- Which channels of distribution should the firm use to market its products abroad?
- Where should the firm produce its products and how should it distribute them in the foreign market?
- What types of representatives, brokers, wholesalers, dealers, distributors, retailers, and so on should the firm use?
- What are the characteristics and capabilities of the available intermediaries?
- Should the assistance of an EMC or ETC be obtained?

Indirect Exporting

The principal advantage of indirect marketing for a smaller U.S. company is that it provides a way to penetrate foreign markets without the complexities and risks of direct exporting. Several kinds of intermediary firms provide a range of export services. Each type of firm offers distinct advantages for the U.S. company.

Commission Agents

Commission or buying agents are finders for foreign firms that want to purchase U.S. products. They seek to obtain the desired items at the lowest possible price and are paid a commission by their foreign clients. In some cases, they may be foreign government agencies or quasi-governmental firms empowered to locate and purchase desired goods. Foreign government purchasing missions are one example.

Export Management Companies

An export management company (EMC) acts as the export department for one or several producers of goods or services. It solicits and transacts business in the names of the producers it represents or in its own name for a commission, salary, or retainer plus commission. Some EMCs provide immediate payment for the producer's products by either arranging financing or directly purchasing products for resale. Typically, only larger EMCs can afford to purchase or finance exports.

EMCs usually specialize either by product or by foreign market or both. Because of their specialization, the best EMCs know their products and the markets they serve very well and usually have well-established networks of foreign distributors already in place. This immediate access to foreign markets is one of the principal reasons for using an EMC, since establishing a productive relationship with a foreign representative may be a costly and lengthy process.

One disadvantage in using an EMC is that a manufacturer may lose control over foreign sales. Most manufacturers are properly concerned that their product and company image be well maintained in foreign markets. An important way for a company to retain sufficient control in such an arrangement is to carefully select an EMC that can meet the company's needs and maintain close communication with it. For example, a company may ask for regular reports on efforts to market its products and may require approval of certain types of efforts, such as advertising programs or service arrangements. If a company wants to maintain this type of relationship with an EMC, it should negotiate points of concern before entering an agreement, since not all EMCs are willing to comply with the company's concerns.

Export Trading Companies

An export trading company (ETC) facilitates the export of U.S. goods and services. Like an EMC, an ETC can either act as the export department for producers or take title to the product and export for its own account. Therefore, the terms ETC and EMC are often used interchangeably. A special kind of ETC is a group organized and operated by producers. These ETCs can be organized along multiple- or single-industry lines and can represent producers of competing products.

Export Trading Company Act of 1982

The goal of the Export Trading Company Act of 1982 is to stimulate U.S. exports by (1) promoting and encouraging the formation of export management and export trading companies; (2) expanding the options available for export financing by permitting bank holding companies to invest in ETCs and reducing restrictions on trade finance provided by financial institutions; and (3) reducing uncertainty about applying U.S. antitrust law to export operations. This legislation allows banks, for the first time in recent history, to make equity investments in commercial ventures that qualify as ETCs. In addition, for the first time, the Export-Import Bank of the United States (Ex-Im Bank) is allowed to make working capital guarantees to U.S. exporters. Through the Office of Export Trading Company Affairs (OETCA) within the ITA, the U.S. Department of Commerce promotes the formation and use of U.S. export intermediaries and issues export trade certificates of review providing limited immunity from U.S. antitrust laws.

OETCA informs the business community of the benefits of export intermediaries through conferences, presentations before trade associations and civic organizations, and publications. The major publication on this subject is the *Export Trading Company Guidebook* (GPO S/N 003-009-00523-0), available for $15 through the Superintendent of Documents, U.S. Government Printing Office, Washington, DC 20402; Tel: (202) 512-1803; Fax: (202) 512-2250; Web site: www.access.gpo.gov/su_docs. OETCA provides counseling to businesses seeking to take advantage of the act.

OETCA also maintains the Contact Facilitation Service (CFS) data base, a listing of U.S. producers of goods and services and of organizations that provide trade facilitation services. Under a public-private sector arrangement, the CFS data base is published annually in a directory entitled *The Export Yellow Pages*, which is available free from local Department of Commerce offices or on the NTDB. The directory provides users with the names and addresses of banks, EMCs, ETCs, freight forwarders, manufacturers, and service organizations and names the export products or export-related services that these firms supply. By obtaining CFS registration forms from Commerce district offices, firms can register in the data base free of charge and be listed in subsequent editions of *The Export Yellow Pages*.

Certificates of Review

The certificates of review are issued by the Secretary of Commerce with the concurrence of the U.S. Department of Justice. Any U.S. corporation or partnership, any resident individual, or any state or local entity may apply for a certificate of review. A certificate can be issued to an applicant if it is determined that the proposed "export trade activities and methods of operation" will not result in a substantial lessening of domestic competition or restraint of trade within the United States. For the conduct covered by the certificate, its holder and any other individuals or firms named as members are given immunity from government suits under U.S. federal and state antitrust laws. In private party actions, liability is reduced from treble to single damages, greatly reducing the probability of nuisance suits. Moreover, in the event of private litigation involving conduct covered by the certificate of review, a prevailing certificate holder recovers the costs of defending the suit, including reasonable attorney's fees.

The certificate of review program provides exporters with an antitrust "insurance policy" intended to foster joint activities where economies of scale and risk diversification can be achieved. The act also amends the Sherman Antitrust Act and the Federal Trade Commission Act to clarify the jurisdictional reach of these statutes to export trade. Both acts now apply to export trade only if there is a "direct substantial and reasonably foreseeable" effect on domestic or import commerce of the United States or the export commerce of a U.S. competitor.

The guidelines for the certificate of review program can be found at 50 FR 1786, and the regulations can be found at 50 FR 1804 (15 CFR Part 325).

Firms and individuals interested in additional information should contact

Office of Export Trading Company Affairs
Room 1104, U.S. Department of Commerce
Washington, DC 20230
Tel: (202) 482-5131; Fax: (202) 482-1790

Export Agents, Merchants, or Remarketers

Export agents, merchants, or remarketers purchase products directly from the manufacturer, packing and marking the products according to their own specifications. They then sell overseas through their contacts in their own names and assume all risks for accounts.

In transactions with export agents, merchants, or remarketers, a U.S. firm relinquishes control over the marketing and promotion of its product, which could have an adverse effect on future sales efforts abroad. For example, the product could be underpriced or incorrectly positioned in the market, or after-sales service could be neglected. On the other hand, the effort required by the manufacturer to market the product overseas is very small and may lead to sales that otherwise would take a great deal of effort to obtain.

Piggyback Marketing

Piggyback marketing is an arrangement in which one manufacturer or service firm distributes a second firm's product or service. The most common piggybacking situation is when a U.S. company has a contract with an overseas buyer to provide a wide range of products or services. Often, this first company does not produce all of the products it is under contract to provide, and it turns to other U.S. companies to provide the remaining products. The second U.S. company thus piggybacks its products to the international market, generally without incurring the marketing and distribution costs associated with exporting. Successful arrangements usually require that the product lines be complementary and appeal to the same customers.

Direct Exporting

The advantages of direct exporting for a U.S. company include more control over the export process, potentially higher profits, and a closer relationship to the overseas buyer and marketplace. These advantages do not come easily, however, since the U.S. company needs to devote more time, personnel, and corporate resources than are needed with indirect exporting.

When a company chooses to export directly to foreign markets, it usually makes internal organizational changes to support more complex functions. A direct exporter normally selects the markets it wishes to penetrate, chooses the best channels of distribution for each market, and then makes specific foreign business connections in order to sell its product. The rest of this chapter discusses these aspects of direct exporting in more detail.

Organizing for Exporting

A company new to exporting generally treats its export sales no differently from domestic sales, using existing personnel and organizational structures. As international sales and inquiries increase, however, the company may separate the management of its exports from that of its domestic sales.

The advantages of separating international from domestic business include the centralization of specialized skills needed to deal with international markets and the benefits of a focused marketing effort that is more likely to lead to increased export sales. A possible disadvantage of such a separation is the less efficient use of corporate resources due to segmentation.

When a company separates international from domestic business, it may do so at different levels in the organization. For example, when a company first begins to export, it may create an export department with a full- or part-time manager who reports to the head of domestic sales and marketing. At later stages a company may choose to increase the autonomy of the export department to the point of creating an international division that reports directly to the president.

Larger companies at advanced stages of exporting may choose to retain the international division or to organize along product or geographic lines. A company with distinct product lines may create an international department in each product division. A company with products that have common end users may organize geographically; for example, it may form a division for Europe, another for the Far East, and so on. A small company's initial needs may be satisfied by a single export manager who has responsibility for the full range of international activities. Regardless of how a company organizes for exporting, it should ensure that the organization facilitates the marketer's job. Good marketing skills can help the firm overcome the handicap of operating in an unfamiliar market. Experience has shown that a company's success in foreign markets depends less on the unique attributes of its products than on its marketing methods.

Once a company has been organized to handle exporting, the proper channel of distribution needs to be selected in each market. These channels include sales representatives, agents, distributors, retailers, and end users.

Sales Representatives

Overseas, a sales representative is the equivalent of a manufacturer's representative in the United States. The representative uses the company's product literature and samples to present the product to potential buyers. A representative usually handles many complementary lines that do not compete. The sales representative usually works on a commission basis, assumes no risk or responsibility, and is under contract for a definite period of time (renewable by mutual agreement). The contract defines territory, terms of sale, method of compensation, reasons and procedures for terminating the agreement, and other details. The sales representative may operate on either an exclusive or a nonexclusive basis.

Agents

The widely misunderstood term agent means a representative who normally has authority, perhaps even power of attorney, to make commitments on behalf of the firm he or she represents. Firms in the United States and other developed countries have stopped using the term and instead rely on the term representative, since agent can imply more than intended. Any contract should state whether the representative or agent does or does not have legal authority to obligate the firm.

Distributors

The foreign distributor is a merchant who purchases merchandise from a U.S. exporter (often at substantial discount) and resells it at a profit. The foreign distributor generally provides support and service for the product, relieving the U.S. company of these responsibilities. The distributor usually carries an inventory of products and a sufficient supply of spare parts and maintains adequate facilities and personnel for normal servicing operations. The distributor typically carries a range of noncompetitive but complementary products. End users do not usually buy from a distributor; they buy from retailers or dealers.

The payment terms and length of association between the U.S. company and the foreign distributor are established by contract. Some U.S. companies prefer to begin with a relatively short trial period and then extend the contract if the relationship proves satisfactory to both parties.

Foreign Retailers

A company may also sell directly to a foreign retailer, although in such transactions, products are generally limited to consumer lines. The growth of major retail chains in markets such as Canada and Japan has created new opportunities for this type of direct sale. The method relies mainly on traveling sales representatives who directly contact foreign retailers, although results may be accomplished by mailing catalogs, brochures, or other literature. The direct mail approach has the benefits of eliminating commissions, reducing traveling expenses, and reaching a broader audience. For best results, however, a firm that uses direct mail to reach foreign retailers should support it with other marketing activities.

American manufacturers with ties to major domestic retailers may also be able to use them to sell abroad. Many large American retailers maintain overseas buying offices and use these offices to sell abroad when practicable.

Direct Sales to End Users

A U.S. business may sell its products or services directly to end users in foreign countries. These buyers can be foreign governments; institutions such as hospitals, banks, and schools; or businesses. Buyers can be identified at trade shows, through international publications, or through U.S. government contact programs, such as the Department of Commerce's Export Contact List Service (ECLS). Chapter 7, "Making Contacts," beginning on page 39, details these and other buyer contact activities and programs.

The U.S. company should be aware that if a product is sold in such a direct fashion, the exporter is responsible for shipping, payment collection, and product servicing unless other arrangements are made. Unless the cost of providing these services is built into the export price, a company could end up making far less than originally intended.

Locating Foreign Representatives and Buyers

A company that chooses to use foreign representatives may meet them during overseas business trips or at domestic or international trade shows. There are other effective methods, too, that can be employed without leaving the United States. Ultimately, the exporter may need to travel abroad to identify, evaluate, and sign overseas representatives; however, a company can save time by first doing homework in the United States. Methods include use of US&FCS contact programs, banks and service organizations, and publications. For more information on these methods, *refer to* Chapter 7, "Making Contacts," beginning on page 39.

Contacting and Evaluating Foreign Representatives

Once the U.S. company has identified a number of potential representatives or distributors in the selected market, it should write directly to each. Just as the U.S. firm is seeking information on the foreign representative, the representative is interested in corporate and product information on the U.S. firm. The prospective representative may want more information than the company normally provides to a casual buyer. Therefore, the firm should provide full information on its history, resources, personnel, the product line, previous export activity, and all other pertinent matters. The firm may wish to include a photograph or two of plant facilities and products or possibly product samples, when practical. (Whenever the danger of piracy is significant, the exporter should guard against sending product samples that could be easily copied.) For more information on correspondence with foreign firms refer to Chapter 9, "Selling Overseas," beginning on page 53.

A U.S. firm should investigate potential representatives of distributors carefully before entering into an agreement. See table 4-1 for an extensive checklist of factors to consider in such evaluations. In brief, the U.S. firm needs to know the following points about the representative or distributor's firm:

- Current status and history, including background on principal officers
- Personnel and other resources (salespeople, warehouse and service facilities, etc.)
- Sales territory covered
- Current sales volume
- Typical customer profiles
- Methods of introducing new products into the sales territory
- Names and addresses of U.S. firms currently represented
- Trade and bank references
- Data on whether the U.S. firm's special requirements can be met
- View of the in-country market potential for the U.S. firm's products. This information is not only useful in gauging how much the representative knows about the exporter's industry, it is also valuable market research in its own right

A U.S. company may obtain much of this information from business associates who currently work with foreign representatives. However, U.S. exporters should not hesitate to ask potential representatives or distributors detailed and specific questions; exporters have the right to explore the qualifications of those who propose to represent them overseas. Well-qualified representatives will gladly answer questions that help distinguish them from less-qualified competitors.

In addition, the U.S. company may wish to obtain at least two supporting business and credit reports to ensure that the distributor or representative is reputable. By using a second credit report from another source, the U.S. firm may gain new or more complete information. Reports are available from commercial firms and from the Department of Commerce's World Traders Data Report (WTDR) program.

The WTDR service provides background reports on specific foreign firms prepared by the US&FCS posts overseas. In addition to information on size, product lines, and financial stability, each WTDR also contains a general narrative statement by the commercial officer who conducted the investigation.

Commercial firms and banks are also sources of credit information on overseas representatives. They can provide information directly or from their correspondent banks or branches overseas. Directories of international companies may also provide credit information on foreign firms.

If the U.S. company has the necessary information, it may wish to contact a few of the foreign firm's U.S. clients to obtain an evaluation of their representative's character, reliability, efficiency, and past performance. To protect itself against possible conflicts of interest, it is also important for the U.S. firm to learn about other product lines that the foreign firm represents.

Once the company has qualified some foreign representatives, it may wish to travel to the foreign country to observe the size, condition, and location of offices and warehouses. In addition, the U.S. company should meet the sales force and try to assess its strength in the marketplace. If traveling to each distributor or representative is difficult, the company may decide to meet with them at U.S. and worldwide trade shows.

Negotiating an Agreement with a Foreign Representative

When the U.S. company has found a prospective representative that meets its requirements, the next step is to negotiate a foreign sales agreement. Department of Commerce district offices and Export Assistance Centers can provide counseling to firms planning to negotiate foreign sales agreements with representatives and distributors.

The potential representative is interested in the company's pricing structure and profit potential. Representatives are also concerned with the terms of payment, product regulation, competitors and their market shares, the amount of support provided by the U.S. firm (sales aids, promotional material, advertising, etc.), training for sales and service staff, and the company's ability to deliver on schedule.

The agreement may contain provisions that the foreign representative

- not have business dealings with competitive firms (this provision may cause problems in some European countries and may also cause problems under U.S. antitrust laws);
- not reveal any confidential information in a way that would prove injurious, detrimental, or competitive to the U.S. firm;
- not enter into agreements binding to the U.S. firm; and

- refer all inquiries received from outside the designated sales territory to the U.S. firm for action.

To ensure a conscientious sales effort from the foreign representative, the agreement should include a requirement that the foreign representative apply the utmost skill and ability to the sale of the product for the compensation named in the contract. It may be appropriate to include performance requirements such as a minimum sales volume and an expected rate of increase.

In the drafting of the agreement, special attention must be paid to safeguarding the exporter's interests in cases in which the representative proves less than satisfactory. (*Refer to* Chapter 11, "Export Regulations, Customs Benefits, and Tax Incentives," beginning on page 60, for recommendations on specifying terms of law and arbitration.) It is vital to include an escape clause in the agreement, allowing the exporter to end the relationship safely and cleanly if the representative does not work out. Some contracts specify that either party may terminate the agreement with written notice 30, 60, or 90 days in advance. The contract may also spell out exactly what constitutes just cause for ending the agreement (e.g., failure to meet specified performance levels). Other contracts specify a certain term for the agreement (usually one year) but arrange for automatic annual renewal unless either party gives notice in writing of its intention not to renew.

In all cases, escape clauses and other provisions to safeguard the exporter may be limited by the laws of the country in which the representative is located. For this reason, the U.S. firm should learn as much as it can about the legal requirements of the representative's country and obtain qualified legal counsel in preparing the contract. These are some of the legal questions to consider:

- How far in advance must the representative be notified of the exporter's intention to terminate the agreement? Three months satisfy the requirements of most countries, but a verifiable means of conveyance (e.g., registered mail) may be needed to establish when the notice was served.
- What is just cause for terminating a representative? Specifying causes for termination in the written contract usually strengthens the exporter's position.
- Which country's laws (or which international convention) govern a contract dispute? Laws in the representative's country may forbid the representative from waiving its nation's legal jurisdiction.
- What compensation is due the representative on dismissal? Depending on the length of the relationship, the added value of the market the representative has created for the exporter, and whether termination is for just cause as defined by the foreign country, the U.S. exporter may be required to compensate the representative for losses.
- What must the representative give up if dismissed? The contract should specify the return of patents, trademarks, name registrations, customer records, and so on.
- Should the representative be referred to as an agent? In some countries, the word agent implies power of attorney. The contract may need to specify that the representative is not a legal agent with power of attorney.
- In what language should the contract be drafted? An English-language text should be the official language of the contract in most cases.

The exporter should also be aware of U.S. laws that govern such contracts. For instance, the U.S. company should seek to avoid provisions that could be contrary to U.S. antitrust laws. The Export Trading Company Act provides a means to obtain antitrust protection when two or more companies combine for exporting. In any case, the U.S. firm should obtain legal advice when preparing and entering into any foreign agreement.

Table 4-1. Factors to Consider When Choosing a Foreign Rep or Distributor

The following checklist should be tailored by each company to its own needs. Key factors vary significantly with the products and countries involved.

Size of sales force

- How many field sales personnel does the representative or distributor have?
- What are its short- and long-range expansion plans?
- Would it need to expand to accommodate your account properly? If so, would it be willing to do so?

Sales record

- Has its sales growth been consistent? If not, why not? Try to determine sales volume for the past five years.
- What is its sales volume per outside salesperson?
- What are its sales objectives for next year? How were they determined?

Territorial analysis

- What territory does it now cover?
- Is it consistent with the coverage you desire? If not, is it able and willing to expand?
- Does it have any branch offices in the territory to be covered?
- If so, are they located where your sales prospects are greatest?
- Does it have any plans to open additional offices?

Product mix

- How many product lines does it represent?
- Are these product lines compatible with yours?
- Would there be any conflict of interest?
- Does it represent any other U.S. firms? If so, which ones?
- If necessary, would it be willing to alter its present product mix to accommodate yours?
- What would be the minimum sales volume needed to justify its handling your lines? Do its sales projections reflect this minimum figure? From what you know of the territory and the prospective representative or distributor, is its projection realistic?

Facilities and equipment

- Does it have adequate warehouse facilities?
- What is its method of stock control?
- Does it use computers? Are they compatible with yours?
- What communications facilities does it have (fax, modem, telex, etc.)?
- If your product requires servicing, is it equipped and qualified to do so? If not, is it willing to acquire the needed equipment and arrange for necessary training? To what extent will you have to share the training cost?
- If necessary and customary, is it willing to inventory repair parts and replacement items?

Marketing policies

- How is its sales staff compensated?
- Does it have special incentive or motivation programs?
- Does it use product managers to coordinate sales efforts for specific product lines?
- How does it monitor sales performance?
- How does it train its sales staff?
- Would it share expenses for sales personnel to attend factory-sponsored seminars?

Customer profile

- What kinds of customers is it currently contacting?
- Are its interests compatible with your product line?
- Who are its key accounts?
- What percentage of its total gross receipts do these key accounts represent?

Principals represented

- How many principals is it currently representing?
- Would you be its primary supplier?
- If not, what percentage of its total business would you represent? How does this percentage compare with other suppliers?

Promotional thrust

- Can it help you compile market research information to be used in making forecasts?
- What media does it use, if any, to promote sales?
- How much of its budget is allocated to advertising? How is it distributed among various principals?
- Will you be expected to contribute funds for promotional purposes? How will the amount be determined?
- If it uses direct mail, how many prospects are on its mailing list?
- What type of brochure does it use to describe its company and the products that it represents?
- If necessary, can it translate your advertising copy?

Chapter 5

Preparing Products for Export

Selecting and preparing a product for export requires not only product knowledge but also knowledge of the unique characteristics of each market being targeted. The market research conducted (as outlined in Chapter 3) and the contacts made with foreign representatives (as outlined in Chapter 4) should give the U.S. company an idea of what products can be sold where. Before the sale can occur, however, the company may need to modify a particular product to satisfy buyer tastes or needs in foreign markets.

The extent to which the company will modify products sold in export markets is a key policy issue to be addressed by management. Some exporters believe the domestic product can be exported without significant changes. Others seek to consciously develop uniform products that are acceptable in all export markets.

If the company manufactures more than one product or offers many models of a single product, it should start with the one best suited to the targeted market. Ideally, the firm chooses one or two products that fit the market without major design or engineering modifications. Doing so is possible when the U.S. company

- Deals with international customers with the same demographic characteristics or with the same specifications for manufactured goods,
- Supplies parts for U.S. goods that are exported to foreign countries without modifications,
- Produces a unique product that is sold on the basis of its status or foreign appeal, or
- Produces a product that has few or no distinguishing features and that is sold almost exclusively on a commodity or price basis.

Product Preparation Considerations

- What foreign needs does the product satisfy?
- Should the firm modify its domestic-market product for sale abroad? Should it develop a new product for the foreign market?
- What product should the firm offer abroad?
- What specific features—design, color, size, packaging, brand, warranty, and so on—should the product have?
- What specific services are necessary abroad at the presale and postsale stages?
- Are the firm's service and repair facilities adequate?

Product Adaptation

To enter a foreign market successfully, a U.S. company may have to modify its product to conform to government regulations, geographic and climatic conditions, buyer preferences, or standard of living. The company may also need to modify its product to facilitate shipment or to compensate for possible differences in engineering or design standards.

Foreign government product regulations are common in international trade and are expected to expand in the future. These regulations can take the form of high tariffs or of nontariff barriers, such as regulations or product specifications. Governments impose these regulations to

- Protect domestic industries from foreign competition,
- Protect the health of their citizens,
- Force importers to comply with environmental controls,
- Ensure that importers meet local requirements for electrical or measurement systems,
- Restrict the flow of goods originating in or having components from certain countries, and
- Protect their citizens from cultural influences deemed inappropriate.

Detailed information on regulations imposed by foreign countries is available from the country desk officers of the Department of Commerce's IEP unit. Where particularly onerous or discriminatory barriers are imposed by a foreign government, a U.S. company may be able to get help from the U.S. government to press for their removal. The firm should contact the nearest U.S. Export Assistance Center, Commerce Department district office or the Office of the U.S. Trade Representative in Washington, D.C. For further information, refer to Appendix II, "Directory of Federal Export Assistance," beginning on page 120, and Appendix III, "State and Local Sources of Assistance," beginning on page 130.

It is often necessary for a company to adapt its product to account for geographic and climatic conditions as well as for availability of resources. Factors such as topography, humidity, and energy costs can affect the performance of a product or even define its use. The cost of petroleum products along with a country's infrastructure, for example, may indicate the demand for a company's energy-consuming products.

Buyer preferences in a foreign market may also lead a U.S. manufacturer to modify its product. Local customs, such as religion or the use of leisure time, often determine whether a product will sell. The sensory impact of a product, such as taste or visual impact, may also be a critical factor. The Japanese desire for beautiful packaging, for example, has led many U.S. companies to redesign cartons and packages specifically for this market.

A country's standard of living can also determine whether a company needs to modify a product. The level of income, the level of education, and the availability of energy are all factors that help predict the acceptance of a product in a foreign market. If a country's standard of living is lower than that of the United States, a manufacturer may find a market for less sophisticated product models that have become obsolete in the United States. Certain high-technology products are inappropriate in some countries not only because of their cost, but also because of their function. For example, a computerized industrial washing machine might replace workers in a country where employment is a high priority. In addition, these products may need a level of servicing that is unavailable in some countries.

Market potential must be large enough to justify the direct and indirect costs involved in product adaptation. The firm should assess the costs to be incurred and the increased revenues expected from adaptation (they may be difficult to determine). The decision to adapt a product is based in part on the degree of commitment to the specific foreign market; two firms, one with short-term goals and the other with long-term goals, may have different perspectives.

Engineering and Redesign

In addition to adaptations related to cultural and consumer preference, the exporter should be aware that even fundamental aspects of its products may require changing. For example, electrical standards in many foreign countries differ from U.S. electrical standards. It is not unusual to find phases, cycles, or voltages (both in home and commercial use) that would damage or impair the operating efficiency of equipment designed for use in the United States. These electrical standards sometimes vary even in the same country. Knowing this requirement, the manufacturer can determine whether a special motor must be substituted or arrange for a different drive ratio to achieve the desired operating revolutions per minute.

Similarly, many kinds of equipment must be engineered in the metric system for integration with other pieces of equipment or for compliance with the standards of a given country. The United States is virtually alone in its adherence to a nonmetric system, and U.S. firms that compete successfully in the global market have found metric measurement to be an important detail in selling to overseas customers. Even instruction or maintenance manuals should take care to give dimensions in centimeters, weights in grams or kilos, and temperatures in degrees Celsius. Information on foreign standards and certification systems is available from

National Center for Standards and Certification Information (NCSCI)
National Institute for Standards and Technology (NIST)
100 Bureau Dr., Stop 2150
Gaithersburg, MD 20899-2150
Tel: (301) 975-4040; Fax: (301) 926-1559; Web site: www.nist.gov/ts

NIST Office of Information Services
Reference Desk
Tel: (301) 975-3052

Since freight charges are usually assessed by weight or volume (whichever provides the greater revenue for the carrier), a company should give some consideration to shipping an item unassembled to reduce delivery costs. Shipping unassembled also facilitates movement on narrow roads or through doorways and elevators.

Branding, Labeling, and Packaging

Consumers are concerned with both the product itself and the product's supplementary features, such as packaging, warranties, and service. Branding and labeling of products in foreign markets raise new considerations for the U.S. company:

- Are international brand names important to promote and distinguish a product? Conversely, should local brands or private labels be employed to heighten local interest?
- Are the colors used on labels and packages offensive or attractive to the foreign buyer? In some countries, certain colors are associated with death, national flags, or other cultural factors.
- Can labels be produced in official or customary languages if required by law or practice?

- Does information on product content and country of origin have to be provided?
- Are weights and measures stated in the local unit?
- Must each item be labeled individually?
- Are local tastes and knowledge considered? A dry cereal box picturing a U.S. athlete may not be as attractive to overseas consumers as the picture of a local sports hero.

A company may find that building international recognition for a brand is expensive. Protection for brand names varies from one country to another, and in some developing countries, barriers to the use of foreign brands or trademarks may exist. In other countries, piracy of a company's brand names and counterfeiting of its products are widespread. To protect its products and brand names, a company must comply with local laws on patents, copyrights, and trademarks. A U.S. firm may find it useful to obtain the advice of local lawyers and consultants where appropriate.

Installation

Another element of product preparation that a company should consider is the ease of installing that product overseas. If technicians or engineers are needed overseas to assist in installation, the company should minimize their time in the field if possible. To do so, the company may wish to preassemble or pretest the product before shipping.

Disassembling the product for shipment and reassembling abroad may be considered by the company. This method can save the firm shipping costs, but it may add to delay in payment if the sale is contingent on an assembled product. Even if trained personnel do not have to be sent, the company should be careful to provide all product information, such as training manuals, installation instructions, and parts lists, in the local language.

Warranties

The company should include a warranty on the product, since the buyer expects a specific level of performance and a guarantee that it will be achieved. Levels of expectation for a warranty vary from country to country depending on its level of development, competitive practices, the activism of consumer groups, local standards of production quality, and other similar factors.

A company may use warranties for advertising purposes to distinguish its product from its competition. Strong warranties may be required to break into a new market, especially if the company is an unknown supplier. In some cases, warranties may be instrumental in making the sale and may be a major element of negotiation. In other cases, however, warranties similar to those in the United States are not expected. By providing an unnecessary warranty, the company may raise the cost of the product higher than the competitors' costs. When considering this point, exporters should keep in mind that servicing warranties will probably be more expensive and troublesome in foreign markets. It is desirable to arrange warranty service locally with the assistance of a representative or distributor.

Servicing

Of special concern to foreign consumers is the service the U.S. company provides for its product. Service after the sale is critical for some products; generally, the more complex the product technology, the greater the demand for presale and postsale service. There is, therefore, pressure in some firms to offer simpler, more robust products overseas to reduce the need for maintenance and repairs. U.S. exporters who rely on a foreign distributor or agent to provide service backup must take steps to ensure an adequate level of service. These steps include training, periodically checking service quality, and monitoring inventories of spare parts. *Refer to* Chapter 15, "After-Sales Service," beginning on page 105, for more on after-sales service.

Chapter 6

Service Exports

The United States is the world's premier producer and exporter of services. Encompassing all economic activity other than agriculture, mining, and manufacturing, the service sector is the largest component of the U.S. economy, accounting for 76 percent of private sector output and 80 percent of private non-farm employment (over 78 million jobs in 1995).

U.S. services exports more than doubled over the last seven years—increasing $100 billion since 1987, and $51 billion just since 1990. In 1994, U.S. services exports exceeded imports by $60 billion (offsetting 36 percent of the deficit on merchandise trade). Major markets for U.S. exports include the European Union ($55 billion in 1994 exports), Japan ($30 billion), and Canada ($17 billion). At $9 billion, Mexico is currently the largest of the emerging markets for services exports. These services exports support millions of U.S. jobs—approximately 3.4 million in 1992—and play a key role in U.S. economic growth.

The income generated and the jobs created through the sale of services abroad are just as important to the U.S. economy as income and jobs resulting from the production and export of goods. In view of the shift toward services both domestically and internationally and the substantial competitive advantage of the United States in the services field, those who have services to offer can become major participants in world trade.

The Trade Promotion Coordinating Committee (TPCC) Services Working Group was established in 1992 because of the importance of services trade. The TPCC/Services Working Group is responsible for coordinating and streamlining Federal Government trade promotion activities, planning and implementing service industries trade promotion activities, and promoting American service industries in new or neglected markets. The Service Industries and Finance sector of Trade Development in the U.S. Department of Commerce is responsible for the TPCC Services Working Group. For further information contact SWG at Tel: (202) 482-5086.

Typical Service Exports

The service sector accounts for a great share of the U.S. economy, although some services are not easily exported. It would be very difficult to export most personal services, such as the service performed by waiters in restaurants; but most business services can be exported—especially those highly innovative, specialized, or technologically advanced services that are efficiently performed in the United States. See "Top 10 Service Exports" on page 38 for some general statistics on U.S. service exports. The following sectors have particularly high export potential:

- ***Construction, design, and engineering.*** The vast experience and technological leadership of the U.S. construction industry, as well as special skills in operations, maintenance, and management, frequently give U.S. firms a competitive edge in international projects. Some U.S. firms with expertise in specialized fields, such as electric power utilities, also export related construction, design, and engineering services, such as power plant design services.
- ***Banking and financial services.*** U.S. financial institutions are very competitive internationally, particularly when offering account management, credit card operations, collection management, and other services they have pioneered.
- ***Insurance services.*** U.S. insurers offer valuable services ranging from underwriting and risk evaluation to insurance operations and management contracts in the international marketplace.
- ***Legal and accounting services.*** Firms in this field typically aid other U.S. firms operating abroad through their international legal and accounting activities. They also use their experience to serve foreign firms in their business operations.
- ***Computer and data services.*** The U.S. computer services and data industries lead the world in marketing new technologies and enjoy a competitive advantage in computer operations, data manipulation, and data transmission.

- ***Teaching services.*** The vast U.S. education sector offers substantial new services for foreign purchasers, particularly in areas such as management, motivation, and the teaching of operational, managerial, and theoretical issues.
- ***Management consulting services.*** Organizations and business enterprises all over the world look to the United States in the field of management. U.S. management consulting firms as well as other U.S. firms that are willing to sell their particular management skills find great potential overseas for export of their services.

Exporting Services versus Products

There are many obvious differences between services and products. Consequently, important features differentiate exporting services from exporting products:

- Services are less tangible than products, providing little in terms of samples that can be seen by the potential foreign buyer. Consequently, communicating a service offer is much more difficult than communicating a product offer. For example, brochures or catalogs explaining services often must show a proxy for the service. A construction company, for instance, can show a picture of a construction site, but a picture of the finished building communicates the actual performance of the service more effectively. Much more attention must be paid to translating the intangibility of a service into a tangible and saleable offer.
- The intangibility of services also makes financing more difficult. Frequently, even financial institutions with international experience are less willing to provide financial support for service exports than for product exports, because the value of services is more difficult to monitor. Customer complaints and difficulties in receiving payments can also appear more troublesome to assess.
- Services are often more time dependent than products. Quite frequently, a service can be offered only at a specific time, and as time passes, the service perishes if it is not used. For example, to offer data transmission through special telephone lines may require providing an open telephone line. If this line is not heavily used, the cost of maintaining it may not be covered.
- Selling services is also more personal than selling products, because it quite often requires direct involvement with the customer. This involvement demands greater cultural sensitivity when services are being provided, since a buffer of indirect communication and interaction does not exist.
- Services are much more difficult to standardize than products. Service activities must frequently be tailored to the specific needs of the buyer. This need for adaptation often necessitates the service client's direct participation and cooperation in the service delivery.

Demand for certain services can derive from product exports. Many of our merchandise exports would not take place if they were not supported by service activities such as banking, insurance, and transportation. Services can be crucial in stimulating product export and are a critical factor in maintaining such exports. However, in such cases, services follow products rather than taking the lead over them.

Marketing Services Abroad

Since service exports are often delivered in the support of product exports, a sensible approach for some beginning exporters is to follow the path of relevant product exports. For years, many large accounting and banking firms have exported by following their major multinational clients abroad and continuing to assist them in their international activities. Smaller service exporters who cooperate closely with manufacturing firms can also determine where these manufacturing firms are operating internationally and aim to provide service support for these manufacturers abroad.

For service providers whose activities are independent from products, a different strategy is needed. These individuals and firms should search for market situations abroad that are similar to the domestic market.

Many opportunities derive from understanding the process and stage of development of relevant trade activities abroad. Just as U.S. society has undergone change, foreign societies are subject to changing economic trends. If, for example, new transportation services are opened up in a country, an expert in the area of containerization may offer services to improve the efficiency of the new system.

Leads for service activities can also be gathered by staying informed about international projects sponsored by organizations such as the World Bank, the Caribbean Development Bank, the Inter-American Development Bank, the UN, and the World Health Organization. Very frequently, such projects are in need of service support.

Government Support for Service Exports

In recognition of the increasing importance of service exports, the U.S. Department of Commerce has made the Office of Service Industries (OSI) responsible for analyzing and promoting services trade. The OSI provides information on opportunities and operations of services abroad. For more information about specific industry sectors, contact the OSI at Tel: (202) 482-3575; Fax: (202) 482-2669; Web site: www.ita.doc.gov/sif/.

The Department of Commerce provides the same overseas exposure in *Commercial News USA* magazine for U.S. service firms as for manufacturers. A brief description of the service with the firm's name and address is listed under the appropriate category. Interested overseas parties are instructed to contact listed firms directly. A modest fee is charged for this service, which distributes the listed information to more than 135,000 agents, distributors, and government officials in 152 countries. An additional two million have electronic access to the information. For more information, *see* "Commercial News USA (CNUSA)" on page 40, or contact your nearest Export Assistance Center or Department of Commerce district offices or call Tel: (202) 482-3334.

Both the Agency for International Development and the Trade and Development Agency offer opportunities for U.S. service firms. For a more complete description of their activities, *see* "Agency for International Development (AID)" on page 45 and "Trade and Development Agency (TDA)" on page 45.

The Engineering Multiplier program of the Ex-Im Bank assists U.S. design, engineering, and architectural firms with foreign contracts. For information on this program, contact the Ex-Im Bank's Engineering and Environment Division at Tel: (202) 565-3570; Fax: (202) 565-3504.

Recent Trade Agreements Liberalizing Services Trade

The General Agreement on Trade in Services (GATS), a result of the Uruguay Round of Multilateral Trade Negotiations, liberalizes trade in services amongst WTO member nations. This is the first multilateral, legally enforcable agreement covering trade and investment in the service industries. Some of its key features include most favored nation (MFN) treatment, national treatment, improved market access, transparency requirements and free flow of payments and transfers. Some of the U.S. industries expected to benefit the most from the GATS include advertising; foreign travel-related businesses; and U.S. professional services, including accounting, architecture, and engineering. In addition, the Government Procurement Agreement opens market access for service providers.

The North American Free Trade Agreement (NAFTA) also provides a number of opportunities to U.S. businesses through improved market access and other liberalizations. Some of the industries most affected by NAFTA are:

- **Transportation services.** U.S. truck and bus companies now have the right to use their own drivers and equipment for cross-border cargo shipment and passenger service with Mexico. NAFTA also creates opportunities for U.S. firms to invest in trucking and bus service, warehousing, intermodal terminals, and landslide port activities in Mexico. It locks in U.S. railroad companies' ability to market rail service directly to customers in Mexico and to operate their trains on Mexican tracks.
- **Financial services.** Mexican reforms in the insurance, banking and securities sectors offer unprecedented access to a previously closed market. NAFTA will eliminate, over a transition period, equity and market share restrictions in Mexico on U.S. financial services providers, including banks and securities firms, insurance companies, leasing and factoring companies and non-bank lenders. For the firs time in 50 years, U.S. financial service providers will be able to operate wholly-owned subsidiaries in Mexico, and receive the same treatment as Mexican-owned firms.
- **Telecommunication services.** Elimination of restrictions on data processing and other telecommunications services allow subsidiaries of U.S. companies in Mexico and Canada to access data processing systems in the United States. The availability of leased lines and the ability to interconnect the private network with the public communications network creates an environment for introducing many new telecommunications technologies into the Mexican market, such as voice and electronic mail systems, online databases and computer processing applications.

Top 10 Service Exports

The values reported here exclude the value of affiliated (intra-firm) sales except for categories marked with an asterisk. By definition, the services exports data also exclude the value of sales by foreign affiliates, which are often a very important channel for U.S. firms marketing their services abroad.

This information was prepared by the International Trade Administration's Office of Service Industries based on Bureau of Economic Analysis estimates that are reported annually in Survey of Current Business. For further information, contact the Office of Service Industries at (202) 482-3575.

	Millions of Dollars
Travel*	**$60,406**
Transportation*	**$43,555**
Includes:	
Freight Services	$9,836
Passenger Fares	$17,477
Port Services	$15,213
Other Transportation Services	$1,029
Commercial, Professional, and Technical Services	**$10,115**
Includes:	
Accounting, Auditing, and Bookkeeping Services	$2,704
Advertising Services	($399)
Construction, Engineering, Architectural, and Mining Services	($2,704)
Franchising Fees	($458)
Industrial Engineering Services	($235)
Industrial Processes	($2,964)
Legal Services	($1,558)
Mailing, Reproduction, and Commercial Art Services	($14)
Management, Consulting, and Public Relations Services	($986)
Personnel Supply Services	($118)
Research Development and Testing Services	($337)
Financial Services	**$8,602**
Includes:	
Financial Services	($6,962)
Insurance (Premiums Received Net of Losses Paid)	($1,640)
Education and Training Services	**$7,510**
Includes:	
Education	($7,140)
Training Services	($370)

	Millions of Dollars
Entertainment Services	**$3,969**
Includes:	
Books, Records, and Tapes	($307)
Broadcasting and Recording of Live Events	($153)
Film and Tape Rentals	($3,448)
Sports and Performing Arts	($61)
Equipment Installation, Maintenance, and Repair Services	**$3,394**
Information Services	**$3,369**
Includes:	
Computer and Data Processing Services	($2,546)
Database and other Information Services	($823)
Telecommunications Services	**$2,757**
Health Care Services	**$812**
Includes:	
Management of Health Care Facilities	($18)
Medical Services	($794)
Other Services* (Including affiliated sales for most catagories above)	**$40,930**
U.S. Private Services Exports TOTAL*	**$185,419**

Chapter 7

Making Contacts

After a company has identified its most promising markets and devised strategies to enter those markets, the next step is to actually locate a buyer. If that buyer is the end user of a company's product or service, a relatively simple transaction may result. In many cases, however, U.S. exporters need an in-country presence through a representative or distributor to reach the eventual buyer. Alternatively, the firm may identify customers through attendance at trade shows, trade missions, direct mail campaigns, and advertising.

Regardless of how the exporter makes contacts and develops sales leads, the exporter faces many questions:

- Specifically who are potential buyers?
- What trade shows are the most effective?
- Which marketing techniques are most successful?

In this chapter U.S. exporters will find the means to answer these questions. The marketing techniques described are by no means exhaustive. However, the chapter describes sources of assistance in locating buyers, evaluating trade missions and shows, and conducting other programs designed to make contacts.

Department of Commerce Contact Programs

The U.S. Department of Commerce can help exporters identify and qualify direct leads for potential buyers, distributors, joint venture partners, and licensees from both private and public sources. Along with its various product, country, and program experts, the Department of Commerce has an extensive network of commercial officers posted in countries that represent 95 percent of the market for U.S. products.

Services and publications available through the Department of Commerce are listed in this section. Exporters should contact the nearest Export Assistance Center or Commerce district office for more information or contact

Office of Export Information and Research Services
U.S. Department of Commerce
Washington, DC 20230
Tel: (202) 482-2000; Fax: (202) 482-3617

International Contact Information

Commercial Service International Contacts (CSIC) provides contact and product information on more than 70,000 firms abroad interested in U.S. products. Country Directories of International Contacts (CDIC) provide the name and contact information for directories of importers, agents, trade associations, government agencies, etc., on a country-by-country basis. Both are available on the NTDB.

Trade Opportunity Program (TOP)

This service provides timely sales leads from overseas firms seeking to buy or represent U.S. products and services. Commercial specialists in U.S. embassies and consulates around the world collect TOP leads at trade shows, through conversations with local buyers, and through market research. They may include direct sales leads, representation offers, investment opportunities, licensing partners, joint venture partnerships, project bids, and foreign government tenders. These prescreened leads are transmitted to the United States every work day by commercial specialists in U.S. embassies and consulates abroad and then immediately posted on Commerce's Economic Bulletin Board (EBB). U.S. exporters respond directly to the contacts listed for the leads of interest. Users can retrieve the TOP files (and all other files) from the EBB each day through a personal computer and modem. Subscribers may use, edit, or redistribute the leads in any way they wish. For more information on subscribing to the EBB, *see* "Sources of General Information" on page 19.

TOP leads are also available through commercial newspapers including the *Journal of Commerce*, major online electronic database services, industry and trade publications, trade associations, state economic development agencies, and World Trade Centers. The NTDB lists the TOP leads for the past two years.

Agent/Distributor Service (ADS)

The ADS is used to locate foreign import agents and distributors.Commercial specialists at U.S. embassies and consulates abroad search the market for qualified agents, distributors, or representatives, according to specifications. Prospects are screened for capability and interest, and within 30 to 60 days information is delivered on up to six of the best qualified candidates.

For each prospect, the U.S. company is given the company name, name and title of key contact person, telephone and fax numbers, level of interest in distributing your product or service, preferred language for correspondence, prospect's opinion on the marketability of your product or service in the targeted market, U.S. Department of Commerce commercial specialist's assessment of each prospect's capability and suitability to distribute your products.

ADS application forms may be obtained from Export Assistance Centers or Commerce district offices. Trade specialists at these offices can help with preparing applications and can provide guidance if there are any factors barring the desired relationship.

Gold Key Service

Through the Gold Key Service, experienced trade professionals in your target country will arrange appointments in overseas markets with prescreened contacts., including representatives, distributors, government contacts, licensing and joint venture partners. Gold Key Service includes customized market and industry briefings prior to your business meetings, plus a debriefing with trade professionals afterwards to discuss the results of your meetings and appropriate follow-up strategies. It can also include hiring interpreters, help with travel and accommodations, providing clerical support, screening business candidates, and setting appointments.

The Gold Key Service is now available in more than 70 markets worldwide, at fees ranging from $150 to $600. To find out more, contact the Export Assistance Center or Commerce district office nearest you.

International Company Profiles

International Company Profiles (ICPs) are thorough background checks on potential clients. Commercial specialists in U.S. embassies and consulates abroad will conduct investigations and deliver the results in 30 to 45 days, at a very reasonable cost. Reports include information such as bank and trade references; principals, key officers and managers; product lines; number of employees; financial data; sales volume; reputation; and market outlook. An ICP may also include reports on subsidiary/parent relationships, recent news items about the firm, the firms' U.S. customers, operational problems, activities of prominent owners, and branch locations. Requests are held in strict confidence—the subject firm does not know who ordered the report.

ICPs are relatively inexpensive, may provide information not available from other investigative services, and will qualify as one of the reports required for foreign credit insurance coverage. Note that these profiles may not be available in countries with well developed commercial credit reporting agencies. Contact the Export Assistance Center or Commerce district office nearest you for more information on ICPs.

Commercial News USA (CNUSA)

CNUSA provides worldwide exposure for U.S. products and services through an illustrated catalog-magazine and electronic bulletin boards. The catalog-magazine is distributed through U.S. embassies and consulates to business readers in 152 countries. Copies are also made available to international visitors at trade events around the world. Current hard-copy distribution averages 137,000 copies, with 10 issues per year. Information in *CNUSA* is further disseminated by US&FCS posts or local organizations that reprint all or part of the publication. *CNUSA*'s electronic distribution reaches an additional two million business readers.

Listings in *CNUSA* describe the major features of an export product or service. The name, address, and telephone and fax numbers of the U.S. manufacturer or distributor are included along with a photo or illustration. Several size formats are available, and prices start at $395; larger formats may contain longer descriptions. The electronic versions of *CNUSA* transmit the complete text of the magazine listings, without illustrations, to EBB subscribers.

The *CNUSA* program covers more than 30 industry categories and focuses on products that have been on the U.S. market no longer than three years. Companies may also market services and trade and technical literature through *CNUSA*. Only pharmaceuticals, raw materials, agricultural commodities, and items on the Federal Register Munitions List are excluded from *CNUSA*. All products in *CNUSA* must be at least 51 percent U.S. parts and 51 percent U.S. labor.

CNUSA also profiles up to three industries per issue with high export potential. In these special industry sections, U.S. firms may promote established products as well as new models. Participants may purchase up to three separate listings per issue, each focusing on a single product model. A new product may be listed four times per year. *CNUSA* does not feature descriptions of entire product lines or accept camera-ready advertisements.

The trade leads generated by *CNUSA* help U.S. firms identify potential export markets and make contacts leading to representation, distributorships, joint venture or licensing agreements, or direct sales. Overseas inquiries come directly to participating U.S. firms and are address coded to allow for tracking and program evaluation. Interested firms should contact the nearest Export Assistance Center or Commerce district office for information, or call the product manager at (202) 482-3334.

Department of Commerce Trade Event Programs

Some products, because of their very nature, are difficult to sell unless the potential buyer has an opportunity to examine them in person. Sales letters and printed literature can be helpful, but they are certainly no substitute for an actual presentation of products in the export market. One way for a company to actually present its products to an overseas market is by participating in trade events such as trade shows, fairs, trade missions, matchmaker delegations, and catalog exhibitions.

In today's international market, trade fairs are "shop windows" where thousands of firms from many countries display their wares. They are marketplaces where buyer and seller can meet with mutual convenience. Some fairs, especially in Europe, have a history that goes back centuries.

Attending trade fairs involves a great deal of planning. The potential exhibitor must take into account the following logistic considerations:

- Choosing the proper fair out of the hundreds that are held every year.
- Obtaining space at the fair, along with designing and constructing the exhibit.
- Shipping products to the show, along with unpacking and setup.
- Providing proper hospitality (refreshments and so on), along with maintaining the exhibit.
- Breaking down and packing the exhibit, and return shipping.

There are many excellent International trade fairs, both privately run and government sponsored. A trade magazine or association can generally provide information on major shows. Because of the many considerations facing exhibitors, a company may wish to attend a Department of Commerce-organized U.S. pavilion overseas. For additional guidance, contact the local Commerce Department office or US&FCS International Operations regional director.

Certified Trade Fair Program

The Department of Commerce Certified Trade Fair Program is designed to encourage private organizations to recruit new-to-market and new-to-export U.S. firms to exhibit in trade fairs overseas. To receive certification, the organization must demonstrate that (1) the fair is a leading international trade event for an industry and (2) the fair organizer is capable of recruiting U.S. exhibitors and assisting them with freight forwarding, customs clearance, exhibit design and setup, public relations, and overall show promotion. The fair organizer must agree to assist new-to-export exhibitors as well as small businesses interested in exporting.

In addition to the services the organizer provides, U.S. exhibitors have the facilities and services of the Department of Commerce available to them, including:

- High-level exposure and added prestige of exhibiting in the U.S. pavilion;
- "Turnkey" booths and other exhibiting options;
- Promotion of the U.S. pavilion through the U.S. Department of Commerce's network of commercial specialists in the target country ;
- Export counseling from U.S. Department of Commerce professional staff before, during, and after the show, including help finding contacts and doing business in the target country.

For additional information contact a local Commerce Department office or

U.S. and Foreign Commercial Service
Export Promotion Services
Trade Fair Certification
Dept. of Commerce, Room 2118
Washington, DC 20230
Tel: (202) 482-2525; Fax: (202) 482-0115; Web site: www.ita.doc.gov.

International Buyer Program

The Department of Commerce encourages foreign buyers to attend selected U.S. trade shows. US&FCS selects more than 20 leading U.S. trade shows with high export potential. U.S. firms are assisted in fulfilling their international business objectives through their participation in selected U.S. trade shows where they can meet foreign buyers, distributors, potential licensees or joint venture partners.

Each show selected for the International Buyer Program receives special promotion through overseas mailings, U.S. embassy and regional commercial newsletters, *CNUSA, Business America,* foreign trade association and chambers of commerce journals, and trade journals overseas. Qualified buyers and prospective representatives and distributors are recruited from all over the world to travel to the show and see U.S. products first-hand. US&FCS works with U.S. companies exhibiting at these shows by helping U.S. firms match their products, marketing objectives, and geographic targets with the needs of the international business visitors.

Through the local Commerce Department offices, international trade specialists are ready to take exhibiting U.S. firms through the exporting process and provide counseling to them before the trade show. In addition, an international trade specialist is available at each show to provide on-the-spot export counseling. The International Buyer Program is also an excellent means for experienced exporters to penetrate new markets.

U.S. exhibitors at selected International Buyer Program shows benefit from complimentary services such as worldwide promotion of products and services through the *Export Interest Directory*, published by the show organizer and distributed to all international visitors at the event, as well as to our commercial offices abroad; export counseling and services to help meet prospective international distributors, representatives, and buyers at the International Business Center; access to hundreds, sometimes thousands, of current international trade leads i; use of the on-site international lounge, business meeting facilities, and interpreter services.

For additional information contact the nearest Export Assistance Center or Commerce district office or call the International Buyer Program at Tel: (202) 482-0481.

Matchmaker Trade Delegations

Matchmaker trade delegations, organized and led by Commerce personnel, enable new-to-export and new-to-market firms to meet prescreened prospects who are interested in their products or services in overseas markets. Matchmaker delegations usually target major markets in two or three countries and limit trips to a week or less. Commercial specialists at U.S. embassies and consulates in the targeted countries prescreen contacts and arrange business appointments. In this way, U.S. firms can interview a maximum number of prospective business partners with a minimum of time away from the office.

Participants also take advantage of group-rate hotels and airfare as well as on-the-spot U.S. embassy support. Thorough briefings on market requirements and business practices and interpreters' services are also provided. Delegation members pay their own expenses and a share of the operating costs of the event.

For a list of upcoming Matchmaker Trade Delegations, contact the Export Assistance Center or Commerce district office nearest you, or contact the product manager at Tel: (202) 482-3119; Fax: (202) 482-0178; Web site: www.ita.doc.gov/uscs/uscsmatc.html.

Multi-State/Catalog Exhibitions

U.S. firms may test foreign markets, develop sales leads, and locate agents or distributors through multi-state/catalog exhibitions sponsored by the US&FCS, in some instances in conjunction with the Department of State's foreign service posts. These exhibitions are done in cooperation with state development offices and feature displays of a large number of U.S. product catalogs, sales brochures, and other graphic sales aids at four to six U.S. embassies and consulates or in conjunction with trade shows in a region.

Because it requires the exporter to make a much smaller investment than a trade mission or other personal visits, this program is particularly well suited for use in developing markets or for smaller companies. To participate, a company must describe its marketing objectives in each targeted country, send catalogs to the exhibition sites abroad, respond promptly to each trade inquiry, and pay a small participation fee. The U.S. Department of Commerce and state representatives will plan, host, and promote exhibitions in the targeted markets abroad; showcase catalogs to local business visitors; personally represent the company at each event, with commercial specialists fluent in the local language to answer questions about the products and services; and send the company contact information for the local companies that expressed an interest in your products and services.

For a list of upcoming events or for more information on the program, contact the nearest Export Assistance Center, local Commerce district office, or

Multi-State/Catalog Exhibition Program
Export Promotion Services
U.S. Department of Commerce
Washington, DC 20230
Tel: (202) 482-3973; Fax: (202) 482-2718.

Other Department of Commerce Programs

Trade Offices and Commercial Offices

There are several Trade Centers and Commercial Centers overseas which are separate from the Embassies and Consulates. Located in Tokyo, Jakarta, Shanghai, Mexico City, and Sao Paulo, these centers may organize and coordinate a range of export promotion programs, including on-site trade shows, U.S. pavilions in international trade fairs, solo U.S. exhibitions, trade seminars, trade missions, catalog exhibitions, video and catalog exhibitions, and special promotions. Each center performs these functions only in the country in which it is located.

When not being used to stage trade exhibitions, centers with exhibit and conference facilities frequently are made available to individual firms or associations. Facilities can be used for sales promotions, seminars, and sales meetings. For a nominal fee, these centers and some commercial offices overseas also provide use of limited office space for traveling U.S. business representatives as well as local telephone use, a market briefing, use of audiovisual equipment, and assistance in making appointments.

Major Projects Program

This program helps U.S. firms win contracts for planning, engineering, and constructing large foreign infrastructure and industrial systems projects, including equipment and turnkey installations. Assistance is provided when requested by a U.S. embassy, a prospective foreign client, or a U.S. firm, either to encourage U.S. companies to bid on a particular project or to help them pursue overseas contracts.

Speed and flexibility in developing a strategy for each case are essential elements in the assistance given U.S. firms. As circumstances warrant, the Infrastructure Division mobilizes and coordinates appropriate support from other U.S. government agencies, including foreign service posts abroad. For further information, contact

Infrastructure Division, Trade Development
International Trade Administration
U.S. Department of Commerce
Washington, DC 20230
Tel: (202) 482-4642; Fax: (202) 482-3352; Web site: www.ita.doc.gov/infrastructure.

Textile and Apparel Export Expansion Program

In recognition of the increasing importance of textile and apparel exports, Commerce has created this program to encourage and assist U.S. manufacturers in initiating or expanding export sales, and to improve foreign market access for these products. To achieve these goals, the program does the following:

- Undertakes policy efforts to identify and negotiate away foreign trade barriers and to examine other methods by which the environment for U.S. textile and apparel exports can be improved.
- Provides vehicles such as sponsoring trade fairs and trade missions to improve exposure for U.S. textile and apparel firms and products in foreign markets.
- Provides information on overseas markets and counseling on methods of entering those markets, and facilitates the exchange of information between industry and government relevant to improving exports of U.S. textile and apparel products.

The program is administered by:

Market Expansion Division
Office of Textiles and Apparel
Tel: (202) 482-5153; Fax: (202) 482-2859

Department of Agriculture Foreign Agricultural Service

Through a network of counselors, attaches, trade officers, commodity analysts, and marketing specialists, USDA's FAS can help arrange contacts overseas and provide promotional assistance. The programs and services offered are described in this section.

Trade Assistance and Promotion Office (TAPO)

The Trade Assistance and Promotion Office of the Foreign Agricultural Service (FAS) serves as the first point of contact for persons who need information on foreign markets for agricultural products. The TAPO staff can provide basic export counseling and direct you to the appropriate USDA offices to answer your specific technical questions on exporting. In addition, the staff can provide country- and commodity specific *Foreign Market Information Reports*, which focus on best market prospects and contain contact information on distributors and importers. Extensive information on the Foreign Agricultural Service is also available through the FAS Home Page on Internet.

Trade Assistance and Promotion Office
Tel: (202) 720-7420; Fax: (202) 205-9728
FAS web site: www.fas.usda.gov

Commodity and Marketing Programs

The Commodity and Marketing area of FAS handles inquiries for specific commodity-related information. Each division provides support for analysis of consumption, trade, stocks, and so on, and marketing information. The eight divisions and their telephone numbers are as follows.

Agricultural Export Services Division (AgExport)
Tel: (202) 720-6343; Fax: (202) 690-0193

Dairy, Livestock, and Poultry Division
Tel: (202) 720-8031; Fax: (202) 720-0617; Web site: www.fas.usda.gov/dlp/infoweb.html

Forest and Fishery Products Division
Tel: (202) 720-0638; Fax: (202) 720-8461; Email: FFPD@fas.usda.gov; Web site: www.fas.usda.gov/ffpd/fpd2.html

Grain and Feed Division
Tel: (202) 720-6219; Fax: (202) 720-0340

Horticultural and Tropical Products Division
Tel: (202) 720-6590; Fax: (202) 720-3799; Web site: www.fas.usda.gov/htp/

Production Estimates and Crop Assement Division
Tel: (202) 720-0888; Fax: (202) 720-8880; Web site: www.fas.usda.gov/pecad/pecad.html

Cotton, Oilseeds, Tobacco and Seeds Division
Tel: (202) 720-9516; Fax: (202) 690-1171; Email: cots@fas.usda.gov; Web site: www.fas.usda.gov/cots/default.htm

Agricultural Export Services Division (AgExport)

AgExport's purpose is to expand overseas markets for U.S. agricultural and food commodities and products through a wide range of services, which are described in this section.

AgExport Connections

AgExport Connections provides information services to help expand and promote agricultural exports. It offers the AgExport Action Kit, which contains information on USDA programs and services that are designed to promote exports of U.S. food, natural fiber and forest products. Among the services described in the Kit are: Trade Leads, Buyer Alert, Foreign Buyer Lists, and U.S. Supplier Lists. Details of these services are given below.

U.S. exporters may request a free copy of the AgExport Action Kit by contacting

AgExport Connections
Ag Box 1052, AGX/FAS/USDA
Washington, DC 20250-1052
Tel: (202) 720-7103; Fax: (202) 690-4374

Trade Leads. These inquiries from overseas buyers in 130 countries looking for U.S. products are sent daily to USDA. Several thousand trade leads are disseminated domestically each year. Trade leads are made available to U.S. exporters on a daily basis through the FAS Internet home page and the Department of Commerce's Electronic Bulletin Board. Trade Leads are also available through a *Trade Leads* Fax Polling System, various trade publications, and the state departments of agriculture and trade development centers. Some of the easiest ways are listed below:

1. ***Trade Leads Fax Service.*** Exporters can receive categorized trade leads by polling the AgExport fax machines each week. The faxed information is free, but the company seeking the information must pay the cost of the call. Interested companies may obtain an information sheet and directions on how to poll the Trade Leads Fax Service units by contacting AgExport Connections Tel: (202) 720-6343; Fax (202) 690-4374.
2. ***Electronic trade leads.*** With a computer, a modem, and communications software, exporters can receive trade leads electronically, either through the Department of Commerce's Economic Bulletin Board (EBB) or through the FAS Web site on the Internet (http://www.fas.usda.gov).
3. ***Journal of Commerce.*** Selected trade leads received by USDA are published several times each week in the "Agricultural Trade Leads" columns of the *Journal of Commerce.* For subscription information call Tel: (800) 221-3777.

Buyer Alert. This biweekly newsletter and inexpensive advertising service for exporters can help introduce U.S. food and agricultural products to foreign buyers. Buyer Alert reaches more than 15,000 buyers in 60 countries. Only agricultural products (no equipment or services) may be announced in Buyer Alert. Each announcement features a product description, an optional indicator price, and specific firm information. To take advantage of the service, contact AgExport Connections, Ag Box 1052, AGX/FAS/USDA, Washington, DC 20250-1052; Tel: (202) 720-7103; Fax: (202) 690-4374.

Foreign Buyer Lists. The AgExport Connection staff maintains a data base of more than 20,000 foreign firms in 80 countries. These foreign firms have expressed interest in importing specific U.S. food and agricultural products. U.S. firms may obtain these lists to match their products with prospective foreign buyers. The Foreign Buyer Lists provide company name; contact name; address; and telephone, fax, and type of product(s) imported. The lists may be ordered for a specific commodity for the entire world or by country for all commodities. These lists are available for distribution only in the United States.

U.S. Supplier Lists. This service offers information on approximately 5,000 U.S. exporters of food and agricultural products. Many of these firms will also supply U.S. brokers or agents. U.S. Supplier Lists are available for more than 500 specific product categories. They provide important information on each firm such as contact person, address, telephone, fax, year started, number of employees, and annual sales.Lists may be ordered by product categories.

Trade Shows

The FAS also organizes U.S. pavilions at major international trade shows and exhibitions. These events provide a cost-effective way of testing a market, checking the competition, meeting foreign buyers and consumers, and establishing new contacts. The Trade Show Coordinators Office can assist U.S. exhibitors with obtaining a booth, advance publicity, product shipment, and customs clearance. In markets without an established international food show, USDA organizes its own American food shows and sales missions. For more information on these programs, contact

Trade Show Office
FAS, USDA
AgBox 1052
Washington, DC 20250-1052
Tel: (202) 690-1182; Fax: (202) 690-4374

Agency for International Development (AID)

AID administers most of the U.S. foreign economic assistance programs. These programs offer export opportunities for U.S. suppliers of professional technical assistance services and commodities (goods, products, equipment, and material). Professional technical assistance services generally offer opportunities for consultant and expert capabilities in agriculture, nutrition, and rural development; education and human resources; health and population; and energy and environmental assessment. Opportunities to export commodities are available through the commodity import programs that AID operates in select AID recipient countries, and through AID's direct procurement of commodities. In addition, AID funds may be available to finance developmentally sound projects in certain recipient countries involving U.S. capital goods and services. U.S. exporters are best positioned to obtain orders by making the local purchasing agencies aware of their products at an early stage. For information on available funds, projects under consideration, and contacts, exporters traveling to developing countries where an AID program is in place may wish to visit the AID mission in the U.S. embassy.

For the most part, AID advertises export opportunities for both professional technical assistance and commodities in the *Commerce Business Daily,* available through paid subscription from the Superintendent of Documents, U.S. Government Printing Office, Washington, DC 20402; Tel: (202) 512-1800; Web site: www.access.gpo.gov/su_docs. The *CBD* is also available through the Internet; contact Loren Data Corp., 4640 Admiralty Way, Suite 430, Marina del Rey, CA 90292; Tel: (310) 827-7400; Email: info@ld.com; Web site: www.ld.com.

Notices of intended procurement of AID-financed commodities are also advertised in the *AID Procurement Information Bulletin,* available through free subscription from AID's Office of Small and Disadvantaged Business Utilization/Minority Resource Center (OSDBU/MRC), Washington, DC 20523-1414; Tel: (202) 712-1500; Fax: (202) 216-3056. The *Bulletin* is also posted on AID's web site. Go to http://www.info.usaid.gov/ and look under "Business & Procurement."

Global Technology Network

Global Technology Network acts as a central point of contact at the United States Agency for International Development (USAID) for the U.S. business community and as a vital link with the developing countries USAID serves. Through Global Technology Network, the opportunities and information generated by USAID activities are made available to the U.S. business community.

Global Technology Network develops and disseminates regional and industry- and sector-specific guides to USAID programs and information and also distributes USAID publications such as the *Guide for Doing Business*. The network provides information on how to obtain the *Procurement Information Bulletin* and USAID documents through the Development Information Service Clearinghouse (DISC).

Global Technology Network also manages the Environmental Technology Network for Asia (ETNA), a service of the U.S.--Asia Environmental Partnership (US-AEP). ETNA electronically matches business leads, submitted by in-country representatives, to appropriate U.S. environmental companies registered within its database, and faxes announcements within 48 hours of receipt of the leads.

Global Technology Network
USAID
Washington, DC 20523
Tel: (800) 872-4348

Trade and Development Agency (TDA)

TDA is an independent U.S. government agency that funds feasibility studies, orientation visits, specialized training grants, business workshops, and various forms of technical assistance in developing and middle-income countries worldwide. Contracts funded by TDA grants must be awarded to U.S. companies, thus helping position potential U.S. suppliers of goods and services for follow-on contracts when these projects are implemented.

Most TDA funding is granted for feasibility studies in sectors that are of high priority to host governments: agriculture; energy; environment; health care; manufacturing; mining and minerals development; telecommunications; transportation; and water resources. To ensure a satisfactory and useful study, the host governments play an active role in awarding and managing the contract. This cooperation also engenders a cooperative relationship between the host country, TDA, and the business community.

In addition, opportunities for technical consultants also

arise in connection with definitional missions to investigate the scope of a project, develop a scope of work for a feasibility study, draw up a budget estimate, and make a recommendation concerning TDA support for the study. TDA selects qualified consultants through use of a consultants data base, for which U.S. small businesses are encouraged to register.

TDA-funded activities generated approximately $7 billion of U.S. exports between the agency's inception in 1981 and 1995, which amounts to nearly $30 in exports for every dollar invested in TDA activities. Hundreds of companies across the U.S. have benefited from activities supported by TDA, both through direct exports and through long-term enhancement of their market position.

TDA's programs are carried out by a Washington-based staff in close coordination with the Department of Commerce, the Export-Import Bank, the Overseas Private Investment Corporation, AID, and other government agencies. TDA also maintains close contact with multilateral and regional development lending institutions to ensure an ongoing exchange of important project information and to keep TDA apprised of critical opportunities for U.S. companies. To be considered for funding, projects must:

- Face strong competition from foreign companies that receive subsidies and other support from their governments;
- Be a development priority of the country where the project is located and have the endorsement of the U.S. embassy in that nation;
- Represent an opportunity for sales of U.S. goods or services that is many times greater than the cost of TDA assistance; and
- Be likely to receive implementation financing, and have a procurement process open to U.S. firms.

General inquiries about TDA's services should be made through TDA's library, located at the agency's office in Rosslyn, Virginia. In addition to providing information about TDA services, the library maintains final reports on all TDA activities. The library also can provide details on purchasing copies of completed feasibility studies through the Department of Commerce's NTIS.

The agency has two regular publications: *The TDA Pipeline,* which is available by subscription, provides U.S. suppliers and manufacturers with timely information on agency-supported projects. The *TDA Update* contains current items of interest on a variety of program activities.

TDA information also is available via the Internet. The home page (at http://www.tda.gov/) features a catalog of TDA library holdings, agency news, information on TDA-sponsored studies, and more.

Requests for proposals to conduct TDA-funded feasibility studies are listed in the *Commerce Business Daily.* For subscription information, contact the Superintendent of Documents, U.S. Government Printing Office, Washington, DC 20402; Tel: (202) 512-1800; Web site: www.access.gpo.gov/su_docs. For an online subscription, contact Loren Data Corp., 4640 Admiralty Way, Suite 430, Marina del Rey, CA 90292; Tel: (310) 827-7400; Email: info@ld.com.

Information on definitional mission opportunities can be obtained by calling TDA's Definitional Mission Hotline at (703) 875-7447. Small and minority U.S. firms that wish to be included in TDA's consultant database and considered for future Definitional Mission solicitations should contact the Contracts Office.

Trade and Development Agency
1621 North Kent St., Suite 300
Arlington, VA 22209-2131
Tel: (703) 875-4357; Fax: (703) 875-4009
Email: info@tda.gov
Web site: http://www.tda.gov/.

State and Local Government Assistance

Most states can provide an array of services to exporters. Many states maintain international offices in major markets; the most common locations are in Western Europe, Japan, and Mexico. Working closely with the commercial sections of U.S. embassies in these countries, they can provide assistance in making contacts in foreign markets, providing such services as:

- Specific trade leads with foreign buyers;
- Assistance for trade missions, such as itinerary planning, appointment scheduling, travel, and accommodations;
- Promotional service for goods or services, including representing the state at trade shows; and
- Help in qualifying potential buyers, agents, or distributors.

In addition, some international offices of state development organizations help organize and promote foreign-buyer missions to the United States, which can be effective avenues of exporting with little effort. Attracting foreign investment and developing tourism are also very important activities of state foreign offices.

Increasingly, many cities and counties are providing these same services. *Refer to* Appendix III, "State and Local Sources of Assistance," beginning on page 130 for contacts at both the state and city levels.

Business and Service Organization Contacts

Contacts made through business colleagues and associations can often prove invaluable to U.S. exporters. A colleague with firsthand experience in an international market may give a personal recommendation for an agent, distributor, or potential buyer. Conversely, the recommendation against the use of a representative for credit or reliability reasons may save the firm a number of problems. Attending export seminars and industry trade shows is an excellent method of networking with business people who have international experience. In addition, trade associations can provide a valuable source of contacts with individuals who may wish to share their experience of identifying and selling to buyers and representatives in foreign markets.

Banks can be another source of assistance in locating overseas representation. The international departments, branches, or correspondent banks of U.S. banks may help locate reputable firms that are qualified and willing to represent U.S. exporters. In addition, freight forwarders, freight carriers, airlines, port authorities, and American chambers of commerce maintain offices throughout the world. These service firms often have contacts with qualified representatives and can make recommendations to the U.S. firm. Foreign embassy and consulate commercial offices may also be able to provide directories and assistance.

Promotion in Publications and Other Media

A large and varied assortment of magazines covering international markets is available to exporters through U.S. publishers. They range from specialized international magazines relating to individual industries such as construction, beverages, and textiles, to worldwide industrial magazines covering many industries. Many consumer publications produced by U.S.-based publishers are also available. Several are produced in national-language editions (Spanish for Latin America, and so on) and also offer "regional buys" for specific export markets of the world. In addition, several business directories published in the United States list foreign representatives geographically or by industry specialization.

Publishers frequently supply potential exporters with helpful market information, make specific recommendations for selling in the markets they cover, help advertisers locate sales representation, and render other services to aid international advertisers. For an extensive list of these international publications, look for the *Gale Directory of Publications & Broadcast Media,* which contains a list of foreign periodicals, with some information on circulation and rates. This directory or others may be available at libraries; Commerce district offices; or in the Department of Commerce's Trade Data Reference Room (Tel: (202) 482-2185; Fax: (202) 482-4614). State departments of commerce, trade associations, business libraries, and major universities may also provide such directories.

Television, radio, and specially produced motion pictures may also be used by a U.S. business for promoting products or services, depending on the country. In areas where programs may be seen and heard in public places, television and radio promotions offer one of the few means of bringing an advertising message to great numbers of people. In many countries, particularly in Latin America, various forms of outdoor advertising (billboards, posters, electric signs, and streetcar and bus cards) are widely used to reach the mass audience.

Because of the specialized knowledge required to advertise and promote successfully in foreign markets, U.S. firms may find useful the services of a U.S. advertising agency with offices or correspondents abroad. Some U.S. agencies handle nothing but foreign advertising, and some marketing consultants specialize in the problems peculiar to selling in foreign markets. The International Advertising Association, can provide names of domestic agencies that handle overseas accounts. Contact the IAA at 521 Fifth Avenue, Suite 1807, New York, NY 10175, Tel: (212) 557-1133; Fax: (212) 983-0455.

Chapter 8
Business Travel Abroad

Business travel abroad can locate and cultivate new customers and improve relationships and communication with current foreign representatives and associates. As in domestic business, there is nothing like a face-to-face meeting with a client or customer.

The following suggestions can help U.S. companies prepare for a trip. By keeping in mind that even little things (such as forgetting to check foreign holiday schedules or neglecting to arrange for translator services) can cost time, opportunity, and money, a firm can get maximum value from its time spent abroad.

Planning the Itinerary

A well-planned itinerary enables a traveler to make the best possible use of time abroad. Although travel time is expensive, care must be taken not to overload the schedule. Two or three definite appointments, confirmed well in advance and spaced comfortably throughout one day, are more productive and enjoyable than a crowded agenda that forces the business person to rush from one meeting to the next before business is really concluded. If possible, an extra rest day to deal with jet lag should be planned before scheduled business appointments. The following travel tips should be kept in mind:

- The travel plans should reflect what the company hopes to accomplish. The traveler should give some thought to the trip's goals and their relative priorities.
- The traveler should accomplish as much as possible before the trip begins by obtaining names of possible contacts, arranging appointments, checking transportation schedules, and so on. The most important meetings should be confirmed before the traveler leaves the United States.
- As a general rule, the business person should keep the schedule flexible enough to allow for both unexpected problems (such as transportation delays) and unexpected opportunities. For instance, accepting an unscheduled luncheon invitation from a prospective client should not make it necessary to miss the next scheduled meeting.
- The traveler should check the normal work days and business hours in the countries to be visited. In many Middle Eastern regions, for instance, the work week typically runs from Saturday to Thursday. In many countries, lunch hours of two to four hours are customary.
- Along the same lines, take foreign holidays into account. The U.S. Department of Commerce's *Business America* magazine annually publishes a list of holidays observed in countries around the world. Information from this useful schedule, entitled "World Commercial Holidays," can be obtained by contacting the local Commerce Department office.
- The potential U.S. traveler should also learn what travel advisories the U.S. Department of State has issued for countries to be visited. *Consular Information Sheets* include such information as location of the U.S. Embassy or Consulate in the subject country, unusual immigration practices, health conditions, minor political disturbances, unusual currency and entry regulations, crime and security information, and drug penalties. *Travel Warnings* are issued when the State Department decides, based on all relevant information, to recommend that Americans avoid travel to a certain country. You can obtain Consular Information Sheets and Travel Warnings through your nearest passport agency, on the State Department's Web site at http://travel.state.gov/travel_warnings.html, or you may call a special number at the State Department (Tel: (202) 647-5225) to listen to recorded travel advisories. Your travel agent may have online access to Consular Information Sheets and Travel Warnings through their reservation system.
- Check with the Centers for Disease Control to find out about any special health risks in areas you are traveling to, or for information on required and recommended vaccinations. This information is available on the CDC's Web site at http://www.cdc.gov/travel/travel.html, or you can call the CDC Travelers Hotline 24 hours a day at (404) 332-4559.
- The U.S. business person should be aware that travel from one country to another may be restricted. For example, a passport containing an Israeli visa may disallow the traveler from entering certain countries in the Middle East.

Other Preparations

Travel agents can frequently arrange for transportation

and hotel reservations quickly and efficiently. They can also help plan the itinerary, obtain the best travel rates, explain which countries require visas, advise on hotel rates and locations, and provide other valuable services. Since travel agents' fees are paid by the hotels, airlines, and other carriers, this assistance and expertise may cost nothing.

The U.S. traveler should obtain the necessary travel documents two to three months before departure, especially if visas are needed. A travel agent can help make the arrangements. A valid U.S. passport is required for all travel outside the United States and Canada. If traveling on an old passport, the U.S. citizen should make sure that it remains valid for the entire duration of the trip.

Passports may be obtained through certain local post offices and U.S. district courts. Check your local telephone directory under the Federal Government blue pages; look for Passport Services under the Department of State or Postal Service listings.

Application may be made in person or, in some cases, by mail. A separate passport is needed for each family member who will be traveling. The applicant must provide (1) proof of citizenship, (2) proof of identity, (3) two identical passport photos, (4) a completed application form, and (5) the appropriate fees. The cost is $55 per passport ($40 for travelers under 18) plus a $10 execution fee for first-time passports or travelers applying in person. The usual processing time for a passport (including time in the mail) is three weeks, but travelers should apply as early as possible, particularly if time is needed to obtain visas, international drivers licenses, or other documents. If you are leaving in less than three weeks you may be eligible for an expidited passport at an additional cost of $30.

Additional information is available from the nearest local passport office or by calling the National Passport Center outside Washington, D.C. Telephone numbers are listed below.

National Passport Center
Tel: (202) 647-0518

Boston, Massachusetts Passport Agency
Tel: (617) 565-6990

Chicago, Illinois Passport Agency
Tel: (312) 341-6020

Honolulu, Hawaii Passport Agency
Tel: (808) 522-8283 or 522-8286

Houston, Texas Passport Agency
Tel: (713) 751-0294

Los Angeles, California Passport Agency
Tel: (310) 575-5700

Miami, Florida Passport Agency
Tel: (305) 539-3600

New Orleans, Louisiana Passport Agency
Tel: (504) 589-6728

New York, New York Passport Agency
Tel: (212) 206-3500

Philadelphia, Pennsylvania Passport Agency
Tel: (215) 597-7480

San Francisco, California Passport Agency
Tel: (415) 538-2700

Seattle, Washington Passport Agency
Tel: (206) 220-7788

Stamford, Connecticut Passport Agency
Tel: (203) 325-4401

Washington, DC Passport Agency
Tel: (202) 647-0518

Visas, which are required by many countries, cannot be obtained through the Office of Passport Services. They are provided for a small fee by the foreign country's embassy or consulate in the United States. To obtain a visa, the traveler must have a current U.S. passport. In addition, many countries require a recent photo. The traveler should allow several weeks to obtain visas, especially if traveling to developing nations (embassies and consulates in the United States are listed in appendix IV). Some countries that do not require visas for tourist travel do require them for business travel. Visa requirements may change from time to time.

Requirements for vaccinations differ from country to country. A travel agent or airline can advise the traveler on various requirements. In some cases, vaccinations against typhus, typhoid, and other diseases are advisable even though they are not required. Check with the Centers for Disease Control by calling the CDC Travelers Hotline at (404) 332-4559 or go to the CDC Travel Information home page on the World Wide Web at www.cdc.gov/travel/travel.html.

Business Preparations for International Travel

Before leaving the United States, the traveler should prepare to deal with language differences by learning whether individuals to be met are comfortable speaking English. If not, plans should be made for an interpreter. Business language is generally more technical than the conversational speech with which many travelers are familiar; mistakes can be costly.

In some countries, exchanging business cards at any first meeting is considered a basic part of good business manners. As a matter of courtesy, it is best to carry business cards printed both in English and in the language of the country being visited. Some international airlines arrange this service.

The following travel checklist covers a number of considerations that apply equally to business travelers and vacationers. A travel agent or various travel publications can help take these considerations into account:

- Seasonal weather conditions in the countries being visited.
- Health care (e.g., what to eat abroad, special medical problems, and prescription drugs).
- Electrical current (a transformer or plug adapter may be needed to use electrical appliances).
- Money (e.g., exchanging currency and using credit cards and travelers' checks).
- Transportation and communication abroad.
- Cultural differences.
- Tipping (who is tipped and how much is appropriate).
- U.S. Customs regulations on what can be brought home.

Assistance from U.S. Embassies and Consulates

Economic and commercial officers in U.S. embassies and consulates abroad can provide assistance to U.S. exporters, both through in-depth briefings and by arranging introductions to appropriate firms, individuals, or foreign government officials. Because of the value and low cost of these services, it is recommended that the exporter visit the U.S. embassy soon after arriving in a foreign country.

When planning a trip, business travelers can discuss their needs and the services available at particular embassies with the staff of the local Commerce district office. It is also advisable to write directly to the U.S. embassy or consulate in the countries to be visited at least two weeks before leaving the United States and to address any communication to the commercial section. The U.S. business traveler should identify his or her business affiliation and complete address and indicate the objective of the trip and the type of assistance required from the post. Also, a description of the firm and the extent of its international experience would be helpful to the post. Addresses of U.S. embassies and consulates are provided in *Key Officers of Foreign Service Posts*, a publication available from the U.S. Government Printing Office, PO Box 371954, Pittsburgh, PA 15250-7954; Tel: (202) 512-1800; Fax: (202) 512-2250; Web site: www.access.gpo.gov/su_docs. The cost for this publication is $5.50 for a single copy. Request GPO S/N 044-000-02499-3.

A program of special value to U.S. business travelers is the Department of Commerce's Gold Key Service, which is custom tailored to U.S. firms visiting overseas markets. This service combines several forms of Commerce assistance, including agent and distributor location, one-on-one business counseling, prescheduled appointments with key contacts, and U.S. embassy assistance with interpreters and translators, clerical support, office services, and so on. The service is not available in all markets and may be known under a different name in some countries (e.g., RepFind in Mexico). Further information and assistance are available from any local Commerce Department office.

Carnets

Foreign customs regulations vary widely from place to place, and the traveler is wise to learn in advance the regulations that apply to each country to be visited. If allowances for cigarettes, liquor, currency, and certain other items are not taken into account, they can be impounded at national borders. Business travelers who plan to carry product samples with them should be alert to import duties they may be required to pay. In some countries, duties and extensive customs procedures on sample products may be avoided by obtaining an ATA (Admission Temporoire) Carnet.

The ATA Carnet is a standardized international customs document used to obtain duty-free temporary admission of certain goods into the countries that are signatories to the ATA Convention. Under the ATA Convention, commercial and professional travelers may take commercial samples; tools of the trade; advertising material; aircraft and road vehicles; containers and packing materials; exhibition and touring facilities; teaching materials; and cinematographic, audiovisual, medical, scientific, or other professional equipment into member countries temporarily without paying customs duties and taxes or posting a bond at the border of each country to be visited. Carnets do not cover consumable goods (such as food and agricultural products), disposable items, or postal traffic.

At press time, the following countries participated in the ATA Carnet system: Algeria, Australia, Austria, Belgium, Bulgaria, Canada, Cyprus, the Czech Republic, Denmark, Finland, France, Germany, Gibraltar, Greece, Hong Kong, Hungary, Iceland, India, Iran, Ireland, Israel, Italy, Ivory Coast, Japan, Luxembourg, Malaysia, Mauritius, Netherlands, New Zealand, Norway, Poland, Portugal, Romania, Senegal, Singapore, Sri Lanka, South Africa, South Korea, Spain, Sweden, Switzerland, Turkey, the United Kingdom, and the United States. Note that many countries will issue carnets for some categories of merchandise and not others.

Since new countries are frequently added to the ATA

Carnet system, the traveler should contact the U.S. Council for International Business if the country to be visited is not included in this list. Applications for carnets should be made to the same organization. A fee is charged, depending on the value of the goods to be covered. A bond, letter of credit, or bank guaranty of 40 percent of the value of the goods is also required to cover duties and taxes that would be due if goods imported into a foreign country by carnet were not reexported and the duties were not paid by the carnet holder. The carnets generally are valid for 12 months.

Contact the U.S. Council for International Business, 1212 Avenue of the Americas, New York, NY 10036; Tel: (212) 354-4480; Fax: (212) 575-0327; Web site: www.uscib.org. The Council also maintains an office in Washington, DC and offices around the country which can issue ATA Carnets. Further information on the ATA Carnet system can be found in *Carnet: Move Goods Duty-free Through Customs,* an informative free brochure published by the council.

Cultural Factors

Business executives who hope to profit from their travel should learn about the history, culture, and customs of the countries to be visited. Flexibility and cultural adaptation should be the guiding principles for traveling abroad on business. Business manners and methods, religious customs, dietary practices, humor, and acceptable dress vary widely from country to country. For example, consider the following:

- Never touch the head of a Thai or pass an object over it; the head is considered sacred in Thailand.
- Avoid using triangular shapes in Hong Kong, Korea, and Taiwan; the triangle is considered a negative shape.
- The number 7 is considered bad luck in Kenya and good luck in the Czech Republic, and it has magical connotations in Benin. The number 10 is bad luck in Korea, and 4 means death in Japan.
- Red is a positive color in Denmark, but it represents witchcraft and death in many African countries.
- A nod means no in Bulgaria, and shaking the head from side to side means yes.
- The "okay" sign commonly used in the United States (thumb and index finger forming a circle and the other fingers raised) means zero in France, is a symbol for money in Japan, and carries a vulgar connotation in Brazil.
- The use of a palm-up hand and moving index finger signals "come here" in the United States and in some other countries, but it is considered vulgar in others.
- In Ethiopia, repeatedly opening and closing the palm-down hand means "come here."

Understanding and heeding cultural variables such as these is critical to success in international business travel and in international business itself. Lack of familiarity with the business practices, social customs, and etiquette of a country can weaken a company's position in the market, prevent it from accomplishing its objectives, and ultimately lead to failure.

Some of the cultural distinctions that U.S. firms most often face include differences in business styles, attitudes toward development of business relationships, attitudes toward punctuality, negotiating styles, gift-giving customs, greetings, significance of gestures, meanings of colors and numbers, and customs regarding titles.

American firms must pay close attention to different styles of doing business and the degree of importance placed on developing business relationships. In some countries, business people have a very direct style, while in others they are much more subtle in style and value the personal relationship more than most Americans do in business. For example, in the Middle East, engaging in small talk before engaging in business is standard practice.

Attitudes toward punctuality vary greatly from one culture to another and, if misunderstood, can cause confusion and misunderstanding. Romanians, Japanese, and Germans are very punctual, whereas people in many of the Latin countries have a more relaxed attitude toward time. The Japanese consider it rude to be late for a business meeting, but acceptable, even fashionable, to be late for a social occasion. In Guatemala, on the other hand, one might arrive anytime from 10 minutes early to 45 minutes late for a luncheon appointment.

When cultural lines are being crossed, something as simple as a greeting can be misunderstood. Traditional greetings may be a handshake, a hug, a nose rub, a kiss, placing the hands in praying position, or various other gestures. Lack of awareness concerning the country's accepted form of greeting can lead to awkward encounters.

People around the world use body movements and gestures to convey specific messages. Sometimes the same gestures have very different meanings, however. Misunderstanding over gestures is a common occurrence in cross-cultural communication, and misinterpretation along these lines can lead to business complications and social embarrassment.

Proper use of names and titles is often a source of confusion in international business relations. In many countries (including the United Kingdom, France, and Denmark) it is appropriate to use titles until use of first names is suggested. First names are seldom used when doing business in Germany. Visiting business people should use the surname preceded by the title. Titles such as "Herr Direktor" are sometimes used to indicate prestige, status, and rank. Thais, on the other hand, address one other by first names and reserve last names for very formal occasions and written communications. In Belgium it is important to address French-speaking business contacts as "Monsieur" or "Madame," while Dutch-speaking contacts should be addressed as "Mr." or "Mrs." To confuse the two is a great insult.

Customs concerning gift-giving are extremely important to understand. In some cultures gifts are expected and failure to present them is considered an insult, whereas in other countries offering a gift is considered offensive. Business executives also need to know when to present gifts—on the initial visit or afterwards; where to present gifts—in public or private; what type of gift to present; what color it should be; and how many to present.

Gift-giving is an important part of doing business in Japan, where gifts are usually exchanged at the first meeting. In sharp contrast, gifts are rarely exchanged in Germany and are usually not appropriate. Gift-giving is not a normal custom in Belgium or the United Kingdom either, although in both countries, flowers are a suitable gift when invited to someone's home.

Customs concerning the exchange of business cards vary, too. Although this point seems of minor importance, observing a country's customs for card giving is a key part of business protocol. In Japan, for example, the Western practice of accepting a business card and pocketing it immediately is considered rude. The proper approach is to carefully look at the card after accepting it, observe the title and organization, acknowledge with a nod that the information has been digested, and perhaps make a relevant comment or ask a polite question.

Negotiating—a complex process even between parties from the same nation—is even more complicated in international transactions because of the added chance of misunderstandings stemming from cultural differences. It is essential to understand the importance of rank in the other country; to know who the decision makers are; to be familiar with the business style of the foreign company; and to understand the nature of agreements in the country, the significance of gestures, and negotiating etiquette.

It is important to acquire, through reading or training, a basic knowledge of the business culture, management attitudes, business methods, and consumer habits of the country being visited. This does not mean that the traveler must go native when conducting business abroad. It does mean that the traveler should be sensitive to the customs and business procedures of the country being visited.

Further Reading

Passport to the World series. A series of books on business cultures in more than 25 different countries. Cost: $6.95 each. Available from World Trade Press, 1450 Grant Ave., Suite 204, Novato, CA 94945; Tel: (415) 898-1124; Fax: (415) 898-1080; Email: WorldPress@aol.com; Web site: www.worldtradepress.com.

Blunders in International Business. By David Ricks. Full of anecdotes covering mistakes and blunders from all aspects of international business including marketing, management, production, translation, and strategy. Cost: $20.95. Available from Blackwell Publishers, 238 Main St., Cambridge, MA 02142; Tel: (617) 876-7000, (800) 903-1181; Web site: www.blackwellpublishers.co.uk.

Do's and Taboos ... A series of paperback books with tips on international business and etiquette. Titles include *Do's and Taboos Around the World, Do's and Taboos of Hosting International Visitors, Do's and Taboos of International Trade, Do's and Tabooos of Preparing for your Trip Abroad,* and *Do's and Taboos of Using English Around the World.* All are by Roger E. Axtell and are published by John Wiley & Sons, 605 Third Ave., New York, NY 10158-0012; Tel: (212) 850-6000, (800) 225-5945 (orders); Fax: (212) 850-6008.

Intercultural Interacting. By V. Lynn Tyler. Explains the elements of interacting with people from other cultures; includes learning exercises. Available from David M. Kennedy Center for International Studies, Publication Services, Brigham Young University, P.O. Box 24538, Provo, UT 84602-4538; Tel: (801) 378-6528, (800) 528-6279.

Chapter 9

Selling Overseas

Many successful exporters first started selling internationally by responding to an inquiry from a foreign firm. Thousands of U.S. firms receive such requests annually, but most firms do not become successful exporters. What separates the successful exporter from the unsuccessful exporter? There is no single answer, but often the firm that becomes successful knows how to respond to inquiries, can separate the wheat from the chaff, recognizes the business practices involved in international selling, and takes time to build a relationship with the client. Although this may seem to be a large number of factors, they are all related and flow out of one another.

Responding to Inquiries

Most but not all, foreign letters of inquiry are in English. A firm may look to certain service providers (such as banks or freight forwarders) for assistance in translating a letter of inquiry in a foreign language. Most large cities have commercial translators who translate for a fee. Many colleges and universities also provide translation services.

A typical inquiry asks for product specifications, information, and price. Some foreign firms want information on purchasing a product for internal use; others (distributors and agents) want to sell the product in their market. A few firms may know a product well enough and want to place an order. Most inquiries want delivery schedules, shipping costs, terms, and, in some cases, exclusivity arrangements.

Regardless of the form such inquiries take, a firm should establish a policy to deal with them. Here are a few suggestions:

- Reply to all correspondents except to those who obviously will not turn into customers. Do not disregard the inquiry merely because it contains grammatical or typographical errors, which may result from the writer knowing English only as a second language. Similarly, if the printing quality of the stationery does not meet usual standards, keep in mind that printing standards in the correspondent's country may be different. Despite first impressions, the inquiry may be from a reputable, well-established firm.
- Reply promptly, completely, and clearly. The correspondent naturally wants to know something about the U.S. firm before doing business with it. The letter should introduce the firm sufficiently and establish it as a reliable supplier. The reply should provide a short but adequate introduction to the firm, including bank references and other sources that confirm reliability. The firm's policy on exports should be stated, including cost, terms, and delivery.
- Enclose information on the firm's goods or services.
- Send the reply airmail. Surface mail can take weeks or even months, whereas airmail usually takes only days. If a foreign firm's letter shows both a street address and a post office box, write to the post office box. In countries where mail delivery is unreliable, many firms prefer to have mail sent to the post office box.
- When speedy communication is called for, send a fax. Unlike telephone communications, fax may be used effectively despite differences in time zones and languages.
- Set up a file for foreign letters. They may turn into definite prospects as export business grows. If the firm has an intermediary handling exports, the intermediary may use the file.
- Sometimes an overseas firm requests a pro forma invoice (*see* "Quotations and Pro Forma Invoices" on page 56), which is a quotation in an invoice format. It is used rarely in domestic business but frequently in international trade.

Separating the Wheat From the Chaff

How can a firm tell if an overseas inquiry is legitimate and from an established source? A U.S. company can obtain more information about a foreign firm making an inquiry by checking with the following sources of information about foreign firms:

- ***Business libraries.*** Several publications list and qualify international firms, including Graham & Whiteside's *Major Companies of ...* series (distributed in the U.S. by Gale Research), Dun and Bradstreet's *Principal International Business,* Kompass directories, and many regional and country directories. Ask the business librarian at a nearby college or public library for recommendations.

- ***International banks.*** Bankers have access to vast amounts of information on foreign firms and are usually very willing to assist corporate customers.
- ***Foreign embassies.*** Foreign embassies are located in Washington, D.C. (*Refer to* Appendix IV, "U.S. and Overseas Contacts for Major Foreign Markets," beginning on page 157), and some have consulates in other major cities. The commercial or business sections of most foreign embassies have directories of firms located in their countries.
- ***U.S. Department of Commerce.*** Commerce can provide information on international firms through its ICPs (*see* "International Company Profiles" on page 40), which are available for a fee through Export Assistance Centers or local Commerce district offices.
- ***Sources of credit information.*** Credit reports on foreign companies are available from many private sector sources, including (in the United States) Dun and Bradstreet and Graydon International. For help in identifying private sector sources of credit reports, contact the nearest Export Assistance Center or Commerce district office. Firms insured by the Foreign Credit Insurance Association (FCIA) can also obtain help from FCIA's headquarters. Contact FCIA, 40 Rector St., 11th Fl., New York, NY 10006; Tel: (212) 306-5000; Fax: (212) 306-5218.

Business Practices in International Selling

Awareness of accepted business practices is paramount to successful international selling. Because cultures vary, there is no single code by which to conduct business. Certain business practices, however, transcend culture barriers:

- Answer requests promptly and clearly.
- Keep promises. The biggest complaint from foreign importers about U.S. suppliers is failure to ship as promised. A first order is particularly important because it shapes a customer's image of a firm as a dependable or an undependable supplier.
- Be polite, courteous, and friendly. It is important, however, to avoid undue familiarity or slang. Some overseas firms feel that the usual brief U.S. business letter is lacking in courtesy.
- Personally sign letters. Form letters are not satisfactory.

Before traveling to a new market, the traveler should learn as much about the culture as possible to avoid embarrassing situations. For example, in Mexico it is customary to inquire about a colleague's wife and family, whereas in many Middle Eastern countries it is taboo. Patting a U.S. colleague on the back for congratulations is a common practice, but in Japan it would be discourteous. Clothes, expressions, posture, and actions are all important considerations in conducting international business.

Another important consideration is religious and national holidays. Trying to conduct business on the Fourth of July in the United States would be difficult, if not impossible. Likewise, different dates have special significance in various countries. Some countries have long holidays by U.S. standards, making business difficult. For example, doing business is difficult in Saudi Arabia during the month of fasting before the Ramadan religious festival.

Numerous seminars, film series, books, and publications exist to help the overseas traveler. Try to obtain cultural information from business colleagues who have been abroad or have expertise in a particular market. A little research and observation in cultural behavior can go a long way in international commerce. Likewise, a lack of sensitivity to another's customs can stop a deal in its tracks. Foreign government consulates in U.S. cities offer a wealth of information on business customs and norms for their countries.

Another good source is the Passport to the World series from World Trade Press. The series of small paperbacks covers business culture, customs and etiquette in more than 25 different countries. Contact World Trade Press, 1450 Grant Ave., Suite 204, Novato, CA 94945; Tel: (415) 898-1124; Fax: (415) 898-1080; Email: WorldPress@aol.com; Web site: www.worldtradepress.com.

Building a Working Relationship

Once a relationship has been established with an overseas customer, representative, or distributor, it is important that the exporter work on building and maintaining that relationship. Common courtesy should dictate business activity. By following the points outlined in this chapter, a U.S. firm can present itself well. Beyond these points, the exporter should keep in mind that a foreign contact should be treated and served like a domestic contact. For example, the U.S. company should keep customers and contacts notified of all changes, including price, personnel, address, and phone numbers.

Because of distance, a contact can "age" quickly and cease to be useful unless communication is maintained. For many companies, this means monthly or quarterly visits to customers or distributors. This level of service, although not absolutely necessary, ensures that both the company and the product maintain high visibility in the marketplace. If the U.S. exporting firm cannot afford such frequent travel, it may use telephone, fax, email, and telex to keep the working relationship active and up to date.

Chapter 10
Pricing, Quotations, and Terms

Proper pricing, complete and accurate quotations, and choice of terms of sale and payment are four critical elements in selling a product or service internationally. Of the four, pricing is the most problematic, even for the experienced exporter.

Pricing Considerations

- At what price should the firm sell its product in the foreign market? Does the foreign price reflect the product's quality? Is the price competitive?
- Should the firm pursue market penetration or market-skimming pricing objectives abroad?
- What type of discount (trade, cash, quantity) and allowances (advertising, trade-off) should the firm offer its foreign customers?
- Should prices differ with market segment?
- What should the firm do about product line pricing?
- What pricing options are available if the firm's costs increase or decrease? Is the demand in the foreign market elastic or inelastic?
- Are the prices going to be viewed by the foreign government as reasonable or exploitative?
- Do the foreign country's dumping laws pose a problem?

As in the domestic market, the price at which a product or service is sold directly determines a firm's revenues. It is essential that a firm's market research include an evaluation of all of the variables that may affect the price range for the product or service. If a firm's price is too high, the product or service will not sell. If the price is too low, export activities may not be sufficiently profitable or may create a net loss.

The traditional components for determining proper pricing are costs, market demand, and competition. These categories are the same for domestic and foreign sales and must be evaluated in view of the firm's objective in entering the foreign market. An analysis of each component from an export perspective may result in export prices that are different from domestic prices.

Foreign Market Objectives

An important aspect of a company's pricing analysis involves determining market objectives. Is the company attempting to penetrate a new market? Looking for long-term market growth? Looking for an outlet for surplus production or outmoded products? For example, many firms view the foreign market as a secondary market and consequently have lower expectations regarding market share and sales volume. Pricing decisions are naturally affected by this view.

Firms also may have to tailor their marketing and pricing objectives for particular foreign markets. For example, marketing objectives for sales to a developing nation where per capita income may be one tenth of per capita income in the United States are necessarily different from the objectives for Europe or Japan.

Costs

The computation of the actual cost of producing a product and bringing it to market or providing a service is the core element in determining whether exporting is financially viable. Many new exporters calculate their export price by the cost-plus method alone. In the cost-plus method of calculation, the exporter starts with the domestic manufacturing cost and adds administration, research and development, overhead, freight forwarding, distributor margins, customs charges, and profit.

The net effect of this pricing approach may be that the export price escalates into an uncompetitive range. For a sample calculation, see the table on page 58. The table shows clearly that if an export product has the same ex-factory price as the domestic product, its final consumer price is considerably higher.

A more competitive method of pricing for market entry is what is termed marginal cost pricing. This method considers the direct, out-of-pocket expenses of producing and selling products for export as a floor beneath which prices cannot be set without incurring a loss. For example, export products may have to be modified for the export market to accommodate different sizes, electrical systems, or labels. Changes of this nature may increase costs. On the other hand, the export product may be a stripped-down version of the domestic product and therefore cost less. Or, if additional products can be produced without increasing fixed costs, the incremental cost of producing additional products for export should be lower than the earlier average production costs for the domestic market.

In addition to production costs, overhead, and research and development, other costs should be allocated to domestic and export products in proportion to the benefit derived from those expenditures. Additional costs often associated with export sales include

- Market research and credit checks;
- Business travel;
- International postage, cable, and telephone rates;
- Translation costs;
- Commissions, training charges, and other costs involving foreign representatives;
- Consultants and freight forwarders; and
- Product modification and special packaging.

After the actual cost of the export product has been calculated, the exporter should formulate an approximate consumer price for the foreign market.

Market Demand

As in the domestic market, demand in the foreign market is a key to setting prices. What will the market bear for a specific product or service?

For most consumer goods, per capita income is a good gauge of a market's ability to pay. Per capita income for most of the industrialized nations is comparable to that of the United States. For the rest of the world, it is much lower. Some products may create such a strong demand—chic goods such as "Levis," for example—that even low per capita income will not affect their selling price. However, in most lower per capita income markets, simplifying the product to reduce selling price may be an answer. The firm must also keep in mind that currency valuations alter the affordability of their goods. Thus, pricing should accommodate wild fluctuations in currency and the relative strength of the dollar, if possible. The firm should also consider who the customers will be. For example, if the firm's main customers in a developing country are expatriates or the upper class, a high price may work even though the average per capita income is low.

Competition

In the domestic market, few companies are free to set prices without carefully evaluating their competitors' pricing policies. This point is also true in exporting, and it is further complicated by the need to evaluate the competition's prices in each export market the exporter intends to enter.

Where a particular foreign market is being serviced by many competitors, the exporter may have little choice but to match the going price or even go below it to establish a market share. If the exporter's product or service is new to a particular foreign market, it may actually be possible to set a higher price than is normally charged domestically.

Pricing Summary

- Determine the objective in the foreign market.
- Compute the actual cost of the export product.
- Compute the final consumer price.
- Evaluate market demand and competition.
- Consider modifying the product to reduce the export price.

Quotations and Pro Forma Invoices

Many export transactions, particularly first-time export transactions, begin with the receipt of an inquiry from abroad, followed by a request for a quotation or a pro forma invoice.

A quotation describes the product, states a price for it, sets the time of shipment, and specifies the terms of sale and terms of payment. Since the foreign buyer may not be familiar with the product, the description of it in an overseas quotation usually must be more detailed than in a domestic quotation. The description should include the following 15 points.

1. Buyer's name and address
2. Buyer's reference number and date of inquiry.
3. Listing of requested products and brief description.
4 Price of each item (it is advisable to indicate whether items are new or used and to quote in U.S. dollars to reduce foreign-exchange risk)
5 Gross and net shipping weight (in metric units where appropriate)
6 Total cubic volume and dimensions (in metric units where appropriate) packed for export
7 Trade discount, if applicable
8 Delivery point
9 Terms of sale
10. Terms of payment

11. Insurance and shipping costs
12. Validity period for quotation
13. Total charges to be paid by customer
14. Estimated shipping date to factory or U.S. port (it is preferable to give U.S. port)
15. Estimated date of shipment arrival

Sellers are often requested to submit a pro forma invoice with or instead of a quotation. Pro forma invoices (*see* page 59, for a sample) are not for payment purposes but are essentially quotations in an invoice format. In addition to the foregoing list of items, a pro forma invoice should include a statement certifying that the pro forma invoice is true and correct and a statement describing the country of origin of the goods. Also, the invoice should be conspicuously marked "pro forma invoice." These invoices are only models that the buyer uses when applying for an import license or arranging for funds. In fact, it is good business practice to include a pro forma invoice with any international quotation, regardless of whether it has been requested. When final collection invoices are being prepared at the time of shipment, it is advisable to check with the U.S. Department of Commerce or some other reliable source for special invoicing requirements that may prevail in the country of destination.

It is very important that price quotations state explicitly that they are subject to change without notice. If a specific price is agreed upon or guaranteed by the exporter, the precise period during which the offer remains valid should be specified.

Terms of Sale

In any sales agreement, it is important that a common understanding exist regarding the delivery terms. The terms in international business transactions often sound similar to those used in domestic business, but they frequently have very different meanings.

Confusion over terms of sale can result in a lost sale or a loss on a sale. For this reason, the exporter must know the terms before preparing a quotation or a pro forma invoice. A complete list of important terms and their definitions will be contained in the new edition of *Incoterms,* which will be published at the end of 1999. It can be purchased from ICC Publishing Corporation, Inc., 156 Fifth Avenue, Suite 308, New York, NY 10010; Tel: (212) 206-1150; Fax: (212) 633-6025. *Guide to Incoterms 1990,* also available from ICC (Price: $49.95), uses illustrations and commentary to explain how buyer and seller divide risks and obligations—and therefore costs—in specific kinds of international transactions. The 1990 update of Incoterms resulted in several new terms and abbreviations; exporters should, therefore, take care to use the correct terms to avoid confusion.

The following are a few of the more common terms used in international trade:

- CIF (cost, insurance, freight) to a named overseas port of import. Under this term, the seller quotes a price for the goods (including insurance), all transportation, and miscellaneous charges to the point of debarkation from the vessel. (Typically used for ocean shipments only.)
- CFR (cost and freight) to a named overseas port of import. Under this term, the seller quotes a price for the goods that includes the cost of transportation to the named point of debarkation. The cost of insurance is left to the buyer's account. (Typically used for ocean shipments only.)
- CPT (carriage paid to) and CIP (carriage and insurance paid to) a named place of destination. Used in place of CFR and CIF, respectively, for shipment by modes other than water.
- EXW (ex works) at a named point of origin (e.g., ex factory, ex mill, ex warehouse). Under this term, the price quoted applies only at the point of origin and the seller agrees to place the goods at the disposal of the buyer at the specified place on the date or within the period fixed. All other charges are for the account of the buyer.
- FAS (free alongside ship) at a named U.S. port of export. Under this term, the seller quotes a price for the goods that includes charges for delivery of the goods alongside a vessel at the port. The seller handles the cost of unloading and wharfage; loading, ocean transportation, and insurance are left to the buyer.
- FCA (free carrier) to a named place. This term replaces the former "FOB named inland port" to designate the seller's responsibility for the cost of loading goods at the named shipping point. It may be used for multimodal transport, container stations, and any mode of transport, including air. FOB (free on board) at a named port of export. The seller quotes the buyer a price that covers all costs up to and including delivery of goods aboard an overseas vessel.

When quoting a price, the exporter should make it meaningful to the prospective buyer. A price for industrial machinery quoted "EXW Saginaw, Michigan, not export packed" would be meaningless to most prospective foreign buyers. Such buyers would have difficulty determining the total cost and, therefore, would hesitate to place an order.

The exporter should quote CIF whenever possible, because it has meaning abroad. It shows the foreign buyer the cost of getting the product to a port in or near the desired country.

If assistance is needed in figuring the CIF price, an international freight forwarder (*see* "Freight Forwarders" on page 80) can provide help to U.S. firms. The exporter should furnish the freight forwarder with a description of the product to be exported and its weight and cubic measurement when packed; the freight forwarder can then compute the CIF price. There is usually no charge for this service.

If at all possible, the exporter should quote the price in U.S. dollars. Doing so eliminates the risk of possible exchange rate fluctuations and the problems of currency conversion. (As a courtesy, the exporter may also wish to include a second pro forma invoice in the foreign currency of the buyer.)

A simple misunderstanding regarding delivery terms may prevent exporters from meeting contractual obligations or make them responsible for shipping costs they sought to avoid. It is important to understand and use delivery terms correctly.

Table 10-1: Sample Cost-Plus Calculation of Product Cost

	Domestic Sale	Export Sale
Factory price	$ 7.50	$7.50
Domestic freight	.70	.70
	8.20	8.20
Export documentation		.50
		8.70
Ocean freight and insurance		1.20
		9.90
Import duty (12 percent of landed cost)		1.19
		11.09
Wholesaler markup (15 percent)	1.23	
	9.43	
Importer/distributor markup (22 percent)		2.44
		13.53
Retail markup (50 percent)	4.72	6.77
Final consumer price	$14.15	$20.30

Figure 10-2: Sample Pro Forma Invoice

Tech International
1000 J Street, N.W.
Washington, DC 20005

Telephone (202) 555-1212 Fax (202) 555-1111

PRO FORMA INVOICE

Date: Jan. 12, 1991

To: Gomez Y. Cartagena
Aptdo. Postal 77
Bogota, Colombia

Your Reference: Ltr., Jan. 6, 1991

Our Reference: Col. 91-14

We hereby quote as follows

Terms of Payment: Letter of Credit
Terms of Sale: CIF Buenaventura

Quantity	Model	Description	Unit	Extension
3	2-50	Separators in accordance with attached specifications	$14,750.00	$44,250.00
3	14-40	First-stage Filter Assemblies per attached specifications	$ 1,200.00	$3,600.00
3	custom	Drive Units—30 hp each (for operation on 3-phase 440 v., 50 cy. current) complete with remote controls	$ 4,235.00	$12,705.00

TOTAL FOB Washington, D.C. domestic packed $60,555.00

Export processing, packaging, prepaid Inland freight to Dulles International Airport & forwarder's handling charges FOB Dulles Airport, Virginia $63,670.00

Estimated air freight and insurance $2,960.00

Est. CIF Buenaventura, Colombia $66,630.00

Estimated gross weight 9,360 lbs. **Estimated cube 520 cu. ft.**

Export packed 4,212 kg. **Export packed 15.6 cu. meters**

PLEASE NOTE

1. All prices quoted herein are U.S. dollars.
2. Prices quoted herein for merchandise only are valid for 60 days from this date.
3. Any changes in shipping costs or insurance rates are for account of the buyer.
4. We estimate ex-factory shipment approximately 60 days from receipt here of purchase order and letter of credit.

Chapter 11

Export Regulations, Customs Benefits, and Tax Incentives

This chapter covers a wide range of regulations, procedures, and practices that fall into three categories: (1) regulations that exporters must follow to comply with U.S. law; (2) procedures that exporters should follow to ensure a successful export transaction; and (3) programs and certain tax procedures that open new markets or provide financial benefits to exporters.

Export Regulations

Most export controls are administered by the Bureau of Export Administration (BXA) in the U.S. Department of Commerce. Exporters should remember that violations of the Export Administration Regulations (EAR) carry both civil and criminal penalties. Whenever there is any doubt about how to comply with export regulations, Department of Commerce officials or qualified professional consultants should be contacted for assistance.

An annual subscription to the EAR provides the basic manual and supplemental updates for about a year. The EAR were restructured in 1996 to clarify the regulatory language, simplify their use, and to generally make the export control regulations more user-friendly. The National Technical Information Service (NTIS) will provide the EAR in electronic or paper formats with three update bulletins (to the those subscribing to the paper version) per cycle. The annual subscription fee is $89.00 for the paper format; $252.00 for the electronic version; and $100 for cd rom. For additional information on the EAR and their availability, contact

National Technical Information Service (NTIS)
5285 Port Royal Road
Springfield, VA 22161
Tel: (703) 605-6060; Fax: (703) 605-6900
Email: info@ntis.fedworld.gov; Web site:
www.fedworld.gov

Some export controls are administered by other U.S. government departments and agencies for national security or foreign policy purposes. These offices include the Department of State, the Office of Foreign Assets Control, the Nuclear Regulatory Commission, and the Patent and Trademark Office.

Export Administration Regulations

Recent Overhaul of the EAR

On September 30, 1993, the Secretary of Commerce submitted to the Congress a report of the Trade Promotion Coordinating Committee (TPCC), which included among its goals to undertake a comprehensive review of the Export Administration Regulations to simplify, clarify, and make the regulations more user-friendly.

In November 1993, BXA organized a Task Group, drawn from several of its offices, to carry out the TPCC recommendation. The interim rule was published in the Federal Register on March 25, 1996 (Volume 61, Number 58, pages 12713–12763. It became effective April 24, 1996, although final compliance with this interim rule was not compelled until November 1, 1996. The repeal of the importer statement requirement for General License GCT was effective immediately, as was the Special Comprehensive License provisions in part 752 are effective immediately. Until March 25, 1997, holders of issued and outstanding special licenses may continue to use those special licenses according to their terms and conditions and according to the special license provisions of the earlier EAR.

Items Subject to the EAR

The following items are subject to the EAR (according to EAR Sec. 734.3(a):

1. All items in the United States, including in a U.S. Foreign Trade Zone or moving in transit through the United States from one foreign country to another;
2. All U.S. origin items wherever located;
3. U.S. origin parts, components, materials or other commodities incorporated abroad into foreign-made products, U.S. origin software commingled with foreign software, and U.S. origin technology commingled with foreign technology, in quantities exceeding de minimis levels as described in EAR Sec. 734.4 and Supplement No. 2 of Sec. 734;
4. Certain foreign-made direct products of U.S. origin technology or software, as described in Sec.

736.2(b)(3) of the EAR. The term "direct product" means the immediate product (including processes and services) produced directly by the use of technology or software; and

5. Certain commodities produced by any plant or major component of a plant located outside the United States that is a direct product of U.S.-origin technology or software, as described in Sec. 736.2(b)(3) of the EAR.

Items Not Subject to the EAR

The following items are not subject to the EAR (according to EAR Sec. 734.3(b):

1. Items that are exclusively controlled for export or reexport by the following departments and agencies of the U.S. Government which regulate exports or reexports for national security or foreign policy purposes:
    - **Department of State.** The International Traffic in Arms Regulations (22 CFR part 121) administered by the Office of Defense Trade Controls relate to defense articles and defense services on the U.S. Munitions List. Section 38 of the Arms Export Control Act (22 USC 2778).
    - **Treasury Department, Office of Foreign Assets Control (OFAC).** Regulations administered by OFAC implement broad controls and embargo transactions with certain foreign countries. These regulations include controls on exports and reexports to certain countries (31 CFR chapter V). Trading with the Enemy Act (50 USC app. section 1 et seq.), and International Emergency Economic Powers Act (50 USC 1701, et seq.)
    - **U.S. Nuclear Regulatory Commission (NRC).** Regulations administered by NRC control the export and reexport of commodities related to nuclear reactor vessels (10 CFR part 110). Atomic Energy Act of 1954, as amended (42 USC part 2011 et seq.).
    - **Department of Energy (DOE).** Regulations administered by DOE control the export and reexport of technology related to the production of special nuclear materials (10 CFR part 810). Atomic Energy Act of 1954, as amended (42 USC section 2011 et seq.).
    - **Patent and Trademark Office (PTO).** Regulations administered by PTO provide for the export to a foreign country of unclassified technology in the form of a patent application or an amendment, modification, or supplement thereto or division thereof (37 CFR part 5). BXA has delegated authority under the Export Administration Act to the PTO to approve exports and reexports of such technology which is subject to the EAR. Exports and reexports of such technology not approved under PTO regulations must comply with the EAR.
2. Prerecorded phonograph records reproducing in whole or in part, the content of printed books, pamphlets, and miscellaneous publications, including newspapers and periodicals; printed books, pamphlets, and miscellaneous publications including bound newspapers and periodicals; children's picture and painting books; newspaper and periodicals, unbound, excluding waste; music books; sheet music; calendars and calendar blocks, paper; maps, hydrographical charts, atlases, gazetteers, globe covers, and globes (terrestrial and celestial); exposed and developed microfilm reproducing, in whole or in part, the content of any of the above; exposed and developed motion picture film and soundtrack; and advertising printed matter exclusively related thereto.
3. Publicly available technology and software that:
    - Are already published or will be published as described in EAR Sec. 734.7;
    - Arise during, or result from, fundamental research, as described in EAR Sec. 734.8;
    - Are educational, as described in EAR Sec. 734.9; or
    - Are included in certain patent applications, as described in EAR Sec. 734.10.
4. Foreign made items that have de minimis U.S. content based on the principles described in EAR Sec. 734.4.

Licensing Requirements

Under the simplified EAR, no license or other authorization is required for any transaction under BXA jurisdiction unless the regulations *affirmatively* state the requirement. Previous regulations stated that *all* exports were prohibited without either a general license or a validated from BXA. In addition, the terms "general license" and "validated license" have been dropped. "License" is now used only to refer to authorization issued by BXA upon application. The many general licenses which previously existed have been converted into a smaller number of exceptions to require the exporter to seek a license when the Commerce Control List indicates that the particular item going to the stated country generally requires a license.

The Ten General Prohibitions

The affirmative statements of the need to obtain a license have been consolidated into ten general prohibitions, found in EAR Sec. 736. They consist, very briefly, of the following:

1. **Exports and reexports.** Export and reexport of controlled items to listed countries.
2. **Parts and components reexports.** Reexport and export from abroad of foreign-made items incorporating more than a de minimis amount of controlled U.S. content.
3. **Foreign-produced direct product reexports.** Reexport and export from abroad of the foreign-produced direct product of U.S. technology and software.
4. **Denial orders.** Engaging in actions prohibited by a denial order.
5. **End-use end-user.** Export or reexport to prohibited end-user or end-users.
6. **Embargo.** Export or reexport to embargoed destinations.
7. **U.S. person proliferation activity.** Support of proliferation activities.
8. **In-Transit.** In-transit shipments and items to be unladen from vessels and aircraft.
9. **Orders, Terms and Conditions.** Violation of any orders, terms, or conditions.
10. **Knowledge Violation to Occur.** Proceeding with transactions with knowledge that a violation has occurred or is about to occur.

Determining Need for a BXA License

Of those exports and reexports subject to the Export Administration Regulations (EAR), a relatively small percentage require a license from BXA. License requirements are dependent upon an item's technical characteristics, the destination, the end-use, and the end-user, and other activities of the end-user. You will need the following five facts to determine your obligations under the EAR:

1. **What is it?**
   What an item is, for export control purposes, depends on its classification, which is its place on the Commerce Control List (see part 774 of the EAR).
2. **Where is it going?**
   The country of ultimate destination for an export or reexport also determines licensing requirements (see parts 738 and 774 of the EAR concerning the Country Chart and the Commerce Control List).
3. **Who will receive it?**
   The ultimate end-user of your item cannot be a bad end-user. See General Prohibition Four (Denial Orders) in Sec. 736.2(b)(4) and parts 744 and 764 of the EAR for a reference to the list of persons you may not deal with.
4. **What will they do with it?**
   The ultimate end-use of your item cannot be a bad end-use. See General Prohibition Five (End-Use End-User) in Sec. 736.2(b)(5) and part 744 of the EAR for general end-use and end-user restrictions.
5. **What else do they do?**
   Conduct such as contracting, financing, and freight forwarding in support of a proliferation project (as described in Sec. 744.6 of the EAR) may prevent you from dealing with someone.

The Department of Commerce, Bureau of Export Administration (BXA) is the primary licensing agency for dual use exports (commercial items which could have military applications). Other departments and agencies have regulatory jurisdiction over certain types of exports and reexports. For example, the State Department licenses the export defense articles and services, while certain nuclear materials and equipment are licensed by the Nuclear Regulatory Commission.

For assistance in determining which U.S. Government agency has licensing jurisdiction over your export *see* "Commodity Jurisdiction" on page 63.

Commodity Classification

To determine licensing requirements, you must first classify your item against the Commerce Control List (CCL). All commodities, technology or software subject to the licensing authority of BXA are included in the CCL which is found in Supplement 1 to Part 774 of the EAR. On the CCL, individual items are identified by an Export Control Classification Number (ECCN).

To classify your product, you should begin with a review of the general characteristics of your item. This will usually guide you to the appropriate category on the CCL. Once the appropriate category is identified, you should match the particular characteristics and functions of your item to a specific ECCN.

You can also request an official commodity classification from BXA. A commodity classification request requires the submission of an application and technical specifications of your commodity, software or technology to BXA. To submit a classification request use Multipurpose Application Form BXA-748P or its electronic equivalent (ERIC).

Dual Use Licensing

The term "dual use" is sometimes used to distinguish the types of items covered by the EAR from those that are covered by the regulations of certain other export licensing agencies. In general, the term dual use serves to distinguish EAR-controlled items that can be used both in sensitive (e.g., military or nuclear) and other, non- sensitive applications from those that are (a) weapons or military-related in use or design and subject to the controls of the Department of State or (b) subject to the nuclear-related controls of the Department of Energy or the Nuclear Regulatory Commission. Note, however, that although the short-hand term dual use may be employed to refer to the entire scope of the EAR, the EAR also apply to some items that have solely civil uses.

U.S. national interests are safeguarded through BXA's effective administration of export control laws relating to dual-use technologies. Controls are maintained on exports from the United States, and reexports of U.S.-origin items from foreign destinations, on strategic commodities and technical data worldwide to prevent the diversion of such strategic items to end-users or end-uses of concern.

The effectiveness of these controls is enhanced by their being maintained as part of multilateral control arrangements. The Wassenaar Arrangement, the Nuclear Suppliers Group, the Australia Group, and the Missile Technology Control Regime are the four multilateral export control regimes in which the United States participates. BXA implements U.S. foreign policy controls such as crime control, antiterrorism and regional stability and is responsible for export controls on terrorist countries. BXA also administers export controls to protect the United States from the adverse impact of the unrestricted export of commodities in short supply (e.g. some crude oil, other petroleum products, and unprocessed western red cedar).

Commodity Jurisdiction

A commodity jurisdiction (CJ) request is used to determine whether an item or service is subject to the export licensing authority of the Department of Commerce or the Department of State, Office of Defense Trade Controls (DTC). BXA is the primary licensing agency for dual use exports (commercial items which could have military applications), while the State Department licenses defense articles and services. If you are not completely sure of the export licensing jurisdiction of an item, you should request a CJ determination. You can also submit a CJ request if you feel that jurisdiction of an item is incorrectly assigned and should be transferred to another agency.

To submit a CJ request, send a letter to DTC, along with technical specifications, brochures, etc. describing the items for consideration. If you believe that the current jurisdiction of the item is incorrectly assigned, provide an explanation outlining the reasons. A CJ determination will only identify the proper licensing authority for an item; it is not a license or approval to export. Once the jurisdiction of an item is established, you should contact the proper licensing agency (Commerce or State) to determine the licensing requirement of the item. For specific instructions you may contact DTC by telephone at (703) 875-6644, or via fax at (703) 875-6647, attention: PM/DTC/CJ.

License Exceptions

If you decide by reviewing the CCL in combination with the Country Chart that a license is required for your destination, you should determine whether a License Exception will except you from that requirement. License Exceptions are generally not available to overcome General Prohibitions Four through Ten. However, selected License Exceptions for embargoed destinations are specified in part 746 of the EAR and License Exceptions for short supply controls are specified in part 754 of the EAR.

Unauthorized Parties

Various requirements of the EAR are dependent upon a person's knowledge of the end-use, end-user, ultimate destination, or other facts relating to a transaction or activity. These provisions include the nonproliferation-related "catch-all" sections and the prohibition against proceeding with a transaction with knowledge that a violation of the EAR has occurred or is about to occur.

If you are being asked to participate in an export transaction that you believe may be illegal, or if you have information that such an illegal transaction may be about to occur, you are encouraged to contact BXA's Office of Export Enforcement immediately at (800) 424-2980 or the Office of Exporter Services at (202) 482-4532.

You may also wish to check the parties to your transaction against the "List of Specially Designated Nationals" maintained by the Department of the Treasury's Office of Foreign Assets Control.

If you think you may be dealing with an "unauthorized party," there are several steps you should take:

- Read and understand the "Know Your Customer Guidance" provided in the EAR (and reprinted below). It will help you recognize and avoid prohibited transactions.
- Be familiar with the "Red Flag Indicators" (listed on page 64) that can help you recognize illegal, or potentially illegal, transactions.
- Always check the parties to your transaction (including freight forwarders, intermediate consignees, and the ultimate consignee) against the most recent "Denied Persons List."

"Know Your Customer" Guidance

Various requirements of the EAR are dependent upon a person's knowledge of the end-use, end-user, ultimate destination, or other facts relating to a transaction or activity. These provisions include the nonproliferation-related "catch-all" sections and the prohibition against proceeding with a transaction with knowledge that a violation of the EAR has occurred or is about to occur.

BXA provides the following guidance on how individuals and firms should act under this knowledge standard. This guidance does not change or interpret the EAR.

1. **Decide whether there are "red flags".**
Take into account any abnormal circumstances in a transaction that indicate that the export may be destined for an inappropriate end-use, end-user, or destination. Such circumstances are referred to as "red flags". Included among examples of red flags are orders for items that are inconsistent with the needs of the purchaser, a customer declining installation and testing when included in the sales price or when normally requested, or requests for equipment configurations that are incompatible with the stated destination (e.g., 120 volts in a country with 220 volts). Commerce has developed lists of such red flags that are not all-inclusive but are intended to illustrate the types of circumstances that should cause reasonable suspicion that a transaction will violate the EAR.

2. **If there are "red flags", inquire.**
If there are no "red flags"' in the information that comes to your firm, you should be able to proceed with a transaction in reliance on information you have received. That is, absent "red flags"' (or an express requirement in the EAR), there is no affirmative duty upon exporters to inquire, verify, or otherwise "go behind" the customer's representations. However, when "red flags" are raised in information that comes to your firm, you have a duty to check out the suspicious circumstances and inquire about the end-use, end- user, or ultimate country of destination. The duty to check out "red flags" is not confined to the use of License Exceptions affected by the "know" or "reason to know" language in the EAR. Applicants for licenses are required by part 748 of the EAR to obtain documentary evidence concerning the transaction, and misrepresentation or concealment of material facts is prohibited, both in the licensing process and in all export control documents. You can rely upon representations from your customer and repeat them in the documents you file unless red flags oblige you to take verification steps.

3. **Do not self-blind.**
Do not cut off the flow of information that comes to your firm in the normal course of business. For example, do not instruct the sales force to tell potential customers to refrain from discussing the actual end-use, end-user, and ultimate country of destination for the product your firm is seeking to sell. Do not put on blinders that prevent the learning of relevant information. An affirmative policy of steps to avoid "bad" information would not insulate a company from liability, and it would usually be considered an aggravating factor in an enforcement proceeding.

4. **Employees need to know how to handle "red flags".**
Knowledge possessed by an employee of a company can be imputed to a firm so as to make it liable for a violation. This makes it important for firms to establish clear policies and effective compliance procedures to ensure that such knowledge about transactions can be evaluated by responsible senior officials. Failure to do so could be regarded as a form of self-blinding.

5. **Reevaluate all the information after the inquiry.**
The purpose of this inquiry and reevaluation is to determine whether the "red flags" can be explained or justified. If they can, you may proceed with the transaction. If the "red flags" cannot be explained or justified and you proceed, you run the risk of having had "knowledge" that would make your action a violation of the EAR.

6. **Refrain from the transaction or advise BXA and wait.**
If you continue to have reasons for concern after your inquiry, then you should either refrain from the transaction or submit all the relevant information to BXA in the form of an application for a validated license or in such other form as BXA may specify.

Industry has an important role to play in preventing exports and reexports contrary to the national security and foreign policy interests of the United States. BXA will continue to work in partnership with industry to make this front line of defense effective, while minimizing the regulatory burden on exporters. If you have any question about whether you have encountered a "red flag", you may contact the Office of Export Enforcement at (800) 424-2980 or the Office of Exporter Services at (202) 482-4532.

Red Flag Indicators

Possible indicators that an unlawful diversion might be planned by your customer include the following:

1. The customer or purchasing agent is reluctant to offer information about the end-use of a product.
2. The product's capabilities do not fit the buyer's line of business; for example, a small bakery places an order for several sophisticated lasers.
3. The product ordered is incompatible with the technical level of the country to which the product is being shipped. For example, semiconductor manufacturing equipment would be of little use in a country without an electronics industry.
4. The customer has little or no business background.

5. The customer is willing to pay cash for a very expensive item when the terms of the sale call for financing.
6. The customer is unfamiliar with the product's performance characteristics but still wants the product.
7. Routine installation, training or maintenance services are declined by the customer.
8. Delivery dates are vague, or deliveries are planned for out- of-the-way destinations.
9. A freight forwarding firm is listed as the product's final destination.
10. The shipping route is abnormal for the product and destination.
11. Packaging is inconsistent with the stated method of shipment or destination.
12. When questioned, the buyer is evasive or unclear about whether the purchased product is for domestic use, export or reexport.

BXA Export Enforcement Programs

The primary roles of BXA's Export Enforcement (EE) program are to:

- prevent the illegal export of dual-use items before they occur;
- Investigate and assist in the prosecution of violators of the Export Administration Regulations (EAR) and the Fastener Quality Act (FQA); and
- Inform and educate exporters, freight forwarders, and manufacturers of their enforcement responsibilities under the EAR and FQA.

Pre-License Checks and Post-Shipment Verification. All export license applications are screened electronically by EE to ensure items are not illegally exported. In addition EE reviews specific individual license applications to assess diversion risks, identify potential violations, and determine the reliability of those receiving controlled U.S.-origin commodities or technical data. In some instances EE, or another Federal agency, requests that a pre-license check be conducted to determine the bona fides of the transaction and suitability of the end-user. The result of this check is factored into the licensing recommendation EE makes to BXA's licensing offices. In addition, EE carries out post-shipment verifications to ensure that a controlled U.S.-origin item has actually been delivered to the authorized ultimate consignee or end-user and that it is being used as claimed on the export license application.

Safeguards Verification Program. EE conducts numerous on-site safeguard verification trips around the world annually. During these trips, pre-license checks and post-shipment verifications are conducted on controlled U.S. goods, especially those of proliferation concern. In cases where EE's Safeguards Verification Teams discover items are being used inappropriately or in a manner that is inconsistent with an export license they work closely with host government officials to correct the situation. The EE verification teams also assess the suitability of foreign firms to receive U.S.-origin goods and technologies that require U.S. validated licenses.

SED Review Program. EE conducts on-site reviews of selected Shipper's Export Declarations (SED) at U.S. ports before goods are exported and again after shipments are made. These on-site reviews are conducted to uncover attempts to export items illegally which require a validated export license from the Department of Commerce. Items for export to destinations of concern and exports of proliferation concern are targeted specifically.

In addition to the preventive enforcement efforts under the SED Review Program, EE's Office of Enforcement Support identifies past shipments that may have violated the Export Administration Regulations and refers them to the Office of Export Enforcement (OEE) for further investigation. Over 450 investigations of suspected export control violations occur annually, based on the routine review of SEDs.

Visa Application Review Program. This program was initiated in 1990 to help prevent the unauthorized access to controlled U.S. technology or technical data by aliens visiting the United States. Under this program, information on visa applications is reviewed to detect and prevent possible violations of the Export Administration Regulations. Each year this program results in a number of recommendations against issuing visas being forwarded to the U.S. Department of State.

BXA Forms

Many BXA forms used in the export licensing process changed during the course of 1996. When ordering forms, check the list below to be certain you are ordering currently accepted forms. Limited quantities are available from BXA's Western Regional Office in California, and most local offices of the Department of Commerce. These forms are only available through the mail; they can not be faxed or sent by email. All forms are available free of charge. If you need more than ten copies of any one form you may submit a request by fax through BXA's Washington D.C. office at Fax: (202) 219-7179, or call the Exporter Counseling Division at Tel: (202) 482-4811.

The following forms remain unchanged:

BXA 645P: International Import Certificate

BXA 647P: Delivery Verification Certificate.

The following new forms are required as of June, 1996:

BXA 748P: Multipurpose Application
(Replaces BXA 622P & BXA685P & BXA699P)

BXA 748P-A: Item Appendix
(Replaces BXA 622P-A)

BXA 748P-B: End User Appendix
(Replaces BXA622P-B)

BXA 752P: Statement by Consignee in support of Special Comprehensive License
(Replaces BXA 6052P)

BXA 711: Statement by Ultimate Consignee and Purchaser
(Replaces BXA 629P)

The following forms have been discontinued:

BXA 648P: Notification of Delivery Verification Requirement

BXA 686P: Statement by Foreign Importer of Aircraft or Vessel Repair Parts

BXA 6026P: Service Supply Statement by U.S. Exporter

For More Information on Export Regulations

BXA Contacts

Web site: www.bxa.doc.gov/

Office of Exporter Services
Tel: (202) 482-0436; Fax: (202) 482-3322

Chemical & Biological Controls and Treaty Compliance
Tel: (202) 482-3825; Fax: (202) 482-0751

Strategic Industries and Economic Security
Tel: (202) 482-4506; Fax: (202) 482-5650

Office of Nuclear and Missile Technology Controls
Tel: (202) 482-4188; Fax: (202) 482-4145

Office of Strategic Trade and Foreign Policy Controls
Tel: (202) 482-0092; Fax: (202) 482-4094

Office of Export Enforcement
Tel: (202) 482-2252; Fax: (202) 482-5889

Office of Export Enforcement, Intelligence and Field Support Division
Tel: (202) 482-1208; Fax: (202) 482-0964

Export License Compliance Division
Tel: (202) 482-5914

Western Regional Office, Orange County, CA
Tel: (949) 660-0144; Fax: (949) 660-9347
Web site: www.primnet.com/~bxawest

Northern Calif. Branch Office, Santa Clara County, CA
Tel: (408) 998-7402; Fax: (408) 998-7470

Publications Related to the EAR

The Table of Denial Orders. Lists entities, domestic and international with whom certain export and export related transactions are prohibited or restricted. The Table of Denial Orders is constantly changing, and exporters are responsible for being up to date with the most current version. The Western Regional Office can mail out a recent, "not current" paper copy of the Table of Denial Orders. An electronic version can be accessed through BXA's Western Regional Office web site at www.primenet.com/~bxawest.

The Specially Designated Nationals List. Lists entities, both domestic and international with whom certain export and export related transactions are prohibited or restricted. The Specially Designated Nationals List is constantly changing, and exporters are responsible for being up to date with the most current version. This list is maintained by the Department of the Treasury Office of Foreign Assets Control and consists primarily of known front runner entities for trade with embargoed entities. An electronic version can be accessed through BXA's Western Regional Office web site at www.primenet.com/~bxawest.

Executive Orders and Federal Register Notices. Changes to the EAR are usually made public in one of two medium. Most often changes to the Export Administration Regulations are made public through publication in the *Federal Register.* Changes are occasionally made public through executive orders issued from the White House. When these orders do not contain an effective date the exporter should check with the local office of the BXA to determine their effective date.

Other Government Agencies Regulating Exports

The list below is organized by commodity. If your commodity is on this list your should check the indicated text Code of Federal Regulations (CFR) and/or contact the agency listed.

- **Carriers and Goods Destined for North Korea**
  Department of Transportation, Office of International Law, General Counsel (See 44 CFR part 403)
  Tel: (202) 366-2972; Fax: (202) 366-9188.
- **Defense Services and Defense Articles**
  Department of State, Office of Defense Trade Controls (See 22 CFR parts 120 through 130)
  Tel: (703) 875-6644; Fax: (703) 875-6647
- **Drugs, Chemicals and Precursors**
  Drug Enforcement Administration, International Chemical Control Unit (See 21 CFR parts 1311 through 1313)
  Tel: (202) 307-7202; Fax: (202) 307-8570
  Web site: www.usdoj.gov/dea/deahome.htm
- **Controlled Substances**
  Drug Enforcement Administration, International Drug Unit (See 21 CFR 1311 through 1313)
  Tel: (202) 307-2414; Fax: (202) 307-8570
  Web site: www.usdoj.gov/dea/deahome.htm

- **Defense-Related Technology**
  Department of Defense, Defense Threat Reduction Agency
  Tel: (703) 604-5196; Fax: (703) 602-5840
- **Drugs and Biologics**
  Food and Drug Administration, Import/ Export (See 21 USC 301 et seq.)
  Tel: (301) 594-3150; Fax: (301) 594-0165
- **Fish and Wildlife; Endangered Species**
  Department of the Interior, Chief Office of Management Authority
  Tel: (703) 358-2093; Fax: (703) 358-2281
  Web site: www.fws.govl
- **Foreign Assets and Transactions Controls**
  Department of Treasury, Office of Foreign Assets Control, Licensing (See 31 CFR parts 500 through 590)
  Tel: (202) 622-2480; Fax: (202) 622-1657
  Web site: www.treas.gov/ofac (Provides direct access to the list of Specially Designated Nationals)
- **Investigational Drugs**
  Food and Drug Administration, International Affairs (See 21 CFR 312.1106)
  Tel: (301) 827-4480; Fax: (301) 443-0235
  Web site: www.fda.gov
- **Medical Devices**
  Food and Drug Administration, Office of Compliance (See 21 USC 301 et seq.)
  Tel: (301) 594-4699; Fax: (301) 594-4715
  Web site: www.fda.gov
- **Natural Gas and Electric Power**
  Department of Energy, Office of Fossil Energy (See 10 CFR 205.300 through 205.379 and part 590)
  Tel: (202) 586-6503; Fax: (202) 586-5146
  Web site: www.fe.doe.gov
- **Nuclear Materials and Equipment**
  Nuclear Regulatory Commission, Office of International Programs (See 10 CFR part 110)
  Tel: (301) 415-2344; Fax: (301) 415-2395
  Web site: www.nrc.gov/NRC/nucmat.html
- **Nuclear Technology, Technical Data for Nuclear Weapons/Special Nuclear Materials**
  Department of Energy, Office of Arms Control and Non Proliferation, Export Control Division (See 10 CFR part 810)
  Tel: (202) 586-2331; Fax: (202) 586-1348
  Web site: http://nn43web.nn.gov/
- **Ocean Freight Forwarders**
  Federal Maritime Commission, Office of Freight Forwarders (See 46 CFR part 510)
  Tel: (202) 523-5843; Fax: (202) 523-5830
  Web site: www.fmc.gov
- **Patent Filing Data Sent Abroad**
  Department of Commerce, Patent and Trademark Office, Licensing and Review (See 37 CFR part 5)
  Tel: (703) 306-4187; Fax: (703) 306-4196
  Web site: www.uspto.gov/
- **Toxic Waste Exports**
  Environmental Protection Agency, Office of Solid Waste, International and Special Projects Branch
  Tel: (703) 308-8751; Fax: (703) 308-0522
  Web site: www.epa.gov/epaoswer/
- **U.S. Flagged or U.S. Manufactured Vessels Over 1,000 Gross Tons**
  U.S. Maritime Administration, Division of Vessel Transfer and Disposal (See 46 CFR part 221)
  Tel: (202) 366-5821; Fax: (202) 493-2180
  Web site: www.marad.dot.gov

Antidiversion, Antiboycott, and Antitrust Requirements

Antidiversion Clause

To help ensure that U.S. exports go only to legally authorized destinations, the U.S. government requires a destination control statement on shipping documents. Under this requirement, the commercial invoice and bill of lading (or air waybill) for nearly all commercial shipments leaving the United States must display a statement notifying the carrier and all foreign parties (the ultimate and intermediate consignees and purchaser) that the U.S. material has been licensed for export only to certain destinations and may not be diverted contrary to U.S. law. Exceptions to the use of the destination control statement are (1) shipments to Canada and intended for consumption in Canada and (2) shipments being made under certain general licenses. Advice on the appropriate statement to be used can be provided by the Department of Commerce, the Commerce district office, an attorney, or the freight forwarder.

Antiboycott Regulations

During the mid-1970's the United States adopted two laws that seek to counteract the participation of U.S. citizens in other nation's economic boycotts or embargoes. These "antiboycott" laws are the 1977 amendments to the Export Administration Act (EAA) and the Ribicoff Amendment to the 1976 Tax Reform Act (TRA). The antiboycott laws were adopted to require U.S. firms to refuse to participate in foreign boycotts that the United States does not sanction. They have the effect of preventing U.S. firms from being used to implement foreign policies of other nations which run counter to U.S. policy.

The antiboycott provisions of the Export Administration Regulations (EAR) apply to all "U.S. persons," defined to include individuals and companies located in the United States and their foreign affiliates. These persons are subject to the law when their activities relate to the sale, purchase, or transfer of goods or services between the United States and a foreign country. This covers U.S. exports and imports, financing, forwarding and shipping, and certain other transactions that may take place wholly offshore.

Generally, the Tax Reform Act applies to all U.S. taxpayers (and their related companies). The TRA's reporting requirements apply to taxpayers' "operations" in, with, or related to boycotting countries or their nationals. Its penalties apply to those taxpayers with Domestic International Sales Corporation, Foreign Sales Corporation, foreign subsidiary deferral, and/or foreign tax credit benefits.

Conduct that may be penalized under the TRA and/or prohibited under the EAR includes:

- Agreements to refuse or actual refusals to do business with or in Israel or with blacklisted companies.
- Agreements to discriminate or actual discrimination against other persons based on race, religion, sex, national origin or nationality.
- Agreements to furnish or actually furnishing information about business relationships with or in Israel or with blacklisted companies.
- Agreements to furnish or the actual furnishing of information about the race, religion, sex, or national origin of another person.
- Furnishing information about business relationships with Israel or with blacklisted persons.
- Implementing letters of credit containing prohibited boycott terms or conditions.

TRA does not "prohibit" conduct, but denies tax benefits for certain types of boycott- related agreements.

The EAR requires U.S. persons to report quarterly any requests they have received to take any action to comply with, further, or support an unsanctioned foreign boycott. EAR reports are filed quarterly on form BXA 621-P, available from the Commerce Department's ITA and BXA field offices or from the Office of Antiboycott Compliance in Washington, D.C.

The TRA requires taxpayers to report "operations" in, with, or related to a boycotting country or its nationals and requests received to participate in or cooperate with an international boycott. The Treasury Department publishes a quarterly list of "boycotting countries." TRA reports are filed with tax returns on IRS Form 5713, available from local IRS offices.

Violations of the antiboycott provisions of the EAR carry the same penalties as those for export control violations. For individuals, this can include fines of up to $250,000, imprisonment for up to ten years, or both. For firms the penalties for each violation can be $1 million or up to five times the value of the exports involved. In addition, for each violation of the EAR any or all of the following may be imposed: revocation of validated export licenses; the general denial of export privileges; the exclusion from practice; and/or the imposition of fines of up to $10,000 per violation, or $100,000. Violations of the TRA involve the denial of all or part of the foreign tax benefits discussed above.

The Department of Commerce's Office of Antiboycott Compliance (OAC) administers the program through ongoing investigations of corporate activities. OAC operates an automated boycott-reporting system providing statistical and enforcement data to Congress and to the public, issuing interpretations of the regulations for the affected public, and offering nonbinding informal guidance to the private sector on specific compliance concerns. U.S. firms with questions about complying with antiboycott regulations should contact OAC's Enforcement Division at Tel: (202) 482-2381 or Fax: (202) 482-0913 or write to

Office of Antiboycott Compliance
Bureau of Export Administration
Room 6098, U.S. Department of Commerce
Washington, DC 20230

Antitrust Laws

The U.S. antitrust laws reflect this nation's commitment to an economy based on competition. They are intended to foster the efficient allocation of resources by providing consumers with goods and services at the lowest price that efficient business operations can profitably offer. Various foreign countries—including the EC, Canada, the United Kingdom, Germany, Japan, and Australia—also have their own antitrust laws that U.S. firms must comply with when exporting to such nations.

Formal written bilateral arrangements exist between the United States and the Federal Republic of Germany, Australia, and Canada. International antitrust cooperation can also occur through mutual legal assistance treaties (MLATs). MLATs currently are in force with over a dozen countries, however, only the MLAT with Canada has been used to date to obtain assistance in antitrust investigations. The Department of Justice and the Federal Trade Commission (FTC) also hold regular consultations with the antitrust officials of Canada, the European Commission, and Japan, and have close, informal ties with the antitrust authorities of many other countries. Since 1990, the U.S. has cooperated closely with countries in the process of establishing competition agencies, assisted by funding provided by the Agency for International Development. On November 2, 1994, President Clinton signed into law the International Antitrust Enforcement Assistance Act of 1994, which authorizes the U.S. to enter into antitrust mutual assistance agreements in accordance with the legislation.

The U.S. antitrust statutes do not provide a checklist of specific requirements. Instead they set forth broad principles that are applied to the specific facts and circumstances of a business transaction. Under the U.S. antitrust laws, some types of trade restraints, known as per se violations, are regarded as conclusively illegal. Per se violations include price-fixing agreements and conspiracies, divisions of markets by competitors, and certain group boycotts and tying arrangements.

Most restraints of trade in the United States are judged under a second legal standard known as the rule of reason. The rule of reason requires a showing that (1) certain acts occurred and (2) such acts had an anticompetitive effect. Under the rule of reason, various factors are considered, including business justification, impact on prices and output in the market, barriers to entry, and market shares of the parties.

In the case of exports by U.S. firms, there are special limitations on the application of the per se and rule of reason tests by U.S. courts. Under Title IV of the Export Trading Company Act (also known as the Foreign Trade Antitrust Improvements Act), there must be a "direct, substantial and reasonably foreseeable" effect on the domestic or import commerce of the United States or on the export commerce of a U.S. person before an activity may be challenged under the Sherman Antitrust Act or the Federal Trade Commission Act (two of the primary federal antitrust statutes). This provision clarifies the particular circumstances under which the overseas activities of U.S. exporters may be challenged under these two antitrust statutes. Under Title III of the Export Trading Company Act the Department of Commerce, with the concurrence of the U.S. Department of Justice, can issue an export trade certificate of review that provides certain limited immunity from the federal and state antitrust laws. *Refer to* Chapter 4, "Methods of Exporting and Channels of Distribution," beginning on page 25, for more information.)

Although the great majority of international business transactions do not pose antitrust problems, antitrust issues may be raised in various types of transactions, among which are

- overseas distribution arrangements;
- overseas joint ventures for research, manufacturing, construction, and distribution;
- patent, trademark, copyright, and know-how licenses;
- mergers and acquisitions involving foreign firms; and
- raw material procurement agreements and concessions.

The potential U.S. and foreign antitrust problems posed by such transactions are discussed in greater detail in Chapter 16, "Technology Licensing and Joint Ventures," beginning on page 108. Where potential U.S. or foreign antitrust issues are raised, it is advisable to obtain the advice and assistance of qualified antitrust counsel.

For particular transactions that pose difficult antitrust issues, and for which an export trade certificate of review is not desired, the Antitrust Division of the Department of Justice can be asked to state its enforcement views in a *business review letter.* The business review procedure is initiated by writing a letter to the Antitrust Division describing the particular business transaction that is contemplated and requesting the department's views on the antitrust legality of the transaction.

Certain aspects of the federal antitrust laws and the Antitrust Division's enforcement policies regarding international transactions are explored in the Department of Justice's *Antitrust Enforcement Guidelines for International Operations*, which were revised in 1995. For more information, contact

Antitrust Division
U.S. Department of Justice
Main Justice Bldg.
Washington, DC 20530
Tel: (202) 514-2401; Fax: (202) 616-2645
Web site: www.usdoj.gov

Foreign Corrupt Practices Act (FCPA)

The FCPA makes it unlawful for any person or firm (as well as persons acting on behalf of the firm) to offer, pay, or promise to pay (or to authorize any such payment or promise) money or anything of value to any foreign official (or foreign political party or candidate for foreign political office) for the purpose of obtaining or retaining business. It is also unlawful to make a payment to any person while knowing that all or a portion of the payment will be offered, given, or promised directly or indirectly, to any foreign official (or foreign political party, candidate, or official) for the purposes of assisting the person or firm in obtaining or retaining business. Knowing includes the concepts of conscious disregard and willful blindness. The FCPA also contains provisions applicable to publicly held companies concerning financial recordkeeping and internal accounting controls.

The Department of Justice enforces the criminal provisions of the FCPA and the civil provisions against "domestic concerns." The Securities and Exchange Commission (SEC) is responsible for civil enforcement against "issuers." The Department of Commerce supplies general information to U.S. exporters who have questions about the FCPA and about international developments concerning the FCPA.

There is an exception to the antibribery provisions for "facilitating payments for routine governmental action." Actions "similar" to the examples listed in the statute are also covered by this exception. A person charged with violating the FCPA's antibribery provisions may assert as a defense that the payment was lawful under the written laws and regulations of the foreign country or that the payment was associated with demonstrating a product or performing a contractual obligation.

Firms are subject to a fine of up to $2 million. Officers, directors, employees, agents, and stockholders are subject to a fine of up to $250,000 and imprisonment for up to five years. The U.S. attorney general can bring a civil action against a domestic concern (and the SEC against an issuer) for a fine of up to $10,000 as well as against any officer, director, employee, or agent of a firm or stockholder acting on behalf of the firm, who willfully violates the antibribery provisions. Under federal criminal law other than the FCPA, individuals may be fined up to $250,000 or up to twice the amount of the gross gain or gross loss if the defendant derives pecuniary gain from the offense or causes a pecuniary loss to another person.

The attorney general (and the SEC, where appropriate) may also bring a civil action to enjoin any act or practice whenever it appears that the person or firm (or a person acting on behalf of a firm) is in violation or about to be in violation of the antibribery provisions.

A person or firm found in violation of the FCPA may be barred from doing business with the federal government. Indictment alone can lead to a suspension of the right to do business with the government.

Conduct that constitutes a violation of the FCPA may give rise to a private cause of action under the Racketeer-Influenced and Corrupt Organizations Act.

The Department of Justice established a new FCPA opinion procedure in the early 1990s; the details of the opinion procedure are provided in 28 CFR Part 80. Under the opinion procedure, any party may request a statement of the Department of Justice's present enforcement intentions under the antibribery provisions of the FCPA regarding any proposed business conduct.

FDA and EPA Restrictions

In addition to the various export regulations that have been discussed, rules and regulations enforced by the Food and Drug Administration (FDA) and the Environmental Protection Agency (EPA) also affect a limited number of exporters.

Food and Drug Administration

The FDA enforces U.S. laws intended to assure the consumer that foods are pure and wholesome, that drugs and devices are safe and effective, and that cosmetics are safe. FDA has promulgated a wide range of regulations to enforce these goals. Exporters of products covered by FDA's regulations are affected as follows:

- If the item is intended for export only, meets the specifications of the foreign purchaser, is not in conflict with the laws of the country to which it is to be shipped, and is properly labeled, it is exempt from the adulteration and misbranding provisions of the Federal Food, Drug, and Cosmetic Act (see 801(e)). This exemption does not apply to "new drugs" or "new animal drugs" that have not been approved as safe and effective or to certain devices.
- If the exporter thinks the export product may be covered by FDA, it is important to contact the nearest FDA field office or the Public Health Service, Food and Drug Administration, 5600 Fishers Lane, Rockville, MD 20857.

Environmental Protection Agency

EPA's involvement in exports is limited to hazardous waste, pesticides, and toxic chemicals. Although EPA has no authority to prohibit the export of these substances, it has an established notification system designed to inform receiving foreign governments that materials of possible human health or environmental concern will be entering their country.

Under the Resource Conservation and Recovery Act (RCRA), generators of waste who wish to export waste considered hazardous are required to notify EPA before shipping a given hazardous waste to a given foreign consignee. EPA then notifies the government of the foreign consignee. Export cannot occur until written approval is received from the foreign government.

As for pesticides and other toxic chemicals, neither the Federal Insecticide, Fungicide, and Rodenticide Act (FIFRA) nor the Toxic Substances Control Act (TSCA) requires exporters of banned or severely restricted chemicals to obtain written consent before shipping. However, the EPA is mandated by FIFRA Section 17 to inform other governments about unregistered pesticides exported from the U.S. and about pesticide regulatory actions taken in the U.S. that may have significance for other countries. The notification program involves both notices of export sent to importing countries, and notices of U.S. regulatory actions sent to all governments world-wide. The revised export policy of 1992 greatly expanded EPA's pesticide export tracking and notification system responsibilities.

An exporter of hazardous waste, unregistered pesticides, or toxic chemicals should contact one or more of the following offices:

- RCRA Hotline
  (For information on compliance with the Resource Conservation and Recovery Act)
  Tel: (703) 412-9810
  Web site: www.epa.gov/
- TSCA Hotline
  (For information on compliance with the Toxic Substances Control Act)
  Tel: (202) 554-1404

- EPA Office of Pesticide Programs
Tel: (703) 305-7090; Fax: (703) 308-4776
- Dept. of Transportation Hazardous Materials Information Center
(For information on transporting hazardous materials)
Tel: (800) 467-4922

U.S. Department of Agriculture

Federal Grain Inspection Service (FGIS)

The FGIS inspects and weighs all exported grain, oilseeds, and related products for domestic and export trade. For more information, contact

FGIS Compliance Division, Regulatory Branch
Tel: (202) 720-8536; Fax: (202) 690-2755
Web site: www.usda.gov/gipsa

Food Safety and Inspection Service (FSIS)

Under the Federal Meat Inspection Act and the Poultry Products Inspection Act, FSIS inspects all meat and poultry sold in interstate and foreign commerce, including imported products. Approximately 7,400 Federal inspectors carry out inspection laws in some 6,200 plants. For further information contact

Food Safety Education
Food Safety and Inspection Service
14th and Independence Ave. SW, Room 2932
Washington, DC 20250
Tel: (202) 720-7943; Fax: (202) 720-1843
Web site: www.fsis.usda.gov

Import Regulations of Foreign Governments

Import documentation requirements and other regulations imposed by foreign governments vary from country to country. It is vital that exporters be aware of the regulations that apply to their own operations and transactions. Many governments, for instance, require consular invoices, certificates of inspection, health certification, and various other documents. For referrals on foreign import regulations related to hazardous substances, contact the United Nations Environmental Programs Office, Tel: (202) 260-5917. For sources of information about foreign government import regulations, *refer to* Chapter 12, "Documentation, Shipping, and Logistics," beginning on page 80.

Customs Benefits for Exporters

Drawback of Customs Duties

Drawback is a form of tax relief in which a lawfully collected customs duty is refunded or remitted wholly or in part because of the particular use made of the commodity on which the duty was collected. U.S. firms that import materials or components that they process or assemble for reexport may obtain drawback refunds of all duties paid on the imported merchandise, less 1 percent to cover customs costs. This practice encourages U.S. exporters by permitting them to compete in foreign markets without the handicap of including in their sales prices the duties paid on imported components. The manufacturer must know, prior to making contractual commitments, that he will be entitled to drawback on his exports. The drawback procedure has been designed to give the manufacturer this assurance and protection.

Several types of drawback are authorized under section 1313, Title 19, United States Code. The Trade and Tariff Act of 1984 revised and expanded drawbacks. Regulations implementing the act have been promulgated in 19 CFR Part 191. Under existing regulations several types of drawback have been authorized, but only two are of interest to most manufacturers:

1. If articles are exported or destroyed, which were manufactured in the United States with the use of imported merchandise, then the duties paid on the imported merchandise used may be refunded as drawback, less one percent, which is retained by Customs to defray costs. (This is Section 1313(a) drawback.)
2. If both imported merchandise and any other merchandise of the same kind and quality are used to manufacture articles, some of which are exported or destroyed before use, then drawback not exceeding 99 percent of the duty which was paid on the imported merchandise is payable on the exports. It is immaterial whether the actual imported merchandise or the domestic merchandise of the same kind and quality was used in the exported articles. This provision makes it possible for firms to obtain drawback without the expense of maintain separate inventories for imported and domestic merchandise. (This is Section 13131(b) drawback—the substitution provision.)

To obtain drawback, the U.S. firm must file a proposal with a regional commissioner of customs (for section 1313(a) drawback) or with the Entry and Carrier Rulings Branch, U.S. Customs Headquarters, at the address at the end of this section (for other types of drawback, including combination 1313 (a) and (b) drawback). There are currently several general drawback contracts available which eliminate the need for submission of a proposal. These have been published in the Customs Bulletin with instructions as to the procedure for adhering to them. A sample drawback proposal to serve as a model may be obtained from regional commissioners for section 1313(a) drawback. For other types of drawback, including combination 1313(a) and (b), contact the Entry and Carrier Rulings Branch of the Customs Service.

The approval of a section 1313(a) proposal takes the form of a letter from a Regional Commissioner of Customs to the applicant. The approval of a section 1313(b) drawback proposal takes the form of a letter from Headquarters, U.S. Customs Service to the Regional Commissioner of Customs where the applicant will file claims. The applicant receives a copy of this letter. Synopses of all contracts are published in the "Customs Bulletin and Decisions." The proposal and approval together are called a drawback contract or drawback rate. If the manufacturer wants to have his rate changed in any way, he should file a new proposal and the procedure is the same as above.

Claims must be filed within three years after exportation of the articles. To prevent tolling by the statute of limitations, a claim may be filed before drawback rate is effective, although no payments will be made until the contract is approved.

Drawback claimants must establish that the articles on which drawback is being claimed were exported within five years after the merchandise in question was imported. Once the request for drawback is approved, the proposal and approval together constitute the manufacturer's drawback rate.

When a claim has been completed by the filing of all required documents, the entry will be liquidated by the Regional Commissioner of Customs to determine the amount of drawback due. Drawback is payable to the exporter unless the manufacturer reserves to himself the right to claim the drawback.

Entry and Carrier Rulings Branch
U.S. Customs Service Headquarters
1301 Constitution Avenue NW
Washington, DC 20229
Tel: (202) 927-2320
Web site: www.customs.ustreas.gov

Effect of NAFTA

The NAFTA provisions on drawback apply to goods imported into the United States and subsequently exported to Canada on or after January 1, 1996. The NAFTA provisions on drawback will apply to goods imported into the United States and subsequently exported to Mexico, on or after January 1, 2001.

Under the NAFTA, the amount of Customs duties that will be refunded, reduced or waived is the lesser of the total amount of Customs duties paid or owed on the goods or materials when imported into the United States and the total amount of Customs duties paid or owed on the finished good in the NAFTA country to which it is exported, for purposes of sections 1313(a), (b), (f), (h), and (g).

No NAFTA country, on condition of export, will refund, reduce or waive the following: antidumping or countervailing duties, premiums offered or collected pursuant to any tendering system with respect to the administration of quantitative import restrictions, tariff rate quotas or trade preference levels, or a fee pursuant to section 22 of the U.S. Agricultural Adjustment Act. Moreover, same condition substitution drawback was eliminated as of January 1, 1994.

U.S. Foreign-Trade Zones

Exporters should also consider the customs privileges of U.S. foreign-trade zones. These zones are domestic U.S. sites that are considered outside U.S. customs territory and are available for activities that might otherwise be carried on overseas for customs reasons. For export operations, the zones provide accelerated export status for purposes of excise tax rebates and customs drawback. For import and reexport activities, no customs duties, federal excise taxes, or state or local ad valorem taxes are charged on foreign goods moved into zones unless and until the goods, or products made from them, are moved into customs territory. This means that the use of zones can be profitable for operations involving foreign dutiable materials and components being assembled or produced here for reexport. Also, no quota restrictions ordinarily apply.

There are now more than 200 approved foreign-trade zones in port communities in 48 states. Associated with these projects are some 200 subzones. These facilities are available for operations involving storage, repacking, inspection, exhibition, assembly, manufacturing, and other processing.

Several thousand business firms use foreign-trade zones every year. The value of merchandise moved to and from the zones in 1995 exceeded $110 billion. Export shipments are a small but quickly growing sector of the trade handled by U.S. FTZs and subzones; in 1995 the value of export shipments was more than $17 billion.

Information about the zones is available from the zone manager, from local Commerce district offices, or from the Executive Secretary, Foreign-Trade Zones Board, International Trade Administration, U.S. Department of Commerce, Washington, DC 20230; Tel: (202) 482-2862; Fax: (202) 482-0002.

Foreign Free Trade Zones and Bonded Warehouses

To encourage and facilitate international trade, there are free ports, free trade zones, and similar customs-privileged facilities are now in operation in some foreign countries worldwide, usually in or near seaports or airports. Many U.S. manufacturers and their distributors use free ports or free trade zones for receiving shipments of goods that are reshipped in smaller lots to customers throughout the surrounding areas.

Bonded warehouses can also be found in many locations. Here, goods can be warehoused without duties being assessed. Once goods are released, they are subject to duties.

Foreign Sales Corporations

One of the most important steps a U.S. exporter can take to reduce federal income tax on export-related income is to set up a foreign sales corporation (FSC). This tax incentive for U.S. exporters replaced the domestic international sales corporation (DISC), except the interest charge DISC. While the interest charge DISC allows exporters to defer paying taxes on export sales, the tax incentive provided by the FSC legislation is in the form of a permanent exemption from federal income tax for a portion of the export income attributable to the offshore activities of FSCs (26 USC, sections 921-927). The tax exemption can be as great as 15 percent on gross income from exporting, and the expenses can be kept low through the use of intermediaries who are familiar with and able to carry out the formal requirements. A firm that is exporting or thinking of exporting can optimize available tax benefits with proper planning, evaluation, and assistance from an accountant or lawyer.

An FSC is a corporation set up in certain foreign countries or in U.S. possessions (other than Puerto Rico) to obtain a corporate tax exemption on a portion of its earnings generated by the sale or lease of export property and the performance of some services. A corporation initially qualifies as an FSC by meeting certain basic formation tests. An FSC (unless it is a small FSC) must also meet several foreign management tests throughout the year. If it complies with those requirements, the FSC is entitled to an exemption on qualified export transactions in which it performs the required foreign economic processes.

FSCs can be formed by manufacturers, nonmanufacturers, or groups of exporters, such as export trading companies. An FSC can function as a principal, buying and selling for its own account, or as a commission agent. It can be related to a manufacturing parent or it can be an independent merchant or broker.

An FSC must be incorporated and have its main office (a shared office is acceptable) in the U.S. Virgin Islands, American Samoa, Guam, the Northern Mariana Islands, or a qualified foreign country. In general, a firm must file for incorporation by following the normal procedures of the host nation or U.S. possession. Taxes paid by an FSC to a foreign country do not qualify for the foreign U.S. tax credit. Some nations, however, offer tax incentives to attract FSCs; to qualify, a company must identify itself as an FSC to the host government. Consult the government tax authorities in the country or U.S. possession of interest for specific information.

A country qualifies as an FSC host if it has an exchange of information agreement with the United States approved by the U.S. Department of the Treasury. Since the Internal Revenue Service (IRS) does not allow foreign tax credits for foreign taxes imposed on the FSC's qualified income, it is generally advantageous to locate an FSC only in a country where local income taxes and withholding taxes are minimized. The vast majority of FSCs are incorporated in the U.S. Virgin Islands or Guam.

The FSC must have at least one director who is not a U.S. resident, must keep one set of its books of account (including copies or summaries of invoices) at its main offshore office, cannot have more than 25 shareholders, cannot have any preferred stock, and must file an election to become an FSC with the IRS. Also, a group may not own both an FSC and an interest charge DISC.

The portion of the FSC gross income from exporting that is exempt from U.S. corporate taxation is 32 percent for a corporate-held FSC if it buys from independent suppliers or contracts with related suppliers at an "arm's-length" price—a price equivalent to that which would have been paid by an unrelated purchaser to an unrelated seller. An FSC supplied by a related entity can also use the special administrative pricing rules to compute its tax exemption. Although an FSC does not have to use the two special administrative pricing rules, these rules may provide additional tax savings for certain FSCs.

Small FSCs and interest charge DISCs are designed to give export incentives to smaller businesses. The tax benefits of a small FSC or an interest charge DISC are limited by ceilings on the amount of gross income that is eligible for the benefits.

The small FSC is generally the same as an FSC, except that a small FSC must file an election with the IRS designating itself as a small FSC—which means it does not have to meet foreign management or foreign economic process requirements. A small FSC tax exemption is limited to the income generated by $5 million or less in gross export revenues.

An exporter can still set up a DISC in the form of an interest charge DISC to defer the imposition of taxes for up to $10 million in export sales. A corporate shareholder of an interest charge DISC may defer the imposition of taxes on approximately 94 percent of its income up to the $10 million ceiling if the income is reinvested by the DISC in qualified export assets. An individual who is the sole shareholder of an interest charge DISC can defer 100 percent of the DISC income up to the $10 million ceiling. An interest charge DISC must meet the following requirements: the taxpayer must make a new election; the tax year of the new DISC must match the tax year of its majority stockholder; and the DISC shareholders must pay interest annually at U.S. Treasury bill rates on their proportionate share of the accumulated taxes deferred.

A shared FSC is an FSC that is shared by 25 or fewer unrelated exporter-shareholders to reduce the costs while obtaining the full tax benefit of an FSC. Each exporter-shareholder owns a separate class of stock and each runs its own business as usual. Typically, exporters pay a commission on export sales to the FSC, which distributes the commission back to the exporter.

States, regional authorities, trade associations, or private businesses can sponsor a shared FSC for their state's companies, their association's members, or their business clients or customers, or for U.S. companies in general. A shared FSC is a means of sharing the cost of the FSC. However, the benefits and proprietary information are not shared. The sponsor and the other exporter-shareholders do not participate in the exporter's profits, do not participate in the exporter's tax benefits, and are not a risk for another exporter's debts.

For more information about FSCs, U.S. companies may contact

Office of Service Industries
U.S. Department of Commerce
Tel: (202) 482-3575; Fax: (202) 482-2669
Web site: www.ita.doc.gov/sif/

The Uruguay Round Trade Agreements

The Uruguay Round Trade Agreements, completed in 1994 under General Agreement on Tariff and Trade (GATT) auspices, produced significant tariff reductions and resulted in some important advances in multilateral trade relations.

The World Trade Organization (WTO) was established in January 1995 as the legal and institutional foundation of the multilateral trading system. The WTO is the embodiment of the results of the Uruguay Round trade negotiations and the successor to the General Agreement on Tariffs and Trade (GATT). WTO members must grant the products of other members no less favorable treatment than that accorded to the products of any other country.

While quotas are generally outlawed, tariffs or customs duties are legal in the WTO. However, significant reductions were made by over 120 countries in the Uruguay Round. These reductions are being phased in over five years and will result in a 40 percent cut in industrial countries' tariffs in industrial products from an average of 6.3 percent to 3.8 percent. The Round also increased the percentage of bound product lines to nearly 100 percent for developed nations and countries in transition and to 73 percent for developing countries. Members have also undertaken an initial set of commitments covering national regulations affecting various services activities. These commitments are, like those for tariffs, contained in binding national schedules.

The WTO extends and clarifies previous GATT rules that laid down the basis on which governments could impose compensating duties on two forms of "unfair" competition: dumping and subsidies. The WTO Agreement on agriculture is designed to provide increased fairness in farm trade. That on intellectual property will improve conditions of competition where ideas and inventions are involved, and another will do the same thing for trade in services.

Some of the benefits of to United States exporters include:

- The total elimination of foreign tariffs imposed on U.S. goods by some major markets for pharmaceuticals; medical, construction, and agricultural equipment; steel; beer; distilled spirits; furniture; paper, pulp, and printed matter; and toys.
- Deep cuts, averaging one-third, in many other foreign tariffs affecting U.S. exports.
- A reduction in paperwork costs due to the simplification and harmonization of customs procedures and licensing.
- Better access to some growing markets such as South Korea, Malaysia, Thailand, Argentina, Brazil, and others.
- Stronger intellectual property protection for U.S. patents, copyrights, trademarks, industrial designs and trade secrets.
- Improved enforcement of GATT rules.
- Strong antidumping and countervailing duty rules.
- More open markets for U.S. service exporters in fields such as accounting, advertising, commuter services, tourism, engineering, and construction.
- Expanded opportunities to compete for foreign government procurement contracts.
- Reduced standards barriers to U.S. exports

For more information on the WTO and GATT, contact

World Trade Organization
154 rue de Lausanne
CH-1211 Geneva 21, Switzerland
Tel: [41] (22) 739-5111; Fax: [41] (22) 739-5458
Web site: www.wto.org.

Office of Multilateral Affairs
U.S. Department of Commerce/ITA
Washington, DC 20230
Tel: (202) 482-0603

There are also a number of documents available on the fax retrieval system operated by the Trade Information Center. Call (800) USA-TRADE and ask for a directory of available documents on the Uruguay Round and WTO.

Intellectual Property Rights Considerations

The United States provides a wide range of protection for intellectual property (i.e., patents, trademarks, service marks, copyrights, trade secrets, and semiconductor mask works). Many businesses—particularly high-technology firms, the publishing industry, chemical and pharmaceutical firms, the recording industry, and computer software companies—depend heavily on the protection afforded their creative products and processes.

In the United States, there are five major forms of intellectual property protection. A U.S. patent confers on its owner the exclusive right for 17 years (14 years for design patents) from the date the patent is granted to manufacture, use, and sell the patented product or process within the United States. The United States and the Philippines are the only two countries that award patents on a first-to-invent basis; all other countries award patents to the first to file a patent application. As of November 16, 1989, a trademark or service mark registered with the U.S. Patent and Trademark Office remains in force for 10 years from the date of registration and may be renewed for successive periods of 10 years, provided the mark continues to be used in interstate commerce and has not been previously canceled or surrendered.

A work created (fixed in tangible form for the first time) in the United States on or after January 1, 1978, is automatically protected by a U.S. copyright from the moment of its creation. Such a copyright, as a general rule, has a term that endures for the author's life plus an additional 50 years after the author's death. In the case of works made for hire and for anonymous and pseudonymous works (unless the author's identity is revealed in records of the U.S. Copyright Office of the Library of Congress), the duration of the copyright is 75 years from publication or 100 years from creation, whichever is shorter. Other, more detailed provisions of the Copyright Act of 1976 govern the term of works created before January 1, 1978.

Trade secrets are protected by state unfair competition and contract law. Unlike a U.S. patent, a trade secret does not entitle its owner to a government-sanctioned monopoly of the discovered technology for a particular length of time. Nevertheless, trade secrets can be a valuable and marketable form of technology. Trade secrets are typically protected by confidentiality agreements between a firm and its employees and by trade secret licensing agreement provisions that prohibit disclosures of the trade secret by the licensee or its employees.

Semiconductor mask work registrations protect the mask works embodied in semiconductor chip products. In many other countries, mask works are referred to as integrated circuit layout designs. The Semiconductor Chip Protection Act of 1984 provides the owner of a mask work with the exclusive right to reproduce, import, and distribute such mask works for a period of 10 years from the earlier of two dates: the date on which the mask work is registered with the U.S. Copyright Office or the date on which the mask work is first commercially exploited anywhere in the world.

Intellectual Property Rights Protections Outside the U.S.

The rights granted under U.S. patent, trademark, or copyright law can be enforced only in the United States, its territories, and its possessions; they confer no protection in a foreign country. The protection available in each country depends on that country's national laws, administrative practices, and treaty obligations. The relevant international treaties set certain minimum standards for protection, but individual country laws and practices can and do differ significantly.

To secure patent and trademark right outside the United States a company must apply for a patent or register a trademark on a country-by-country basis. The laws of many countries differ in various respects from the patent law of the United States. In most foreign countries, publication of the invention before the date of the application will bar the right to a patent. In most foreign countries maintenance fees are required. Most foreign countries require that the patented invention must be manufactured in that country after a certain period, usually three years. If there is no manufacture within this period, the patent may be void in some countries, although in most countries the patent may be subject to the grant of compulsory licenses to any person who may apply for a license.

The Paris Convention for the Protection of Industrial Property, relating to patents, is adhered to by 100 countries, including the United States. It provides that each country guarantees to the citizens of the other countries the same rights in patent and trademark matters that it gives to its own citizens. The treaty also provides for the right of priority in the case of patents, trademarks and industrial designs (design patents). This right means that, on the basis of a regular first application filed in one of the member countries, the applicant may, within a certain period of time, apply for protection in all the other member countries. These later applications will then be regarded as if they had been filed on the same day as the first application. Thus, these later applicants will have priority over applications for the same invention which may have been filed during the same period of time by other persons. Moreover, these later applications, being based on the first application, will not be invalidated by any acts accomplished in the interval, such as, for example, publication or exploitation of the invention, the sale of copies of the design, or use of the trademark. The period of time mentioned above, within which the subsequent applications may be filed in the other countries, is 12 months in the case of first applications for patent and six months in the case of industrial designs and trademarks.

Another treaty, known as the Patent Cooperation Treaty, was negotiated at a diplomatic conference in Washington, D.C., in June of 1970. The treaty came into force on January 24, 1978, and is presently adhered to by 44 countries, including the United States. The treaty facilitates the filing of applications for patent on the same invention in member countries by providing, among other things, for centralized filing procedures and a standardized application format.

The timely filing of an international application affords applicants an international filing date in each country which is designated in the international application and provides both a search of the invention and a later time period within which the national applications for patent must be filed.

A number of patent attorneys specialize in obtaining patents in foreign countries. In general, an inventor should be satisfied that he could make some profit from foreign patents or that there is some particular reason for obtaining them, before he attempts to apply for foreign patents.

Under United States law it is necessary, in the case of inventions made in the United States, to obtain a license from the Commissioner of Patents and Trademarks before applying for a patent in a foreign country. Such a license is required if the foreign application is to be filed before an application is filed in the United States or before the expiration of six months from the filing of an application in the United States. The filing of an application for patent constitutes the request for a license and the granting or denial of such request is indicated in the filing receipt mailed to each applicant. After six months from the United States filing, a license is not required unless the invention has been ordered to be kept secret. If the invention has been ordered to be kept secret, the consent to the filing abroad must be obtained from the Commissioner of Patents and Trademarks during the period the order of secrecy is in effect.

The level and scope of copyright protection available within a country also depends on that country's domestic laws and treaty obligations. In most countries, the place of first publication is an important criterion for determining whether foreign works are eligible for copyright protection. Works first published in the United States on or after March 1, 1989—the date on which U.S. adherence to the Berne Convention for the Protection of Literary and Artistic Works became effective—are, with few exceptions, automatically protected in the more than 110 countries that comprise the Berne Union. Exporters of goods embodying works protected by copyright in the United States should find out how individual Berne Union countries deal with older U.S. works, including those first published (but not first or simultaneously published in a Berne Union country) before March 1, 1989.

The United States maintains copyright relations with a number of countries under a second international agreement called the Universal Copyright Convention (UCC). UCC countries that do not also adhere to Berne often require compliance with certain formalities to maintain copyright protection. Those formalities can be either or both of the following: (1) registration and (2) the requirement that published copies of a work bear copyright notice, the name of the author, and the date of first publication. The United States has bilateral copyright agreements with more than 40 countries, and the laws of these countries may or may not be consistent with either of the copyright conventions. Before first publication of a work anywhere, it is advisable to investigate the scope of and requirements for maintaining copyright protection for those countries in which copyright protection is desired.

Intellectual property rights owners should be aware that after valuable intellectual property rights have been secured in foreign markets, enforcement must be accomplished through local law. As a general matter, intellectual property rights are private rights to be enforced by the rights owner. Ease of enforcement varies from country to country and depends on such factors as the attitude of local officials, substantive requirements of the law, and court procedures. U.S. law affords a civil remedy for infringement (with money damages to a successful plaintiff) and criminal penalties (including fines and jail terms) for more serious offenses. The availability of criminal penalties for infringement, either as the exclusive remedy or in addition to private suits, also varies among countries.

A number of countries are parties to only some, or even none, of the treaties that have been discussed here. Therefore, would-be U.S. exporters should carefully evaluate the intellectual property laws of their potential foreign markets, as well as applicable multilateral and bilateral treaties and agreements (including bilateral trade agreements), *before* making a decision to do business there. The intellectual property considerations that arise can be quite complex and, if possible, should be explored in detail with an attorney.

In summary, U.S. exporters with intellectual property concerns should consider taking the following steps:

1. Obtaining protection under all applicable U.S. laws for their inventions, trademarks, service marks, copyrights, and semiconductor mask works.
2. Researching the intellectual property laws of countries where they may conduct business. The US&FCS has information about intellectual property laws and practices of particular countries, although it does not provide legal advice.
3. Securing the services of competent local counsel to file appropriate patent, trademark, or copyright applications within priority periods.
4. Adequately protecting their trade secrets through appropriate confidentiality provisions in employment, licensing, marketing, distribution, and joint venture agreements.

For more information on intellectual property rights issues, contact

U.S. Patent and Trademark Office
U.S. Department of Commerce
101 Independence Ave. SE
Washington, DC 20231
Tel: (703) 308-4357; Fax: (703) 308-5258
Web site: www.uspto.gov

U.S. Copyright Office
LM 455, Library of Congress
Washington, D.C. 20559
Tel: (202) 707-3000
Web site: www.loc.gov/copyright

Uruguay Round TRIPs Agreement

The Uruguay Round Agreement on Trade Related Aspects of Intellectual Property Rights (also known as the TRIPs Agreement) recognizes that widely varying standards in the protection and enforcement of intellectual property rights and the lack of a multilateral framework of principles, rules and disciplines dealing with international trade in counterfeit goods have been a growing source of tension in international economic relations. To that end, the agreement addresses the applicability of basic GATT principles and those of relevant international intellectual property agreements; the provision of adequate intellectual property rights; the provision of effective enforcement measures for those rights; multilateral dispute settlement; and transitional arrangements.

The implementation periods varies. Developed countries, such as the United States, were given only one year to bring their legislation and practices into conformity. Developing and least-developed countries have been assigned transition periods ranging from 5 to 11 years. On December 8, 1994, President Clinton signed the Uruguay Round Agreements Act (URAA). The URAA implements the Uruguay Round GATT, which includes an agreement on TRIPs.

Some of the notable intellectual and industrial rights protections offered by the TRIPs agreement cover the following:

- **National-treatment commitment.** The nationals of other parties must be given treatment no less favorable than that accorded to a party's own nationals with regard to the protection of intellectual property. In addition, any advantage a party gives to the nationals of another country must be extended immediately and unconditionally to the nationals of all other parties.
- **Patents.** There is a general obligation to comply with the main provisions of the Paris Convention. In addition, the agreement requires that 20-year patent protection be available for all inventions, whether of products or processes, in almost all fields of technology. Detailed conditions are laid down for compulsory licensing or governmental use of patents without the authorization of the patent owner.
- **Copyrights.** Parties must comply with most major provisions of the Paris version of the Berne Convention. Important additions to existing international rules in the area of copyright and related rights are the provisions on rental rights; authors of computer programs and producers of sound recordings are given the right to authorize or prohibit the commercial rental of their works to the public. A similar exclusive right applies to films where commercial rental has led to widespread copying. The draft also requires performers to be given protection from unauthorized recording and broadcast of live performances, commonly known as bootlegging.
- **Trademarks and service marks.** The agreement defines what types of signs must be eligible for protection as a trademark or service mark and what the minimum rights conferred on their owners must be. Marks that have become well-known in a particular country enjoy additional protection. In addition, the agreement lays down a number of obligations with regard to the use of trademarks and service marks, their term of protection, and their licensing or assignment.
- **Industrial designs.** These are protected under the

agreement for a period of 10 years. Owners of protected designs would be able to prevent the manufacture, sale or importation of articles with a design which is a copy of the protected design.

- **Layout designs of integrated circuits.** The agreement requires parties to provide protection on the basis of the Washington Treaty on Intellectual Property in Respect of Integrated Circuits, but with a number of additions: protection must be available for a minimum period of 10 years; the rights must extend to articles incorporating infringing layout designs; innocent infringers must be allowed to use or sell stock in hand or ordered before learning of the infringement against a suitable royalty: and compulsory licensing and government use is only allowed under a number of strict conditions.

Arbitration of Disputes in International Transactions

The parties to a commercial transaction may provide in their contract that any disputes over interpretation or performance of the agreement will be resolved through arbitration. In the domestic context, arbitration may be appealing for a variety of reasons. Frequently cited advantages over conventional courtroom litigation include potential savings in time and expense, confidentiality of the proceedings, and expertise of the arbitrators.

For export transactions, in which the parties to the agreement are from different countries, additional important advantages are neutrality (international arbitration allows each party to avoid the domestic courts of the other should a dispute arise) and ease of enforcement (foreign arbitral awards can be easier to enforce than foreign court decisions).

In an agreement to arbitrate (usually just inserted as a term in the contract governing the transaction as a whole), the parties also have broad power to agree on many significant aspects of the arbitration. The arbitration clause may do the following:

- Specify the location (a "neutral site") where the arbitration will be conducted, although care must be taken to select a country that has adopted the UN Convention on the Recognition and Enforcement of Foreign Awards (or another convention providing for the enforcement of arbitral awards).
- Establish the rules that will govern the arbitration, usually by incorporating a set of existing arbitration rules such as the UN Commission on International Trade Law (UNCITRAL) Model Rules.
- Appoint an arbitration institute to administer the arbitration. The International Chamber of Commerce based in Paris, the American Arbitration Association in New York, and the Arbitration Institute of the Stockholm Chamber of Commerce in Sweden are three such prominent institutions.
- Choose the law that will govern procedural issues or the merits of the dispute, for example, the law of the State of New York.
- Place certain limitations on the selection of arbitrators, for example, by agreeing to exclude nationals of the parties to the dispute or by requiring certain qualifications or expertise.
- Designate the language in which the arbitral proceedings will be conducted.

For international arbitration to work effectively, the national courts in the countries of both parties to the dispute must recognize and support arbitration as a legitimate alternative means for resolving disputes. This support is particularly crucial at two stages in the arbitration process. First, should one party attempt to avoid arbitration after a dispute has arisen, the other party must be able to rely on the judicial system in either country to enforce the agreement to arbitrate by compelling arbitration. Second, the party that wins in the arbitration proceeding must be confident that the national courts will enforce the decision of the arbitrators. This will ensure that the arbitration process is not ultimately frustrated at the enforcement stage if the losing party refuses to pay or otherwise satisfy the arbitral award.

The strong policy of U.S. federal law is to approve and support resolution of disputes by arbitration. Through the UN Convention on the Recognition and Enforcement of Foreign Arbitral Awards (popularly known as the New York Convention), which the United States ratified in 1970, more than 80 countries have undertaken international legal obligations to recognize and enforce arbitral awards. While several other arbitration treaties have been concluded, the New York Convention is by far the most important international agreement on commercial arbitration and may be credited for much of the explosive growth of arbitration of international disputes in recent decades.

Providing for arbitration of disputes makes good sense in many international commercial transactions. Because of the complexity of the subject, however, legal advice should be obtained for specific export transactions. For more information on arbitration, contact

American Arbitration Association
1633 Broadway
New York, NY 10019
Tel: (212) 484-4000; Fax: (212) 307-4387
Web site: www.adr.org

The United Nations Sales Convention

The UN Convention on Contracts for the International Sale of Goods (CISG) became the law of the United States on January 1, 1988. It establishes uniform legal rules to govern the formation of international sales contracts and the rights and obligations of the buyer and seller. The CISG is expected to facilitate and stimulate international trade.

The CISG applies automatically to all contracts for the sale of goods between traders from two different countries that have both ratified the CISG. This automatic application takes place unless the parties to the contract expressly exclude all or part of the CISG or expressly stipulate to law other than the CISG. Parties can also expressly choose to apply the CISG when it would not automatically apply.

As of 1996, the following countries and territories applied the CISG: Argentina, Australia, Austria, Bosnia-Herzegovina, Bulgaria, Belarus, Canada, Chile, China, Cuba, the Czech Republic, Denmark, Ecuador, Egypt, Estonia, Finland, France, Georgia, Germany, Ghana, Guinea, Hungary, Iraq, Italy, Lithuania, Lesotho, Mexico, Moldova, the Netherlands, New Zealand, Norway, Poland, Romania, Russia, Singapore, the Slovak Republic, Slovenia, Spain, Sweden, Switzerland, Syria, Uganda, Ukraine, United States, Venezuela, Yugoslavia (Serbia-Montenegro), and Zambia.

The United States made a reservation, the effect of which is that the CISG will apply only when the other party to the transaction also has its place of business in a country that applies the CISG.

Convention Provisions

The provisions and scope of the CISG are similar to Article 2 of the Uniform Commercial Code (effective in the United States except Louisiana). The CISG comprises four parts:

- Part I, Sphere of Application and General Provisions (Articles 1-13), provides that the CISG covers the international sale of most commercial goods.
- Part II, Formation of the Contract (Articles 14-24), provides rules on offer and acceptance.
- Part III, Sale of Goods (Articles 25-88), covers obligations and remedies of the seller and buyer and rules governing the passing of risk and damages.
- Part IV, Final Provisions (Articles 89-101), covers the right of a country to disclaim certain parts of the convention.

Applying (or Excluding) the CISG

U.S. businesses can avoid the difficulties of reaching agreement with foreign parties on choice-of-law issues because the CISG text is available as a compromise. Using the CISG may decrease the time and legal costs otherwise involved in research of different unfamiliar foreign laws. Further, the CISG may reduce the problems of proof and foreign law in domestic and foreign courts.

Application of the CISG may especially make sense for smaller firms and for American firms contracting with companies in countries where the legal systems are obscure, unfamiliar, or not suited for international sales transactions of goods. However, some larger, more experienced firms may want to continue their current practices, at least with regard to parties with whom they have been doing business regularly.

When a firm chooses to exclude the CISG, it is not sufficient to simply say "the laws of New York apply," because the CISG would be the law of the State of New York under certain circumstances. Rather, one would say "the provisions of the Uniform Commercial Code as adopted by the State of New York, and not the UN Convention on Contracts for the International Sale of Goods, apply."

After it is determined whether or not the CISG governs a particular transaction, the related documentation should be reviewed to ensure consistency with the CISG or other governing law. For agreements about to expire, companies should make sure renewals take into account the applicability (or nonapplicability) of the CISG.

The CISG can be found in the Federal Register (March 2, 1987; Vol. 52, No. 40, p. 6262) along with a notice by the U.S. Department of State, and in the pocket part to 15 USCA app. at 29. To obtain an up to date listing of ratifying or acceding countries and their reservations call the UN Treaty Section at Tel: (212) 963-5047; Fax: (212) 963-3693, or visit the UN's Web site (www.un.org). For further information contact the Office of the Assistant Legal Adviser for Private International Law, U.S. Department of State (Tel: (202) 776-8420; Fax: (202) 776-8482), or the Office of the Chief Counsel for International Commerce, U.S. Department of Commerce (Tel: (202) 482-0937; Fax: (202) 482-4076).

Chapter 12

Documentation, Shipping, and Logistics

When preparing to ship a product overseas, the exporter needs to be aware of packing, labeling, documentation, and insurance requirements. Because the goods are being shipped by unknown carriers to distant customers, the new exporter must be sure to follow all shipping requirements to help ensure that the merchandise is

- Packed correctly so that it arrives in good condition;
- Labeled correctly to ensure that the goods are handled properly and arrive on time and at the right place;
- Documented correctly to meet U.S. and foreign government requirements as well as proper collection standards; and
- Insured against damage, loss, and pilferage and, in some cases, delay.

Because of the variety of considerations involved in the physical export process, most exporters, both new and experienced, rely on an international freight forwarder to perform these services.

Freight Forwarders

The international freight forwarder acts as an agent for the exporter in moving cargo to the overseas destination. These agents are familiar with the import rules and regulations of foreign countries, methods of shipping, U.S. government export regulations, and the documents connected with foreign trade.

Freight forwarders can assist with an order from the start by advising the exporter of the freight costs, port charges, consular fees, cost of special documentation, and insurance costs as well as their handling fees—all of which help in preparing price quotations. Freight forwarders may also recommend the type of packing for best protecting the merchandise in transit; they can arrange to have the merchandise packed at the port or containerized. The cost for their services is a legitimate export cost that should be figured into the price charged to the customer.

When the order is ready to ship, freight forwarders should be able to review the letter of credit, commercial invoices, packing list, and so on to ensure that everything is in order. They can also reserve the necessary space on board an ocean vessel, if the exporter desires.

If the cargo arrives at the port of export and the exporter has not already done so, freight forwarders may make the necessary arrangements with customs brokers to ensure that the goods comply with customs export documentation regulations. In addition, they may have the goods delivered to the carrier in time for loading. They may also prepare the bill of lading and any special required documentation. After shipment, they forward all documents directly to the customer or to the paying bank if desired.

Packing

In packing an item for export, the shipper should be aware of the demands that exporting puts on a package. Four problems must be kept in mind when an export shipping crate is being designed: breakage, weight, moisture, and pilferage.

Most general cargo is carried in containers, but some is still shipped as breakbulk cargo. Besides the normal handling encountered in domestic transportation, a breakbulk shipment moving by ocean freight may be loaded aboard vessels in a net or by a sling, conveyor, chute, or other method, putting added strain on the package. In the ship's hold, goods may be stacked on top of one another or come into violent contact with other goods during the voyage. Overseas, handling facilities may be less sophisticated than in the United States and the cargo may be dragged, pushed, rolled, or dropped during unloading, while moving through customs, or in transit to the final destination.

Moisture is a constant problem because cargo is subject to condensation even in the hold of a ship equipped with air conditioning and a dehumidifier. The cargo may also be unloaded in the rain, and some foreign ports do not have covered storage facilities. In addition, unless the cargo is adequately protected, theft and pilferage are constant threats.

Since proper packing is essential in exporting, often the buyer specifies packing requirements. If the buyer does not so specify, be sure the goods are prepared with the following considerations in mind.

- Pack in strong containers, adequately sealed and filled when possible.
- To provide proper bracing in the container, regardless of size, make sure the weight is evenly distributed.
- Goods should be packed in oceangoing containers, if possible, or on pallets to ensure greater ease in handling.
- Packages and packing filler should be made of moisture-resistant material.
- To avoid pilferage, avoid mentioning contents or brand names on packages. In addition, strapping, seals, and shrink wrapping are effective means of deterring theft.

One popular method of shipment is the use of containers obtained from carriers or private leasing concerns. These containers vary in size, material, and construction and can accommodate most cargo, but they are best suited for standard package sizes and shapes. Some containers are no more than semi-truck trailers lifted off their wheels and placed on a vessel at the port of export. They are then transferred to another set of wheels at the port of import for movement to an inland destination. Refrigerated and liquid bulk containers are readily available.

Normally, air shipments require less heavy packing than ocean shipments, but they must still be adequately protected, especially if highly pilferable items are packed in domestic containers. In many instances, standard domestic packing is acceptable, especially if the product is durable and there is no concern for display packaging. In other instances, high-test (at least 250 pounds per square inch) cardboard or tri-wall construction boxes are more than adequate.

For both ocean and air shipments, freight forwarders and carriers can advise on the best packaging. Marine insurance companies are also available for consultation. It is recommended that a professional firm be hired to package for export if the exporter is not equipped for the task. This service is usually provided at a moderate cost.

Finally, because transportation costs are determined by volume and weight, special reinforced and lightweight packing materials have been devised for exporting. Care in packing goods to minimize volume and weight while giving strength may well save money while ensuring that goods are properly packed.

Labeling

Specific marking and labeling is used on export shipping cartons and containers to

- Meet shipping regulations,
- Ensure proper handling,
- Conceal the identity of the contents, and
- Help receivers identify shipments.

The overseas buyer usually specifies export marks that should appear on the cargo for easy identification by receivers. Many markings may be needed for shipment. Exporters need to put the following markings on cartons to be shipped:

- Shipper's mark
- Country of origin (USA)
- Weight marking (in pounds and in kilograms)
- Number of packages and size of cases (in inches and centimeters)
- Handling marks (international pictorial symbols)
- Cautionary markings, such as "This Side Up" or "Use No Hooks" (in English and in the language of the country of destination)
- Port of entry
- Labels for hazardous materials (universal symbols adapted by the International Maritime Organization)

Legibility is extremely important to prevent misunderstandings and delays in shipping. Letters are generally stenciled onto packages and containers in waterproof ink. Markings should appear on three faces of the container, preferably on the top and on the two ends or the two sides. Old markings must be completely removed.

In addition to port marks, customer identification code, and indication of origin, the marks should include the package number, gross and net weights, and dimensions. If more than one package is being shipped, the total number of packages in the shipment should be included in the markings. The exporter should also include any special handling instructions on the package. It is a good idea to repeat these instructions in the language of the country of destination. Standard international shipping and handling symbols should also be used.

Exporters may find that customs regulations regarding freight labeling are strictly enforced; for example, most countries require that the country of origin be clearly labeled on each imported package. Most freight forwarders and export packing specialists can supply necessary information regarding specific regulations.

Documentation

Exporters should seriously consider having the freight forwarder handle the formidable amount of documentation that exporting requires; freight forwarders are specialists in this process. The following documents are commonly used in exporting; which of them are actually used in each case depends on the requirements of both the U.S. government and the government of the importing country.

- ***Commercial invoice.*** As in a domestic transaction, the commercial invoice is a bill for the goods from the buyer to the seller. A commercial invoice should include basic information about the transaction, including a description of the goods, the address of the shipper and seller, and the delivery and payment terms. The buyer needs the invoice to prove ownership and to arrange payment. Some governments use the commercial invoice to assess customs duties.
- ***Bill of lading.*** Bills of lading are contracts between the owner of the goods and the carrier (as with domestic shipments). There are two types. A *straight bill of lading* is nonnegotiable. A *negotiable* or *shipper's order bill of lading* can be bought, sold, or traded while goods are in transit and is used for letter-of-credit transactions. The customer usually needs the original or a copy as proof of ownership to take possession of the goods.
- ***Consular invoice.*** Certain nations require a consular invoice, which is used to control and identify goods. The invoice must be purchased from the consulate of the country to which the goods are being shipped and usually must be prepared in the language of that country.
- ***Certificate of origin.*** Certain nations require a signed statement as to the origin of the export item. Such certificates are usually obtained through a semiofficial organization such as a local chamber of commerce. A certificate may be required even though the commercial invoice contains the information.
- ***Inspection certification.*** Some purchasers and countries may require a certificate of inspection attesting to the specifications of the goods shipped, usually performed by a third party. Inspection certificates are often obtained from independent testing organizations.
- ***Dock receipt and warehouse receipt.*** These receipts are used to transfer accountability when the export item is moved by the domestic carrier to the port of embarkation and left with the international carrier for export.
- ***Destination control statement.*** This statement appears on the commercial invoice, ocean or air waybill of lading, and SED to notify the carrier and all foreign parties that the item may be exported only to certain destinations.
- ***Insurance certificate.*** If the seller provides insurance, the insurance certificate states the type and amount of coverage. This instrument is negotiable.
- ***Shipper's Export Declaration.*** The SED is used to control exports and compile trade statistics and must be prepared and submitted to the customs agent for shipments by mail valued at more than $500 and for shipments by means other than mail valued at more than $2,500. For more information, *see* "Shipper's Export Declarations (SEDs)" on page 83.
- ***Export license.*** U.S. export shipments may be required by the U.S. government to have an export license. (*Refer to* Chapter 11, "Export Regulations, Customs Benefits, and Tax Incentives," beginning on page 60, for a complete discussion of licensing.)
- ***Export packing list.*** Considerably more detailed and informative than a standard domestic packing list, an export packing list itemizes the material in each individual package and indicates the type of package: box, crate, drum, carton, and so on. It shows the individual net, legal, tare, and gross weights and measurements for each package (in both U.S. and metric systems). Package markings should be shown along with the shipper's and buyer's references. The packing list should be attached to the outside of a package in a waterproof envelope marked "packing list enclosed." The list is used by the shipper or forwarding agent to determine (1) the total shipment weight and volume and (2) whether the correct cargo is being shipped. In addition, customs officials (both U.S. and foreign) may use the list to check the cargo.

Documentation must be precise. Slight discrepancies or omissions may prevent U.S. merchandise from being exported, result in U.S. firms not getting paid, or even result in the seizure of the exporter's goods by U.S. or foreign government customs. Collection documents are subject to precise time limits and may not be honored by a bank if out of date. Much of the documentation is routine for freight forwarders or customs brokers acting on the firm's behalf, but the exporter is ultimately responsible for the accuracy of the documentation.

The number of documents the exporter must deal with varies depending on the destination of the shipment. Because each country has different import regulations, the exporter must be careful to provide proper documentation. If the exporter does not rely on the services of a freight forwarder, there are several methods of obtaining information on foreign import restrictions:

- Country desk officers in the Department of Commerce are specialists in individual country conditions.
- Industry specialists in the Department of Commerce can advise on product classifications.
- Foreign government embassies and consulates in the United States can often provide information on import regulations.
- The International Air Transport Association (IATA) has a number of publications with information on tariff rules, air waybills, and other international air cargo regulations. Contact the North American office of IATA at 800 Place Victoria, P.O. Box 113, Montreal, Quebec H4z 1M1, Canada; Tel: (800) 716-6326, (514) 874-0202; Fax: (514) 874-9632; Web site: www.iataonline.com.
- The Bureau of National Affairs *Export Reference Manual* contains complete country-by-country shipping information as well as tariff systems, import and exchange controls, mail regulations, and other special information. Contact the Bureau of National Affairs, Inc., 9435 Key West Ave., Rockville, MD 20850; Tel: (800) 372-1033; Fax: (800) 253-0332.
- *Exporters' Encyclopedia* contains information on trade regulations and documentation for more than 220 world markets. Contact Dun's Marketing Services, Business Reference Solutions Dept., 3 Sylvan Way, Parsippany, NJ 07054-3896; Tel: (800) 526-0651 or (973) 605-6000.

Shipping

The handling of transportation is similar for domestic orders and export orders. The export marks should be added to the standard information shown on a domestic bill of lading and should show the name of the exporting carrier and the latest allowed arrival date at the port of export. The exporter should also include instructions for the inland carrier to notify the international freight forwarder by telephone on arrival.

International shipments are increasingly being made on a through bill of lading under a multimodal contract. The multimodal transport operator (frequently one of the modal carriers) takes charge of and responsibility for the entire movement from factory to the final destination.

When determining the method of international shipping, the exporter may find it useful to consult with a freight forwarder. Since carriers are often used for large and bulky shipments, the exporter should reserve space on the carrier well before actual shipment date (this reservation is called the booking contract).

The exporter should consider the cost of shipment, delivery schedule, and accessibility to the shipped product by the foreign buyer when determining the method of international shipping. Although air carriers are more expensive, their cost may be offset by lower domestic shipping costs (because they may use a local airport instead of a coastal seaport) and quicker delivery times. These factors may give the U.S. exporter an edge over other competitors, whose service to their accounts may be less timely.

Before shipping, the U.S. firm should be sure to check with the foreign buyer about the destination of the goods. Buyers often wish the goods to be shipped to a free-trade zone or a free port, where goods are exempt from import duties.

Insurance

Export shipments are usually insured against loss, damage, and delay in transit by cargo insurance. For international shipments, the carrier's liability is frequently limited by international agreements and the coverage is substantially different from domestic coverage. Arrangements for cargo insurance may be made by either the buyer or the seller, depending on the terms of sale. Exporters are advised to consult with international insurance carriers or freight forwarders for more information.

Damaging weather conditions, rough handling by carriers, and other common hazards to cargo make marine insurance important protection for U.S. exporters. If the terms of sale make the U.S. firm responsible for insurance, it should either obtain its own policy or insure cargo under a freight forwarder's policy for a fee. If the terms of sale make the foreign buyer responsible, the exporter should not assume (or even take the buyer's word) that adequate insurance has been obtained. If the buyer neglects to obtain coverage or obtains too little, damage to the cargo may cause a major financial loss to the exporter.

Shipper's Export Declarations (SEDs)

Shipper's Export Declarations (SEDs) are used for compiling the official U.S. export statistics and for export control purposes. Separate SEDs are required for each shipment (including each rail car, truck, or other vehicle). A shipment is defined as all merchandise moving from one exporter to one consignee on one exporting carrier.

The SED must be prepared in English, typewritten or in other non-erasable medium. The original should be signed by the exporter or his duly authorized agent. Exporters may list more than one general license and validated license or a combination of general and validated licenses on the same SED.

Where two or more items are classified under the same Schedule B number, the Schedule B number should appear only once on the SED with a single quantity, shipping weight, and value, unless a validated license requires otherwise or, the shipment consists of a combination of foreign and domestic merchandise classified under the same Schedule B number. Shipments involving multiple invoices or packages should be reported on the same SED.

SEDs are not required for the following types of shipments:

- Shipments (excluding postal shipments) where the value of commodities classified under each individual Schedule B number is $2,500 or less and for which a validated export license is not required and when shipped to countries in groups T and V as listed in Supplement 1 to Section 770 of the Export Administration Regulations.
- Shipments from the United States to Canada, except those: (1) Requiring a Department of Commerce validated export license; (2) Subject to the Department of State, International Traffic in Arms Regulations regardless of license requirements; or (3) Subject to Department of Justice, Drug enforcement Administration, export declaration requirements.
- Shipments through the U.S. Postal Service that do not require a validated license when the shipment is: (1) valued $500 or under, (2) either the consignee or the consignor is not a business concern, or (3) the shipment is not for commercial consideration.
- In-transit shipments not requiring a validated export license and leaving for a foreign destination by means other than vessel.
- Shipments from one point in the United States to another point in the United by routes passing through Mexico, and shipments from one point in Mexico by routes passing through the United States.
- Shipments to the U.S. Armed Services.
- Shipments to U.S. government agencies and employees for their exclusive use.
- Other miscellaneous shipments:

  1. Diplomatic pouches and their contents.

  2. Human remains and accompanying receptacles and flowers.

  3. Shipments of gift parcels moving under General License GIFT.

  4. Shipments of interplant correspondence and other business records from a U.S. firm to its subsidiary or affiliate.

  5. Shipments of pets as baggage, accompanying or not accompanying persons leaving the United States.
- Merchandise not moving as cargo under a bill of lading or air waybill and not requiring a validated export license.

  1. Baggage and household effects and tools of trade of persons leaving the United States when such are owned by the person, in his possession at the time of departure and not intended for sale.

  2. Carriers' stores, supplies, equipment, bunker fuel, and so forth, when not intended for unlading in a foreign country.

  3. Usual and reasonable kinds and quantities of dunnage necessary to secure and stow cargo. (For sole use on board the carrier.)

SED Forms

SED form 7525-V, its continuation sheet, and the SED for in-transit goods, Form 7513 may be purchased from the Government Printing Office (Tel: (202) 512-1800; Web site: www.access.gpo.gov/su_docs), local Customs District Directors, or privately printed. SED Form 7525-V-Alternate (Intermodal) and its continuation sheet must be privately printed. Privately printed SEDs must conform in every respect to the official forms.

Exporters, freight forwarders and carriers may be authorized to submit monthly reports via electronic medium in lieu of filing an individual SED for each shipment. For additional information on the Automated Export System (AES), check the web site at www.customs.ustreas.gov (follow links for Import/Export AES).

For More Information on SEDs

Detailed legal requirements regarding the SED and its preparation are contained in the Foreign Trade Statistics Regulations (FTSR) (15 CFR, Part 30). Questions concerning the FTSR may be directed to the Regulations Branch, Foreign Trade Division, Bureau of the Census, (301) 457-2238; Fax: (301) 457-3765.

Information concerning export control laws and regulations including additional SED requirements is contained in the Export Administration Regulations (15 CFR Parts 768-799) which may be purchased from the Superintendent of Documents, U.S. Government Printing Office, Washington, DC 20402; Tel: (202) 512-1800; Web site: www.access.gpo.gov/su_docs.

A sample SED Form 7525-V, with comments, is supplied at the end of this chapter. For assistance in filling out SEDs, try the following offices:

Bureau of the Census, Foreign Trade Division
Tel: (301) 457-3041; Fax: (301) 457-2647

Bureau of the Census, Foreign Trade Division, Commodity Classification Assistance,
Tel: (301) 457-1084; Fax: (301) 457-2647

Bureau of the Census, Foreign Trade Division, Regulations
Tel: (301) 457-2238; Fax. (301) 457-3765

Bureau of Export Administration, Export Control, Washington, DC
Tel: (202) 482-4811

Bureau of Export Administration, Export Control, Newport Beach, CA
Tel: (949) 660-0144; Fax: (949) 660-9347

Bureau of Export Administration, Export Control, Santa Clara, CA
Tel: (408) 998-7402

U.S. State Dept., Office of Defense Trade Controls
Tel: (703) 875-6644; Fax: (703) 875-6647

U.S. Customs Service, Office of Finance, Budget Division
Tel: (202) 927-0310 (user fees), 927-0034 (harbor maintenance fees); Fax: (202) 927-1818

Information Reported on SED Form 7525-V

1 (a). Exporter The name and address of the U.S. exporter—the principal party responsible for effecting export from the United States. The exporter as named on the validated export license. Report only the first five digits of the ZIP code.

1 (b). Exporter Identification Number The exporter's Internal Revenue Service Employer Identification Number (EIN) or Social Security Number (SSN) if no EIN has been assigned. Report the 9-digit numerical code as reported on your latest Employer's Quarterly Federal Tax Return, Treasury Form 941. The EIN is usually available from your accounting or payroll department.

1(c). Related Party Transaction One between a U.S. exporter and foreign consignee, (e.g., parent company or sister company), where there is at least 10 percent ownership of each by the same U.S. or foreign person or business enterprise.

2. Date of Exportation The date of departure or date of clearance, if date of departure is not known. This is not required for vessel and postal shipments.

3. Bill of Lading or Air Waybill Number The exporting carrier's bill of lading or air waybill number.

4 (a). Ultimate Consignee The name and address of the party actually receiving the merchandise for the designated end-use or the party so designated on the validated export license. For overland shipments to Mexico, also include the Mexican state in the address.

4 (b). Intermediate Consignee The name and address of the party in a foreign country who makes delivery of the merchandise to the ultimate consignee or the party so named on the export license.

5. Agent of Exporter The name and address of the duly authorized forwarding agent.

6. Point (State) of Origin or Foreign Trade Zone (FTZ) Number Use one of the following: (1) the two-digit U.S. Postal Service abbreviation of the state in which the merchandise actually starts its journey to the port of export; or (2) the state of the commodity of the greatest value, or (3) the state of consolidation, or (3) the Foreign Trade Zone Number for exports leaving an FTZ.

7. Country of Ultimate Destination The country in which the merchandise is to be consumed, further processed, or manufactured; the final country of destination as known to the exporter at the time of shipment; or the country of ultimate destination as shown on the validated export license. Two-digit (alpha character) International Standards Organization (ISO) codes may also be used.

8. Loading Pier The number or name of the pier at which the merchandise is laden aboard the exporting vessel. (For vessel shipments only)

9. Method of Transportation The mode of transport by which the merchandise is exported. Specify by name, i.e., vessel, air, rail, truck, etc. Specify "own power" if applicable.

10. Exporting Carrier The name of the carrier transporting the merchandise out of the United States. For vessel shipments, give the vessel's flag also.

11. U.S. Port of Export Overland shipments: The U.S. Customs port at which the surface carrier crosses the border. Vessel and air shipments: The U.S. Customs port where the merchandise is loaded on the carrier which is taking the merchandise out of the United States. Postal shipments: The U.S. Post Office where the merchandise is mailed.

12. Foreign Port of Unloading The foreign port and country at which the merchandise will be unladen from the exporting carrier. For vessel and air shipments only.

13. Containerized Cargo originally booked as containerized cargo and placed in containers at the vessel operator's option. For vessel shipments only.

14. Commodity Description A sufficient description of the commodity to permit verification of the Schedule B Commodity Number or the description shown on the export license.

15. Marks, Numbers, and Kinds of Packages Marks, numbers, or other identification shown on the packages and the numbers and kinds of packages (boxes, barrels, baskets, etc.).

16. "D" (Domestic) or "F" (Foreign) Domestic exports: Merchandise grown, produced, or manufactured in the United States (including imported merchandise which has been enhanced in value or changed from the form in which imported by further manufacture or processing in the United States). Foreign exports: Merchandise that has entered the United States and is being reexported in the same condition as when imported.

17. Schedule B Commodity Number The ten-digit commodity number as provided in Schedule B - Statistical Classification of Domestic and Foreign Commodities Exported From the United States. Check Digit (CD) is no longer required.

18. Net Quantity Report whole unit(s) as specified in Schedule B with the unit indicated. Report also the unit specified on the validated export license if the units differ.

19. Gross Shipping Weight The gross shipping weight in kilograms for each Schedule B number, including the weight of containers but excluding carrier equipment (Lbs. multiplied by 0.4536 = kils. Report whole units.) For vessel and air shipments only.

20. Value Selling price or cost if not sold, including freight, insurance, and other charges to U.S. port of export, but excluding unconditional discounts and commissions (nearest whole dollar, omit cents). Report one value for each Schedule B number.

21. Export License Number or General License Symbol Validated export license number and expiration date or general license symbol.

22. Export Control Classification Number (When required) ECCN number of commodities listed on the Commerce Control List in the Export Administration Regulations.

23. Designation of Agent Signature of exporter authorizing the named agent to effect the export when such agent does not have formal power of attorney.

24. Signature/Title/Date Signature of exporter or authorized agent certifying the truth and accuracy of the information on the SED, title of exporter or authorized agent, and date of signature.

25. Authentication For Customs use only.

Sample Shipper's Export Declaration

FORM 7525-V (1-1-88) **SHIPPER'S EXPORT DECLARATION** OMB No. 0607-0018

1a. EXPORTER'S *(Name and address including ZIP code)*

ZIP CODE

2. DATE OF EXPORTATION

3. BILL OF LADING/AIR WAYBILL NO.

b. EXPORTER'S EIN (IRS) NUMBER

c. PARTIES TO TRANSACTION

☐ Related ☐ Non-related

4a. ULTIMATE CONSIGNEE

b. INTERMEDIATE CONSIGNEE

5. FORWARDING AGENT

6. POINT (STATE) OF ORIGIN OR FTZ NO.

7. COUNTRY OF ULTIMATE DESTINATION

8. LOADING PIER *(Vessel Only)*

9. MODE OF TRANSPORT *(Specify)*

10. EXPORTING CARRIER

11. PORT OF EXPORT

12. PORT OF UNLOADING *(VESSEL and AIR ONLY)*

13. CONTAINERIZED *(Vessel only)*

☐ Yes ☐ No

14. SCHEDULE B DESCRIPTION OF COMMODITIES,
15. MARKS, NOS., AND KINDS OF PACKAGES
(Use columns 17-19)

D/F (16)	SCHEDULE B NUMBER (17)	CHECK DIGIT	QUANTITY – SCHEDULE B UNIT(S) (18)	SHIPPING WEIGHT *(Kilos)* (19)	VALUE (U.S. dollars, omit cents) *(Selling price or cost if not sold)* (20)

21. VALIDATED LICENSE NO./GENERAL LICENSE SYMBOL

22. ECCN *(When required)*

23. Duly authorized officer or employee

The exporter authorizes the forwarder named above to act as forwarding agent for export control and customs purposes.

24. I certify that all statements made and all information contained herein are true and correct and that I have read and understand the instructions for preparation of this document, set forth in the "**Correct Way to Fill Out the Shipper's Export Declaration.**" I understand that civil and criminal penalties, including forfeiture and sale, may be imposed for making false or fraudulent statements herein, failing to provide the requested information or for violation of U.S. laws on exportation (13 U.S.C. Sec. 305; 22 U.S.C. Sec. 401; 18 U.S.C. Sec. 1001; 50 U.S.C. App. 2410).

Signature

Confidential - For use solely for official purposes authorized by the Secretary of Commerce (13 U.S.C. 301 (g).

Title

Export shipments are subject to inspection by U.S. Customs Service and/or Office of Export Enforcement.

Date

25. AUTHENTICATION *(When required)*

The "Correct Way to Fill Out the Shipper's Export Declaration" is available from the Bureau of the Census, Washington, D.C. 20233.

Chapter 13

Methods of Payment

There are several basic methods of receiving payment for products sold abroad. As with domestic sales, a major factor that determines the method of payment is the amount of trust in the buyer's ability and willingness to pay. For sales within the United States, if the buyer has good credit, sales are usually made on open account; if not, cash in advance is required. For export sales, these same methods may be used; however, other methods are also often used in international trade. Ranked in order from most secure for the exporter to least secure, the basic methods of payment are

1. Cash in advance,
2. Letter of credit,
3. Documentary collection or draft,
4. Open account, and
5. Other payment mechanisms, such as consignment sales.

Since getting paid in full and on time is of utmost concern to exporters, risk is a major consideration. Many factors make exporting riskier than domestic sales. However, there are also several methods of reducing risks. One of the most important factors in reducing risks is to know what risks exist. For that reason, exporters are advised to consult an international banker to determine an acceptable method of payment for each specific transaction.

Note: An excellent short book on the topic is *A Short Course in International Payments* by Edward G. Hinkelman, available from World Trade Press.

Cash in Advance

Cash in advance before shipment may seem to be the most desirable method of all, since the shipper is relieved of collection problems and has immediate use of the money if a wire transfer is used. Payment by check, even before shipment, may result in a collection delay of four to six weeks and therefore frustrate the original intention of payment before shipment. On the other hand, advance payment creates cash flow problems and increases risks for the buyer. Thus, cash in advance lacks competitiveness; the buyer may refuse to pay until the merchandise is received.

Documentary Letters of Credit and Drafts

The buyer may be concerned that the goods may not be sent if the payment is made in advance. To protect the interests of both buyer and seller, documentary letters of credit or drafts are often used. Under these two methods, documents are required to be presented before payment is made. Both letters of credit and drafts may be paid immediately, at sight, or at a later date. Drafts that are to be paid when presented for payment are called *sight drafts.* Drafts that are to be paid at a later date, which is often after the buyer receives the goods, are called *time drafts* or *date drafts.*

Since payment under these two methods is made on the basis of documents, all terms of sale should be clearly specified. For example, "net 30 days" should be specified as "net 30 days from acceptance" or "net 30 days from date of bill of lading" to avoid confusion and delay of payment. Likewise, the currency of payment should be specified as "US$XXX" if payment is to be made in U.S. dollars. International bankers can offer other suggestions to help.

Banks charge fees—usually a small percentage of the amount of payment—for handling letters of credit and less for handling drafts. If fees charged by both the foreign and U.S. banks for their collection services are to be charged to the account of the buyer, this point should be explicitly stated in all quotations and on all drafts. The exporter usually expects the buyer to pay the charges for the letter of credit, but some buyers may not accept terms that require this added cost. In such cases the exporter must either absorb the letter of credit costs or lose that potential sale.

Letters of Credit

A letter of credit adds a bank's promise of paying the

exporter to that of the foreign buyer when the exporter has complied with all the terms and conditions of the letter of credit. The foreign buyer applies for issuance of a letter of credit to the exporter and therefore is called the *applicant*; the exporter is called the *beneficiary*.

Payment under a documentary letter of credit is based on documents, not on the terms of sale or the condition of the goods sold. Before payment, the bank responsible for making payment verifies that all documents are exactly as required by the letter of credit. When they are not as required, a discrepancy exists, which must be *cured* before payment can be made. Thus, the full compliance of documents with those specified in the letter of credit is mandatory.

Often a letter of credit issued by a foreign bank is confirmed by a U.S. bank. This means that the U.S. bank, which is the confirming bank, adds its promise to pay to that of the foreign, or issuing, bank. Letters of credit that are not confirmed are advised through a U.S. bank and are called *advised* letters of credit. U.S. exporters may wish to confirm letters of credit issued by foreign banks not only because they are unfamiliar with the credit risk of the foreign bank but also because there may be concern about the political or economic risk associated with the country in which the bank is located. An international banker or the local U.S. Department of Commerce district office can help exporters evaluate these risks to determine what might be appropriate for each specific export transaction.

A letter of credit may be either *irrevocable* (that is, it cannot be changed unless both the buyer and the seller agree to make the change) or *revocable* (that is, either party may unilaterally make changes). A revocable letter of credit is inadvisable. A letter of credit may be *at sight*, which means immediate payment upon presentation of documents, or it may be a *time* or *date* letter of credit with payment to be made in the future. *See* "Drafts" on page 90.

Any change made to a letter of credit after it has been issued is called an amendment. The fees charged by the banks involved in amending the letter of credit may be paid by either the exporter or the foreign buyer, but who is to pay which charges should be specified in the letter of credit. Since changes can be time-consuming and expensive, every effort should be made to get the letter of credit right the first time.

An exporter is usually not paid until the advising or confirming bank receives the funds from the issuing bank. To expedite the receipt of funds, wire transfers may be used. Bank practices vary, however, and the exporter may be able to receive funds by discounting the letter of credit at the bank, which involves paying a fee to the bank for this service. Exporters should consult with their international bankers about bank policy.

A Typical Letter of Credit Transaction

Here is what typically happens when payment is made by an irrevocable letter of credit confirmed by a U.S. bank:

1. After the exporter and customer agree on the terms of a sale, the customer arranges for its bank to open a letter of credit. (Delays may be encountered if, for example, the buyer has insufficient funds.)
2. The buyer's bank prepares an irrevocable letter of credit, including all instructions to the seller concerning the shipment.
3. The buyer's bank sends the irrevocable letter of credit to a U.S. bank, requesting confirmation. The exporter may request that a particular U.S. bank be the confirming bank, or the foreign bank selects one of its U.S. correspondent banks.
4. The U.S. bank prepares a letter of confirmation to forward to the exporter along with the irrevocable letter of credit.
5. The exporter reviews carefully all conditions in the letter of credit. The exporter's freight forwarder should be contacted to make sure that the shipping date can be met. If the exporter cannot comply with one or more of the conditions, the customer should be alerted at once.
6. The exporter arranges with the freight forwarder to deliver the goods to the appropriate port or airport.
7. When the goods are loaded, the forwarder completes the necessary documents.
8. The exporter (or the forwarder) presents to the U.S. bank documents indicating full compliance.
9. The bank reviews the documents. If they are in order, the documents are airmailed to the buyer's bank for review and transmitted to the buyer.
10. The buyer (or agent) gets the documents that may be needed to claim the goods.
11. A draft, which may accompany the letter of credit, is paid by the exporter's bank at the time specified or may be discounted at an earlier date.

Example of a Confirmed Irrevocable Letter of Credit

The example of a confirmed irrevocable letter of credit on page 94 illustrates the various parts of a typical letter of credit. In this sample, the letter of credit was forwarded to the exporter, The Walton Building Supplies Company (A) by the drawee bank, C&S/Sovran Corporation (B) as a result of the letter of credit being issued by the First Hong Kong Bank, Hong Kong (C), for the account of the importer, BBH Hong Kong (D). The date of issue was March 8, 1996 (E), and the exporter must submit proper documents (e.g., a commercial invoice in one original and three copies) (F) by June 23, 1996 (G) in order for a sight draft (H) to be honored.

Tips on Using a Letter of Credit

When preparing quotations for prospective customers, exporters should keep in mind that banks pay only the amount specified in the letter of credit—even if higher charges for shipping, insurance, or other factors are documented.

Upon receiving a letter of credit, the exporter should carefully compare the letter's terms with the terms of the exporter's pro forma quotation. This point is extremely important, since the terms must be precisely met or the letter of credit may be invalid and the exporter may not be paid. If meeting the terms of the letter of credit is impossible or any of the information is incorrect or misspelled, the exporter should get in touch with the customer immediately and ask for an amendment to the letter of credit to correct the problem.

The exporter must provide documentation showing that the goods were shipped by the date specified in the letter of credit or the exporter may not be paid. Exporters should check with their freight forwarders to make sure that no unusual conditions may arise that would delay shipment. Similarly, documents must be presented by the date specified for the letter of credit to be paid. Exporters should verify with their international bankers that sufficient time will be available for timely presentation.

Exporters should always request that the letter of credit specify that partial shipments and transshipment will be allowed. Doing so prevents unforeseen problems at the last minute.

International letters of credit are usually governed by uniform customs and practices UCP 500. International bankers or publications of the International Chamber of Commerce may be consulted for more information.

ICC Publishing Inc.
156 Fifth Avenue
New York, NY 10010
Tel: (212) 206-1150; Fax: (212) 633-6025
Web site: www.icc-ibcc.org.

Drafts

A draft, sometimes also called a bill of exchange, is analogous to a foreign buyer's check. Like checks used in domestic commerce, drafts sometimes carry the risk that they will be dishonored.

Sight Drafts

A sight draft is used when the seller wishes to retain title to the shipment until it reaches its destination and is paid for. Before the cargo can be released, the original ocean bill of lading must be properly endorsed by the buyer and surrendered to the carrier, since it is a document that evidences title.

Air waybills of lading, on the other hand, do not need to be presented in order for the buyer to claim the goods. Hence, there is a greater risk when a sight draft is being used with an air shipment.

In actual practice, the bill of lading or air waybill is endorsed by the shipper and sent via the shipper's bank to the buyer's bank or to another intermediary along with a sight draft, invoices, and other supporting documents specified by either the buyer or the buyer's country (e.g., packing lists, consular invoices, insurance certificates). The bank notifies the buyer when it has received these documents; as soon as the amount of the draft is paid, the bank releases the bill of lading, enabling the buyer to obtain the shipment.

When a sight draft is being used to control the transfer of title of a shipment, some risk remains because the buyer's ability or willingness to pay may change between the time the goods are shipped and the time the drafts are presented for payment. Also, the policies of the importing country may change. If the buyer cannot or will not pay for and claim the goods, then returning or disposing of them becomes the problem of the exporter.

Exporters should also consider which foreign bank should negotiate the sight draft for payment. If the negotiating bank is also the buyer's bank, the bank may favor its customer's position, thereby putting the exporter at a disadvantage. Exporters should consult their international bankers to determine an appropriate strategy for negotiating drafts.

Time Drafts and Date Drafts

If the exporter wants to extend credit to the buyer, a time draft can be used to state that payment is due within a certain time after the buyer accepts the draft and receives the goods, for example, 30 days after acceptance. By signing and writing "accepted" on the draft, the buyer is formally obligated to pay within the stated time. When this is done the draft is called a trade acceptance and can be either kept by the exporter until maturity or sold to a bank at a discount for immediate payment.

A date draft differs slightly from a time draft in that it specifies a date on which payment is due, for example, December 1, 19XX, rather than a time period after the draft is accepted. When a sight draft or time draft is used, a buyer can delay payment by delaying acceptance of the draft. A date draft can prevent this delay in payment but still must be accepted.

When a bank accepts a draft, it becomes an obligation of the bank and a negotiable investment known as a banker's acceptance is created. A banker's acceptance can also be sold to a bank at a discount for immediate payment.

Credit Cards

Many U.S. exporters of consumer and other products (generally of low dollar value) that are sold directly to the end user accept Visa and MasterCard in payment for export sales. In international credit card transactions, merchants are normally required to deposit drafts in the currency of their country; for example, a U.S. exporter would deposit a draft in U.S. dollars. U.S. merchants may find that domestic rules and international rules governing credit card transactions differ somewhat and should contact their credit card processor for more specific information.

International credit card transactions are typically placed by telephone or fax, methods that facilitate fraudulent transactions. Merchants should determine the validity of transactions and obtain proper authorizations.

Open Account

In a foreign transaction, an open account is a convenient method of payment and may be satisfactory if the buyer is well established, has demonstrated a long and favorable payment record, or has been thoroughly checked for creditworthiness. Under open account, the exporter simply bills the customer, who is expected to pay under agreed terms at a future date. Some of the largest firms abroad make purchases only on open account.

Open account sales do pose risks, however. The absence of documents and banking channels may make legal enforcement of claims difficult to pursue. The exporter may have to pursue collection abroad, which can be difficult and costly. Also, receivables may be harder to finance, since drafts or other evidence of indebtedness are unavailable.

Before issuing a pro forma invoice to a buyer, exporters contemplating a sale on open account terms should thoroughly examine the political, economic, and commercial risks and consult with their bankers if financing will be needed for the transaction.

Other Payment Mechanisms

Consignment Sales

In international consignment sales, the same basic procedure is followed as in the United States. The material is shipped to a foreign distributor to be sold on behalf of the exporter. The exporter retains title to the goods until they are sold by the distributor. Once the goods are sold, payment is sent to the exporter. With this method, the exporter has the greatest risk and least control over the goods and may have to wait quite a while to get paid.

When this type of sale is contemplated, it may be wise to consider some form of risk insurance. In addition, it may be necessary to conduct a credit check on the foreign distributor (*see* "Decreasing Credit Risks Through Credit Checks" on page 92). Furthermore, the contract should establish who is responsible for property risk insurance covering merchandise until it is sold and payment received.

Foreign Currency

A buyer and a seller in different countries rarely use the same currency. Payment is usually made in either the buyer's or the seller's currency or in a mutually agreed-on currency that is foreign to both parties.

One of the uncertainties of foreign trade is the uncertainty of the future exchange rates between currencies. The relative value between the dollar and the buyer's currency may change between the time the deal is made and the time payment is received. If the exporter is not properly protected, a devaluation in the foreign currency could cause the exporter to lose dollars in the transaction. For example, if the buyer has agreed to pay 500,000 French francs for a shipment and the franc is valued at 20 cents, the seller would expect to receive $100,000. If the franc later decreased in value to be worth 19 cents, payment under the new rate would be only $95,000, a loss of $5,000 for the seller. On the other hand, if the foreign currency increases in value the exporter would get a windfall in extra profits. However, most exporters are not interested in speculating on foreign exchange fluctuations and prefer to avoid risks.

One of the simplest ways for a U.S. exporter to avoid this type of risk is to quote prices and require payment in U.S. dollars. Then the burden and risk are placed on the buyer to make the currency exchange. Exporters should also be aware of problems of currency convertibility; not all currencies are freely or quickly convertible into U.S. dollars. Fortunately, the U.S. dollar is widely accepted as an international trading currency, and American firms can often secure payment in dollars.

If the buyer asks to make payment in a foreign currency, the exporter should consult an international banker before negotiating the sales contract. Banks can offer advice on the foreign exchange risks that exist; further, some international banks can help one hedge against such a risk if necessary, by agreeing to purchase the foreign currency at a fixed price in dollars regardless of the value of the currency when the customer pays. The bank charges a fee or discount on the transaction. If this mechanism is used, the fee should be included in the price quotation.

Countertrade and Barter

International countertrade is a trade practice whereby a supplier commits contractually, as a condition of sale, to undertake specified initiatives that compensate and benefit the other party. The resulting linked trade fulfills financial (e.g., lack of foreign exchange), marketing, or public policy objectives of the trading parties. Not all suppliers consider countertrade an objectionable imposition; many U.S. exporters consider countertrade a necessary cost of doing business in markets where U.S. exports would otherwise not occur.

Simple barter is the direct exchange of goods or services between two parties; no money changes hands. Pure barter arrangements in international commerce are rare, because the parties' needs for the goods of the other seldom coincide and because valuation of the goods may pose problems. The most common form of compensatory trade practiced today involves contractually linked, parallel trade transactions each of which involves a separate financial settlement. For example, a countertrade contract may provide that the U.S. exporter will be paid in a convertible currency as long as the U.S. exporter (or another entity designated by the exporter) agrees to export a related quantity of goods from the importing country.

U.S. exporters can take advantage of countertrade opportunities by trading through an intermediary with countertrade expertise, such as an international broker, an international bank, or an export management company. Some export management companies offer specialized countertrade services. Exporters should bear in mind that countertrade often involves higher transaction costs and greater risks than simple export transactions.

The Department of Commerce can advise and assist U.S. exporters faced with countertrade requirements. The Finance and Countertrade Division of the Office of Finance monitors countertrade trends, disseminates information (including lists of potentially beneficial countertrade opportunities), and provides general assistance to enterprises seeking barter and countertrade opportunities. For information, contact

Finance and Countertrade Division, Office of Finance
International Trade Administration
U.S. Department of Commerce
Washington, DC 20230
Tel: (202) 482-4471; Fax: (202) 482-5702

A guide to countertrade contracts is available from United Nations Publications. *UNCITRAL: Legal Guide on International Countertrade Transactions* focuses on contractual clauses, and discusses those clauses that are essential for establishing a countertrade transaction and possible approaches to the structure of such transactions. The guide also provides suggestions as to how certain issues might be settled. The United Nations sales number is E.93.V.7 92-1-133444-6; the price is $30. For more information or to order, contact

United Nations Publications
Room DC2-0853
New York, NY 10017
Tel: (212) 963-8302; Fax: (212) 963-3489
Web site: www.un.org/publications

Decreasing Credit Risks Through Credit Checks

Generally, it is a good idea to check a buyer's credit even if credit risk insurance or relatively safe payment methods are employed. Banks are often able to provide credit reports on foreign companies, either through their own foreign branches or through a correspondent bank.

The Department of Commerce's International Company Profiles also provide useful information for credit checks (*see* "International Company Profiles" on page 40). For a fee, an ICP may be requested on any foreign company. Although the ICP is itself not a credit report, it does contain some financial information and also identifies other U.S. companies that do business with the reported firm. The exporter may then contact those companies directly to find out about their payment experience. Private credit reporting services also are available. Several U.S. services compile financial information on foreign firms (particularly larger firms) and make it available to subscribers.

Collection Problems

In international trade, problems involving bad debts are more easily avoided than rectified after they occur. Credit checks and the other methods that have been discussed can limit the risks involved. Nonetheless, just as in a company's domestic business, exporters occasionally encounter problems with buyers who default on payments. When these problems occur in international trade, obtaining payment can be both difficult and expensive. Even when the exporter has insurance to cover commercial credit risks, a default by a buyer still requires time, effort, and cost. The exporter must exhaust all reasonable means of obtaining payment before an insurance claim is honored, and there is often a significant delay before the insurance payment is made.

The simplest (and least costly) solution to a payment problem is to contact and negotiate with the customer. With patience, understanding, and flexibility, an exporter can often resolve conflicts to the satisfaction of both sides.

This point is especially true when a simple misunderstanding or technical problem is to blame and there is no question of bad faith. Even though the exporter may be required to compromise on certain points—perhaps even on the price of the committed goods—the company may save a valuable customer and profit in the long run.

If, however, negotiations fail and the sum involved is large enough to warrant the effort, a company should obtain the assistance and advice of its bank, legal counsel, and other qualified experts. If both parties can agree to take their dispute to an arbitration agency, this step is preferable to legal action, since arbitration is often faster and less costly. The International Chamber of Commerce handles the majority of international arbitrations and is usually acceptable to foreign companies because it is not affiliated with any single country. For information contact

Vice President for Arbitration
U.S. Council of the International Chamber of Commerce
1212 Avenue of the Americas
New York, NY 10036
Tel: (212) 354-4480; Fax: (212) 575-0327
Web site: www.uscib.org

The American Arbitration Association is also a reputable arbitration agency that handles international disputes; for information contact

American Arbitration Association
1633 Broadway
New York, NY 10019
Tel: (212) 484-4000; Fax: (212) 307-4387
Web site: www.adr.org

U.S. Government Trade Complaint Service

The Trade Complaint Service is available to aid U.S. exporters who find themselves in a trade dispute as a result of a specific overseas commercial transaction. These disputes, which are processed through the Department of Commerce's district offices, must meet certain criteria. After a firm has made every effort to settle the complaint without U.S. government assistance, cases are accepted when it can be clearly shown that communications have broken down and the value of the claim is more than $1,000. Simple collection claims are not accepted.

Commerce makes every effort to restore communications between the parties to the dispute in order to arrive at an amicable settlement. When legal proceedings are initiated, U.S. government assistance is normally withdrawn. Contact the Office of Domestic Operations, U.S. Department of Commerce; Tel: (202) 482-3347; Fax: (202) 482-0687; Web site: www.ita.doc.gov.

Figure 13-1: Sample Confirmed Irrevocable Letter of Credit

ORIGINAL

INTERNATIONAL BANKING GROUP

C&S/Sovran Corporation

P.O. Box 4899, ATLANTA, GEORGIA 30302-4889
CABLE ADDRESS: CITSOUTH
TELEX NO. 3737650
SWIFT NO. CSBKUS33

OUR ADVICE NUMBER: EA00000091
ADVICE DATE: 08MAR96
ISSUE BANK REF: 3312/HBI/22341
EXPIRY DATE: 23JUN96

******AMOUNT******
USD**25,000.00**

BENEFICIARY:
THE WALTON BUILDING SUPPLIES CO.
2356 SOUTH BELK STREET
ATLANTA, GEORGIA 30345

APPLICANT:
BBH HONG KONG
34 INDUSTRIAL DRIVE
CENTRAL, HONG KONG

WE HAVE BEEN REQUESTED TO ADVISE TO YOU THE FOLLOWING LETTER OF CREDIT AS ISSUED BY:

FIRST HONG KONG BANK
1 CENTRAL TOWER
HONG KONG

PLEASE BE GUIDED BY ITS TERMS AND CONDITIONS AND BY THE FOLLOWING:

CREDIT IS AVAILABLE BY NEGOTIATION OF YOUR DRAFT(S) IN DUPLICATE AT SIGHT FOR 100 PERCENT OF INVOICE VALUE DRAWN ON US ACCOMPANIED BY THE FOLLOWING DOCUMENTS:

1. **SIGNED COMMERCIAL INVOICE IN 1 ORIGINAL AND 3 COPIES.**
2. **FULL SET 3/3 OCEAN BILLS OF LADING CONSIGNED TO THE ORDER OF FIRST HONG KONG BANK, HONG KONG NOTIFY APPLICANT AND MARKED FREIGHT COLLECT.**
3. **PACKING LIST IN 2 COPIES.**

EVIDENCING SHIPMENT OF: 500 PINE LOGS—WHOLE—8 TO 12 FEET
FOB SAVANNAH, GEORGIA

SHIPMENT FROM: SAVANNAH, GEORGIA TO: HONG KONG
LATEST SHIPPING DATE: 02JUN96

PARTIAL SHIPMENTS NOT ALLOWED TRANSSHIMENT NOT ALLOWED

ALL BANKING CHARGES OUTSIDE HONG KONG ARE FOR BENEFICIARYS ACCOUNT.
DOCUMENTS MUST BE PRESENTED WITHIN 21 DAYS FROM B/L DATE.

AT THE REQUEST OF OUR CORRESPONDENT, WE CONFIRM THIS CREDIT AND ALSO ENGAGE WITH YOU THAT ALL DRAFTS DRAWN UNDER AND IN COMPLIANCE WITH THE TERMS OF THIS CREDIT BY DULY HONORED BY US.

PLEASE EXAMINE THIS INSTRUMENT CAREFULLY. IF YOU ARE UNABLE TO COMPLY WITH THE TERMS OR CONDITIONS, PLEASE COMMUNICATE WITH YOUR BUYER TO ARRANGE FOR AN AMENDMENT.

Chapter 14

Financing Export Transactions

Exporters naturally want to get paid as quickly as possible, and importers usually prefer delaying payment at least until they have received and resold the goods. Because of the intense competition for export markets, being able to offer good payment terms is often necessary to make a sale. Exporters should be aware of the many financing options open to them so that they may choose the one that is most favorable for both the buyer and the seller.

An exporter may need (1) preshipment financing to produce or purchase the product or to provide a service or (2) postshipment financing of the resulting account or accounts receivable, or both. The following factors are important to consider in making decisions about financing:

1. **The need for financing to make the sale.**
   In some cases, favorable payment terms make a product more competitive. If the competition offers better terms and has a similar product, a sale can be lost. In other cases, the exporter may need financing to produce the goods that have been ordered or to finance other aspects of a sale, such as promotion and selling expenses, engineering modifications, and shipping costs. Various financing sources are available to exporters, depending on the specifics of the transaction and the exporter's overall financing needs.
2. **The cost of different methods of financing.**
   Interest rates and fees vary. The total costs and their effect on price and profit should be well understood before a pro forma invoice is submitted to the buyer.
3. **The length of time financing is required.**
   Costs increase with the length of terms. Different methods of financing are available for short, medium, and long terms. However, exporters also need to be fully aware of financing limitations so that they can obtain the financing required to complete the transaction.
4. **The risks associated with financing the transaction.**
   The greater the risks associated with the transaction—whether they actually exist or are only perceived by the lender—the greater the costs to the exporter as well as the more difficult financing will be to obtain. Financing will also be more costly.

   The creditworthiness of the buyer directly affects the probability of payment to the exporter, but it is not the only factor of concern to a potential lender. The political and economic stability of the buyer's country also can be of concern. To provide financing for either accounts receivable or the production or purchase of the product for sale, the lender may require the most secure methods of payment, a letter of credit (possibly confirmed), or export credit insurance.

   If a lender is uncertain about the exporter's ability to perform, or if additional credit capacity is needed, a government guarantee program may enable the lender to provide additional financing.
5. **The availability of the exporter's own financial resources.**
   The company may be able to extend credit without seeking outside financing, or the company may have sufficient financial strength to establish a commercial line of credit. If neither of these alternatives is possible or desirable, other options may exist, but the exporter should fully explore the available options before issuing the pro forma invoice.

   For assistance in determining which financing options may be available, the following sources may be consulted:

   - The exporter's international or domestic banker,
   - The exporter's state export promotion or export finance office,
   - The nearest Export Assistance Center or Commerce Department district office,
   - The Small Business Administration, and/or
   - The Ex-Im Bank, Washington, DC

Extending Credit to Foreign Buyers

Exporters need to weigh carefully the credit or financing they extend to foreign customers. Exporters should follow the same careful credit principles they follow for domestic customers. An important reason for controlling the credit period is the cost incurred, either through use of working capital or through interest and fees paid. If the buyer is not responsible for paying these costs, then the exporter should factor them into the selling price.

A useful guide for determining the appropriate credit period is the normal commercial terms in the exporter's industry for internationally traded products. Buyers generally expect to receive the benefits of such terms. With few exceptions, normal commercial terms range from 30 to 180 days for off-the-shelf items like consumer goods, chemicals, and other industrial raw materials, agricultural commodities, and spare parts and components. Custom-made or higher-value capital equipment, on the other hand, may warrant longer repayment periods. An allowance may have to be made for longer shipment times than are found in domestic trade, because foreign buyers are often unwilling to have the credit period start before receiving the goods.

Foreign buyers often press exporters for longer payment periods, and it is true that liberal financing is a means of enhancing export competitiveness. The exporter should recognize, however, that longer credit periods increase any risk of default for which the exporter may be liable.

Thus, the exporter must exercise judgment in balancing competitiveness against considerations of cost and safety. Also, credit terms once extended to a buyer tend to set the precedent for future sales, so the exporter should carefully consider any credit terms extended to first-time buyers.

Customers are frequently charged interest on credit periods of a year or longer but infrequently on short-term credit (up to 180 days). Most exporters absorb interest charges for short-term credit unless the customer pays after the due date.

Obtaining cash immediately is usually a high priority with exporters. One way they do so is by converting their export receivables to cash at a discount with a bank. Another way is to expand working capital resources. A third approach, suitable when the purchase involves capital goods and the repayment period extends a year or longer, is to arrange for project financing. In this case, a lender makes a loan directly to the buyer for the project and the exporter is paid immediately from the loan proceeds while the bank waits for payment and earns interest. A fourth method, when financing is difficult to obtain for a buyer or market, is to engage in countertrade to afford the customer an opportunity to generate earnings with which to pay for the purchase. *See* "Countertrade and Barter" on page 92.

The options that have been mentioned normally involve the payment of interest, fees, or other costs. Some options are more feasible when the amounts are in larger denominations. Exporters should also determine whether they incur financial liability should the buyer default.

Commercial Banks

The same type of commercial loans that finance domestic activities—including loans for working capital and revolving lines of credit—are often sought to finance export sales until payment is received. However, banks do not usually extend credit solely on the basis of an order.

A logical first step in obtaining financing is for an exporter to approach its local commercial bank. If the exporter already has a loan for domestic needs, then the lender already has experience with the exporter's ability to perform. Many exporters have very similar, if not identical, preshipment needs for both their international and their domestic transactions. Many lenders, therefore, would be willing to provide financing for export transactions if there were a reasonable certainty of repayment. By using letters of credit or export credit insurance, an exporter can reduce the lender's risk.

When a lender wishes greater assurance than is afforded by the transaction, a government guarantee program may enable a lender to extend credit to the exporter. *See* "Government Assistance Programs" on page 98.

For a company that is new to exporting or is a small or medium-sized business, it is important to select a bank that is sincerely interested in serving businesses of similar type or size. If the exporter's bank lacks an international department, it will refer the exporter to a correspondent bank that has one. The exporter may want to visit the international department—of the exporter's own bank or a correspondent bank—to discuss its export plans, available banking facilities, and applicable fees.

When selecting a bank, the exporter should ask the following questions:

- What are the charges for confirming a letter of credit, processing drafts, and collecting payment?
- Does the bank have foreign branches or correspondent banks? Where are they located?
- Can the bank provide buyer credit reports? At what cost?

- Does it have experience with U.S. and state government financing programs that support small business export transactions? If not, is it willing to consider participating in these programs?
- What other services, such as trade leads, can it provide?

Banker's Acceptances and Discounting

A time draft under an irrevocable letter of credit confirmed by a prime U.S. bank presents relatively little risk of default. Also, some banks or other lenders may be willing to buy time drafts that a creditworthy foreign buyer has accepted or agreed to pay at a specified future date. In some cases, banks agree to accept the obligations of paying a draft, usually of a customer, for a fee; this is called a *banker's acceptance.*

However, to convert these instruments to cash immediately, an exporter must obtain a loan using the draft as collateral or sell the draft to an investor or a bank for a fee. When the draft is sold to an investor or bank, it is sold at a discount. The exporter receives an amount less than the face value of the draft so that when the draft is paid at its face value at the specified future date, the investor or bank receives more than it paid to the exporter. The difference between the amount paid to the exporter and the face amount paid at maturity is called a *discount* and represents the fees or interest (or both) the investor or bank receives for holding the draft until maturity. Some drafts are discounted by the investor or bank without recourse to the exporter in case the party that is obligated to pay the draft defaults; others may be discounted with recourse to the exporter, in which case the exporter must reimburse the investor or bank if the party obligated to pay the draft defaults. The exporter should be certain of the terms and conditions of any financing arrangement of this nature.

Project Finance

Some export sales, especially sales of capital equipment, may sometimes require financing terms tailored to the buyer's cash flow and may involve payments over several years. Often the buyer obtains a loan from its own bank or arranges for other financing to enable it to pay cash to the exporter. If other project financing is required, either the exporter or the foreign buyer can initiate the proposal.

U.S. exporters frequently benefit from project finance in which federal agencies such as the Ex-Im Bank and OPIC participate. Although these programs are designed to support the purchase of U.S. goods and services, many U.S. companies export without being parties to the project finance or even being aware of its existence.

Other Private Sources

Factoring, Forfaiting, and Confirming

Factoring is the discounting of a foreign account receivable that does not involve a draft. The exporter transfers title to its foreign accounts receivable to a factoring house (an organization that specializes in the financing of accounts receivable) for cash at a discount from the face value. Although factoring is often done without recourse to the exporter, the specific arrangements should be verified by the exporter. Factoring of foreign accounts receivable is less common than factoring of domestic receivables.

Forfaiting is the selling, at a discount, of longer term accounts receivable or promissory notes of the foreign buyer. These instruments may also carry the guarantee of the foreign government. Both U.S. and European forfaiting houses, which purchase the instruments at a discount from the exporter, are active in the U.S. market. Because forfaiting may be done either with or without recourse to the exporter, the specific arrangements should be verified by the exporter.

Confirming is a financial service in which an independent company confirms an export order in the seller's country and makes payment for the goods in the currency of that country. Among the items eligible for confirmation (and thereby eligible for credit terms) are the goods themselves; inland, air, and ocean transportation costs; forwarding fees; custom brokerage fees; and duties. For the exporter, confirming means that the entire export transaction from plant to end user can be fully coordinated and paid for over time. Although confirming is common in Europe, it is still in its infancy in the United States.

Export Intermediaries

In addition to acting as export representatives, many export intermediaries, such as ETCs and EMCs, can help finance export sales. Some of these companies may provide short-term financing or may simply purchase the goods to be exported directly from the manufacturer, thus eliminating any risks associated with the export transaction as well as the need for financing. Some of the larger companies may make countertrade arrangements that substitute for financing in some cases.

Buyers and Suppliers as Sources of Financing

Foreign buyers may make down payments that reduce the need for financing from other sources. In addition, buyers may make progress payments as the goods are completed, which also reduce other financing requirements. Letters of credit that allow for progress payments upon inspection by the buyer's agent or receipt of a statement of the exporter that a certain percentage of the product has been completed are not uncommon.

In addition, suppliers may be willing to offer terms to the exporter if they are comfortable that they will receive payment. Suppliers may be willing to accept assignment of a part of the proceeds of a letter of credit or a partial transfer of a transferable letter of credit. However, some banks allow only a single transfer or assignment of a letter of credit. Therefore, the exporter should investigate the policy of the bank that will be advising or confirming the letter of credit.

Government Assistance Programs

Several federal government agencies, as well as a number of state and local ones, offer programs to assist exporters with their financing needs. Some are guarantee programs that require the participation of an approved lender; others provide loans or grants to the exporter or a foreign government.

Government programs generally aim to improve exporters' access to credit rather than to subsidize the cost at below-market levels. With few exceptions, banks are allowed to charge market interest rates and fees; part of those fees is paid to the government agencies to cover the agencies' administrative costs and default risks.

Government guarantee and insurance programs are used by commercial banks to reduce the risk associated with loans to exporters. Lenders concerned with an exporter's ability to perform under the terms of sale, and with an exporter's ability to be paid, often use government programs to reduce the risks that would otherwise prevent them from providing financing.

In overview, the Export-Import Bank of the United States is the federal government's general trade finance agency, offering numerous programs to address a broad range of needs. Credit insurance from Ex-Im Bank protects against default on exports sold under open account terms and drafts and letters of credit that are not the obligation of a U.S. entity. (Excluded are drafts that have been accepted by a U.S. bank or corporation and letters of credit confirmed by a U.S. bank.) Other guarantee and loan programs extend project finance and medium-term credit for durable goods.

Other agencies fill various market niches. USDA offers a variety of programs to foster agricultural exports. The TDA provides grant financing for project planning activities conducted by U.S. firms and thereby seeks to give a U.S. "imprint" on project feasibility studies and design. (*See* "Trade and Development Agency (TDA)" on page 45 for more information on TDA programs) SBA offers programs to address the needs of smaller exporters. OPIC provides specialized assistance to U.S. firms through its performance bond and contractor insurance programs. AID provides grants to developing nations that can be used to purchase U.S. goods and services. (*See* "Agency for International Development (AID)" on page 45 for more information on AID programs.)

Although the Department of Commerce does not offer any financing programs of its own, export counseling is available through its district offices. In addition, current articles on export finance programs are periodically published in *Business America*.

Export-Import Bank of the United States

The Export-Import Bank of the United States, or Ex-Im Bank, is an independent U.S. government agency with the primary purpose of facilitating the export of U.S. goods and services. Ex-Im Bank meets this objective by providing loans, guarantees, and insurance coverage to U.S. exporters and foreign buyers, normally on market-related credit terms.

Ex-Im Bank's insurance and guarantee programs are structured to encourage private financial institutions to fund U.S. exports by reducing the commercial risks (such as buyer insolvency and failure to pay) and political risks (such as war and currency inconvertibility) exporters face. The financing made available under Ex-Im Bank's guarantees and insurance is generally on market terms, and most of the commercial and political risks are borne by Ex-Im Bank.

Ex-Im Bank's loan program, on the other hand, is structured to neutralize interest rate subsidies offered by foreign governments. By responding with its own subsidized loan assistance, Ex-Im Bank enables U.S. financing to be competitive on specific sales with that offered by foreign exporters.

Ex-Im Bank programs are outlined below. If you require further information, contact your nearest U.S. Export Assistance Center, a regional Ex-Im Bank office, or

Ex-Im Bank, Marketing and Program Division
811 Vermont Avenue NW
Washington, DC 20571
Tel: (800) 565-EXIM, (202) 565-3946
Fax Retrieval (800) 565-EXIM (press 1, then 2 at voice prompts)
Web site: www.exim.gov

U.S. Content Requirements

Ex-Im Bank has a mandate to support the export sale and lease of goods and services of U.S. origin. The products sold must be produced or manufactured in the United States. For short-term sales, at least one half of the value (excluding price mark-up) must have been added by labor or material exclusively of U.S. origin. Goods must be shipped from the United States. No value may be added to the product by the insured after export from the United States. Services must be performed by U.S.-based personnel or U.S. personnel temporarily assigned in the host country. Services may be performed in the United States or in the buyer's country.

Ex-Im Bank recognizes that there may be export opportunities which involve products that do not meet foreign content guidelines. Insurance agreements with certain foreign government export credit agencies may enable Ex-Im Bank to provide support for such transactions. These transactions may involve content coming from Canada, Finland, France, Mexico, Sweden and Switzerland.

Country Limitation Schedule

Economic and political conditions vary widely among nations. A Country Limitation Schedule has been established that details special conditions on short- and medium-term insurance covering the repayment risks on buyers in various countries. The schedule is updated when country risk perceptions change. To confirm current conditions for transactions in a particular country, call the Ex-Im Bank regional office nearest you.

City/State Program

Ex-Im Bank has established the City/State Program, consisting of state and municipal organizations whose staff receive training in Ex-Im Bank programs and can guide the exporter through the application process.

All Ex-Im Bank resources are available through its City/State partners, including the Working Capital Guarantee Program and the Export Credit Insurance Program. City/State partners also represent Ex-Im Bank in the U.S. Export Assistance Centers set up around the country. By 1996, City/State programs were operating in 32 states, one county, a Chamber of Commerce and the Commonwealth of Puerto Rico. A listing of the participants in this program is available from Ex-Im Bank. For more information, contact your nearest Export Assistance Center or the Ex-Im Bank Office of Communication at Tel: (202) 565-3200; Fax: (202) 565-3210.

Working Capital Guarantee Program

Ex-Im Bank's Working Capital Guarantee Program encourages commercial lenders to make loans to U.S. businesses for various export-related activities. The program helps small and medium-sized businesses that have exporting potential but need funds to buy or produce goods, and/or to provide services, for export. It may be used to cover working capital loans to a U.S. business if the lender shows that the loan would not have been made without Ex-Im Bank's guarantee, and Ex-Im Bank determines that the exporter is creditworthy.

The exporter may use the guaranteed financing to:

- Purchase raw materials and finished products for export;
- Pay for materials, labor and overhead to produce goods and/or to provide services for export; or
- Cover standby letters of credit serving as bid bonds, performance bonds, or payment guarantees.

Ex-Im Bank's working capital guarantee covers 90 percent of the loan's principal and accrued interest. Guaranteed loans must be fully collateralized at all times. Acceptable collateral may include export-related inventory, export-related accounts receivable, or other assets. For companies in the service sector, costs such as engineering, design, and allocable overhead may be treated as collateral. The loan can be structured to finance one or more specified transactions, or as a revolving line of credit.

Exporters must demonstrate a successful track record of past performance including at least one full year of operations and a positive net worth. Financial statements must show sufficient strength to accommodate the requested debt.

Exporters may apply directly to Ex-Im Bank for a preliminary commitment for a guarantee. If approved, the exporter may then approach various lenders to secure the most attractive loan package. A preliminary commitment is valid for six months. The lender must apply for the final commitment.

Ex-Im Bank imposes no interest rate ceilings or maximum fee limitations; however, lenders should take into account that 90 percent of the risk is covered by an agency of the U.S. Government and price their loans accordingly.

Export Credit Insurance Program

An exporter may reduce foreign risks by purchasing Ex-Im Bank export credit insurance through an insurance broker or directly from Ex-Im Bank. A wide range of policies is available to accommodate many different export credit insurance needs. Insurance coverage:

- protects the exporter against the failure of foreign buyers to pay their credit obligations for commercial or political reasons;
- encourages exporters to offer foreign buyers competitive terms of payment;

- supports an exporter's prudent penetration of higher risk foreign markets; and
- because the proceeds of the policies are assignable from the insured exporter to a financial institution, it gives exporters and their banks greater financial flexibility in handling overseas accounts receivable.

Small Business Insurance Policy

Ex-Im Bank offers a short-term (up to 180 days) insurance policy geared to meet the particular credit requirements of smaller, less experienced exporters. Products typically supported under short-term policies are spare parts, raw materials, and consumer goods. Under the policy, Ex-Im Bank assumes 95 percent of the commercial and 100 percent of the political risk involved in extending credit to the exporter's overseas customers. This policy frees the exporter from "first loss" commercial risk deductible provisions that are usually found in regular insurance policies. It is a multi-buyer type policy which requires the exporter to insure all export credit sales. It offers a special "hold-harmless" assignment of proceeds which makes the financing of insured receivables more attractive to banks. The special coverage is available to companies which have an average annual export credit sales volume of less than $3 million for the two years prior to application and which meet the Small Business Administration's definition of a small business.

Umbrella Policy

The Umbrella Policy allows state agencies, export trading and management companies, insurance brokers, and similar agencies to act as intermediaries (administrators) between Ex-Im Bank and their clients by assisting their clients in obtaining export credit insurance. The coverage and eligibility requirements are the same as for the Small Business Policy.

Short-Term Single Buyer Policy

For those exporters who do not want to insure all their short-term export credit sales under a multi-buyer type of policy, the single buyer policy is available to cover single or repetitive sales. The policy offers 90 percent to 100 percent cover for both political and commercial risks of default (depending on the type of buyer, terms of sale, and product) and has no deductible. A special reduced minimum premium is available to small businesses.

Medium-Term Insurance

Medium-term insurance is available for exporters of capital goods or services in amounts less than $10 million and terms up to five years. Ex-Im Bank offers 100 percent commercial and political risk protection. Although similar to the guarantee program, medium-term insurance applications will usually be decided on in a more timely fashion because of their conditional nature.

Other Policies Available from Ex-Im Bank

- **Short Term Multibuyer Policy** Provides regular coverage for short-term export sales to many different buyers.
- **Financial Institution Buyer Credit Policy** Protects financial institutions against losses on short-term direct credit loans or reimbursement loans to foreign entities for importing U.S. goods and services.
- **Bank Letter of Credit Policy** Protects banks against losses on irrevocable letters of credit issued by foreign banks in support of U.S. exports.
- **Financing or Operating Leases** Insures both the stream-of-lease payments and the fair market value of the leased product.
- **Insurance Special Policies** Provides insurance on environmentally related goods and services, and insurance administered by trade associations.

Repayment Terms

Ex-Im Bank-supported financing follows the repayment term guidelines customary in international trade. For capital goods sales, the guidelines are:

Contract Value	Maximum Term
Less than $75,000	2 years
$75,001 - $150,000	3 years
$150,001 - $300,000	4 years
$300,001 or more	5-10 years, depending on the nature of the sale and the OECD classification of the buyer's country

Loans for projects and large product acquisitions, such as aircraft, are eligible for longer terms while lower unit value items such as automobiles and appliances receive shorter terms.

Other Ex-Im Bank Programs

Ex-Im Bank will support the export of environmental goods and services through a short- term environmental insurance policy with coverage of 95 percent of the commercial and 100 percent of the political risks of default without a deductible. Medium-term environmental exports will have enhanced guarantee coverage with local cost coverage equal to 15 percent of the U.S. contract price and capitalization of interest during construction.

Ex-Im Bank has established the Project Finance Division to analyze transactions where the repayment of the financing is based on a project's cash flow instead of a bank or government guarantee.

Seminars & Briefing Programs

Ex-Im Bank offers briefing programs which are available to the small business community. The program includes regular seminars, group briefings and individual discussions held both at Ex-Im Bank and around the country. For a seminar brochure and scheduling information contact

Ex-Im Bank Seminar Information
Tel: (202) 565-3912; Fax: (202)565-3723

Accelerated Processing For Lenders

Ex-Im Bank offers lenders accelerated processing of requests through the Priority Lending Program (PLP) and Delegated Authority Program (DA). Under the PLP, lenders who have made at least two transactions operative under the Working Capital Guarantee Program may submit a complete write-up of the exporter and transaction and be given a 10-day turnaround on their application. Since October 1994, Ex-Im Bank has given DA to qualified lenders which allows them to commit Ex-Im Bank's guarantee as soon as they have made their credit decision. No further analysis is done by Ex-Im Bank.

Department of Agriculture

The Foreign Agricultural Service (FAS) of the USDA administers several programs to help make U.S. exporters competitive in international markets and make U.S. products affordable to countries that have greater need than they have ability to pay.

One effort to boost U.S. agricultural sales overseas is the Export Credit Guarantee Program, which offers risk protection for U.S. exporters against nonpayment of foreign banks. The program guarantees payment for commercial as well as noncommercial risks. Private U.S. banking institutions provide the operating funds. The guarantee program makes it easier for exporters to obtain bank financing and to meet credit competition from other exporting countries.

FAS also helps carry out food aid programs that provide emergency food donations and long-term concessional and commercial financing for U.S. agricultural products. These sales are intended to stimulate long-range improvements in foreign economies and development of export markets for U.S. farm products.

The Trade Assistance and Promotion Office (TAPO) of the Foreign Agricultural Service (FAS) serves as the first point of contact for persons who need information on foreign markets for agricultural products or assistance in accessing government programs. For more information, contact

Foreign Agricultural Service
Trade Assistance and Promotion Office
Tel: (202) 720-7420; Fax (202) 205-9728
Web site: www.fas.usda.gov

The Commodity Credit Corporation (CCC)

The Commodity Credit Corporation (CCC) administers two export credit guarantee programs established to insure financing for sales of U.S. agricultural commodities overseas. The Export Credit Guarantee Program (GSM-102) provides coverage for financing with repayment terms from 90 days to three years. The intermediate Export Credit Guarantee Program (GSM-103) provides coverage on credit terms longer than three years to ten years. Currently, maximum terms under GSM-103 do not exceed seven years. Through these programs, the U.S. Department of Agriculture (USDA) makes about $5 billion in GSM-102 coverage available globally each fiscal year and about $500 million in GSM-103.

These programs allow foreign buyers to purchase U.S. agricultural commodities from private U.S. exporters, with U.S. banks providing financing to the importers' banks on commercial terms. Under both programs, CCC is the guarantor and does not finance the export of the commodities. CCC typically insures up to 98 percent of the principal and a portion of the interest. Both guarantee programs provide variable interest rate coverage, which is based on a percentage of the average investment rate of the 52-week treasury bill.

These programs operate in countries where credit is necessary to increase or maintain U.S. exports and where private financial institutions may be unwilling to provide financing without the CCC's guarantee. These programs are designed to increase U.S. exports by assisting overseas buyers in making commercial purchases.

The CCC also oversees several other programs for agricultural exporters, as described below. Basic information required to participate in the programs described below is contained in the Code of Federal Regulations 7 CFR Part 1494, Subpart B. Copies of press releases and summaries of activities, are available through fax polling at (202) 720-1728. For a copy of regulations or to learn more about the programs, contact

CCC Operations Division
Room 4519-South
14th & Independence Avenue SW
Washington, D.C. 20250-1000
Tel: (202) 720-26211; Fax: (202) 720-2949

Dairy Export Incentive Program (DEIP)

The Dairy Export Incentive Program (DEIP) helps exporters of U.S. dairy products meet prevailing world prices for targeted dairy products and destinations. Under the program, the U.S. Department of Agriculture pays cash to exporters as bonuses, allowing them to sell certain U.S. dairy products at prices below the exporter's costs of acquiring them. Major objectives of the program are to challenge unfair trade practices, to encourage other countries exporting agricultural commodities to undertake serious negotiations on agricultural trade problems, and to expand U.S. agricultural exports.

The DEIP helps U.S. agricultural producers, processors, and exporters gain access to foreign markets. The program makes possible sales of U.S. agricultural products that would otherwise not have been made due to subsidized prices offered by competitor countries.

Commodities eligible under DEIP initiatives are milk powder, butterfat, and Cheddar, mozzarella, Gouda, feta, cream, and processed American cheeses.

Export Enhancement Program (EEP)

The Export Enhancement Program (EEP) helps products produced by U.S. farmers meet competition from subsidizing countries, especially the European Union. Under the program, the U.S. Department of Agriculture pays cash to exporters as bonuses, allowing them to sell U.S. agricultural products in targeted countries at prices below the exporter's costs of acquiring them. Major objectives of the program are to challenge unfair trade practices, to encourage other countries exporting agricultural commodities to undertake serious negotiations on agricultural trade problems, and to expand U.S. agricultural exports.

The EEP helps U.S. agricultural producers, processors, and exporters gain access to foreign markets. The program makes possible sales of U.S. agricultural products that would otherwise not have been made due to subsidized prices offered by competitor countries.

Commodities eligible under EEP initiatives are wheat, wheat flour, semolina, rice, frozen poultry, frozen pork, barley, barley malt, table eggs, and vegetable oil. USDA operates similar programs to assist in the export of dairy products and sunflowerseed and cottonseed oils.

Market Promotion Program (MPP)

The Market Promotion Program (MPP) uses funds from the CCC to help U.S. producers, exporters, and other trade organizations finance promotional activities for U.S. agricultural products. The MPP encourages the development, maintenance, and expansion of commercial export markets for agricultural commodities. Activities financed include consumer promotions, market research, technical assistance, and trade servicing.

The Export Incentive Program (EIP)—a subcomponent of the MPP—helps U.S. commercial entities conduct brand promotion activities including advertising, trade shows, in-store demonstrations, and trade seminars. Generally, the CCC reimburses EIP participants for no more than 50 percent of a brand promotion activity.

The MPP and EIP helps develop new markets and increase U.S. agricultural exports. Exports not only provide income for U.S. farmers and their suppliers, but also generate employment throughout the U.S. economy. About 80 percent of MPP funds have been allocated to high-value products-the fastest growing component of the world's agricultural trade.

New MPP regulations to strengthen compliance and standards were put into place in February 1995. Among the changes reflected in the new regulations are the following: 1) small businesses are given priority assistance; 2) paperwork requirements are reduced; 3) program terms, application procedures, and approval criteria are clarified and simplified; 4) program performance measures and compliance standards are strengthened; and 5) program assistance for promotion of brand products in a single country is generally limited to no more than 5 years.

USDA has approved MPP proposals to promote a wide variety of U.S. commodities in almost every region of the world. Among those U.S. food and fiber products are: apples, asparagus, canned peaches and fruit cocktail, catfish, cherries, citrus, cotton, dairy products, dry beans, eggs, feed grains, frozen potatoes, ginseng, feed grains, grapes, honey, hops, kiwifruit, meat, mink pelts, peanuts, pears, pet food, pistachios, poultry meat, prunes, raisins, rice, salmon, soybeans, strawberries, sunflower seeds, surimi, tallow, tomato products, walnuts, and wheat.

To submit a MPP proposal or to find out the status of programs under consideration, contact the Marketing Operations Staff, Tel: (202) 720-5521; Fax: (202) 720-9361.

Sunflowerseed Oil Assistance Program (SOAP) and Cottonseed Oil Assistance Program (COAP)

The Sunflowerseed Oil Assistance Program (SOAP) and the Cottonseed Oil Assistance Program (COAP) are designed to help U.S. exporters meet prevailing world prices for sunflowerseed oil and cottonseed oil in targeted markets. Under the programs, the U.S. Department of Agriculture (USDA) pays cash to U.S. exporters as bonuses, making up the difference between the higher U.S. cost of acquiring these vegetable oils and the lower world price at which they are sold.

The SOAP and COAP help U.S. sunflowerseed and cottonseed producers, processors, and vegetable oil exporters gain access to foreign markets.

Overseas Private Investment Corporation

The Overseas Private Investment Corporation (OPIC) facilitates U.S. foreign direct investment in nearly 140 developing nations worldwide. OPIC is an independent, financially self-supporting corporation, fully owned by the U.S. government.

OPIC encourages U.S. investment projects overseas by offering political risk insurance; financing businesses through guaranties and direct loans; supporting private investment funds to provide equity for U.S. companies investing in overseas projects; and engaging in outreach activities to inform the U.S. business community of overseas investment opportunities. Projects must have a positive effect on U.S. employment, are financially sound, and promise benefits to the social and economic development of the host country.

For more information, call OPIC's automated information retrieval systems. The InfoLine allows callers to listen to brief recorded program descriptions, request that printed information be sent to them via fax or email, or speak with an OPIC Information Officer (during business hours). You may bypass the InfoLine and proceed directly to OPIC FactsLine, and automated fax retrieval system.

Overseas Private Investment Corporation
1100 New York Ave. NW
Washington, DC 20527
Tel: (202) 336-8400; Fax: (202) 408-9859
OPIC InfoLine, Tel: (202) 336-8799
OPIC FactsLine, Tel: (202) 336-8700
Email: OPIC/S=INFO@mhs.attmail.com
Web site: www.opic.gov

OPIC Investment Insurance

U.S. exporters and contractors operating abroad can benefit from OPIC programs covering wrongful calling of performance, bid, and down payment bonds and contract repudiation. Under other programs, OPIC ensures against expropriation of construction equipment temporarily located abroad, spare parts warehoused abroad, and some cross-border operating and capital loans.

OPIC political risk insurance protects U.S. investment ventures abroad against the risks of three political risks:

- **Currency inconvertibility** Deterioration of the investor's ability to convert profits, debt service and other remittances from local currency into U.S. dollars.
- **Expropriation** Loss of investment due to expropriation, nationalization, or confiscation by a foreign government
- **Political violence** Loss of assets or income due to war, revolution, insurrection, or politically motivated civil strife, terrorism, and sabotage.

OPIC also has several insurance programs for financial institutions, oil and gas projects, natural resource projects, leasing arrangements, and contractors and exporters.

The term of an insurance policy may extend to a maximum of 20 years, depending on the type of policy. OPIC requires that investors bear at least 10 percent of the risk of loss, with a few exceptions.

Interested investors must first register their projects with OPIC with *OPIC Form 50: Request for Registration* for Political Risk Investment Insurance. Once this has been confirmed and the final form of investment is determined, the investor submits *OPIC Form 52: Application for Political Risk Investment Insurance.*

OPIC Investment Finance

Project Financing

OPIC provides project financing through direct loans and loan guarantees that provide medium- to long-term funding to ventures involving significant equity and/or management participation by U.S. businesses. OPIC does not participate in projects that can secure adequate financing from commercial sources. Project financing looks for repayment from the cash flow generated by projects. Many of OPIC's financings involve at least one other lender or independent investor, and large projects may involve several such institutions.

OPIC may assist in designing the financial plan and in coordinating it with other lenders and investors. OPIC can generally participate in up to 50 percent of the total costs of a new venture.

Small business or cooperative projects are commonly financed through direct loans in the $2 million to $10 million range. Larger projects are more often funded through loan guaranties ranging from $10 million to $100 million, although they may go as high as $200 million.

To apply for OPIC financing, the project sponsor should submit OPIC *Form 115: Application for Financing* and a business plan for the proposed project.

OPIC also provides services to facilitate wider participation by smaller U.S. businesses in overseas investment, including investment missions, a computerized data bank, and investor information services.

Investment Funds

OPIC can provide financing to support privately owned and managed direct investment funds that can provide equity capital to facilitate business formation and expansion. One fund invests exclusively in small businesses, while another invests only in new or expanding companies that improve the natural environment. Other regional and sectoral funds are planned. Each portfolio company must have a significant business connection with the U.S. economy and must meet various OPIC standards.

Small Business Administration Assistance

The Small Business Administration (SBA) also provides financial assistance programs for U.S. exporters. Applicants must qualify as small businesses under the SBA's size standards and meet other eligibility criteria. The major programs are outlined below. For more specific information on SBA's financial assistance programs, policies, and requirements, contact the nearest SBA field office or U.S. Export Assistance Center (USEAC) or SBA's Small Business Answer Desk at Tel: (800) 8-ASK-SBA.

Export Working Capital Program (EWCP)

SBA's Export Working Capital Program (EWCP), which replaces the former Export Revolving Line of Credit, provides short-term, transaction-specific financing for loans of $833,333 or less. Exporters may use this program for pre-export financing of labor and materials, financing receivables generated from these sales; and/or standby letters of credit used as performance bonds or payment guarantees to foreign buyers. The EWCP provides repayment guarantees of 75 percent or $750,000 (whichever is less) to commercial lenders and offers exporters preliminary commitments (PCs) that encourage lenders to provide credit. To be eligible, the small business concern must have been in operation, though not necessarily exporting, for at least 12 months. The EWCP offers a simplified application form. Interest rates and fees are negotiable between the lender and the small business exporter.

International Trade Loan Program (ITL)

The ITL helps small businesses that are engaged or preparing to engage in international trade, as well as small businesses adversely affected by competition from imports. SBA can guarantee up to $1.25 million, less the amount of SBA's guaranteed portion of other loans outstanding, to the borrower under SBA's regular lending program. Loans are made by lending institutions with the SBA guaranteeing a portion of the loan. The applicant must establish either that the loan proceeds will significantly expand existing export markets, or develop new export markets, or that the small business is adversely affected by import competition. Proceeds may be used for working capital and/or facilities or equipment. Maturities of loans for facilities or equipment may extend to the 25-year maximum.

Although SBA loans are generally limited to $750,000 to $1.25 million, larger loans can be financed by using a cooperative agreement between SBA and Ex-Im Bank. This option may be attractive to a company with an existing SBA loan or one whose bank would prefer to work through a local SBA office, since Ex-Im Bank is based in Washington, D.C.

Both the EWCP and the ILP programs are guarantee programs that require the participation of an eligible commercial bank. Most bankers are familiar with SBA's guarantee programs.

In addition, other SBA programs may meet specific needs of exporters. These include loans from the SBA's regular 7(1) Loan Guaranty Program, Small Business Investment Company (SBIC) Financing, and various business development and legal assistance programs.

State and Local Export Finance Programs

Several cities and states have funded and operational export financing programs, including preshipment and postshipment working capital loans and guarantees, accounts receivable financing, and export insurance. To be eligible for these programs, an export sale must generally be made under a letter of credit or with credit insurance coverage. A certain percentage of state or local content may also be required. However, some programs may require only that certain facilities, such as a state or local port, be used; therefore, exporters may have several options.

Exporters should contact an Export Assistance Center or Department of Commerce district office or their state economic development agency for more information. (*Refer to* Appendix III, "State and Local Sources of Assistance" on page 130.)

Chapter 15

After-Sales Service

Three factors are critical to the success of any export sales effort: quality, price, and service. Quality and price are dealt with in other chapters. Service should be an integral part of any company's export strategy from the start. Properly handled, service can be a foundation for growth. Ignored or left to chance, it can cause an export effort to fail.

Service is the prompt delivery of the product. It is courteous sales personnel. It is a localized user manual or service manual. It is ready access to a service facility. It is knowledgeable, cost-effective maintenance, repair, or replacement. Service is location. Service is dealer support.

Service varies by the product type, the quality of the product, the price of the product, and the distribution channel employed. For export products that require no service—such as food products, some consumer goods, and commercial disposables—the issue is resolved once distribution channels, quality criteria, and return policies have been identified.

On the other hand, the characteristics of consumer durables and some consumables demand that service be available. For such products, service is a feature expected by the consumer. In fact, foreign buyers of industrial goods typically place service at the forefront of the criteria they evaluate when making a purchase decision.

All foreign markets are sophisticated, and each has its own expectations of suppliers and vendors. U.S. manufacturers or distributors must therefore ensure that their service performance is comparable to that of the predominant competitors in the market. This level of performance is an important determinant in ensuring a reasonable competitive position, given the other factors of product quality, price, promotion, and delivery.

An exporting firm's strategy and market entry decision may dictate that it does not provide after-sale service. It may determine that its export objective is the single or multiple opportunistic entry into export markets. Although this approach may work in the short term, subsequent product offerings will be less successful as buyers recall the failure to provide expected levels of service. As a result, market development and sales expenditures may result in one-time sales. Instead of saving money by cutting back on service, the company will see lower profits (because expenses are not spread over longer production runs), ongoing sales programs, and multiple sales to developed buyers.

Service Delivery Options

Service is an important factor in the initial export sale and ongoing success of products in foreign markets. U.S. firms have many options for the delivery of service to foreign buyers.

A high-cost option—and the most inconvenient for the foreign retail, wholesale, commercial, or industrial buyer—is for the product to be returned to the manufacturing or distribution facility in the United States for service or repair. The buyer incurs a high cost and loses the use of the product for an extended period, while the seller must incur the export cost of the same product a second time to return it. Fortunately, there are practical, cost-effective alternatives to this approach.

If the selected export distribution channel is a joint venture or other partnership arrangement, the overseas partner may have a service or repair capability in the markets to be penetrated. An exporting firm's negotiations and agreements with its partner should include explicit provisions for repairs, maintenance, and warranty service. The cost of providing this service should be negotiated into the agreement.

For goods sold at retail outlets, a preferred service option is to identify and use local service facilities. Doing so requires front-end expenses to identify and train local service outlets, but such costs are more than repaid in the long run.

An excellent case study on this issue involves a foreign firm's service approach to the U.S. market. A leading Canadian manufacturer of consumer personal care items uses U.S. distributors and sales representatives to generate purchases by large and small retailers across the United States. The products are purchased at retail by individual consumers. The Canadian firm contracted with local consumer electronic repair facilities in leading U.S. cities to provide service or replacement for its product line. Consequently, the manufacturer can include a certificate with each product listing "authorized" local warranty and service centers.

There are administrative, training, and supervisory overhead costs associated with such a warranty and service program. The benefit, however, is that the company is now perceived to be a local company that competes on equal footing with domestic U.S. manufacturers. U.S. exporters should keep this example in mind when entering foreign markets.

Exporting a product into commercial or industrial markets may dictate a different approach. For the many U.S. companies that sell through distributors, selection of a representative to serve a region, a nation, or a market should be based not only on the distributing company's ability to sell effectively but also on its ability and willingness to service the product.

Assessing that ability to service requires that the exporter ask questions about existing service facilities; about the types, models, and age of existing service equipment; about training practices for service personnel; and about the firm's experience in servicing similar products.

If the product being exported is to be sold directly to end users, service and timely performance are critical to success. The nature of the product may require delivery of on-site service to the buyer within very specific time parameters. These are negotiable issues for which the U.S. exporter must be prepared. Such on-site service may be available from service organizations in the buyer's country; or the exporting company may have to send personnel to the site to provide service. The sales contract should anticipate a reasonable level of on-site service and should include the associated costs. Existing performance and service history can serve as a guide for estimating service and warranty requirements on export sales, and sales can be costed accordingly. This practice is accepted among small and large exporters alike.

At some level of export activity, it may become cost-effective for a U.S. company to establish its own branch or subsidiary operation in the foreign market. The branch or subsidiary may be a one-person operation or a more extensive facility staffed with sales, administration, service, and other personnel, most of whom are nationals in the market. This high-cost option enables the exporter to ensure sales and service quality, provided that personnel are trained in sales, products, and service on an ongoing basis. The benefits of this option include the control it gives to the exporter and the ability to serve multiple markets in a single region.

Manufacturers of similar or related products may find it cost-effective to consolidate service, training, and support in each export market. Service can be delivered by U.S.-based personnel, a foreign facility under contract, or a jointly owned foreign-based service facility. Despite its cost benefits, this option raises a number of issues. Such joint activity may be interpreted as being in restraint of trade or otherwise market controlling or monopolistic. Exporters that are considering it should therefore obtain competent legal counsel when developing this joint operating arrangement. Exporters may wish to consider obtaining an export trade certificate of review, which provides limited immunity from U.S. antitrust laws.

Legal Considerations

Service is a very important part of many types of representation agreements. For better or worse, the quality of service in a country or region affects the U.S. manufacturer's reputation there.

Quality of service also affects the intellectual property rights of the manufacturer. A trademark is a mark of source, with associated quality and performance. If quality control is not maintained, the manufacturer can lose its rights to the product, because one can argue that, within that foreign market, the manufacturer has abandoned the trademark to the distributor.

It is, therefore, imperative that agreements with a representative be specific about the form of the repair or service facility, the number of people on the staff, inspection provisions, training programs, and payment of costs associated with maintaining a suitable facility. The depth or breadth of a warranty in a given country or region should be tied to the service facility to which the manufacturer has access in that market; it is important to promise only what can be delivered.

Another part of the representative agreement may detail the training the exporter will provide to its foreign representative. This detail can include frequency of training, who must be trained, where the training is provided, and which party absorbs travel and per diem costs.

New Sales Opportunities and Improved Customer Relations

Foreign buyers of U.S.-manufactured products typically have limited contact with the manufacturer or its personnel. The foreign service facility is, in fact, one of the major contact points between the exporter and the buyer. To a great extent, the U.S. manufacturer's reputation is made by the overseas service facility.

The service experience can be a positive and reinforcing sales and service encounter. It can also be an excellent sales opportunity if the service personnel are trained to take advantage of the situation. Service personnel can help the customer make life cycle decisions regarding the efficient operation of the product, how to update it for more and longer cost-effective operation, and when to replace it as the task expands or changes. Each service contact is an opportunity to educate the customer and expand the exporter's sales opportunities.

Service is also an important aspect of selling solutions and benefits rather than product features. More than one leading U.S. industrial products exporter sells its products as a "tool to do the job" rather than as a "truck" or a "cutting machine" or "software." Service capability enables customers to complete their jobs more efficiently with the exporter's "tool." Training service managers and personnel in this type of thinking vitalizes service facilities and generates new sales opportunities.

Each foreign market offers a unique opportunity for the U.S. exporter. Care and attention to the development of in-country sales and distribution capabilities is paramount. Delivery of after-sales service is critical to the near- and long-term success of the U.S. company's efforts in any market.

Senior personnel should commit to a program of regular travel to each foreign market to meet with the company's representatives, clients, and others who are important to the success of the firm in that market. Among those persons would be the commercial officer at the US&FCS post and representatives of the American chamber of commerce and the local chamber of commerce or business association.

The benefits of such a program are twofold. First, executive management learns more about the foreign marketplace and the firm's capabilities. Second, the in-country representative appreciates the attention and understands the importance of the foreign market in the exporter's long-term plans. As a result, such visits help build a strong, productive relationship.

Chapter 16

Technology Licensing and Joint Ventures

Technology Licensing

Technology licensing is a contractual arrangement in which the licenser's patents, trademarks, service marks, copyrights, or know-how may be sold or otherwise made available to a licensee for compensation negotiated in advance between the parties. Such compensation, known as *royalties*, may consist of a *lump sum royalty*, a *running royalty* (royalty based on volume of production), or a combination of both. U.S. companies frequently license their patents, trademarks, copyrights, and know-how to a foreign company that then manufactures and sells products based on the technology in a country or group of countries authorized by the licensing agreement.

A technology licensing agreement usually enables a U.S. firm to enter a foreign market quickly, yet it poses fewer financial and legal risks than owning and operating a foreign manufacturing facility or participating in an overseas joint venture. Licensing also permits U.S. firms to overcome many of the tariff and nontariff barriers that frequently hamper the export of U.S.-manufactured products. For these reasons, licensing can be a particularly attractive method of exporting for small companies or companies with little international trade experience, although licensing is profitably employed by large and small firms alike. Technology licensing can also be used to acquire foreign technology (e.g., through cross-licensing agreements or *grantback clauses* granting rights to improvement technology developed by a licensee).

Technology licensing is not limited to the manufacturing sector. Franchising is also an important form of technology licensing used by many service industries. In franchising, the franchisor (licenser) permits the franchisee (licensee) to employ its trademark or service mark in a contractually specified manner for the marketing of goods or services. The franchisor usually continues to support the operation of the franchisee's business by providing advertising, accounting, training, and related services and in many instances also supplies products needed by the franchisee.

As a form of exporting, technology licensing has certain potential drawbacks. The negative aspects of licensing are that (1) control over the technology is weakened because it has been transferred to an unaffiliated firm and (2) licensing usually produces fewer profits than exporting goods or services produced in the United States. In certain Third World countries, there also may be problems in adequately protecting the licensed technology from unauthorized use by third parties.

In considering the licensing of technology, it is important to remember that foreign licensees may attempt to use the licensed technology to manufacture products that are marketed in the United States or third countries in direct competition with the licenser or its other licensees. In many instances, U.S. licensers may wish to impose territorial restrictions on their foreign licensees, depending on U.S. or foreign antitrust laws and the licensing laws of the host country. Also, U.S. and foreign patent, trademark, and copyright laws can often be used to bar unauthorized sales by foreign licensees, provided that the U.S. licenser has valid patent, trademark, or copyright protection in the United States or the other countries involved. In addition, unauthorized exports to the United States by foreign licensees can often be prevented by filing unfair import practices complaints under section 337 of the Tariff Act of 1930 with the U.S. International Trade Commission and by recording U.S. trademarks and copyrights with the U.S. Customs Service. Contact the Office of Unfair Import Investigations at Tel: (202) 205-2558; Fax: (202) 205-2158, for information on filing a complaint.

As in all overseas transactions, it is important to investigate not only the prospective licensee but the licensee's country as well. The government of the host country often must approve the licensing agreement before it goes into effect. Such governments, for example, may prohibit royalty payments that exceed a certain rate or contractual provisions barring the licensee from exporting products manufactured with or embodying the licensed technology to third countries.

The prospective licenser must always take into account the host country's foreign patent, trademark, and copyright laws; exchange controls; product liability laws; possible countertrading or barter requirements; antitrust and tax laws; and attitudes toward repatriation of royalties and dividends. The existence of a tax treaty or bilateral investment treaty between the United States and the prospective host country is an important indicator of the overall commercial relationship. Prospective U.S. licensers, especially of advanced technology, also should determine whether they need to obtain an export license from the U.S. Department of Commerce.

International technology licensing agreements, in a few instances, can unlawfully restrain trade in violation of U.S. or foreign antitrust laws. U.S. antitrust law, as a general rule, prohibits international technology licensing agreements that unreasonably restrict imports of competing goods or technology into the United States or unreasonably restrain U.S. domestic competition or exports by U.S. persons.

Whether or not a restraint is reasonable is a fact-specific determination that is made after consideration of the availability of competing goods or technology; market shares; barriers to entry; the business justifications for and the duration of contractual restraints; valid patents, trademarks, and copyrights; and certain other factors. The U.S. Department of Justice's *Antitrust Enforcement Guidelines for International Operations* (Revised in1995) contains useful advice regarding the legality of various types of international transactions, including technology licensing. In those instances in which significant federal antitrust issues are presented, U.S. licensers may wish to consider applying for an export trade certificate of review from the Department of Commerce (*refer to* Chapter 4, "Methods of Exporting and Channels of Distribution," beginning on page 25) or requesting a Department of Justice business review letter.

Foreign countries, particularly the EC, also have strict antitrust laws that affect technology licensing. The EC has issued detailed regulations governing patent and know-how licensing. These block exemption regulations are entitled "Commission Regulation (EEC) No. 2349/84 of 23 July 1984 on the Application of Article 85(3) of the Treaty [of Rome] to Certain Categories of Patent Licensing Agreements" and "Commission Regulation (EEC) No. 556/89 of 30 November 1988 on the Application of Article 85(3) of the Treaty to Certain Categories of Know-how Licensing Agreements." These regulations should be carefully considered by anyone currently licensing or contemplating the licensing of technology to the EC.

Because of the potential complexity of international technology licensing agreements, firms should seek qualified legal advice in the United States before entering into such an agreement. In many instances, U.S. licensors should also retain qualified legal counsel in the host country in order to obtain advice on applicable local laws and to receive assistance in securing the foreign government's approval of the agreement. Sound legal advice and thorough investigation of the prospective licensee and the host country increase the likelihood that the licensing agreement will be a profitable transaction and help decrease or avoid potential problems.

Joint Ventures

There are a number of business and legal reasons why unassisted exporting may not be the best export strategy for a U.S. company. In such cases, the firm may wish to consider a joint venture with a firm in the host country. International joint ventures are used in a wide variety of manufacturing, mining, and service industries and are frequently undertaken in conjunction with technology licensing by the U.S. firm to the joint venture.

The host country may require that a certain percentage (often 51 percent) of manufacturing or mining operations be owned by nationals of that country, thereby requiring U.S. firms to operate through joint ventures. In addition to such legal requirements, U.S. firms may find it desirable to enter into a joint venture with a foreign firm to help spread the high costs and risks frequently associated with foreign operations.

Moreover, the local partner may bring to the joint venture its knowledge of the customs and tastes of the people, an established distribution network, and valuable business and political contacts. Having local partners also decreases the foreign status of the firm and may provide some protection against discrimination or expropriation, should conditions change.

There are, of course, possible disadvantages to international joint ventures. A major potential drawback to joint ventures, especially in countries that limit foreign companies to 49 percent or less participation, is the loss of effective managerial control. A loss of effective managerial control can result in reduced profits, increased operating costs, inferior product quality, and exposure to product liability and environmental litigation and fines. U.S. firms that wish to retain effective managerial control will find this issue an important topic in negotiations with the prospective joint venture partner and frequently the host government as well.

Like technology licensing agreements, joint ventures can raise U.S. or foreign antitrust issues in certain circumstances, particularly when the prospective joint venture partners are major existing or potential competitors in the affected national markets. Firms may wish to consider applying for an export trade certificate of review from the Department of Commerce (*see* "Export Trading Company Act of 1982" on page 26 for more information) or a business review letter from the Department of Justice when significant federal antitrust issues are raised by the proposed international joint venture.

Because of the complex legal issues frequently raised by international joint venture agreements, it is very important, before entering into any such agreement, to seek legal advice from qualified U.S. counsel experienced in this aspect of international trade. Many of the export counseling sources in Chapter 2, "Export Advice," beginning on page 6, can help direct a U.S. company to local counsel suitable for its needs.

U.S. firms contemplating international joint ventures also should consider retaining experienced counsel in the host country. U.S. firms can find it very disadvantageous to rely upon their potential joint venture partners to negotiate host government approvals and advise them on legal issues, since their prospective partners' interests may not always coincide with their own. Qualified foreign counsel can be very helpful in obtaining government approvals and providing ongoing advice regarding the host country's patent, trademark, copyright, tax, labor, corporate, commercial, antitrust, and exchange control laws.

Export Glossary

Acronyms

ABC	Asia Business Center
ADS	Agent/Distributor Service
AES	Automated Export System
AgExport	Agricultural Export Services Division
AGRICOLA	Agricultural OnLine Access database
ALF	Agricultural Libraries Forum
AID	Agency for International Development
AmCham	American Chamber of Commerce
APHIS	Animal and Plant Health Inspection Service
ANSI	American National Standards Institute
BISNIS	Business Information Service for the Newly Independent States
BXA	Bureau of Export Administration
CBD	Commerce Business Daily
CCC	Commodity Credit Corporation
CCG	Country Commercial Guide
CCL	Commerce Control List
CDC	Centers for Disease Control
CDIC	Country Directory of International Contacts
CEEBIC	Central and Eastern Europe Business Information Center
CFR	Code of Federal Regulations
CFR	cost and freight
CFS	Contact Facilitation Service
CIF	cost, insurance, freight
CIP	carriage and insurance paid to
CIMS	Commercial Information Management System
CISG	Contracts for the International Sale of Goods
CJ	commodity jurisdiction
CMA	Customized Market Analysis
CMP	country marketing plan
CNUSA	*Commercial News USA*
COAP	Cottonseed Oil Assistance Program
CPT	carriage paid to
CSIC	Commercial Service International Contacts
CTIS	Center for Trade & Investment Services
DA	Delegated Authority Program
DEC	district export council
DEIP	Dairy Export Incentive Program
DISC	Domestic International Sales Corporation
DOC	U.S. Department of Commerce
DOE	Department of Energy
DOSFAN	
DTSA	Defense Technology and Security Administration
EAA	Export Administration Act
EAC	Export Assistance Center
EAR	Export Administration Regulations
EBB	Economic Bulletin Board
ECCN	Export Control Classification Number
ECLS	Export Contact List Service
EE	Export Enforcement
EEP	Export Enhancement Program
EIN	Employer Identification Number
EIP	Export Incentive Program
ELAN	Export Legal Assistance Network
EMC	export management company
EPA	Environmental Protection Agency
ERIC	
ERS	Economic Research Service
ETC	export trading company
ETCA	Export Trading Company Act
ETNA	Environmental Technology Network for Asia
EU	European Union
EWCP	Export Working Capital Program
Ex-Im Bank	Export-Import Bank of the United States
EXW	ex works
FAS	Foreign Agricultural Service
FAS	free alongside ship
FBA	Federal Bar Association
FDA	Food and Drug Administration
FCA	free carrier

FCIA	Foreign Credit Insurance Association
FCPA	Foreign Corrupt Practices Act
FIFRA	Federal Insecticide, Fungicide, and Rodenticide Act
FOB	free on board
FR	Federal Register
FGIS	Federal Grain Inspection Service
FSC	Foreign Sales Corporation
FSIS	Food Safety and Inspection Service
FTSR	Foreign Trade Statistics Regulations
FTZ	Foreign-Trade Zone
GATS	General Agreement on Trade in Services
GATT	General Agreement on Tariffs and Trade
GPO	Government Printing Office
IAA	International Advertising Association
ICC	International Chamber of Commerce
ICP	International Company Profile
IEP	International Economic Policy
IFS	International Financial Statistics
IMF	International Monetary Fund
IRS	Internal Revenue Service
ISA	Industry Sector Analysis
ISI	International Market Insights
ISIS	Integrated System for Information Services
ITA	International Trade Administration
ITL	International Trade Loan Program
JEIC	Japan Export Information Center
L/C	letter of credit
MBDA	Minority Business Development Agency
MBDC	Minority Business Development Center
MBE	minority business enterprise
MFN	most favored nation
MPP	Market Promotion Program
MRC	Minority Resource Center
NAFTA	North American Free Trade Agreement
NCSCI	National Center for Standards and Certification Information
NOAA	National Oceanic and Atmospheric Administration
NMFS	National Marine Fisheries Service
NTDB	National Trade Data Bank
NIST	National Institute of Standards and Technology
NRC	Nuclear Regulatory Commission
OAC	Office of Antiboycott Compliance
OECD	Organization for Economic Cooperation and Development
OEE	Office of Export Enforcement
OETCA	Office of Export Trading Company Affairs
OIT	Office of International Trade
OPIC	Overseas Private Investment Corporation
OSDBU	Office of Small and Disadvantaged Business Utilization
OSI	Office of Service Industries
PCs	preliminary commitments (
PLP	Priority Lending Program
RCRA	Resource Conservation and Recovery Act
RSVP	Research Strategic Venture Partners
SED	Shipper's Export Declaration
SBA	Small Business Administration
SBAtlas	SBA's Automated Trade Locator Assistance System
SBDC	Small Business Development Center
SBI	Small Business Institute
SBIC	Small Business Investment Company
SCORE	Service Corps of Retired Executives
SEC	Securities and Exchange Commission
SED	Shipper's Export Declarations
SOAP	Sunflowerseed Oil Assistance Program
TAPO	Trade Assistance and Promotion Office
TDA	Trade and Development Agency
TIC	Trade Information Center
TOP	Trade Opportunity Program
TPCC	Trade Promotion Coordinating Committee
TRA	Tax Reform Act
TRIPs	Trade Related Aspects of Intellectual Property Rights Agreement
TSCA	Toxic Substances Control Act
UN	United Nations
UNCITRAL	UN Commission on International Trade Law
URAA	Uruguay Round Agreements Act
US&FCS	U.S. and Foreign Commercial Service
US-AEP	U.S.-Asia Environmental Partnership
USAID	U.S. Agency for International Development
USDA	U.S. Department of Agriculture
USEAC	U.S. Export Assistance Center
USITC	U.S. International Trade Commission
WTC	World Trade Center
WTCA	World Trade Centers Association
WTDR	World Traders Data Report
WTO	World Trade Organization

Definitions

Note: These definitions are excerpted from the World Trade Press *Dictionary of International Trade,* © 1999.

acceptance

(law) (a) An unconditional assent to an offer. (b) An assent to an offer conditioned on only minor changes that do not affect any material terms of the offer.

(shipping) Receipt by the consignee of a shipment thus terminating the common carrier liability.

ad valorem

Literally: according to value.

(general) Any charge, tax, or duty that is applied as a a percentage of value.

(taxation) A tax calculated on the value of the property subject to the tax.

(shipping) A freight rate set at a certain percentage of the declared value of an article.

(U.S. Customs) Ad valorem duty. A duty assessed as a percentage rate or value of the imported merchandise. For example, 5% ad valorem. *See also* duty.

advance against collection

(banking) A short term loan or credit extended to the seller (usually the exporter) by the seller's bank once a draft has been accepted by the buyer (generally the importer) of the seller's goods. Once the buyer pays the loan is paid off. If the buyer does not pay the draft, the seller must still make good on the loan.

advising bank

(banking) The bank (also referred to as the seller's or exporter's bank) which receives a letter of credit or amendment to a letter of credit from the issuing bank (the buyer's bank) and forwards it to the beneficiary (seller/exporter) of the credit. *See also* letter of credit.

advisory capacity

A term indicating that a shipper's agent or representative is not empowered to make definitive decisions or adjustments without approval of the group or individual represented. *Compare to* without reserve.

agent

(law) An individual or legal entity authorized to act on behalf of another individual or legal entity (the principal). An agent's authorized actions will bind the principal. A sales representative, for example, is an agent of the seller.

air waybill (airbill)

(Shipping) A shipping document used by the airlines for air freight. It is a contract for carriage that includes carrier conditions of carriage including such items as limits of liability and claims procedures. The air waybill also contains shipping instructions to airlines, a description of the commodity and applicable transportation charges. Air waybills are used by many truckers as through documents for coordinated air/truck service.

Air waybills are not negotiable. The airline industry has adopted a standard formatted air waybill that accommodates both domestic and international traffic. The standard document was designed to enhance the application of modern computerized systems to air freight processing for both the carrier and the shipper. *See also* bill of lading.

alongside

(shipping) A phrase referring to the side of a ship. (a) Goods to be delivered "alongside" are to be placed on the dock or lighter within reach of the transport ship's tackle so that they can be loaded aboard the ship. (b) Goods delivered to the port of embarkation, but without loading fees.

arbitrage

(banking/finance/foreign exchange) The simultaneous buying and selling (or borrowing and lending) of identical securities, currencies, or commodities in two or more markets to take advantage of price differentials.

ATA Carnet

(customs) ATA stands for the combined French and English words Admission Temporair/Temporary Admission." An ATA Carnet is an international customs document which may be used for the temporary duty-free admission of certain goods into a country in lieu of the usual customs documents required. The carnet serves as a guarantee against the payment of customs duties which may become due on goods temporarily imported and not re-exported. Quota compliance may be required on certain types of merchandise.

ATA Carnets are issued by National Chambers of Commerce affiliated with the Paris-based International Chamber of Commerce (ICC). These associations guarantee the payment of duties to local customs authorities should good imported under cover of a foreign-issued carnet not be re-exported.

The issuing and guaranteeing organization in the United States is: U.S. Council, International Chamber of Commerce, 1212 Avenue of the Americas, New York, NY 10036; Tel: (212) 354-4480. Additional information can be obtained from The Roanoke Companies, agents for the U.S. Council for International Business. Address: The Roanoke Companies, 1930 Thoreau Drive, Suite 101, Schaumburg, IL 60173; Tel: (800) ROANOKE (800-762-6653), or (847) 490-5940.

See also carnet.

balance of trade

(economics) The difference between a country's total imports and exports over a set period. (a) A balance of trade deficit is when a country imports more than it exports. (b) A balance of trade surplus is when a country exports more than it imports.

barter

The direct exchange of goods for other goods without the use of money as a medium of exchange and without involvement of a third party. *See also* countertrade.

beneficiary

(banking/letter of credit) The individual or company in whose favor a letter of credit is opened.

(insurance) The person or legal entity named to receive the proceeds or benefits of an insurance policy.

bill of exchange

(banking) An unconditional order in writing, signed by a person (drawer) such as a buyer, and addressed to another person (payee), often a seller, on demand or at a fixed or determinable future time. The most common versions of a bill of exchange are sight drafts, time drafts, and promissory notes. The most common versions of a bill of exchange are:

(a) A *draft,* wherein the drawer instructs the drawee to pay a certain amount to a named person, usually in payment for the transfer of goods or services. *Sight drafts* are payable when presented. *Time drafts* (also called usance drafts) are payable at a future fixed (specific) date or determinable (30, 60, 90 days, etc.) date. Time drafts are used as a financing tool to give the buyer time to pay for his purchase.

(b) A *promissory note,* wherein the issuer promises to pay a certain amount.

For more information, *refer to* Chapter 13, "Methods of Payment," beginning on page 88.

bill of lading

A document issued by a carrier to a shipper, signed by the captain, agent, or owner of a vessel, furnishing written evidence regarding receipt of the goods (cargo), the conditions on which transportation is made (contract of carriage), and the engagement to deliver goods at the prescribed port of destination to the lawful holder of the bill of lading. A bill of lading is, therefore, both a receipt for merchandise and a contract to deliver it as freight. *See also* air waybill, inland bill of lading, ocean bill of lading, and through bill of lading.

bonded warehouse

(U.S. Customs) A warehouse owned by persons approved by the Treasury Department, and under bond or guarantee for the strict observance of the revenue laws of the United States; utilized for storing goods until the goods enter the Customs Territory of the United States. The goods are not subject to duties if reshipped to foreign points.

booking

(shipping) The act of recording arrangements for the movement of goods by vessel.

buying agent

See purchasing agent.

carnet

(customs) A customs document permitting the holder to carry or send merchandise temporarily into certain foreign countries (for display, demonstration, or similar purposes) without paying duties or posting bonds. *See also* ATA Carnet.

carrier

(law/shipping) An individual or legal entity that is in the business of that transporting passengers or goods for hire. Shipping lines, airlines, trucking companies and railroad companies are all carriers.

(a) A common carrier is one that by law must convey passengers or goods without refusal, provided the party requesting conveyance has paid the charge for transport. By U.S. government regulation, a common carrier publishes stated rates for carriage and must accept andy passengers or goods for transport so long as space is available and the published rate is paid.

(b) A private or contract carrier is one that transports only those persons or goods that it selects.

cash against documents (CAD)

Payment for goods in which a commission house or other intermediary transfers title documents to the buyer upon payment in cash.

cash in advance (CIA)

Payment for goods in which the price is paid in full before shipment is made. This method is usually used only for small purchases or when the goods are built to order.

cash with order (CWO)

Payment for goods in which the buyer pays when ordering and in which the transaction is binding on both parties.

certificate of inspection

A document certifying that merchandise (such as perishable goods) was in good condition at the time of inspection, usually immediately prior to shipment. Pre-shipment inspection is a requirement for importation of goods into many developing countries. Often used interchangeably with certificate of analysis. *See also* phytosanitary inspection certificate.

certificate of manufacture

A document (often notarized) in which a producer of goods certifies that the manufacturing has been completed and that the goods are now at the disposal of the buyer.

certificate of origin

A document attesting to the country of origin of goods. A certificate of origin is often required by customs authorities of a country as part of the entry process. Such certificates are usually obtained through an official or quasi-official organization in the country of origin, such as a consular office or local chamber of commerce. A certificate of origin may be required even though the commercial invoice contains the information.

cost and freight ... (named port of destination) (CFR)

(Incoterm) "Cost and Freight" (CFR) means that the seller must pay the costs and freight necessary to bring the goods to the named port of destination but the risk of loss of or damage to the goods, as well as any additional costs due to events occurring after the time the goods have been delivered on board the vessel, is transferred from the seller to the buyer when the goods pass the ship's rail in the port of shipment. The CFR term requires the seller to clear the goods for export. For more information, *refer to* Chapter 10, "Pricing, Quotations, and Terms," beginning on page 55.

charter party

A lease or agreement to hire an airplane, vessel, or other means of conveyance to transport goods on a designated voyage to one or more locations.

cost, insurance, freight ... (named port of destination) (CIF)

(Incoterm) "Cost, Insurance, Freight" (CIF) means that the seller has the same obligations as under cost and freight (CFR) but with the addition that he has to procure marine insurance against the buyer's risk of loss of or damage to the goods during the carriage. For more information, *refer to* Chapter 10, "Pricing, Quotations, and Terms," beginning on page 55.

clean bill of lading

(shipping) A bill of lading receipted by the carrier for goods received in "apparent good order and condition," without damages or other irregularities, and without the notation "Shippers Load and Count." *See also* bill of lading

clean draft

(banking) A sight or date draft which has no documents attached to it. This is to be distinguished from documentary draft.

collection papers

All documents (invoices, bills of lading, etc.) submitted to a buyer for the purpose of receiving payment for a shipment.

commercial attache

The commerce expert on the diplomatic staff of his or her country's embassy or large consulate.

commercial invoice

(general) A document identifying the seller and buyer of goods or services, identifying numbers such as invoice number, date, shipping date, mode of transport, delivery and payment terms, and a complete listing and description of the goods and services being sold including prices, discounts and quantities.

(customs) A commercial invoice is often used by governments to determine the true (transaction) value of goods for the assessment of customs duties and also to prepare consular documentation. Governments using the commercial invoice to control imports often specify its form, content, number of copies, language to be used, and other characteristics.

confirmed letter of credit

(banking) A letter of credit which contains a guarantee on the part of both the issuing and advising banks of payment to the seller so long as the seller's documentation is in order and the terms of the letter of credit are met. Confirmation is only added to irrevocable letters of credit, usually available with the advising bank. *See also* letter of credit. *Refer to* Chapter 13.

consignment

(shipping) Shipment of one or more pieces of property, accepted by a carrier for one shipper at one time, receipted for in one lot, and moving on one bill of lading.

(commerce) Delivery of merchandise from an exporter (the consignor) to an agent (the consignee) under agreement that the agent sell the merchandise for the account of the exporter. The consignor retains title to the goods until sold. The consignee sells the goods for commission and remits the net proceeds to the consignor.

consular declaration

A formal statement, made in a country of export by the consul of an importing country, describing goods to be shipped to the importing country. See also consular invoice.

consular invoice

(customs) An invoice covering a shipment of goods certified (usually in triplicate) by the consul of the country for which the merchandise is destined. This invoice is used by customs officials of the country of entry to verify the value, quantity, and nature of the merchandise imported. See also commercial invoice. Refer to Chapter 12).

convertible currency

A currency that can be easily exchanged, bought and sold for other currencies.

correspondent bank

(banking) A bank that acts as a depository for another bank, accepting deposits and collecting items (such as drafts) on a reciprocal basis. Correspondent banks are often in foreign countries.

countertrade

An umbrella term for several sorts of trade in which the seller is required to accept goods or other instruments or trade, in partial or whole payment for its products.

Countertrade transactions include barter, buy-back or compensation, counterpurchase, offset requirements, swap, switch, or triangular trade, evidence or clearing accounts.

countervailing duty

A special duty imposed on imports to offset the benefits of subsidies to producers or exporters in the exporting country. Countervailing duties in the U.S. can only be imposed after the International Trade Commission has determined that the imports are causing or threatening to cause material injury to a U.S. industry.

carriage paid to ... (named port of destination) (CPT)

(Incoterm) "Carriage paid to ... " (CPT) means that the seller pays the freight for the carriage of the goods to the named destination. The risk of loss of or damage to the goods, as well as any additional costs due to events occurring after the time the goods have been delivered to the carrier, is transferred from the seller to the buyer when the goods have been delivered into the custody of the carrier.

carriage and insurance paid to ... (named port of destination) (CIP)

(Incoterm) "Carriage and insurance paid to ... " (CIP) means that the seller has the same obligations as under CPT (carriage paid to) terms, but with the addition that the seller has to procure cargo insurance against the buyer's risk of loss of or damage to the goods during the carriage. The seller contracts for insurance and pays the insurance premium.

credit risk insurance

Insurance designed to cover risks of nonpayment for delivered goods.

customs broker

An individual or firm licensed to act for importers in handling the sequence of customs formalities and other details critical to the legal and speedy exporting and importing of goods.

customs

A government authority designated to regulate the flow of goods to/from a country and to collect duties levied by a country on imports and exports. The term also applies to the procedures involved in such collection.

date draft

A draft that matures in a specified number of days after the date it is issued, without regard to the date of acceptance. *See also* bill of exchange. Also *refer to* Chapter 13, "Methods of Payment," beginning on page 88.

deferred payment letter of credit

(banking) A letter of credit which enables the buyer to take possession of the title documents and the goods by agreeing to pay the issuing bank at a fixed time in the future. *See also* letter of credit.

destination control statement

Any of various statements that the U.S. government requires to be displayed on export shipments and that specify the destinations for which export of the shipment has been authorized. For more information, *refer to* Chapter 12, "Documentation, Shipping, and Logistics," beginning on page 80.

devaluation

(economics) The lowering of the value of a national currency in terms of the currency of another nation. Devaluation tends to reduce domestic demand for imports in a country by raising their prices in terms of the devalued currency and to raise foreign demand for the country's exports by reducing their prices in terms of foreign currencies. Devaluation can therefore help to correct a balance of payments deficit and sometimes provide a short-term basis for economic adjustment of a national economy.

domestic international sales corporation (DISC)

(U.S.) A special U.S. corporation authorized by the U.S. Revenue Act of 1971, as amended by the Tax Reform Act of 1984, to borrow from the U.S. Treasury at the average one-year Treasury Bill interest rate to the extent of income tax liable on 94 percent of its annual corporate income. For more information, *see* "Foreign Sales Corporations" on page 73.

discrepancies

(banking/letter of credit) The non-compliance of documents with the terms and conditions of a letter of credit. Information (or missing information or missing documents/papers, etc.) in the documents submitted under a letter of credit, which: (1) is not consistent with its terms and conditions; (2) is inconsistent with other documents submitted; (3) does not meet the requirements of the Uniform Customs and Practice for Documentary Credits (UCPDC), 1993 revision.

If the documents show discrepancies of any kind, the issuing bank is no longer obligated to pay and, in the case of a confirmed letter of credit, neither is the confirming bank (strict documentary compliance).

See also letter of credit.

dispatch

(shipping) (a) An amount paid by a vessel's operator to a charterer if loading or unloading is completed in less time than stipulated in the charter party. (b) The release of a container to an interline carrier.

distributor

An agent who sells directly for a supplier and maintains an inventory of the supplier's products.

dock receipt

(shipping) A receipt issued by a warehouse supervisor or port officer certifying that goods have been received by the shipping company. The dock receipt is used to transfer accountability when an export item is moved by the domestic carrier to the port of embarkation and left with the international carrier for movement to its final destination. *See also* warehouse receipt.

documentary collection

(banking) A method of effecting payment for goods whereby the seller/exporter ships goods to the buyer, but instructs his bank to collect a certain sum from the buyer/importer in exchange for the transfer of title, shipping and other documentation enabling the buyer/importer to take possession of the goods. The two types of documentary collection are:

(a) *Documents against payment (D/P),* where the bank releases the documents to the buyer/importer only against a cash payment in a prescribed currency; and

(b) *Documents against acceptance (D/A),* where the bank releases the documents to the buyer/importer against acceptance of a bill of exchange (draft) guaranteeing payment at a later date.

documents against acceptance (D/A)

See documentary collection.

documents against payment (D/P)

See documentary collection.

draft

See bill of exchange.

drawback—refund of duties

(U.S. Customs) The refund of all or part of customs duties, or domestic tax paid on imported merchandise which was subsequently either manufactured into a different article or reexported. The purpose of drawback is to enable a domestic manufacturer to compete in foreign markets without the handicap of including in his costs, and consequently his sales price, the duty paid on imported raw materials or merchandise used in the subsequent manufacture of the exported goods.

drawee

The individual or firm on whom a draft is drawn and who owes the indicated amount. In a documentary collection, the drawee is the buyer.

drawer

The individual or firm that issues or signs a draft and thus stands to receive payment of the indicated amount from the drawee. In a documentary collection, the drawer is the seller.

dumping

(customs) The sale of a commodity in a foreign market at less than fair value, usually considered to be a price lower than at which it is sold within the exporting country to third countries.

"Fair value" can also be the constructed value of the merchandise plus a mandatory 8 percent profit margin.

Dumping is generally recognized as an unfair trade practice because it can disrupt markets and injure producers of competitive products in an importing country.

duty

(customs) A tax levied by a government on the import, export or consumption of goods. Usually a tax imposed on imports by the customs authority of a country. Duties are generally based on the value of the goods (ad valorem duties), some other factor such as weight or quantity (specific duties), or a combination of value and other factors (compound duties). *See also* ad valorem.

Eurodollars

(banking) U.S. dollar-denominated deposits in banks and other financial institutions outside of the United States. Originating from, but not limited to, the large quantity of U.S. dollar deposits held in western Europe.

ex ... (named point of origin)

(trade term) A term of sale where the price quoted applies only at the point of origin and the seller agrees to place the goods at the disposal of the buyer at the specified place on the date or within the period fixed. All other charges are for the account of the buyer.

exchange permit

(foreign exchange) A government permit sometimes required by the importer's government to enable the import firm to convert its own country's currency into foreign currency with which to pay a seller in another country.

exchange rate

(foreign exchange) The price of one currency expressed in terms of another, i.e., the number of units of one currency that may be exchanged for one unit of another currency.

export broker

An individual or firm that brings together buyers and sellers for a fee but does not take part in actual sales transactions.

export commission house

An organization which, for a commission, acts as a purchasing agent for a foreign buyer.

export declaration

See shipper's export declaration.

export license

A document prepared by a government authority, granting the right to export a specified quantity of a commodity to a specified country. This document may be required in some countries for most or all exports and in other countries only under special circumstances.

export management company (EMC)

A private firm that serves as the export department for several manufacturers, soliciting and transacting export business on behalf of its clients in return for a commission, salary, or retainer plus commission. *See also* "Export Management Companies" on page 25.

export trading company (ETC)

A corporation or other business unit organized and operated principally for the purpose of exporting goods and services, or of providing export-related services to other companies. An ETC can be owned by foreigners, and can import, barter, and arrange sales between third countries, as well as export. *See also* "Export Trading Companies" on page 26.

(U.S.) The Export Trading Company Act of 1982 exempts authorized trading companies from certain provisions of U.S. antitrust laws.

factoring houses

Certain companies which purchase domestic or foreign accounts receivables (e.g., the as yet unpaid invoices to domestic and foreign buyers) at a discounted price, usually about 2 to 4 percent less than their face value. *See also* "Factoring, Forfaiting, and Confirming" on page 97.

free alongside ship ... (named port of shipment) (FAS)

(Incoterm) "Free Alongside Ship" (FAS) means that the seller fulfills his obligation to deliver when the goods have been placed alongside the vessel on the quay or in lighters at the named port of shipment. This means that the buyer has to bear all costs and risks of loss of or damage to the goods from that moment. The FAS term requires the buyer to clear the goods for export. It should not be used when the buyer cannot carry out directly or indirectly the export formalities. For more information, *refer to* Chapter 10, "Pricing, Quotations, and Terms," beginning on page 55.

free carrier ... (named place) (FCA)

"Free carrier" (FCA) means that the seller fulfills his obligation to deliver when he has handed over the goods, cleared for export, into the charge of the carrier named by the buyer at the named place or point. If no precise point is indicated by the buyer, the seller may choose within the place or range stipulated where the carrier shall take the goods into his charge. When, according to commercial practice, the seller's assistance is required in making the contract with the carrier (such as in rail or air transport) the seller may act at the buyer's risk and expense. For more information, *refer to* Chapter 10, "Pricing, Quotations, and Terms," beginning on page 55.

free in (FI)

(shipping) A pricing term indicating that the loading charges are for the account of the supplier.

free out (FO)

(shipping) A pricing term indicating that unloading charges are for the account of the receiver.

free on board ... (named port of shipment) (FOB)

(Incoterm) "Free on board" (FOB) means that the seller fulfills his obligation to deliver when the goods have passed over the ship's rail at the named port of shipment. This means that the buyer has to bear all costs and risks of loss of or damage to the goods from that point. The FOB term requires the seller to clear the goods for export. For more information, *refer to* Chapter 10, "Pricing, Quotations, and Terms," beginning on page 55.

force majeure

(shipping) Any condition or set of circumstances, such as earthquakes, floods, or war, beyond the carrier's control that prevents the carrier from performing fulfillment of their obligations.

foreign exchange

(banking/foreign exchange) Current or liquid claims payable in foreign currency and in a foreign country (bank balances, checks, bills of exchange). Not to be confused with foreign bank notes and coin, which are not included in this definition.

foreign sales agent

An individual or firm that serves as the foreign representative of a domestic supplier and seeks sales abroad for the supplier.

foreign trade zone (FTZ)

FTZs (or free zones, free ports, or bonded warehouses) are special commercial and industrial areas in or near ports of entry where foreign and domestic merchandise, including raw materials, components, and finished goods, may be brought in without being subject to payment of customs duties. Merchandise brought into these zones may be stored, sold, exhibited, repacked, assembled, sorted, graded, cleaned, or otherwise manipulated prior to reexport or entry into the national customs territory.

foul bill of lading

(shipping) A receipt for goods issued by a carrier with an indication that the goods were damaged or short in quantity when received.

free port

An area, such as a port city, into which imported merchandise may legally be moved without payment of duties. *See also* foreign trade zone.

freight forwarder

(shipping) A person engaged in the business of assembling, collection, consolidating, shipping and distributing less-than-carload or less-than-truckload freight. Also, a person acting as agent in the transshipping of freight to or from foreign countries and the clearing of freight through customs, including full preparation of documents, arranging for shipping, warehousing, delivery and export clearance.

General Agreement on Tariffs and Trade (GATT)

A multilateral trade agreement aimed at expanding international trade. The main goals of GATT are to liberalize world trade an place it on a secure basis thereby contributing to economic growth and development and the welfare of the world's people. GATT is the only multilateral instrument that lays down agreed rules for international trade.

gross weight

The full weight of a shipment, including goods and packaging. *Compare with* tare weight.

import license

(customs) A document required and issued by some national governments authorizing the importation of goods into their individual countries.

inland bill of lading

A bill of lading used in transporting goods overland to the exporter's international carrier. Although a through bill of lading can sometimes be used, it is usually necessary to prepare both an inland bill of lading and an ocean bill of lading for export shipments. *See also* air waybill, ocean bill of lading, and through bill of lading.

irrevocable letter of credit

(banking) A letter of credit which cannot be amended or cancelled without prior mutual consent of all parties to the credit. Such a letter of credit guarantees payment by the bank to the seller/exporter so long as all the terms and conditions of the credit have been met. *See also* letter of credit.

letter of credit (L/C)

(banking) Formal term: Documentary credit or documentary letter of credit.

A letter of credit (L/C) is a document issued by a bank stating its commitment to pay someone (supplier/seller) a stated amount of money on behalf of a buyer (importer) so long as the seller meets specific terms and conditions. Letters of credit are more formally called documentary letters of credit because the banks handling the transaction deal in documents as opposed to goods. Letters of credit are the most common method of making international payments, because the risks of the transaction are shared by both the buyer and the seller.

licensing agreement

(law) A contract whereby the holder of a trademark, patent, or copyright transfers a limited right to use a process, sell or manufacture an article, or furnish specialized services covered by the trademark, patent or copyright to another firm.

manifest

(document) A document giving the description of a ship's cargo or the contents of a car or truck.

marine insurance

Insurance covering loss of, or damage to, goods at sea. Marine insurance typically compensates the owner of merchandise for losses in excess of those which can be legally recovered from the carrier that are sustained by fire, shipwreck, piracy, and various other causes.

ocean bill of lading

(shipping) A receipt for the cargo and a contract for transportation between a shipper and the ocean carrier. It may also be used as an instrument of ownership (negotiable bill of lading) which can be bought, sold, or traded while the goods are in transit. To be used in this manner, it must be a negotiable "order" bill of lading.

on board

(shipping) Notation on a bill of lading indicating that the goods have been loaded on board or shipped on a named ship. In the case of received for shipment bills of lading, the following four parties are authorized to add this "on board" notation: (1) the carrier, (2) the carrier's agent, (3) the master of the ship, and (4) the master's agent. *See also* ocean bill of lading, bill of lading.

open account

Credit extended that is not supported by a note, mortgage, or other formal written evidence of indebtedness (e.g., merchandise for which a buyer is later billed). Because this method poses an obvious risk to the supplier, it is essential that the buyer's integrity be unquestionable.

open policy

(insurance) An insurance contract (policy) which remains in force until cancelled and under which individual successive shipments are reported or declared and automatically covered on or after the inception date. The open policy saves time and expense for all concerned, whether underwater, agent or assured.

order bill

(law) A bill of lading that states that goods are consigned to the order of the person named in the bill.

packing list

(shipping) A document prepared by the shipper listing the kinds and quantities of merchandise in a particular shipment. A copy is usually sent to the consignee to assist in checking the shipment when received. Also referred to as a bill of parcels. For more information, *refer to* Chapter 12, "Documentation, Shipping, and Logistics," beginning on page 80.

Private Export Funding Corporation (PEFCO)

(U.S.) PEFCO works with the Export-Import Bank in using private capital to finance U.S. exports. PEFCO acts as a supplemental lender to traditional banking sources by making loans to public and private borrowers located outside of the United States who require medium- and/or longer-term financing of their purchases of U.S. goods and services.

phytosanitary inspection certificate

(U.S.) A certificate issued by the U.S. Department of Agriculture to satisfy import regulations of foreign countries, indicating that a U.S. export shipment has been inspected and is free from harmful pests and plant diseases.

political risk

(economics) Extraordinary measures of foreign countries and political events abroad which make it impossible for a debtor to comply with a contract or which leads to the loss, confiscation of or damage to goods belonging to the exporter (e.g., war, revolution, annexation, civil war) which can have detrimental effect upon the exporter. An exporter may be able to cover this risk by utilizing a confirmed letter of credit or by applying for cover from export credit agencies.

pro forma invoice

An invoice provided by a supplier prior to a sale or shipment of merchandise, informing the buyer of the kinds and quantities of goods to be sent, their value, and important specifications (weight, size, etc.). A pro forma invoice is used: (1) as a preliminary invoice together with a quotation; (2) for customs purposes in connection with shipments or samples, advertising materials, etc.

purchasing agent
An agent who purchases goods in his/her own country on behalf of foreign buyers such as government agencies and private businesses.

quota
(customs) A limitation on the quantity of goods that may be imported into a country from all countries or from specified countries during a set period of time.

quotation
(foreign exchange) The price quotation of a currency can be made either directly or indirectly. (a) The *direct quotation* gives the equivalent of a certain amount of foreign currency (normally in units of 100 or one) in domestic currency. (b) In an *indirect price quotation* (less common) the domestic currency is valued in units of foreign currency.

remitting bank
(banking) In a documentary collection, a bank which acts as an intermediary, forwarding the remitter's documents to, and payments from the collecting bank.

revocable letter of credit
A letter of credit which can be cancelled or altered by the drawee (buyer) after it has been issued by the drawee's bank. Due to the low level of security of this type of credit, they are extremely rare in practice. *Compare* Irrevocable letter of credit. *Refer to* Chapter 13.)

shipper's export declaration (SED)
A form required for some U.S. export shipments by mail valued at more than $500 or non-mail shipments with declared value of greater than $2,500. Prepared by shipper indicating the value, weight, destination, and other basic information about the shipment. The shipper's export declaration is used to control exports and compile trade statistics. *See also* "Shipper's Export Declarations (SEDs)" on page 83.

ship's manifest
(shipping) A list, signed by the captain of a ship, of the individual shipments constituting the ship's cargo. *See also* manifest.

sight draft (S/D)
(banking) A financial instrument payable upon presentation or demand. A bill of exchange may be made payable, for example, at sight or after sight, which means it is payable upon presentation or demand, or within a particular period after demand is made. *See also* bill of exchange.

spot exchange
(foreign exchange) The purchase and sale of foreign exchange for delivery and payment at the time of the transaction.

standard industrial classification (SIC)
(U.S.) The classification standard underlying all establishment-based U.S. economic statistics classified by industry.

standard international trade classification (SITC)
One of a number of numerical commodity codes developed by the United Nations and used solely by international organizations for reporting international trade. The SITC has been revised several times; the current version is Revision 3. *See also* Harmonized System.

straight bill of lading
(shipping) A nonnegotiable bill of lading that designates a consignee who is to receive the goods and that obligates the carrier to deliver the goods to that consignee only. A straight bill of lading cannot be transferred by endorsement.

tare weight
The weight of a container and/or packing materials, but without the weight of the goods being shipped. The gross weight of a shipment minus the net weight of the goods being shipped. *Compare with* gross weight.

tenor
(law/banking) The period between the formation of a debt and the date of expected payment.

through bill of lading
(shipping) A single bill of lading covering receipt of the cargo at the point of origin for delivery to the ultimate consignee, using two or more modes of transportation. *See also* bill of lading.

time draft
(banking) A financial instrument that is payable at a future fixed or determinable date.

tramp steamer
(shipping) A steamship which does not operate under any regular schedule from one port to another, but calls at any port where charge may be obtained.

trust receipt
(banking) A declaration by a client to a bank that ownership in goods released by the bank are retained by the bank, and that the client has received the goods in trust only.

Release of merchandise by a bank to a buyer in which the bank retains title to the merchandise. The buyer, who obtains the goods for manufacturing or sales purposes, is obligated to maintain the goods (or the proceeds from their sale) distinct from the remainder of his/her assets and to hold them ready for repossession by the bank.

Trust receipts are used under letters of credit or collections so that the buyer may receive the goods before paying the issuing bank or collecting bank.

warehouse receipt
(shipping) An instrument (document) listing the goods or commodities deposited in a warehouse. It is a receipt for the commodities listed, and for which the warehouse is the bailee. Warehouse receipts may be either nonnegotiable or negotiable.

wharfage
(shipping) (a) A charge assessed by a pier or dock owner for handling incoming or outgoing cargo. (b) The charge made for docking vessels at a wharf.

without reserve
(shipping) A term indicating that a shipper's agent or representative is empowered to make definitive decisions and adjustments abroad without approval of the group or individual represented. *Compare with* advisory capacity.

Appendix II

Directory of Federal Export Assistance

A. Department of Commerce

The U.S. Department of Commerce can provide a wealth of information to exporters. The first step an exporter should take is to contact the nearest Department of Commerce Export Assistance Center or district office (listed by state in Appendix III), which can help guide the exporter to the right person or office.

U.S. Department of Commerce
14th and Constitution Avenue NW
Washington, DC 20230
Tel: (202) 482-2000
Web site: www.doc.gov

Stat-USA
Tel: (202) 482-1986
Email: stat-usa@doc.gov
Web site: www.stat-usa.gov/

International Trade Administration

Web site: www.ita.doc.gov

Trade Information Center
Tel: (800) USA-TRADE
Web site: www.ita.doc.gov/how_to_export

Trade Compliance Center
Tel: (202) 482-1191
Web site: www.mac.doc.gov/tcc/index.html

Foreign-Trade Zones Board
Tel: (202) 482-2862; Fax: (202) 482-0002
Web site: www.ita.doc.gov/import_admin/records/

U.S. and Foreign Commercial Service

Domestic Operations
Tel: (202) 482-4767; Fax: (202) 482-0687
Web site: www.ita.doc.gov

Export Promotion Services

Office of Export Information & Research Services
Tel: (202) 482-2000; Fax: (202) 482-3617

Office of Public/Private Initiatives
Tel: (202) 482-4231; Fax: (202) 482-0115

Office of Trade Events Management
Tel: (202) 482-2107

International Operations

Office of International Operations
Tel: (202) 482-6228; Fax: (202) 482-3159

Foreign Services Personnel Office
Tel: (202) 482-2368; Fax: (202) 482-5013

International Economic Policy (IEP) Division

Note: For a complete breakdown of offices in IEP, refer to "Department of Commerce International Economic Policy Division" on page 125.

Africa
Tel: (202) 482-4925; Fax: (202) 482-6083

Asia and Pacific
Tel: (202) 482-0543; Fax: (202) 482-4473

Europe
Tel: (202) 482-5638; Fax: (202) 482-4098

Japan
Tel: (202) 482-2427; Fax: (202) 482-0469

Western Hemisphere
Tel: (202) 482-5324; Fax: (202) 482-4736

Office of Multilateral Affairs
Tel: (202) 482-0603; Fax: (202) 482-5444

Trade Development

Advocacy Center
Tel: (202) 482-3896; Fax: (202) 482-3508

Office of Export Promotion Coordination
Tel: (202) 482-4501; Fax: (202) 482-1999

Office of Planning, Coordination and Resource Mgmt.
Tel: (202) 482-4921; Fax: (202) 482-4462

Office of Trade and Economic Analysis
Tel: (202) 482-5145
Web site: www.ita.doc.gov/industry/otea/otea.html

Basic Industries
Tel: (202) 482-0614; Fax: (202) 482-5666

- Office of Automotive Affairs
  Tel: (202) 482-0554; Fax: (202) 482-0674
- Office of Metals, Materials, and Chemicals
  Tel: (202) 482-0575; Fax: (202) 482-0378
- Office of Energy and Infrastructure
  Tel: (202) 482-1466; Fax: (202) 482-0170

Environmental Technologies Exports
Tel: (202) 482-5225; Fax: (202) 482-5665

Services Industries and Finance
Tel: (202) 482-5261; Fax: (202) 482-4775

- Office of Export Trading Company Affairs
  Tel: (202) 482-5131; Fax: (202) 482-1790
- Office of Finance
  Tel: (202) 482-3277; Fax: (202) 482-5702
  Finance & Countertrade Div., Tel: (202) 482-4471
- Office of Service Industries
  Tel: (202) 482-3575; Fax: (202) 482-2669
  Web site: www.ita.doc.gov/industry/osi/

Technology and Aerospace Industries
Tel: (202) 482-1872; Fax: (202) 482-0856

- Office of Aerospace
  Tel: (202) 482-1228; Fax: (202) 482-3113
- Office of Computers and Business Equipment
  Tel: (202) 482-0571; Fax: (202) 482-0952
- Office of Microelectronics, Medical Equipment and Instrumentation
  Tel: (202) 482-2470; Fax: (202) 482-0975
- Office of Telecommunications
  Tel: (202) 482-4466; Fax: (202) 482-5834

Textiles, Apparel and Consumer Goods Industries
Tel: (202) 482-3737; Fax: (202) 482-2331

- Office of Textiles and Apparel
  Tel: (202) 482-5078; Fax: (202) 482-2331
- Office of Consumer Goods
  Tel: (202) 482-0337; Fax: (202) 482-3981

Bureau of Export Administration

Web site: www.bxa.doc.gov/

Office of Exporter Services
Tel: (202) 482-0436; Fax: (202) 482-3322

- Exporter Counseling Division
  Tel: (202) 482-4811; Fax: (202) 482-3617
- Export Seminar Division
  Tel: (202) 482-6031; Fax: (202) 482-2927
- Regulatory Policy Division
  Tel: (202) 482-2240; Fax: (202) 482-3355
- Compliance & Special Licenses Division
  Tel: (202) 482-0062; Fax: (202) 501-6750
- System for Tracking Export License Applications (STELA)
  Tel: (202) 482-2752
- Public Affairs Office
  Tel: (202) 482-2721; Fax: (202) 482-2421

Chemical & Biological Controls and Treaty Compliance
Tel: (202) 482-3825; Fax: (202) 482-0751

Strategic Industries and Economic Security
Tel: (202) 482-4506; Fax: (202) 482-5650

Office of Nuclear and Missile Technology Controls
Tel: (202) 482-4188; Fax: (202) 482-4145

Office of Strategic Trade and Foreign Policy Controls
Tel: (202) 482-0092; Fax: (202) 482-4094

Office of Antiboycott Compliance
Tel: (202) 482-2381; Fax: (202) 482-0913

- Compliance Policy Division
  Tel: (202) 482-5942; Fax: (202) 482-0913
- Enforcement Division
  Tel: (202) 482-2381; Fax: (202) 482-0913

Office of Export Enforcement
Tel: (202) 482-2252; Fax: (202) 482-5889

Office of Enforcement Support
Tel: (202) 482-4255; Fax: (202) 482-0971

- Export License Compliance Division
  Tel: (202) 482-5914

Western Regional Office, Orange County, CA
Tel: (949) 660-0144; Fax: (949) 660-9347
Web site: www.primnet.com/~bxawest

Northern Calif. Branch Office, Santa Clara County, CA
Tel: (408) 998-7402

Minority Business Development Agency (MBDA)

Minority Business Development Agency
Office of Program and Policy Development
Tel: (202) 482-5001, Fax: (202) 501-4698
Email: mbda@doc.govt
Web site: www.mbda.gov

Economic Development Administration

Web site: www.doc.gov/eda/

Trade Adjustment Assistance Division
Tel: (202) 482-2127; Fax: (202) 482-0466

National Institute of Standards and Technology

National Institute of Standards and Technology (NIST)
100 Bureau Dr.
Gaithersburg, MD 20899
Tel: (301) 975-2000; Fax: (301) 948-1935
Web site: www.nist.gov

- The Metric Program
  Tel: (301) 975-3690; Fax: (301) 948-1416
  Email: metric_prg@nist.gov
  Web site: www.nist.gov/metric

National Center for Standards and Certification Information (NCSCI),
100 Bureau Dr., Stop 2150
Gaithersburg, MD 20899-2150
Tel: (301) 975-4040, 975-4038, 975-4036, 975-5155
Fax: (301) 926-1559

Technical assistance
Tel: (301) 975-4033

GATT/WTO Standards Hotline
Tel: (301) 975-4041

EU Standards Hotline
Tel: (301) 921-4164

Bureau of the Census

Web site: www.census.gov/

Census Customer Services
Tel: (301) 457-4100
Fax: (301) 457-4714 (General info), 457-3842 (Orders)

Foreign Trade Information
Tel: (301) 457-3041; Fax; (301) 457-1158

Bureau of Export Administration
Tel: (202) 482-2721
Web site: www.census.gov

Shippers' Export Declaration Assistance
Tel: (301) 457-2238; Fax: (301) 457-3765

U.S. Patent and Trademark Office

U.S. Patent and Trademark Office
U.S. Department of Commerce
Washington, DC 20231
Tel: (703) 308-4357; Fax: (703) 305-7786
Web site: www.uspto.gov

USPTO Licensing and Review
Tel: (703) 306-4187; Fax: (703) 306-4196

B. Small Business Administration

All export programs administered through the Small Business Administration (SBA) are available through SBA field offices (see Appendix III). More information about the programs can be obtained through

Small Business Administration
Office of International Trade
409 Third Street SW, 8th Floor
Washington, DC 20416
Tel: (202) 205-6720; Fax: (202) 205-7064
SBA Answer Desk: (800) 8-ASK-SBA (or 827-5722)
Web site: www.sbaonline.sba.gov

C. Export-Import Bank

Export-Import Bank of the United States
811 Vermont Avenue NW
Washington, DC 20571
Tel: (800) 565-3946, (202) 565-3946;
Fax: (202) 565-3380
Web site: www.exim.gov

Marketing and Program Division
Tel: (800) 565-EXIM, (202) 565-3946

Fax Retrieval Service
Tel: (800) 565-EXIM (press 1, then 2 at voice prompts)

Export Trading Company Assistance
Tel: (800) 565-3946

Engineering & Environment Division
Tel: (202) 565-3570; Fax: (202) 565-3584

Seminar Information
Tel: (202) 565-3912; Fax (202)565-3723

Office of Communication
Tel: (202) 565-3200; Fax: (202) 565-3210

D. Department of Agriculture

U.S. Department of Agriculture
14th Street and Independence Avenue SW
Washington, DC 20250
Tel: (202) 720-2791
Web site: www.usda.gov

Animal and Plant Health Inspection Service (APHIS)

Animal Exports, Tel: (301) 734-3277; Fax: (301) 734-8226

Animal Products Exports, Tel: (301) 734-8364; Fax: (301) 734-6402

Plant Exports (Phytosanitary Certificates), Tel: (301) 734-8537; Fax: (301) 734-5007

Federal Grain Inspection Service (FGIS)
Tel: (202) 720-5091 (Public Affairs and Information); Fax: (202) 205-9237

FGIS Compliance Division, Regulatory Branch
Tel: (202) 720-8536; Fax: (202) 690-2755
Web site: www.usda.gov/gipsa

Economic Research Service
Tel: (202) 694-5000; Fax: (202) 694-5103

Commodity Credit Corporation (CCC)
Operations Division
Tel: (202) 720-6211; Fax: (202) 720-2949

Food and Drug Administration

Web site: www.fda.gov

Food and Drug Administration, Import/ Export Office
Tel: (301) 594-3150; Fax: (301) 594-0165

Food and Drug Administration, International Affairs
Tel: (301) 827-4480; Fax: (301) 443-0235

Office of Compliance
Tel: (301) 594-4699

Food Safety and Inspection Service (FSIS)
Tel: (202) 720-7943; Fax: (202) 720-1843
Web site: www.fsis.usda.gov

FSIS Food Safety Education
Tel: (202) 720-7943; Fax: (202) 720-1843

Foreign Agricultural Service (FAS)
Tel: (202) 720-7115; Fax: (202) 720-1727
Web site: www.fas.usda.gov

AgExport Services Division
Tel: (202) 720-6343; Fax: (202) 690-0193

Marketing Operations Staff
Tel: (202) 720-4327; Fax: (202) 720-9361

Trade Assistance and Promotion Office (TAPO)
Tel: (202) 720-7420; Fax: (202) 205-9728

Trade Show Office
Tel: (202) 690-1182; Fax: (202) 690-4374

Office of Foreign Agricultural Affairs (FAA)
Tel: (202) 720-6138; Fax: (202) 690-0059
Call the FAA for a directory of overseas FAS posts.

- Europe
  Tel: (202) 720-2144; Fax: (202) 720-5183
- Western Hemisphere
  Tel: (202) 720-3221; Fax: (202) 720-5183
- Africa and Middle East
  Tel: (202) 720-7053; Fax: (202) 720-5183
- South, Southeast Asia and Pacific
  Tel: (202) 720-3080; Fax: (202) 720-8316
- North Asia
  Tel: (202) 720-3080; Fax: (202) 720-8316

E. Overseas Private Investment Corporation (OPIC)

Overseas Private Investment Corporation
1100 New York Ave. NW
Washington, DC 20527-0001
Tel: (202) 336-8400; Fax: (202) 408-9859
InfoLine Tel: (202) 336-8799 (24 hours)
FactsLine Tel: (202) 336-8700 (24 hours)
Email: info@opic.gov
Web site: www.opic.gov

F. Department of State

U.S. Department of State
2201 C Street NW
Washington, DC 20520
Tel: (202) 647-4000
Web site: www.state.gov

Consular Information Sheets and Travel Warnings
Tel: (202) 647-5225
Web site: travel.state.gov/travel_warnings.html

National Passport Center
Tel: (202) 647-0518

Office of Defense Trade Controls
Tel: (703) 875-6644; Fax: (703) 875-6647
Web site: www.pmdtc.org

U.S. Department of State Commercial Coordinators

Bureau of Economic and Business Affairs
Tel: (202) 647-7727; Fax: (202) 647-5713

Bureau of Int'l Communications and Info. Policy
Tel: (202) 647-5832; Fax: (202) 647-5957

Office of the Coordinator for Business Affairs
Tel: (202) 647-1625; Fax (202) 647-3953

Bureau of African Affairs
Tel: (202) 647-7371; Fax: (202) 736-4872

Bureau of East Asian and Pacific Affairs
Tel: (202) 647-4835; Fax: (202) 647-0136

Bureau of European Regional Affairs
Tel: (202) 647-6925; Fax: (202) 647-5116

Bureau of Western Hemisphere Affairs
Tel: (202) 647-1232; Fax: (202) 736-7618

Bureau of Near East Affairs
Tel: (202) 647-5150; Fax: (202) 647-4465

Bureau of South Asian Affairs
Tel: (202) 736-4255; Fax: (202) 736-4259

G. Department of the Treasury

U.S. Department of the Treasury
1500 Pennsylvania Avenue NW
Washington, DC 20220
Web site: www.ustreas.gov

Office of Foreign Assets Control, Licensing
Tel: (202) 622-2480; Fax: (202) 622-1657
Web site: www.treas.gov/ofac (Provides direct access to the list of Specially Designated Nationals)

U.S. Customs Service
1300 Pennsylvania Ave. NW
Washington, DC 20229
Web site: www.customs.ustreas.gov

Strategic Investigations Division (Exodus Command Center)
Tel: (202) 927-1540; Fax: (202) 927-1181

Automated Export System (AES)
Web site: www.customs.ustreas.gov (follow links for Import/Export AES)

Entry and Carrier Rulings Branch
Tel: (202) 927-2320; Fax: (202) 927-1873

Office of Finance, Budget Division
Tel: (202) 927-0310 (user fees), 927-0034 (harbor maintenance fees), Fax: (202) 927-1010

H. Agency for International Development

Agency for International Development
Ronald Reagan Building
Washington, DC 20523-0016
Tel: (202) 712-4810; Fax: (202) 216-3524
Web site: www.info.usaid.gov

Office of Small and Disadvantaged Business Utilization/ Minority Resource Center (OSDBU/MRC)
Tel: (202) 712-1500; Fax: (202) 216-3056

Global Technology Network
Tel: (800) 872-4348, (202) 712-0474
Fax: (202) 216-3526
Web site: www.info.usaid.gov

I. Office of the U.S. Trade Representative

Office of the U.S. Trade Representative
600 17th Street NW
Washington, DC 20508
Tel: (888) 473-8787; Fax: (202) 395-3911
Web site: www.ustr.gov

Assistant U.S. Trade Representatives:

Intergovernmental and Public Liaison
Tel: (202) 395-6120; Fax: (202) 395-3692

Asia & the Pacific/Asia-Pacific Economic Cooperation (APEC)
Tel: (202) 395-3430; Fax: (202) 395-9515

Europe & Mediterranean
Tel: (202) 395-4620; Fax: (202) 395-3974

China
Tel: (202) 395-5050; Fax: (202) 395-3512

Japan
Tel: (202) 395-5070; Fax: (202) 395-3597

Western Hemisphere
Tel: (202) 395-6135; Fax: (202) 395-9517

World Trade Organization (WTO) Affairs
Tel: (202) 395-6843; Fax: (202) 395-5674

Agricultural Affairs
Tel: (202) 395-6127; Fax: (202) 395-4579

Industry Policy
Tel: (202) 395-5656

Environment & Natural Resources
Tel: (202) 395-7320; Fax: (202) 395-4579

Services, Investment & Intellectual Property
Tel: (202) 395-4510; Fax: (202) 395-3891

Trade & Development
Tel: (202) 395-6971

J. Other Federal Export Assistance Resources

Department of Defense

U.S. Department of Defense
The Pentagon
Washington, DC 20301
Tel: (703) 545-6700

Defense Threat Reduction Agency
Tel: (703) 604-8084; Fax: (703) 602-5838

Department of the Interior

U.S. Department of the Interior
1849 C Street NW
Washington, DC 20240
Tel: (202) 208-3100
Web site: www.doi.gov

Chief Office of Management Authority
Tel: (703) 358-2093; Fax: (703) 358-2280
Web site: www.fws.gov/who/usfws.html

Department of Labor

U.S. Department of Labor
200 Constitution Avenue NW
Washington, DC 20210
Tel: (202) 219-6666
Web site: www.dol.gov

Department of Transportation

U.S. Department of Transportation
400 Seventh Street, SW
Washington, DC 20590
Tel: (202) 366-4000
Web site: www.dot.gov

Office of International Law, General Counsel
Tel: (202) 366-2972; Fax: (202) 366-9188

Hazardous Materials Information Center
Tel: (800) 467-4922

Department of Energy

U.S. Department of Energy
1000 Independence Avenue SW
Washington, DC 20585
Tel: (202) 586-5000
Web site: www.doe.gov

Office of Fossil Energy
Tel: (202) 586-6503; Fax: (202) 586-5146
Web site: www.fe.doe.gov

Office of Arms Control and Non Proliferation
Export Control Division
Tel: (202) 586-2331; Fax: (202) 586-1348
Web site: http://nn43web.nn.gov/

Department of Justice

U.S. Department of Justice
Main Justice Bldg.
Washington, DC 20530

Antitrust Division
Tel: (202) 514-2401; Fax: (202) 616-2645
Web site: www.usdoj.gov

Drug Enforcement Administration
Web site: www.usdoj.gov/dea

DEA, International Chemical Control Unit
Tel: (202) 307-7202; Fax: (202) 307-8570

DEA, International Drug Unit
Tel: (202) 307-2414; Fax: (202) 307-7503

Environmental Protection Agency

Environmental Protection Agency
401 M Street SW
Washington, DC 20460-0003
Tel: (202) 260-2090
Web site: www.epa.gov

Office of Pesticide Programs
Tel: (703) 305-7090; Fax: (703) 308-4776

Office of Solid Waste
International and Special Projects Branch
Tel. (703) 308-8751; Fax: (703) 308-0522
Web site: www.epa.gov/epaoswer/

RCRA Hotline
(For information on compliance with the Resource Con servation and Recovery Act)
Tel: (703) 412-9810
Web site: www.epa.gov/

TSCA Hotline
(For information on compliance with the Toxic Substances Control Act)
Tel: (202) 554-1404

National Institute of Standards and Technology (NIST)

National Institute of Standards and Technology
Office of Information Services
Reference Desk
Tel: (301) 975-3052
Web site: www.nist.gov

National Center for Standards and Certification Information (NCSCI)
National Institute of Standards and Technology (NIST)
100 Bureau Dr., Stop 2150
Gaithersburg, MD 20899-2150
Tel: (301) 975-4040, 975-4038, 975-4036, 975-5155
Technical assistance Tel: (301) 975-4033
WTO Hotline Tel: (301) 975-4041
EU Standards Hotline Tel: (301) 921-4164
Fax: (301) 926-1559
Email: ncsci@nist.gov

The Metric Program
Tel: (301) 975-3690; Fax: (301) 948-1416
Email: metric_prg@nist.gov
Web site: www.nist.gov/metric

National Marine Fisheries Service

Office of Industry and Trade
National Marine Fisheries Service
1315 East-West Highway
Building 3, Room 3670
Silver Spring, MD 20910
Tel: (301)-713-2379; Fax: (301) 713-2384
Web site: www.nmfs.gov

Seafood Inspection Program
Tel: (301) 713-2351; Fax: (301) 713-1081

Inspection Services Division
Tel: (301) 713-2355; Fax: (301) 713-1081

National Technical Information Service (NTIS)

National Technical Information Service (NTIS)
5285 Port Royal Road
Springfield, VA 22161
Tel: (703) 605-6060; Fax: (703) 605-6900
Email: info@ntis.fedworld.gov
Web site: www.fedworld.gov

Nuclear Regulatory Commission

Nuclear Regulatory Commission
Office of International Programs
Tel: (301) 415-2344; Fax: (301) 415-2395
Web site: www.nrc.gov/NRC/nucmat.html

U.S. Government Printing Office

U.S. Government Printing Office
P.O. Box 371954
Pittsburgh, PA 15250-7954
Tel: (202) 512-1800; Fax: (202) 512-2250
Web site: www.access.gpo.gov/su_docs

U.S. Trade and Development Agency (TDA)

U.S. Trade and Development Agency
1621 North kent St., Suite 300
Arlington, VA 22209-2131
Tel: (703) 875-4357; Fax: (703) 875-4009
Email: info@tda.gov
Web site: www.tda.gov

TDA Definitional Mission Hotline
Tel: (703) 875-7447

U.S. Information Agency

U.S. Information Agency
301 4th Street SW
Washington, DC 20547
Tel: (202) 619-4355
Email: inquiry@usia.gov
Web site: www.usia.gov/usis.html

International Trade Commission

U.S. International Trade Commission
500 E Street, SW
Washington, DC 20436
Tel: (202) 205-1819; Fax: (202) 205-2798
Web site: www.usitc.gov/

Department of Commerce International Economic Policy Division

The International Trade Administration's International Economic Policy Division has an office or an individual Country Desk Officer assigned to each country of the world. The Country Desk Officers deal strictly with policy issues. The list given here is divided into the following regions of the world:

A. The Americas

North America
Caribbean
Central and South America

B. Europe and Central Asia

Western Europe
Central and Eastern Europe
Former Soviet States

C. Africa and Near East

Near East and Northern Africa
Western and Central Africa
West Central Africa

Southern Africa (Except South Africa)
South Africa

Eastern Africa

D. Asia and the Pacific

Asia and the Pacific (Except Japan)
Japan

A. The Americas

North America

There are no individual Country Desk Officers for North America. All inquiries are handled by:

Office of NAFTA (North American Free Trade Agreement)
Tel: (202) 482-0305; Fax: (202) 482-4473
Web site: www.itaiep.doc.gov
The countries handled by the Office of NAFTA are:

- Canada
- Mexico

Caribbean

The country desk officers for the Caribbean are:

Michelle Brooks (Primarily East Caribbean)
Tel: (202) 482-1658; Fax: (202) 482-0464

Mark Siegelman (Primarily Caribbean Basin)
Tel: (202) 482-0704; Fax: (202) 482-0464; Email: siegelma@usita.gov
The countries in the Caribbean and their desk officer assignments are:

- Anguilla (Michelle Brooks)
- Antigua/Barbuda (Michelle Brooks)
- Aruba (Michelle Brooks)
- Bahamas (Michelle Brooks)
- Barbados (Michelle Brooks)
- Belize (Michelle Brooks)
- Bermuda (Michelle Brooks)
- Cayman Islands (Michelle Brooks)
- Cuba (Michelle Brooks)
- Dominica (Michelle Brooks)
- Dominican Republic (Mark Siegelman)
- Grenada (Michelle Brooks)
- Guadeloupe (Michelle Brooks)
- Haiti (Mark Siegelman)
- Jamaica (Mark Siegelman)
- Martinique (Michelle Brooks)
- Montserrat (Michelle Brooks)
- Netherlands Antilles (Michelle Brooks)
- Puerto Rico (Michelle Brooks)
- St. Barthelemey (Michelle Brooks)
- St. Kitts-Nevis (Michelle Brooks)
- St. Lucia (Michelle Brooks)
- St. Martin (Michelle Brooks)
- St. Vincent & the Grenadines (Michelle Brooks)
- Trinidad & Tobago (Michelle Brooks)
- Turks & Caicos Islands (Michelle Brooks)
- Virgin Islands (UK) (Michelle Brooks)
- Virgin Islands (US) (Michelle Brooks)

Central and South America

The Country Desk officers for South America are:

Michelle Brooks
Tel: (202) 482-1658; Fax: (202) 482-0464

Valerie Dees
Tel: (202) 482-0477; Fax: (202) 482-4726
Email: dees@usita.gov

Matt Gaisford
Tel: (202) 482-0057; Fax: (202) 482-0464
Email: gaisford@usita.gov

Tom Welch
Tel: (202) 482-0475; Fax: (202) 482-0464

Elizabeth Jaffee
Tel: (202) 482-4302; Fax: (202) 482-4726

Paulo Mendes
Tel: (202) 482-3872; Fax: (202) 482-4157
Email: mendes@usita.gov

Randy Mye
Tel: (202) 482-1744

Mark Siegelman
Tel: (202) 482-0704; Fax: (202) 482-0464
Email: siegelma@usita.gov

Laura Zeiger-Hatfield
Tel: (202) 482-0703
Email: zeiger@usita.gov

Carlo Cavagna
Tel: (202) 482-0428; Fax: (202) 482-4157

The countries in Central and South America and their desk officer assignments are:

- Argentina (Valerie Dees)
- Bolivia (Tom Welch)
- Brazil (Carlo Cavagna)
- Colombia (Matt Gaisford)
- Costa Rica (Mark Siegelman)
- Chile (Laura Zeiger-Hatfield)
- Ecuador (Matt Gaisford)
- El Salvador (Elizabeth Jaffee)
- Guatemala (Elizabeth Jaffee)
- Guyana (Michelle Brooks)
- Honduras (Elizabeth Jaffee)

- MERCOSUR (Paulo Mendes)
- Nicaragua (Elizabeth Jaffee)
- Panama (Matt Gaisford)
- Paraguay (Valerie Dees)
- Peru (Tom Welch)
- Suriname (Michelle Brooks)
- Uruguay (Laura Zeiger-Hatfield)
- Venezuela (Tom Welch)

B. Europe and Central Asia

Western Europe

The Country Desk officers for Western Europe are:

Ann Corro
Tel: (202) 482-2177; Fax: (202) 482-2897
Email: corro@usita.gov

Paul Dasher
Tel: (202) 482-3310; Fax: (202) 482-2897

Lisa Tomlinson
Tel: (202) 482-2434; Fax: (202) 482-2897

Robert McLaughlin
Tel: (202) 482-3748; Fax: (202) 482-2897

David DeFalco
Tel: (202) 482-2178; Fax: (202) 482-2897

Leakomey Norim
Tel: (202) 482-4414; Fax: (202) 482-2897

The countries in Western Europe and their desk officer assignments are:

- Austria (Lisa Tomlinson)
- Belgium (Paul Dasher)
- Cyprus (Ann Corro)
- Denmark (Leaksmey Norim)
- Finland (Leaksmey Norim)
- France (Paul Dasher)
- Germany (Lisa Tomlinson)
- Greece (Ann Corro)
- Iceland (Leaksmey Norim)
- Ireland (Robert McLaughlin)
  Northern Ireland and Border Counties web site:
  www.itaiep.doc.gov/ire/intro.html
- Italy (David DeFalco)
- Luxembourg (Paul Dasher)
- Malta (Ann Corro)
- Netherlands (Paul Dasher)
- Norway (Leaksmey Norim)
- Portugal (Ann Corro)
- Spain (Ann Corro)
- Sweden (Leaksmey Norim)
- Switzerland (Lisa Tomlinson)
- Turkey (David DeFalco)
- United Kingdom (Robert McLaughlin)
  N. Ireland and Border Counties web site:
  www.itaiep.doc.gov/ire/intro.html

Central and Eastern Europe

There are no individual Country Desk Officers for Central and Eastern Europe. All inquiries are handled by:

Central and Eastern Europe Business Information Center (CEEBIC)
Tel: (202) 482-2645; Fax: (202) 501-0787
Email: ceebic@usita.gov
Web site: www.mac.doc.gov.eebic/ceebic.html
The countries handled by CEEBIC are:

- Albania
- Balkan States
- Bosnia-Herzegovina
- Bulgaria
- Croatia
- Czech Republic
- Estonia
- Hungary
- Latvia
- Lithuania
- Macedonia (FYR)
- Poland
- Romania
- Slovak Republic
- Slovenia
- Yugoslavia (Serbia-Montenegro)

Former Soviet States

There are no individual Country Desk Officers for the Newly Independent States of the Soviet Union. All inquiries are handled by:

Business Information Service for the Newly Independent States (BISNIS)
Tel: (202) 482-4655; Fax: (202) 482-2293
Web site: www.mac.doc.gov/bisnis.html
Note that the Baltic States are handled by CEEBIC. The countries handled by BISNIS are:

- Armenia
- Azerbaijan
- Belarus
- Georgia
- Kazakhstan
- Kyrgsz Republic
- Moldova
- Russia
- Tajikistan
- Turkmemistan
- Ukraine
- Uzbekistan

C. Africa and the Near East

Near East and North Africa

All inquiries regarding the countries of the Near East and North Africa are handled by:

Office of Near East
Tel: (202) 482-1860; Fax: (202) 482-0878
Web site: www.mac.doc.gov/tcc
The Country Desk Officers for this region are:

David Guglielmi
Tel: (202) 482-1860; Fax: (202) 482-0878
Email: guglielmi@usita.gov

Cherie Loustaunau
Tel: (202) 482-1860; Fax: (202) 482-0878

Thomas Sams
Tel: (202) 482-1860; Fax: (202) 482-0878
Email: sams@usita.gov

Paul Thanos
Tel: (202) 482-1860; Fax: (202) 482-0878
Email: thanos@usita.gov

The countries in the Near East and North Africa and their desk officer assignments are:

Algeria (David Guglielmi)

- Bahrain (David Guglielmi)
- Egypt (Thomas Sams)
- Iran (Paul Thanos)
- Iraq (Thomas Sams)
- Israel (Paul Thanos)
- Jordan (Paul Thanos)
- Kuwait (Cherie Loustaunau)
- Lebanon (Thomas Sams)
- Libya (David Gugliemi)
- Morocco (David Gugliemi)
- Oman (Cherie Loustaunau)
- Qatar (Cherie Loustaunau)
- Saudi Arabia (David Guglielmi)
- Syria (Thomas Sams)
- Tunisia (David Guglielmi)
- United Arab Emirates (David Guglielmi)
- West Bank/Gaza Strip (Paul Thanos)
- Yemen (Cherie Loustaunau)

Western and Central Africa

The countries in this region, as listed below, are handled by:

Philip Michelini (Central Africa)
Tel: (202) 482-4388; Fax: (202) 482-5198

Douglas Wallace (Western Africa)
Tel: (202) 482-5149

- Burkina Faso
- Burundi
- Cape Verde
- Central African Rep.
- Chad
- Cote d'Ivoire
- Equatorial Guinea
- Gambia
- Guinea
- Guinea-Bissau
- Ivory Coast
- Liberia
- Mali
- Mauritania
- Niger
- Rwanda
- São Tome & Principe
- Senegal
- Sierra Leone
- Zaire

Gulf of Guinea

The countries in this region, as listed below, are handled by:

Alicia Robinson
Tel: (202) 482-4228; Fax: (202) 482-5198
Email: robinsa@usita.gov

- Benin
- Cameroon
- Congo
- Gabon
- Ghana
- Nigeria
- Togo

Southern Africa (except South Africa)

The countries in this region, as listed below, are handled by:

Alicia Robinson
Tel: (202) 482-4228; Fax: (202) 482-5198
Email: robinsa@usita.gov

- Angola
- Botswana
- Lesotho
- Malawi
- Mozambique
- Namibia
- Swaziland
- Tanzania
- Zambia
- Zimbabwe

South Africa

The Republic of South Africa is handled by:

Finn Holm-Olsen
Tel: (202) 482-5149; Fax: (202) 482-5198

Eastern Africa

The countries in this region, listed below, are handled by:

Alicia Robinson
Tel: (202) 482-4228; Fax: (202) 482-5198
Email: robinsa@usita.gov

- Comoros
- D'Jibouti
- Eritrea
- Ethiopia
- Kenya
- Madagascar
- Mauritius
- Seychelles
- Somalia
- Sudan
- Uganda

D. Asia and the Pacific

Asia and the Pacific (Except Japan)

There are no individual Country Desk Officers for Asia and the Pacific, with the exception of Japan. All inquiries are handled by:

Trade Information Center
Tel: (800) USA-TRADE; Fax: (202) 482-4473
Web site: www.ita.doc.gov/how_to_export
The countries handled by TIC are:

- Afghanistan
- ASEAN
- Australia
- Bangladesh
- Bhutan
- Brunei
- Burma (Myanmar)
- Cambodia (Kampuchea)
- China (People's Republic of)
- Hong Kong
- India
- Indonesia
- Korea (South)
- Laos
- Macau
- Malaysia
- Maldives
- Mongolia
- Nepal
- New Zealand
- Pacific Islands
- Pakistan
- Philippines
- Singapore
- Sri Lanka
- Taiwan
- Thailand
- Vietnam

Japan

Tel: (202) 482-2427; Fax: (202) 482-0469
The Country Desk Officer for Japan is:

Eric Kennedy (Email: kennedy@usita.gov)

Appendix III
State and Local Sources of Assistance

Organization

The following list gives contact information for offices and organizations offering export assistance in each state and in Puerto Rico and the U.S. Virgin Islands. This is not intended to be an exhaustive directory, merely a starting point with some of the most important U.S. government, state government, and local offices.

U.S. Government Offices

The U.S. government delivers the majority of its exporter assistance programs through the Commerce Department and Small Business Administration offices scattered throughout the U.S. These offices should be a first stop for anyone contemplating exporting and are listed first under each state heading.

The Commerce Department has undergone some reorganization in recent years, most notably through its U.S. Export Assistance Centers. Fifteen USEACs opened in 1994 and 1995; they are located in Baltimore, Chicago, Miami and Los Angeles (Long Beach), Seattle, Dallas, Denver, Cleveland, St. Louis, New York, Atlanta, Philadelphia, New Orleans, Boston and Detroit. USEACs offer a full range of federal export programs and services under one roof. Clients receive assistance by professionals from the SBA, the Department of Commerce, the Export-Import Bank, and other public and private organizations. Each USEAC provides export marketing and trade finance assistance, customized counseling, and customer service. In 1996 a number of Commerce Department district and branch offices were renamed as "Export Assistance Centers" in an effort to continue the centralization of export assistance and to emphasize the role of the Commerce Department as a promoter of U.S. exports. For more information on Commerce Department programs, see "Department of Commerce" on page 6.

Some of the Small Business Administration (SBA) offices have specific services for exporters, while others may refer export queries to the nearest Export Assistance Center. The SBA also oversees the Small Business Development Centers, located throughout the U.S. We have indicated only the network office for each state (Texas has four), which can describe their services and programs and refer you to the nearest appropriate SBDC. For more information on SBA programs, see "Small Business Administration" on page 12.

Other U.S. government-operated offices listed include Minority Business Development Centers (see "Minority Business Development Agency (MBDA)" on page 10 for information), the Ex-Im Bank (see "Export-Import Bank of the United States" on page 98 for more information), and the U.S. Agency for International Development (see "Agency for International Development (AID)" on page 45 for information).

State Government Offices

Most states offer some export assistance, promotion, counseling, or other services through an economic development office. Some have specific offices devoted to international trade and may have overseas offices or representatives. The location of such overseas offices or representatives has been indicated; contact the designated state office for more information. The export of agricultural goods is generally promoted through agriculture departments, which have also been listed. In addition, some states offer financing for exporters. This may be arranged through the financing office noted or through Ex-Im Bank's City/State Program. Some port authorities may offer information or assistance for exporters as well.

Other Contacts

The World Trade Centers Association has dozens of member organizations in the United States and even more abroad. Services and facilities vary considerably, but if there is a WTC in your area they may be the best source of information and contacts beyond government assistance programs and fees are usually modest. An assortment of other international trade clubs and groups have been listed below; there are certainly many more, but those included are among the more active.

Some other valuable contacts include District Export Councils (DECs) and local chambers of commerce. Assistance from DECs may be obtained through the Department of Commerce district offices with which they are affiliated. These DECs assist in many of the workshops and seminars on exporting arranged by the district offices or they may sponsor their own. DEC members may also provide direct, personal counseling to less experienced exporters, suggesting marketing strategies, trade contacts, and ways to maximize success in overseas markets. Check your local telephone directory for chamber of commerce listings; chambers in larger cities are most likely to be active in promoting international trade for its members.

Alabama

U.S. Department of Commerce
Export Assistance Center
950 22nd St. North, Suite 707
Birmingham, AL 35203
Tel: (205) 731-1331; Fax: (205) 731-0076
Email: OBirming@doc.gov

U.S. Small Business Administration District Office
2121 8th Ave. North, Suite 200
Birmingham, AL 35203-2398
Tel: (205) 731-1344; Fax: (205) 731-1404

Small Business Development Center
University of Alabama
1717 - 11th Ave. South, Suite 419
Birmingham, AL 35294-4410
Tel: (205) 934-7260; Fax: (205) 934-7645
Email: sandefur@uab.edu
Web site: www.asbdc.org

Alabama Development Office
401 Adams Avenue, Ste 600
Montgomery, AL 36130
Tel: (334) 242-0400; Fax: (334) 242-2414
Web site: www.ado.state.al.us
Overseas offices: Hanover, Germany; Tokyo, Japan; Seoul, South Korea

Foreign Trade Relations Commission
International Trade Center, Suite 131
250 N. Water Street
Mobile, AL 36602
Tel: (334) 433-1151; Fax: (334) 438-2711

Alabama Dept. of Agriculture & Industries
Marketing and Economic Division
P.O. Box 3336
Beard Bldg
Montgomery, AL 36109-0336
Tel: (334) 240-7245; Fax: (334) 240-7270

North Alabama International Trade Association
P.O. Box 2457
Huntsville, AL 35804
Tel: (256) 536-1854; Fax: (256) 539-0945
Web site: www.naita.org

Center for International Trade & Commerce
250 N Water St., Ste 131
Mobile, AL 36602
Tel: (334) 441-7012; Fax: (334) 438-2711
Email: citcmob@maf.mobile.al.us
Web site: www.maf.mobile.al.us/~citcmob/

Madison County Commission
International Trade Program
100 Northside Square
Huntsville, AL 35801-4820
Tel: (256) 532-3505; Fax: (256) 532-3704
Email: ped@co.madison.al.us

Alabama International Trade Center
University of Alabama
P.O. Box 870396
Tuscaloosa, AL 35487-0396
Tel: (205) 348-7621; Fax: (205) 348-6974

Alaska

U.S. Department of Commerce
Export Assistance Center
3601 C Street, Suite 700
Anchorage, AK 99503
Tel: (907) 271-6237; Fax: (907) 271-6242
Email: OAnchora@doc.gov

U.S. Small Business Administration District Office
222 West 8th Ave.
Anchorage, AK 99513-7559
Tel: (907) 271-4022; Fax: (907) 271-4545

Small Business Development Center
State Network Office
University of Alaska at Anchorage
430 West 7th Ave., Suite 110
Anchorage, AK 99501
Tel: (907) 274-7232; Fax: (907) 274-9524
Email: anjaf@uaa.alaska.edu

Alaska Office of International Trade
3601 C Street, Suite 700
Anchorage, AK 99503
Tel: (907) 269-8100; Fax: (907) 269-8125
Web site: www.state.ak.us
Overseas offices: Tokyo, Japan; Seoul, South Korea; Taipei, Taiwan

Alaska Department of Natural Resources
Division of Agriculture
1800 Glen Highway, Suite 12
Palmer, AK 99645-6736
Tel: (907) 745-7200; Fax: (907) 745-7112
Web site: www.dnr.state.ak.us

Alaska Industrial Development & Export Authority (AIDEA)
480 West Tudor Road
Anchorage, AK 99503
Tel: (907) 269-3000; Fax: (907) 269-3044
Web site: www.aidea.org

World Trade Center Alaska/Anchorage
421 W. First Ave., Ste 300
Anchorage, AK 99501
Tel: (907) 278-7233; Fax: (907) 278-2982
Email: WTCAK@compuserve.com

Arizona

U.S. Department of Commerce
Export Assistance Center
2901 N. Central Avenue, Suite 970
Phoenix, AZ 85012
Tel: (602) 640-2513; Fax: (602) 640-2518
Email: OPhoenix@doc.gov

Export Assistance Center
166 West Alameda
Tuscon, Arizona 85726
Tel: (520) 670-5540; Fax: (520) 791-5413

U.S. Small Business Administration District Office
2828 N. Central Avenue
Phoenix, AZ 85004-1025
Tel: (602) 640-2316; Fax: (602) 640-2360

Small Business Development Center
Maricopa County Community College
2411 W 14th Street, Suite 132
Tempe, AZ 85281
Tel: (602) 230-7308; Fax: (602) 230-7989
Email: york@maricopa.edu
Web site: www.dist.maricopa.edu/sbdc

Arizona Department of Commerce
International Trade and Investment Division
3800 N. Central, Suite 1500
Phoenix, AZ 85012
Tel: (602) 280-1371; Fax: (602) 280-1378
Web site: www.state.az.us/ep/commhome.html
Overseas offices: London, England; Hermosillo, Mexico; Mexico City, Mexico; Tokyo, Japan; Taipei, Taiwan

Arizona Department of Agriculture
International Services
1688 West Adams
Phoenix, AZ 85007
Tel: (602) 542-0982; Fax: (602) 542-0969
Web site: http://agriculture.state.az.us

World Trade Center - Arizona
201 N Central Ave., Ste 2700
Phoenix, AZ 85073-2700
Tel: (602) 495-6480; Fax: (602) 253-9488
Email: wtcaz@mail.com

City of Tuscon, Office of Economic Development
International Trade Program
P.O. Box 27210
Tucson, AZ 85726-7210
Tel: (520) 791-5093; Fax: (520) 791-5413
Email: Bbourla1@ci.tuscon.az.us

Arizona-Mexico Commission
1700 W. Washington
State Capitol Bldg., Suite 180
Phoenix, AZ 85007
Tel: (602) 542-1345; Fax: (602) 542-1411
Web site: www.azmc.org

Arkansas

U.S. Department of Commerce
Export Assistance Center
Suite 700, TCBY Tower Building
425 West Capitol Avenue
Little Rock, AR 72201
Tel: (501) 324-5794; Fax: (501) 324-7380
Email: OLittleR@doc.gov

U.S. Small Business Administration District Office
2120 Riverfront Drive, Suite 100
Little Rock, AR 72202
Tel: (501) 324-5278; Fax: (501) 324-6072

Small Business Development Center (SBDC)
State Network Office
University of Arkansas at Little Rock
College of Business Administration
100 South Main, Suite 401
Little Rock, AR 72201
Tel: (501) 324-9043; Fax: (501) 324-9049
Web site: www.ualr.edu/~sbdcdept/

Arkansas Dept. of Economic Development
Foreign Trade and Investment Division/ADED
One State Capitol Mall
Little Rock, AR 72201
Tel: (501) 682-2460; Fax: (501) 324-9856
Web site: www.1800arkansas.com
Overseas offices: Brussels, Belgium; Tokyo, Japan; Mexico City, Mexico; Kuala Lumpur, Malaysia

Arkansas Development Finance Authority (ADFA)
100 S. Main, Suite 200
Little Rock, AR 72201
Tel: (501) 682-5900; Fax: (501) 682-3350

Arkansas Dept. fo Economic Development
One State Capitol Mall, 4th Floor
Little Rock, AR 72201
Tel: (501) 682-1121; Fax: (501) 682-3456

Arkansas International Center
University of Arkansas at Little Rock
Stabler Hall, Room 304
2801 South University
Little Rock, AR 72204
Tel: (501) 569-3282; Fax: (501) 569-8347
Web site: www.ualr.edu/~lsdept/headpage.htm

California (Southern)

U.S. Department of Commerce
Export Assistance Center
One World Trade Center, Ste. 1670
Long Beach, CA 90831
Tel: (562) 980-4550; Fax: (562) 980-4561
Email: OLongBea@doc.gov

U.S. Department of Commerce
Export Assistance Center
350 South Figueroa Street, Suite 172
Los Angeles, CA 90071
Tel: (213) 894-8784; Fax: (213) 894-8789

U.S. Department of Commerce
Export Assistance Center
2940 Inland Empire Blvd., Suite 121
Ontario, CA 91764
Tel: (909) 466-4134; Fax: (909) 466-4140
Email: OOntario@doc.gov

U.S. Department of Commerce
Export Assistance Center
6363 Greenwich Drive, Suite 230
San Diego, CA 92122
Tel: (619) 557-5395; Fax: (619) 557-6176
Email: OSanDieg@doc.gov

U.S. Department of Commerce
Export Assistance Center
3300 Irvine Avenue, Suite 345
Newport Beach, CA 92660
Tel: (949) 660-0144; Fax: (949) 660-9347
Web site: www.primenet.com/~bxawest

U.S. Small Business Administration District Office
550 West C Street, Suite 550
San Diego, CA 92101-3500
Tel: (619) 557-7250; Fax: (619) 557-5894

U.S. Small Business Administration District Office
200 W. Santa Ana Blvd., Suite 700
Santa Ana, CA 92701
Tel: (714) 550-7420; Fax: (714) 550-0191

Small Business Development Center
330 N. Brand Blvd., Suite 190
Glendale, CA 91203-2304
Tel: (818) 552-3254; Fax: (818) 398-3059

Small Business Development Center
4275 Executive Square, Suite 920
La Jolla, CA 92037
Tel: (619) 453-9388; Fax: (619) 450-1997
Email: sbdc@smallbiz.org
Web site: www.smallbiz.org

Export Small Business Development Center of Southern California
222 N. Sepulveda, Suite 1600
El Segundo, CA 90245
Tel: (800) 371-1110; Fax: (310) 606-0155
Email: info@exportsbdc.org
Web site: www.exportsbdc.org

Ex-Im Bank Western Regional Office
One World Trade Center, Suite 1670
Long Beach, CA 90831
Tel: (562) 980-4580; Fax: (562) 980-4590
Web site: www.exim.gov

California International Trade and Investment Agency
Office of Export Development
One World Trade Center, Suite 990
Long Beach, CA 90831
Tel: (562) 590-5965; Fax: (562) 590-5958
Web site: www.commerce.ca.gov/international

California Export Finance Office (CEFO)
California Trade and Commerce Agency
One World Trade Center, Suite 900
Long Beach, CA 90831-0900
Tel: (562) 499-6014; Fax: (562) 499-6080

Greater Los Angeles World Trade Center Association
One World Trade Center, Suite 295
Long Beach, CA 90831-0205
Tel: (562) 495-7070; Fax: (562) 495-7071
Email: infola@wtcala-lb.com

Greater Los Angeles World Trade Center
350 S. Figueroa Street, Suite 172
Los Angeles, CA 90071
Tel: (213) 680-1888; Fax: (213) 680-1878
Email: infola@wtcala-lb.com

World Trade Center Association of Orange County
Tel: (949) 724-9822; Fax: (949) 760-8873

Economic Development Corporation of Los Angeles County
515 South Flower Street, Suite 3200
Los Angeles, CA 90071
Tel: (213) 622-4300; Fax: (213) 622-7100

Foreign Trade Association of Southern California
900 Wilshire Boulevard, Suite 1434
Los Angeles, CA 90017
Tel: (213) 627-0634; Fax: (213) 627-0398
Email: foreigntrade@earthlink.net
Web site: www.ftasc.org

California (Northern)

U.S. Department of Commerce
Export Assistance Center
101 Park Center Plaza, Suite 1001
San Jose, CA 95113

U.S. Department of Commerce
Export Assistance Center
250 Montgomery Street, 14th Floor
San Francisco, CA 94104
Tel: (415) 705-2300; Fax: (415) 705-2297
Email: OSanFran@doc.gov

U.S. Department of Commerce
Export Assistance Center
5201 Great America Parkway, Suite 456
Santa Clara, CA 95054
Tel: (408) 970-4610; Fax: (408) 970-4618
Email: OSantaCl@doc.gov

U.S. Small Business Administration District Office
455 Market Street, Suite 2200
San Francisco, CA 94105
Tel: (415) 744-2118; Fax: (415) 744-2119

San Francisco Small Business Development Center
711 Van Ness Ave., Suite. 305
San Francisco, CA 94102
Tel: (415) 561-1890; Fax: (415) 561-1894
Email: sfsbdc@ziplink.net

Port of Oakland
530 Water Street
Oakland, CA 94607
Tel: (510) 272-1100; Fax: (510) 839-5104
Web site: www.portofoakland.com

World Trade Center of San Francisco
250 Montgomery Street, 14th Floor
San Francisco, CA 94104
Tel: (415) 392-2705; Fax: (415) 392-1710
Email: pyap@bawtc.baytrade.org
Web site: www.wtcsf.org

Asian Business League of San Francisco
233 Sansome St., Suite 1108
San Francisco, CA 94104
Tel: (415) 788-4664; Fax: (415) 788-4756

California Council for International Trade
580 Washington Street, Suite 305
San Francisco, CA 94111
Tel: (415) 788-4127; Fax: (415) 788-5356
Email: ccit@well.com
Web site: ccit.net

California-Southeast Asia Business Council
1946 Embarcadero, Suite 200
Oakland, CA 94606
Tel: (510) 536-1967; Fax: (510) 261-9598
Web site: www.calsea.org

City of San Jose Office of Economic Development
International Program
50 W. San Fernando Street, Suite 900
San Jose, CA 95113
Tel: (408) 277-3439, 277-5880; Fax: (408) 277-3615

Vista Community College
Center for International Trade Development
2020 Milvia Street
Berkeley, CA 94704
Tel: (510) 841-8860 x271

World Affairs Council of Northern California
312 Sutter Street, Suite 200
San Francisco, CA 94108
Tel: (415) 982-2541; Fax: (415) 982-5028
Web site: www.wacsf.org

California (Central)

U.S. Department of Commerce
Export Assistance Center
917 7th Street, 2nd Floor
Sacramento, CA 95814
Tel: (916) 498-5155; Fax: (916) 498-5923

U.S. Small Business Administration District Office
2719 N. Air Fresno Dr.
Fresno, CA 93727-1547
Tel: (559) 487-5791; Fax: (559) 487-5292

U.S. Small Business Administration District Office
660 J Street, Suite 215
Sacramento, CA 95814-2413
Tel: (916) 498-6410; Fax: (916) 498-6422

Small Business Development Center
California Trade and Commerce Agency
801 K Street, Suite 1700
Sacramento, CA 95814
Tel: (800) 303-6600, (916) 324-5068; Fax: (916) 322-5084
Web site: http://commerce.ca.gov/business/small/starting/sb_sbdcl.html

California International Trade and Investment Agency
801 K Street
Sacramento, CA 95814
Tel: (916) 324-5511; Fax: (916) 324-5791
Email: iti@smpp.doc.ca.gov
Web site: www.commerce.ca.gov
Overseas offices: London, England; Frankfurt, Germany; Hong Kong; Jakarta, Indonesia; Jerusalem, Israel; Tokyo, Japan; Mexico City, Mexico; Johannesburg, South Africa; Taipei, Taiwan

California Department of Food and Agriculture
Export Program
1220 N Street, Suite A280
Sacramento, CA 95814
Tel: (916) 654-0389; Fax: (916) 653-2604
Web site: www.cdfa.ca.gov/exports

California Central Coast World Trade Center Assoc.
300 Esplanade Drive, Suite 1900
Oxnard, CA 93030
Tel: (805) 988-1406; Fax: (805) 988-1862
Email: infor@worldtradecenter.org
Web site: www.worldtradecenter.org

Colorado

U.S. Department of Commerce
Export Assistance Center
1625 Broadway, Suite 680
Denver, CO 80202
Tel: (303) 844-6623; Fax: (303) 844-5651
Email: Odenver@doc.gov

U.S. Small Business Administration District Office
721 - 19th Street, Suite 500
Denver, CO 80202
Tel: (303) 844-0500; Fax: (303) 844-0506

Small Business Development Center
Front Range Community College
3645 West 112th Ave.
Westminster, CO 80030
Tel: (303) 460-1032; Fax: (303) 469-7143
Email: fr_henry@cccs.ccoes.edu

Colorado International Trade Office
Governor's Office
1625 Broadway, Suite 900
Denver, CO 80202
Tel: (303) 892-3850; Fax: (303) 892-3820
Email: ito@state.co.us
Web site: www.state.co.us/gov.gir/govnr.dir/ito/intl_trade.gov.htm
Overseas offices: London, England; Tokyo, Japan; Mexico City, Mexico

Colorado Department of Agriculture
Markets Division
700 Kipling Street, Suite 4000
Lakewood, CO 80215-5894
Tel: (303) 239-4100; Fax: (303) 239-4125
Web site: www.state.co.us/gov_dir/ag_dir/ag_home.html

World Trade Center Denver
1625 Broadway, Suite 680
Denver, CO 80202
Tel: (303) 592-5760; Fax: (303) 592-5228
Email: wtcdn@worldnet.att.net
Web site: www.wtcdn.com

Connecticut

U.S. Department of Commerce
Export Assistance Center
213 Court Street, Suite 903
Middletown, CT 06457-3346
Tel: (860) 638-6950; Fax: (860) 638-6970
Email: OHartfor@doc.gov

U.S. Small Business Administration District Office
330 Main St.
Hartford, CT 06106
Tel: (860) 240-4700; Fax: (860) 240-4659

Service Corps of Retired Executives (SCORE)
24 Belden Ave.
Norwalk, CT 06850
Tel: (203) 847-7348; Fax: (203) 849-9308

Small Business Development Center
University of Connecticut
2 Bourne Place, Box U94
Storrs, CT 06269-5094
Tel: (860) 486-4135; Fax: (860) 486-1576
Email: statedirector@ct.sbdc.uconn.edu
Web site: www.sbdc.uconn.edu

Connecticut Department of Economic Development
International Division
505 Hudson Street
Hartford, CT 06106
Tel: (860) 270-8067; Fax: (860) 270-8070
Email: DECD@po.state.ct.us
Web site: www.state.ct.us/ecd/international

Connecticut Department of Agriculture
Bureau of Marketing and Technology
765 Asylum Avenue
Hartford, CT 06105-2822
Tel: (860) 713-2503; Fax: (860) 713-2516
Email: ctdeptag@po.state.ct.us
Web site: www.state.ct.uc/doag

Connecticut Development Authority
999 West Street
Rocky Hill, CT 06067
Tel: (860) 258-7800; Fax: (860) 257-7582

Connecticut Foreign Trade Association
P.O. Box 1601
Norwalk, CT 06852-1601
Tel: (203) 406-6628; Fax: (203) 406-6084

Connecticut International Trade Association
P.O. Box 974
East Gramby, CT 06026
Tel: (860) 653-7765; Fax: (860) 653-2705

Connecticut World Trade Center
330 Water St.
Bridgeport, CT 06604
Tel: (203) 336-5353; Fax: (203) 331-9959
Email: NickCwta@aol.com
Web site: www.imex.com/cwta.html

Delaware

U.S. Department of Commerce
Delaware is served by the Philadelphia office:

U.S. Department of Commerce
Export Assistance Center
615 Chestnut Street, Suite 1501
Philadelphia, PA 19106
Tel: (215) 597-6101; Fax: (215) 597-6123
Email: OPhilade@doc.gov

U.S. Small Business Administration Branch Office
824 N. Market St.
Wilmington, DE 19801-3011
Tel: (302) 573-6294; Fax: (302) 573-6060

Small Business Development Center
University of Delaware
102 MBNA America Hall
Newark, DE 19716-2711
Tel: (302) 831-1555; Fax: (302) 831-1423
Email: clinton.tymes@mvs.udel.edu
Web site: www.be.udel.edu/sbdc

State of Delaware Development Office
Division of Economic Development
99 Kings Highway
Dover, DE 19901
Tel: (302) 739-4271; Fax: (302) 739-5749
Web site: www.state.de.us (Follow links for "Economic Development")
Overseas offices: Tokyo, Japan; Merida, Mexico; Veracruz, Mexico

Delaware Department of Agriculture
c/o Delaware Development Office
99 Kings Highway
Dover, DE 19901-7305
Tel: (302) 739-4271; Fax: (302) 739-5749
Web site: www.state.de.us

Port of Wilmington
P.O. Box 1191
Wilmington, DE 19899
Tel: (302) 571-4600; Fax: (302) 571-4646

World Trade Center Delaware, Inc.
831 Washington Street, Suite 100
Wilmington, DE 19801
Tel: (302) 656-7905; Fax: (302) 656-7956
Email: wtcde@dca.net

District of Columbia

U.S. Department of Commerce
Washington, DC is served by the Baltimore office:

U.S. Department of Commerce
Export Assistance Center
World Trade Center, Suite 2432
401 East Pratt Street
Baltimore, MD 21202
Tel: (410) 962-4539; Fax: (410) 962-4529
Email: OBaltimo@doc.gov

U.S. Small Business Administration District Office
1110 Vermont Ave. NW
Washington, DC 20005
Tel. (202) 606-4000; Fax: (202) 606-4225

Small Business Development Center
Howard University
2600 Sixth Street NW, Room 128
Washington, DC 20059
Tel: (202) 806-1550; Fax: (202) 806-1777
Email: husbdc@cldc.howard.edu
Web site: www.cldc.howard.edu/husbdc

District of Columbia Office of International Business
717 14th Street NW
Suite 1100, Box 4
Washington, DC 20005
Tel: (202) 727-1576; Fax: (202) 727-1588

Greater Washington Board of Trade
1129 20th Street, NW, Suite 200
Washington, DC 20036
Tel: (202) 857-5900; Fax: (202) 223-2648
Email: info@bot.org
Web site: www.bot.org

Export-Import Bank of the U.S.
Washington, DC Office
811 Vermont Avenue, NW
Washington, DC 20571
Tel: (800) 565-EXIM, (202) 565-EXIM; Fax: (202) 565-3380

World Trade Center Washington
1300 Pennsylvania Avenue, NW, Suite M1 100
Washington, DC 20004
Tel: (202) 418-4224; Fax: (202) 418-4238
Web site: www.itcdc.com

Florida

U.S. Department of Commerce
Export Assistance Center
5600 NW 36th St., Suite 617
Miami, FL 33166
Tel: (305) 526-7425; Fax: (305) 526-7434
Email: OMiami@doc.gov

U.S. Department of Commerce
Export Assistance Center
Eola Park Centre, Suite 1270
200 E. Robinson Street
Orlando, FL 32801
Tel: (407) 648-6235; Fax: (407) 648-6756
Email: OOrlando@doc.gov

U.S. Department of Commerce
Export Assistance Center
The Capitol, Suite 2001
Tallahassee, FL 32399-0001
Tel: (850) 488-6469; Fax: (850) 487-3014
Email: OTallaha@doc.gov

U.S. Department of Commerce
Export Assistance Center
1130 Cleveland Street
Clearwater, FL 33755
Tel: (727) 441-1742; Fax: (727) 449-2889
Email: OClearwa@doc.gov

U.S. Small Business Administration District Office
100 S. Biscayne Blvd., 7th Floor
Miami, FL 33131
Tel: (305) 536-5521; Fax: (305) 536-5058

U.S. Small Business Administration District Office
7825 Bay Meadows Way, Suite 100B
Jacksonville, FL 32256-7504
Tel: (904) 443-1900; Fax: (904) 443-1980

Small Business Development Center
University of West Florida
19 West Garden Street, Suite 300
Pensacola, FL 32501
Tel: (800) 644-SBDC, (904) 444-2060; Fax: (904) 444-2070

Minority Business Development Center
1 SW 1st Avenue, Box 25
Miami, FL 33130
Tel: (305) 536-5054; Fax: (305) 350-7068
Web site: www.mbda.gov

Ex-Im Bank Southeast Regional Office
P.O. Box 590570
Miami, FL 33159-0570
Tel: (305) 526-7425; Fax: (305) 526-7435
Web site: www.exim.gov

Enterprise Florida
Office of International Trade
2801 Ponce de Leon Blvd., Suite 700
Coral Gables, FL 33134
Tel: (305) 569-2650; Fax: (305) 569-2686

Florida Trade Data Center
P.O. Box 590750
Miami, FL 33159-0750
Tel: (305) 876-9747; Fax: (305) 876-9433

Florida State Department of Agriculture
Mayo Building, Room 413
409 South Calhoun St.
Tallahassee, FL 32399-0800
Tel: (850) 488-4366; Fax: (850) 922-0374
Web site: www.sl-ag.com

Florida Export Finance Corp.
P.O. Box 526524
Miami, FL 33152-6524
Tel: (305) 870-5027; Fax: (305) 870-5017

Jacksonville Port Authority
P.O. Box 3005
Jacksonville, FL 32206
Tel: (904) 630-3080; Fax: (904) 630-3010
Web site: www.jaxport.com

World Trade Center Ft. Lauderdale
200 East Las Olas Boulevard, Suite 100
Ft. Lauderdale, FL 33301
Tel: (954) 761-9797; Fax: (954) 761-9990
Web site: www.worldtradefl.com
Email: mail@worldtradefl.com

World Trade Center Miami
P.O. Box 590508
Miami, FL 33159-0508
Tel: (305) 871-7910; Fax: (305) 871-7904
Web site: www.worldtrade.org
Email: info@worldtrade.org

World Trade Center Orlando
201 S. Orange Avenue, Suite 1070
Orlando, FL 32801
Tel: (407) 649-1899; Fax: (407) 649-1486
Email: wtcor@gdi.net
Web site: www.gdi.net/wtc

World Trade Center Tampa Bay
800 Second Avenue South, Suite 340
St. Petersburg, FL 33701
Tel: (727) 822-2492; Fax: (727) 823-8128
Email: wtctb@gate.ne
Web site: www.worldcommerce.org

Georgia

U.S. Department of Commerce
Export Assistance Center
285 Peachtree Center Ave. NE, Suite 200
Atlanta, GA 30303-1229
Tel: (404) 657-1900; Fax: (404) 657-1970
Email: OAtlanta@doc.gov

U.S. Department of Commerce
Export Assistance Center
6001 Chatham Center Drive, Suite 100
Savannah, GA 31405
Tel: (912) 652-4204; Fax: (912) 652-4241
Email: OSavanna@doc.gov

U.S. Small Business Administration Regional Office
1720 Peachtree Rd. NW, Suite 496
Atlanta, GA 30309-2482
Tel: (404) 347-4999; Fax: (404) 347-2355

U.S. Small Business Administration District Office
1720 Peachtree Rd. NW, 6th Floor
Atlanta, GA 30309
Tel: (404) 347-4147; Fax: (404) 347-4745

Small Business Development Center
University of Georgia
Chicopee Complex
1180 East Broad St.
Athens, GA 30602-5412
Tel: (706) 542-6762; Fax: (706) 542-6776
Email: hlogan@sbdc.uga.edu
Web site: www.sbdc.uga.edu

Minority Business Development Center
270 Peachtree Street, Suite 140
Atlanta, GA 30303
Tel: (404) 577-7734; Fax: (404) 577-7737
Web site: www.atlmbdc.com

International Trade Division
Georgia Dept. of Industry, Trade and Tourism
285 Peachtree Center Avenue, NE, Suite 1100
Atlanta, GA 30303
Tel: (404) 656-3571; Fax: (404) 651-6505
Email: trade@georgia.org
Web site: www.georgia.org
Overseas offices: Brussels, Belgium; Sao Paulo, Brazil; Toronto, Canada; Shanghai, China; Jerusalem, Israel; Tokyo, Japan; Seoul, South Korea; Mexico City, Mexico; Johannesburg, South Africa; Taipei, Taiwan

Georgia Department of Agriculture
International Trade Division
19 Martin Luther King Jr. Drive
Capitol Square
340 Agriculture Building
Atlanta, GA 30334
Tel: (404) 656-3740; Fax: (404) 656-0380

Georgia Housing & Finance Authority
60 Executive Park South, NE
Atlanta, GA 30329
Tel: (404) 657-1958
Web site: www.dca.state.ga.us

Georgia Ports Authority (Savannah)
P.O. Box 2406
Savannah, GA 31402
Tel: (912) 964-3811; Fax: (912) 964-3921
Web site: www.gaports.com

World Trade Center Atlanta
303 Peachtree Street NE
Lower Lobby 100
Atlanta, GA 30308-3252
Tel: (404) 880-1550; Fax: (404) 880-1555
Email: wtcatl@mindspring.com
Web site: www.wtcatlanta.com/

Hawaii

U.S. Department of Commerce
Export Assistance Center
P.O. Box 50026
Honolulu, HI 96850
Tel: (808) 522-8040; Fax: (808) 522-8045
Email: OHonolul@doc.gov

U.S. Small Business Administration District Office
300 Ala Moana Blvd.
Honolulu, HI 96850-4981
Tel: (808) 541-2990; Fax: (808) 541-2976

Small Business Development Center
University of Hawaii at Hilo
200 West Kawili Street
Hilo, HI 96720-4091
Tel: (808) 974-7515; Fax: (808) 974-7683
Email: darrylm@interpac.net

Hawaii Department of Agriculture
Market Development Branch
P.O. Box 22159
Honolulu, HI 96823-2159
Tel: (808) 973-9595; Fax: (808) 973-9590
Web site: www.hawaiiag.org:591

Hawaii Dept. of Business, Economic Development & Tourism
Product Trade Branch
P.O. Box 2359
Honolulu, HI 96804
Tel: (808) 587-2717; Fax: (808) 587-3388

State of Hawaii World Trade Center, Honolulu
250 South Hotel Street, 5th Floor
Honolulu, HI 96813
Tel: (808) 587-2750; Fax: (808) 587-3833
Email: dling@dbedthawaii.gov
Web site: www.hawaii.gov/dbedt/

Business Action Center
1130 North Nimitz Highway, Room A-254
Honolulu, HI 96817
Tel: (808) 586-2545; Fax: (808) 586-2544

Pacific Business Center Program
College of Business Administration
University of Hawaii at Manoa
2404 Maile Way, Rm. A413
Honolulu, HI 96822-2220
Tel: (808) 956-6286; Fax: (808) 956-6278
Web site: www.cba.hawaii.edu/pbcp

Idaho

U.S. Department of Commerce
Export Assistance Center
700 West State Street, 2nd Floor
Boise, ID 83720
Tel: (208) 334-3857; Fax: (208) 334-2783
Email: OBoise@doc.gov

U.S. Small Business Administration District Office
1020 Main Street
Boise, ID 83702
Tel: (208) 334-1696; Fax: (208) 334-1696

Small Business Development Center
Boise State University
1910 University Drive
Boise, ID 83725
Tel: (208) 426-1640; Fax: (208) 426-3877
Email: jhogge@bsu.idbsu.edu
Web site: www.idbsu.edu/isbdc

Idaho Department of Commerce
Division of International Business Development
700 West State Street, 2nd Floor
P.O. Box 83720
Boise, ID 83720-0093
Tel: (208) 334-3857; Fax: (208) 334-2783

Idaho Department of Agriculture
Agriculture Marketing
P.O. Box 790
Boise, ID 83701
Tel: (208) 332-8530; Fax: (208) 334-2879
Web site: www.agri.state.id.us

Illinois

U.S. Department of Commerce
Export Assistance Center
Xerox Center, Suite 2440
55 West Monroe St.
Chicago, IL 60603
Tel: (312) 353-8045; Fax: (312) 353-8120
Email: OChicago@doc.gov

U.S. Department of Commerce
Export Assistance Center
515 North Court Street
Rockford, IL 61103
Tel: (815) 987-8123; Fax: (815) 963-7943
Email: ORockfor@doc.gov

U.S. Department of Commerce
Export Assistance Center
610 Central Avenue, Suite 150
Highland Park, IL 60035
Tel: (847) 681-8010; Fax: (847) 681-8012

U.S. Small Business Administration District Office
500 W. Madison St.
Chicago, IL 60661-2511
Tel: (312) 353-4528; Fax: (312) 886-5688

U.S. Small Business Administration Branch Office
511 W. Capitol Ave., Suite 302
Springfield, IL 62704
Tel: (217) 492-4416; Fax: (217) 492-4867

Small Business Development Center
Department of Commerce & Community Affairs
620 East Adams Street, 3rd Floor
Springfield, IL 62701
Tel: (217) 524-5856; Fax: (217) 785-6328
Web site: www.commerce.state.il.us

Ex-Im Bank Midwest Regional Office
55 West Monroe St., Suite 2440
Chicago, IL 60603
Tel: (312) 353-8081; Fax: (312) 353-8098
Web site: www.exim.gov

Illinois Dept. of Commerce & Community Affairs
Illinois International Business Division
100 West Randolph, Suite 3-400
Chicago, IL 60601
Tel: (312) 814-2089; Fax: (312) 814-6581
Overseas offices: Brussels, Belgium; Hong Kong; Budapest, Hungary; Tokyo, Japan; Mexico City, Mexico; Warsaw, Poland

Illinois Department of Agriculture
International Trade and Marketing Division
P.O. Box 19281
State Fairgrounds
Springfield, IL 62794-9281
Tel: (217) 782-6675; Fax: (217) 524-5960
Web site: www.agr.state.il.us

Illinois Development Finance Authority
233 S. Wacker Drive, Suite 4000
Chicago, IL 60606
Tel: (312) 627-1434; Fax: (312) 496-0578
Web site: www.idfa.com

Illinois World Trade Center Association
200 World Trade Center, Suite 2400
Chicago, IL 60654
Tel: (312) 467-0550; Fax: (312) 467-0615
Email: info@wtcc.org
Web site:: www.wtcc.org

International Trade Club of Chicago
203 N. Wabash, Suite 2208
Chicago, IL 60601
Tel: (312) 368-9197; Fax: (312) 368-0673

Indiana

U.S. Department of Commerce
Export Assistance Center
11405 N. Pennsylvania St., Suite 106
Carmel, IN 46032
Tel: (317) 582-2300; Fax: (317) 582-2301
Email: OIndiana@doc.gov

U.S. Small Business Administration District Office
429 N. Pennsylvania St.
Indianapolis, IN 46204-1873
Tel: (317) 226-7272; Fax: (317) 226-7259

Small Business Development Center
342 North Senate Avenue
Indianapolis, IN 46204
Tel: (317) 261-3030; Fax: (317) 261-3053

Small Business Development Center
Export Assistance Center
216 West Allen St.
Bloomington, IN 47403
Tel: (812) 339-8937; Fax: (812) 335-7352

Minority Business Development Center
c/o Gary Chamber of Commerce
504 Broadway, Suite 328
Gary, IN 46402
Tel: (219) 885-7407; Fax: (219) 885-7408

Indiana Department of Commerce
International Trade Division
One North Capitol, Suite 700
Indianapolis, IN 46204-2288
Tel: (317) 233-4337; Fax: (317) 233-1680
Email: abrown@commerce.state.in.us
Web site: www.state.in.us/doc/indiresidents/intmarket/index.html
Overseas offices: Toronto, Canada; Beijing, China; Yokohama, Japan; Seoul, South Korea; Mexico City, Mexico; Amsterdam, Netherlands; Taipei, Taiwan

Indiana Office of the Commissioner of Agriculture
ISTA Center, Suite 414
150 West Market Street
Indianapolis, IN 46204
Tel: (317) 232-8770; Fax: (317) 232-1362
Web site: www.ai.org/oca

Indiana Manufacturers' Association
2400 One American Sq., Box 82012
Indianapolis, IN 46282
Tel: (317) 632-2474; Fax: (317) 231-2320
Web site: www.imaweb.com

Michiana World Trade Club
c/o Chamber of Commerce of St. Joseph County
P.O. Box 1677
South Bend, IN 46634-1677
Tel: (219) 234-0051; Fax: (219) 289-0358

Iowa

U.S. Department of Commerce
Export Assistance Center
601 Locust Street, Suite 100
Des Moines, IA 50309
Tel: (515) 288-8614; Fax: (515) 288-1437
Email: ODesMoin@doc.gov

U.S. Small Business Administration District Office
215 Fourth Ave. SE, Suite 200
Cedar Rapids, IA 52401-1806
Tel: (319) 362-6405; Fax: (319) 362-7861
Web site: www.sba.gov/

U.S. Small Business Administration District Office
210 Walnut Street, Room 749
Des Moines, IA 50309
Tel: (515) 284-4422; Fax: (515) 284-4572

Small Business Development Center
137 Lynn Avenue
Ames, IA 50014
Tel: (800) 373-7232, (515) 292-6351; Fax: (515) 292-0020
Email: rmanning@iastate.edu
Web site: www.iowasbdc.org/staff.html

Iowa Department of Economic Development
Department of International Trade
200 East Grand Avenue
Des Moines, IA 50309
Tel: (515) 242-4729; Fax: (515) 242-4918
Email: international@idcd.state.ia.us
Web site: www.state.ia.us/government/ided
Overseas offices: Frankfurt, Germany; Hong Kong; Tokyo, Japan; Seoul, South Korea; Mexico City, Mexico

Kansas

U.S. Department of Commerce
Export Assistance Center
209 East William, Suite 300
Wichita, KS 67202-4001
Tel: (316) 269-6160; Fax: (316) 269-6111
Email: OWichita@doc.gov

U.S. Small Business Administration District Office
100 East English St., Suite 510
Wichita, KS 67202
Tel: (316) 269-6616; Fax: (316) 269-6499

Small Business Development Center
Fort Hays State University
109 W. 10th Street
Hays, KS 67601
Tel: (785) 628-6786; Fax: (785) 628-0533
Email: sbdc@fhsuvm.fhsu.edu

Kansas Department of Commerce & Housing
Trade Development Division
700 SW Harrison Street, Suite 1300
Topeka, KS 66603-3712
Tel: (785) 296-4027; Fax: (785) 296-5263
Web site: www.kansascommerce.com
Overseas offices: Sydney, Australia; Brussels, Belgium; Tokyo, Japan

Kansas Department of Commerce & Housing
Agriculture Products Development Division
700 SW Harrison, Suite 1300
Topeka, KS 66603-3712
Tel: (785) 296-3736; Fax: (785) 296-3776
Web site: www.kansascommerce.com

Kansas World Trade Center, Wichita
350 West Douglas Avenue
Wichita, KS 67202-2970
Tel: (316) 262-3232; Fax: (316) 262-3585
Email: mail@kansaswtc.org

The World Trade Council of Wichita, Inc/CIBA
Barton School of Business.
Wichita State University
Campus Box 88
Wichita, KS 67260-0088
Tel: (316) 978-3176; Fax: (316) 978-3698

Kentucky

U.S. Department of Commerce
Export Assistance Center
601 West Broadway, Room 634B
Louisville, KY 40202
Tel: (502) 582-5066; Fax: (502) 582-6573
Email: OLouisvl@doc.gov

U.S. Department of Commerce
Export Assistance Center
2292 S. Highway 27, Suite 320
Somerset, KY 42501
Tel: (606) 677-6160; Fax: (606) 677-6161

U.S. Small Business Administration District Office
Federal Office Building, Room 188
600 Dr. M.L. King Jr. Place
Louisville, KY 40202
Tel: (502) 582-5971; Fax: (502) 582-5009

Small Business Development Center
University of Kentucky
225 Gatton Business and Economics Bldg.
Lexington, KY 40506-0034
Tel: (606) 257-7668; Fax: (606) 323-1907

Minority Business Development Center
609 West Main Street, 3rd Floor
Louisville, KY 40202
Tel: (502) 589-6232; Fax: (502) 589-3228

Kentucky International Trade Office
Cabinet for Economic Development
Capital Plaza Tower, Suite 2400
500 Mero Street
Frankfort, KY 40601
Tel: (800) 626-2930; Fax: (502) 564-3256
Web site: www.think-ky.com
Overseas offices: Brussels, Belgium; Tokyo, Japan

Kentucky Department of Agriculture
Capitol Plaza Tower, 7th floor
500 Mero Street
Frankfort, KY 40601
Tel: (502) 564-4696; Fax: (502) 564-2133

Kentucky World Trade Center
333 West Vine Street
Lexington, KY 40507
Tel: (606) 258-3139; Fax: (606) 233-0658
Email: kwtclex@uky.campuscw.net
Web site: www.kwtc.org

North Kentucky International Trade Association
P.O. Box 668
Florence, KY 41022-0668
Tel: (606) 283-1885; Fax: (606) 283-8178
Email: nkadd@aol.com
Web site: www.pol.com/nkadd

Louisville/Jefferson County Office for Economic Development
600 West Main Street, Suite 400
Louisville, KY 40202-4266
Tel: (502) 574-3051; Fax: (502) 574-3026

Louisiana

U.S. Department of Commerce
Export Assistance Center
365 Canal Street, Suite 2150
New Orleans, LA 70130
Tel: (504) 589-6546; Fax: (504) 589-2337
Email: ONewOrle@doc.gov

U.S. Small Business Administration District Office
365 Canal Street
New Orleans, LA 70130
Tel: (504) 589-6685; Fax: (504) 589-2339

Small Business Development Center
Northeast Louisiana University
College of Business Administration
700 University Avenue, Admin 2-57
Monroe, LA 71209
Tel: (318) 342-5506; Fax: (318) 342-5510

Minority Business Development Center
7240 Crowder Boulevard, Suite 203
New Orleans, LA 70127
Tel: (504) 241-8664; Fax: (504) 241-8902

Louisiana Department of Economic Development
P.O. Box 94185
Baton Rouge, LA 70804-9185
Tel: (225) 342-4320; Fax: (225) 342-5389
Web site: www.lded.state.la.us
Overseas offices: Herborn, Germany; Mexico City, Mexico; Taipei, Taiwan

Louisiana Department of Agriculture
P.O. Box 3334
Baton Rouge, LA 70821-3334
Tel: (225) 922-1280; Fax: (225) 922-1289
Web site: www.ldaf.state.la.us/

Louisiana Economic Development Corp.
P.O. Box 44153
Baton Rouge, LA 70804
Tel: (225) 342-5675; Fax: (225) 342-0142
Web site: www.lded.state.la.us/new

Jefferson Parish Economic Development Commission (JEDCO)
3445 N. Causeway Blvd., Suite 300
Metairie, LA 70002
Tel: (504) 833-1881; Fax: (504) 833-7676
Web site: www.jedco.com

World Trade Center of New Orleans
Executive Offices, Suite 2900
2 Canal Street
New Orleans, LA 70130
Tel: (504) 529-1601; Fax: (504) 529-1691
Web site: www.wtc-no.org/

Southern United States Trade Association (SUSTA)
World Trade Center, Suite 1540
2 Canal Street
New Orleans, LA 70130
Tel: (504) 568-5986; Fax: (504) 568-6010
Email: anna@susta.org

Louisiana International Trade Center
2926 World Trade Center
New Orleans, LA 70130
Tel: (504) 568-8222; Fax: (504) 568-8228
Web site: www.awsg.com/litc

Maine

U.S. Department of Commerce
Export Assistance Center
c/o Maine International Trade Center
511 Congress St.
Portland, ME 04101
Tel: (207) 541-7400; Fax: (207) 541-7420
Email: OPortlan@doc.gov

U.S. Small Business Administration District Office
40 Western Ave., Suite 512
Augusta, ME 04330
Tel: (207) 622-8378; Fax: (207) 622-8277

Small Business Development Center
University of Southern Maine
P.O. Box 9300
Portland, ME 04104-9300
Tel: (207) 780-4949; Fax: (207) 780-4810
Email: msbdc@portland.maine.edu
Web site: www.usm.maine.edu/~sbdc

Maine Dept. of Economic and Community Development
Office of Business Development
59 State House Station
Augusta, ME 04333
Tel: (207) 287-3153; Fax: (207) 287-5701
Web site: www.econdevmaine.com

Maine Dept. of Agriculture
Market Development Division
Food and Rural Resources
Deering Building (AMHI)
State House, Station 28
Augusta, ME 04333
Tel: (207) 287-3491; Fax: (207) 287-7548

Maryland

U.S. Department of Commerce
Export Assistance Center
World Trade Center, Suite 2432
401 East Pratt Street
Baltimore, MD 21202
Tel: (410) 962-4539; Fax: (410) 962-4529
Email: OBaltimo@doc.gov

U.S. Small Business Administration District Office
10 S. Howard St., 6th Fl.
Baltimore, MD 21201-2525
Tel: (410) 962-4392; Fax: (410) 962-1805

Maryland Small Business Development Center
7100 Baltimore Ave., Suite 401
College Park, MD 20740
Tel: (301) 403-8300; Fax: (301) 403-8303
Web site: www.mbs.umd.edu/sbdc

Small Business Development Center
Small Business Resource Center
Towson State University
3 West Baltimore Street
Baltimore, MD 21201
Tel: (410) 659-1930; Fax: (410) 659-1939

Maryland Department of Economic Development
400 Washington Avenue
Courthouse Mezzanine
Towson, MD 21204
Tel: (410) 887-8000; Fax: (410) 887-8017
Web site: www.co.ba.md.us

Maryland Department of Agriculture
Marketing Division
50 Harry S. Truman Parkway
Annapolis, MD 21401
Tel: (410) 841-5770; Fax: (410) 841-5987

Maryland Trade Finance Program
217 E. Redwood Street, 22nd Floor
Baltimore, MD 21202
Tel: (410) 767-6382; Fax: (410) 333-4302

World Trade Center, Baltimore
The World Trade Center, Suite 232
Baltimore, MD 21202
Tel: (410) 576-0022; Fax: (410) 576-0751
Email: menziea@wtci.org
Web site: www.wtci.org

Greater Baltimore Committee
111 South Calvert Street, Suite 1700
Baltimore, MD 21202
Tel: (410) 727-2820; Fax: (410) 539-5705
Web site: www.gbc.org

Massachusetts

U.S. Department of Commerce
Export Assistance Center
164 Northern Avenue
World Trade Center, Suite 307
Boston, MA 02210
Tel: (617) 424-5990; Fax: (617) 424-5992
Email: OBoston@doc.gov

U.S. Department of Commerce
Export Assistance Center
100 Granger Boulevard, Unit 102
Marlborough, MA 01752
Tel: (508) 624-6000; Fax: (508) 624-7145

U.S. Small Business Administration District Office
10 Causeway St., Room 265
Boston, MA 02222-1093
Tel: (617) 565-5590; Fax: (617) 565-5598

U.S. Small Business Administration Branch Office
1441 Main St., Suite 410
Springfield, MA 01103
Tel: (413) 785-0268; Fax: (413) 785-0267

Small Business Development Center
University of Massachusetts - Amherst
School of Management, Room 205
Amherst, MA 01003-4935
Tel: (413) 545-6301; Fax: (413) 545-1273

Massachusetts Office of International Trade
10 Park Plaza, Suite 3720
Boston, MA 02116
Tel: (617) 367-1830; Fax: (617) 227-3488
Email: moiti@state.ma.us
Web site: www.magnet.state.ma.us/moiti/
Overseas offices: Guangzhou, China; Berlin, Germany; Jerusalem, Israel

Massachusetts Department of Food and Agriculture
100 Cambridge Street, 21st Floor
Boston, MA 02202
Tel: (617) 727-3000 x172; Fax: (617) 727-7235
Web site: www.massgrown.org

Massachusetts Industrial Finance Agency (MIFA)
75 Federal Street, 10th Floor
Boston, MA 02110
Tel: (617) 451-2477; Fax: (617) 451-3429
Web site: www.massdevelopment.com

Massachusetts Port Authority (MASSPORT)
International Marketing
One Harborside Drive, Suite 200S
East Boston, MA 02128
Tel: (617) 478-4100; Fax: (617) 478-4160
Web site: www.massport.com

World Trade Center Boston
164 Northern Avenue, Suite 50
Boston, MA 02210-2004
Tel: (617) 385-5000; Fax: (617) 385-5033
Email: wti@wtcb.com
Web site: www.wtcb.com/

Smaller Business Association of New England, Inc.
204 2nd Avenue
Waltham, MA 02451
Tel: (781) 890-9070; Fax: (781) 890-4567
Email: infor@sbane.org
Web site: www.sbane.org

Associated Industries of Massachusetts
P.O. Box 763
Boston, MA 02117-0763
Tel: (617) 262-1180; Fax: (617) 536-6785
Web site: www.aimnet.org

Michigan

U.S. Department of Commerce
Export Assistance Center
211 West Fort St., Suite 2220
Detroit, MI 48226
Tel: (313) 226-3650; Fax: (313) 226-3657
Email: ODetroit@doc.gov

U.S. Department of Commerce
Export Assistance Center
Oakland Pointe Office Building
250 Elizabeth Lake Road, Suite 1300 West
Pontiac, MI 48341
Tel: (248) 975-9600; Fax: (248) 975-9606
Email: OPontiac@doc.gov

U.S. Department of Commerce
Export Assistance Center
425 S. Main St., Suite 103
Ann Arbor, MI 48104
Tel: (734) 741-2430; Fax: (734) 741-2432
Email: OAnnArbo@doc.gov

U.S. Department of Commerce
Export Assistance Center
301 West Fulton St., Suite 718-S
Grand Rapids, MI 49504-6495
Tel: (616) 458-3564; Fax: (616) 458-3872
Email: OGrandRa@doc.gov

U.S. Small Business Administration District Office
Patrick V. McNamara Building, Room 515
477 Michigan Avenue
Detroit, MI 48226
Tel: (313) 226-6075; Fax: (313) 226-4769

U.S. Small Business Administration Branch Office
501 South Front St.
Marquette, MI 49855
Tel: (906) 225-1108; Fax: (906) 225-1109

Small Business Development Center
2727 Second Avenue, Suite 107
Detroit, MI 48201
Tel: (313) 964-1798; Fax: (313) 964-3648

Michigan Economic Development Corporation
201 N. Washington Square, 4th Floor
Lansing, MI 48913
Tel: (517) 241-3518; Fax: 241-3686
Overseas offices: Brussels, Belgium; Toronto, Canada; Hong Kong; Tokyo, Japan; Mexico City, Mexico

World Trade Center Detroit/Windsor
1251 Fort Street
Trenton, MI 48183
Tel: (734) 479-2345; Fax: (734) 479-5733
Email: wtcdw@sprintmail.com
Web site: www.wtcdw.com

Minnesota

U.S. Department of Commerce
Export Assistance Center
45 South 7th Street, Suite 2240
Minneapolis, MN 55402
Tel: (612) 348-1638; Fax: (612) 348-1650
Email: OMinneap@doc.gov

U.S. Small Business Administration District Office
Butler Square
100 North 6th Street, Suite 610-C
Minneapolis, MN 55403-1563
Tel: (612) 370-2324; Fax: (612) 370-2303

Small Business Development Center
500 Metro Square
121 Seventh Place East
St. Paul, MN 55101-2146
Tel: (651) 297-5770; Fax: (651) 296-1290
Email: mary.kruger@dted.state.mn.us

Minnesota Trade Office
1000 Minnesota World Trade Center
30 East Seventh Street
St. Paul, MN 55101-4902
Tel: (651) 297-4222; Fax: (651) 296-3555
Email: mto@state.mn.us
Web site: www.dted.state.mn.us
Overseas offices: Sydney, Australia; Brussels, Belgium; London, England; Paris, France; Frankfurt, Germany; Budapest, Hungary; Tokyo, Japan; Kobe, Japan; Mexico City, Mexico; Oslo, Norway; Stockholm, Sweden; Taipei, Taiwan

Minnesota Department of Agriculture
90 West Plato Blvd.
St. Paul, MN 55107-2094
Tel: (651) 297-2200; Fax: (651) 297-5522
Web site: www.mda.state.mn.us

Minnesota Export Finance Authority
Minnesota World Trade Center, Suite 1000
30 East 7th Street
St. Paul, MN 55101-4902
Tel: (651) 297-4658; Fax: (651) 296-3555
Email: ndoja@dted.state.mn.us
Web site: www.dted.state.mn.us

Minnesota World Trade Center Corporation
400 Minnesota World Trade Center
30 East 7th Street, Suite 400
St. Paul, MN 55101
Tel: (651) 297-1580; Fax: (651) 297-4812
Web site: www.copycatdigital.com/twc

Red River Trade Corridor
P.O. Box 685
Crookstone, MN 56716
Tel: (218) 281-8459; Fax: (218) 281-8457
Web site: www.rrtrade.org

Mississippi

U.S. Department of Commerce
Export Assistance Center
704 East Main Street
Raymond, MS 39154
Tel: (601) 857-0128; Fax: (601) 857-0026
Email: OJackson@doc.gov

U.S. Small Business Administration District Office
101 W. Capitol St., Suite 400
Jackson, MS 39201
Tel: (601) 965-4378; Fax: (601) 965-4294

U.S. Small Business Administration Branch Office
One Government Plaza
2909 - 13th St., Suite 203
Gulfport, MS 39501-1949
Tel: (228) 863-4449; Fax: (228) 864-0179

Small Business Development Center
University of Mississippi
Old Chemistry Building, Suite 216
University, MS 38677
Tel: (601) 232-5001; Fax: (601) 232-5650
Email: msbdc@olemiss.edu
Web site: www.olemiss.edu/depts/mssbdc

Mississippi Department of Economic and Community Development
International Development Division
P.O. Box 849
Jackson, MS 39205
Tel: (601) 359-6672; Fax: (601) 359-2832
Web site: www.mississippi.org
Overseas offices: Frankfurt, Germany; Santiago, Chile

Mississippi Department of Agriculture and Commerce
P.O. Box 1609
Jackson, MS 39215-1000
Tel: (601) 359-1158; Fax: (601) 354-6001
Web site: www.mdac@state.ms.us

International Trade Center
Hinds Community College
1500 Raymond Lake Road
Raymond, MS 39154
Tel: (601) 857-3536/7; Fax: (601) 857-3474
Email: hherbert@codec.ro

Missouri

U.S. Department of Commerce
Export Assistance Center
8182 Maryland Avenue, Suite 303
St. Louis, MO 63105
Tel: (314) 425-3302; Fax: (314) 425-3381
Email: OStLouis@doc.gov

U.S. Department of Commerce
Export Assistance Center
2345 Grand, Suite 650
Kansas City, MO 64108
Tel: (816) 410-9201; Fax: (816) 410-9208

U.S. Department of Commerce
Export Assistance Center
601 East 12th Street, Room 635
Kansas City, MO 64106
Tel: (816) 426-3141; Fax: (816) 426-3140

U.S. Small Business Administration District Office
323 West Eighth St., Suite 501
Kansas City, MO 64105-1500
Tel: (816) 374-6708; Fax: (816) 374-6759

U.S. Small Business Administration District Office
815 Olive Street
St. Louis, MO 63101
Tel: (314) 539-6600; Fax: (314) 539-3785

U.S. Small Business Administration Branch Office
620 S. Glenstone St., Suite 110
Springfield, MO 65802-3200
Tel: (417) 864-7670; Fax: (417) 864-4108

Small Business Development Center
University of Missouri
300 University Place
Columbia, MO 65211
Tel: (573) 882-0344; Fax: (573) 884-4297
Email: summersm@missouri.edu

Missouri Department of Economic Development
International Business Office
301 W. High Street, Room 720C
P.O. Box 118
Jefferson City, MO 65102
Tel: (800) 523-1434, (573) 751-4999
Fax: (573) 751-7384
Web site: www.ecodev.state.mo.us/intermark/
Overseas offices: Dusseldorf, Germany; Tokyo, Japan; Seoul, South Korea; Guadalajara, Mexico; Taipei, Taiwan

Missouri Department of Agriculture
International Marketing Program
P.O. Box 630
1616 Missouri Boulevard
Jefferson City, MO 65102-0630
Tel: (573) 751-5613; Fax: (573) 751-2868
Email: mexport@mail.state.mo.us
Web site: www.mda.state.mo.us

Missouri Development Finance Board
301 West High Street, Room 680
Harry S. Truman Building
Jefferson City, MO 65102
Tel: (573) 751-8479; Fax: (573) 526-4418

World Trade Center of Kansas City, Inc.
2600 Commerce Tower
911 Main Street
Kansas City, MO 64105
Tel: (816) 374-5483; Fax: (816) 221-7440
Email: pyle@kcchamber.com
Web site: www.kansaswtc.org

World Trade Center of St. Louis
121 S. Meramec, Suite 1111
St. Louis, MO 63105
Tel: (314) 854-6141; Fax: (314) 862-0102
Email: wtcst@co.st-louis.mo.us
Web site: www.st-louis.mo.us/st-louis/county/wtc

Montana

U.S. Department of Commerce
Montana is served by the Boise, Idaho:

U.S. Department of Commerce
Export Assistance Center
700 West State Street, 2nd Floor
Boise, ID 83720
Tel: (208) 334-3857; Fax: (208) 334-2783
Email: OBoise@doc.gov

U.S. Small Business Administration District Office
301 South Park, Room 334
Helena, MT 59626
Tel: (406) 441-1081; Fax: (406) 441-1090

Small Business Development Center
1424 Ninth Avenue
Helena, MT 59620
Tel: (406) 444-4780; Fax: (406) 444-1872
Email: rkloser@state.mt.us
or rhampton@mt.gov

Montana Department of Commerce
Trade Program
P.O. Box 2005050505
Helena, MT 59620
Tel: (406) 444-4380; Fax: (406) 444-2903
Overseas offices: Kumamoto City, Japan; Taipei, Taiwan

Montana Department of Agriculture
P.O. Box 200201
Helena, MT 59620-0201
Tel: (406) 444-3144; Fax: (406) 444-5409
Email: agr@state.mt.us
Web site: www.agr.state.mt.us

Nebraska

U.S. Department of Commerce
Export Assistance Center
11135 O Street
Omaha, NE 68137
Tel: (402) 221-3664; Fax: (402) 221-3668
Email: OOmaha@doc.gov

U.S. Small Business Administration District Office
11145 Mill Valley Rd.
Omaha, NE 68154
Tel: (402) 221-4691; Fax: (402) 221-3680

Small Business Development Center
University of Nebraska at Omaha
60th & Dodge Streets, CBA Room 407
Omaha, NE 68182-0248
Tel: (402) 554-2521; Fax: (402) 554-3473
Email: rberniew@unomaha.edu

Nebraska Office of International Trade & Foreign Investment
Department of Economic Development
301 Centennial Mall South
Lincoln, NE 68509
Tel: (402) 471-3111; Fax: (402) 471-3778
Web site: www.ded.state.ne.us

Nebraska Department of Agriculture
Agriculture Promotion and Development Div.
301 Centennial Mall South
Lincoln, NE 68509
Tel: (402) 471-4876; Fax: (402) 471-2759
Web site: www.agr.state.ne.us/

Nevada

U.S. Department of Commerce
Export Assistance Center
1755 E. Plumb Lane, Room 152
Reno, NV 89502
Tel: (702) 784-5203; Fax: (702) 784-5343
Email: OReno@doc.gov

U.S. Small Business Administration District Office
300 Las Vegas Blvd. South, Suite 1100
Las Vegas, NV 89101
Tel: (702) 388-6611; Fax: (702) 388-6469

Small Business Development Center
University of Nevada in Reno
College of Business Administration
Mail Stop 032
Reno, NV 89557-0100
Tel: (702) 784-1717; Fax: (702) 784-4337

Nevada Commission on Economic Development
International Trade Program
555 E. Washington, Suite 5400
Las Vegas, NV 89101
Tel: (702) 486-2700; Fax: (702) 486-2701

Nevada Department of Business & Industry
Division of Agriculture
350 Capitol Hill Ave.
Reno, NV 89502
Tel: (702) 688-1180; Fax: (702) 688-1178
Web site: www.state.nv.us/b&i/ad

Nevada State Development Corporation
350 S. Center Street, Suite 310
Reno, NV 89501
Tel: (702) 323-3625; Fax: (702) 323-1997
Email: nsdc_rno@is.netcom.com

Nevada World Trade Center
925 East Desert Inn Rd.
Las Vegas, NV 89109
Tel: (702) 387-5581; Fax: (702) 893-2339
Email: wtcibsadmin@earthlink.net
Web site: www.wtcnevada.com

New Hampshire

Office of International Commerce
International Trade Resource Center
17 New Hampsire Avenue
Portsmouth, NH 03801
Tel: (603) 334-6074; Fax: (603) 334-6110
Email: oic@dred.state.nh.us
Web site: www.ded.state.nh.us/oic/trade

U.S. Department of Commerce
Export Assistance Center
17 New Hampshire Avenue
Portsmouth, NH 03801-2838
Tel: (603) 334-6074; Fax: (602) 334-6110

U.S. Small Business Administration District Office
143 N. Main St.
Concord, NH 03301
Tel: (603) 225-1400; Fax: (603) 225-1409

Small Business Development Center
University of New Hampshire
108 McConnell Hall
Durham, NH 03824-3593
Tel: (603) 862-2200; Fax: (603) 862-4876

N.H. Department of Resources and Economic Development
International Trade Resource Center
17 New Hampshire Avenue
Portsmouth, NH 03801-2838
Tel: (603) 334-6074; Fax: (603) 334-6110
Web site: www.ded.state.nh.us/oic/trade

N.H. Department of Agriculture, Markets and Food
P.O. Box 2042
Concord, NH 03302-2042
Tel: (603) 271-2505; Fax: (603) 271-1109
Email: GMcWilliam@compuserve.com

Greater Nashua Chamber of Commerce
146 Main Street, Second Floor
Nashua, NH 03060
Tel: (603) 881-8333; Fax: (603) 881-7323
Web site: www.nashua.chamber.com

New Jersey

U.S. Department of Commerce
Export Assistance Center
3131 Princeton Pike
Building 4, Suite 105
Trenton, NJ 08648
Tel: (609) 989-2100; Fax: (609) 989-2395
Email: OTrenton@doc.gov

U.S. Department of Commerce
Export Assistance Center
Gateway One, 9th Floor
Newark, NJ 07102
Tel: (973) 645-4682; Fax: (973) 645-4783
Email: ONewark@doc.gov

U.S. Small Business Administration District Office
Two Gateway Ctr., 15th Fl.
Newark, NJ 07102
Tel: (973) 645-2434; Fax: (973) 645-6265

Small Business Development Center
Rutgers U. Graduate School of Management
University Heights - 49 Bleeker Street
Newark, NJ 07102-1993
Tel: (973) 353-1927; Fax: (973) 353-1110
Email: bhopper@andromeda.rutgers.edu
Web site: www.nj.com/njsbdc

New Jersey Department of Commerce & Economic Development
Division of International Trade
20 West State Street; Box 838
Trenton, NJ 08625-0838
Tel: (609) 633-3606; Fax: (609) 633-3672
Overseas offices: Raanana, Israel; Tokyo, Japan

New Jersey Department of Agriculture
P.O. Box 330
Trenton, NJ 08625
Tel: (609) 292-5536; Fax: (609) 984-2508
Web site: www.state.nj.us

New Mexico

U.S. Department of Commerce
Export Assistance Center
c/o New Mexico Dept. of Economic Development
P.O. Box 20003
Santa Fe, NM 87504-5003
Tel: (505) 827-0350; Fax: (505) 827-0263
Email: OSantaFe@doc.gov

U.S. Small Business Administration District Office
625 Silver Ave. SW
Albuquerque, NM 87102
Tel: (505) 346-7909; Fax: (505) 346-6711

Small Business Development Center
Santa Fe Community College
6401 Richards Avenue
Santa Fe, NM 87505
Tel: (505) 428-1343; Fax: (505) 428-1469

State of New Mexico Trade Division
1100 St. Francis Drive
Santa Fe, NM 87503
Tel: (505) 827-0307; Fax: (505) 827-0263
Email: trade@edd.state.nm.us
Web site: www.edd.state.nm.us/TRADE/
Overseas offices: Mexico City, Mexico

New Mexico Department of Agriculture
Marketing and Development Division
P.O. Box 30005, Dept. 5600
Las Cruces, NM 88003-0005
Tel: (505) 646-4929; Fax: (505) 646-3303

New Mexico Border Authority
505 South Main, Suite 134
Las Cruces, NM 88001
Tel: (505) 525-5622; Fax: (505) 525-5623

New York

U.S. Department of Commerce
Export Assistance Center
163 West 125th Stgreet, Suite 904
New York, NY 10027
Tel: (212) 860-6200; Fax: (212) 860-6203
Email: OHarlem@doc.gov

U.S. Department of Commerce
Export Assistance Center
111 West Huron St., Rm. 1304
Buffalo, NY 14202
Tel: (716) 551-4191; Fax: (716) 551-5290
Email: OBuffalo@doc.gov

U.S. Department of Commerce
Export Assistance Center
1550 Franklin Ave., Suite 207
Mineola, NY 11501
Tel: (516) 739-1765; Fax: (516) 739-3310
Email: OLongIsl@doc.gov

U.S. Department of Commerce
Export Assistance Center
6 World Trade Center, Room 635
New York, NY 10048
Tel: (212) 466-5222; Fax: (212) 264-1356
Email: ONew York@doc.gov

U.S. Department of Commerce
Export Assistance Center
707 Westchester Ave., Suite 209
White Plains, NY 10604
Tel: (914) 682-6712; Fax: (914) 682-6698
Email: OWestche@doc.gov

U.S. Small Business Administration District Office
111 West Huron St., Room 1311
Buffalo, NY 14202
Tel: (716) 551-4301; Fax: (716) 551-4418

U.S. Small Business Administration District Office
26 Federal Plaza, Room 3100
New York, NY 10278
Tel: (212) 264-2454; Fax: (212) 264-7751

U.S. Small Business Administration District Office
401 S. Salina Street, 5th Floor
Syracuse, NY 13202
Tel: (315) 471-9393; Fax: (315) 471-9288

U.S. Small Business Administration Branch Office
333 East Water St., 4th Fl.
Elmira, NY 14901
Tel: (607) 734-8130; Fax: (607) 733-4656

U.S. Small Business Administration Branch Office
35 Pinelawn Road, Suite 207W
Melville, NY 11747
Tel: (516) 454-0750; Fax: (516) 454-0769

U.S. Small Business Administration Branch Office
100 State St., Room 410
Rochester, NY 14614
Tel: (716) 263-6700; Fax: (716) 263-3146

Small Business Development Center
State University of New York
SUNY Plaza, S-523
Albany, NY 12246
Tel: (518) 443-5398; Fax: (518) 465-4992
Email: kingjl@cc.sunycentral.edu

Minority Business Development Center
350 5th Avenue, Suite2202
New York, NY 10118
Tel: (212) 947-5351; Fax: ((212) 947-1506

Ex-Im Bank Northeast Regional Office
6 World Trade Center, Suite 635
New York, NY 10048
Tel: (212) 466-2950; Fax: (212) 466-2959
Web site: www.exim.gov

N.Y. State Dept. of Trade and Economic Development
International Division
633 Third Ave., 33rd Fl.
New York, NY 10017
Tel: (212) 803-2300; Fax: (212) 803-2399
Overseas offices: Montreal, Canada; Toronto, Canada; London, England; Frankfurt, Germany; Hong Kong; Milan, Italy; Tokyo, Japan

N.Y. State Dept. of Agriculture & Markets
Agricultural Protection & Development Services
1 Winners Circle
Albany, NY 12235
Tel: (518) 457-7076; Fax: (518) 457-2716
Email: kimballb@nysnet.net
Web site: www.agmkt.state.ny.us

Erie County Industrial Development Agency
Suite 300 - Liberty Building
424 Main Street
Buffalo, NY 14202
Tel: (716) 856-6525; Fax: (716) 856-6754

World Trade Center New York
The Port Authority of New York & New Jersey
One World Trade Center, Suite 88 West
New York, NY 10048
Tel: (212) 435-168; Fax: (212) 435-2810
Email: dmay@panynj.gov

World Trade Center Schenectady-Capital District
Schenectady County Community College
78 Washington Ave.
Schenectady, NY 12305
Tel: (518) 381-1317; Fax: (518) 346-7511
Email: crwtc@gw.suny.sccc.edu
Web site: crisny.org/education/capreg/sccc/crwtc.htm

Harlem International Trade Center
Harlem State Office Building
163 West 125th Street, Room 904
New York, NY 10027
Tel: (212) 860-6200; Fax: (212) 860-6203
Web site: www.nyuseac.org

Western New York International Trade Council
300 Main Place Tower
Buffalo, NY 14202
Tel: (716) 852-7160; Fax: (716) 852-2761

North Carolina

U.S. Department of Commerce
Export Assistance Center
400 West Market Street, Suite 102
Greensboro, NC 27401
Tel: (336) 333-5345; Fax: (336) 333-5158
Email: Office.greensboro@mail.doc.gov

U.S. Department of Commerce
Export Assistance Center
521 East Morehead Street, Suite 435
Charlotte, NC 28202
Tel: (704) 333-4886; Fax: (704) 332-2681

U.S. Small Business Administration District Office
200 N. College St., Suite A2015
Charlotte, NC 28202-2173
Tel: (704) 344-6563; Fax: (704) 344-6769

Small Business and Technology Development Center
333 Fayetteville St., Suite 1150
Raleigh, NC 27610-1742
Tel: (800) 2580-UNC, (919) 715-7272
Fax: (919) 715-7777
Email: sdaugherty@sbtdc.org
Web site: www.sbtdc.org

North Carolina Department of Commerce
International Trade Division
301 N. Wilmington St.
P.O. Box 29571
Raleigh, NC 27626-0571
Tel: (919) 733-7193; Fax: (919) 733-0110
Web site: www.commerce.state.nc.us
Overseas offices: Dusseldorf, Germany; Hong Kong; Tokyo, Japan; Mexico City, Mexico

North Carolina Department of Agriculture
Export Marketing Division
2 W. Edenton Street
Raleigh, NC 27601
Tel: (919) 733-7887; Fax: (919) 733-0999
Web site: www.agr.state.nc.us

World Trade Center North Carolina
2 Hannover Square, Suite 1200
Raleigh, NC 27601
Tel: (919) 743-0177; Fax: (919) 743-0188
Email: wtcnc@wtcnc.org
Web site: www.wtcnc.org

North Carolina State University
International Programs Office
NCSU Box 7112
Raleigh, NC 27695-7112
Tel: (919) 515-3201; Fax: (919) 515-6835
Email: vrdavis2@gw.fis.ncsu.edu

North Dakota

U.S. Department of Commerce
North Dakota is served by the Minneapolis office:

U.S. Department of Commerce
Export Assistance Center
45 South 7th Street, Suite 2240
Minneapolis, MN 55402
Tel: (612) 348-1638; Fax: (612) 348-1650
Email: OMinneap@doc.gov

U.S. Small Business Administration District Office
657 2nd Ave. North, Room 219
P.O. Box 3086
Fargo, ND 58108
Tel: (701) 239-5131; Fax: (701) 239-5645

Small Business Development Center
University of North Dakota
118 Gamble Hall; Box 7308
Grand Forks, ND 58202-7308
Tel: (701) 777-3700; Fax: (701) 777-3225

North Dakota Department of Economic Development and Finance
International Trade Division
1833 East Bismarck Expressway
Bismarck, ND 58504-6708
Tel: (701) 328-5300; Fax: (701) 328-5320
Email: ccmail.ndef@state.nd.us
Web site: www.growingnorthdakota.state.nd.us

North Dakota Department of Agriculture
Division of Marketing
600 East Boulevard, Dept. 602
Bismarck, ND 58505-0020
Tel: (701) 328-2231; Fax: (701) 328-4567
Email: ndda@pioneer.state.nd.us
Web site: www.state.nd.us/agr

Ohio

U.S. Department of Commerce
Export Assistance Center
Bank One Center
600 Superior Ave. East, Suite 700
Cleveland, OH 44114
Tel: (216) 522-4750; Fax: (216) 522-2235
Email: OClevela@doc.gov

U.S. Department of Commerce
Export Assistance Center
36 East 7th Street, Suite 2650
Cincinnati, OH 45202
Tel: (513) 684-2944; Fax: (513) 684-3227
Email: OCincinn@doc.gov

U.S. Department of Commerce
Export Assistance Center
Two Nationawide Plaza, Suite 1400
Columbus, OH 43215
Tel: (614) 365-9510; Fax: (614) 365-9598
Email: OColumbu@doc.gov

U.S. Department of Commerce
Export Assistance Center
300 Madison Avenue
Toledo, OH 43604
Tel: (419) 241-0683; Fax: (419) 241-0684
Email: OToledo@doc.gov

U.S. Small Business Administration District Office
1111 Superior Ave., Suite 630
Cleveland, OH 44144-2507
Tel: (216) 522-4180; Fax: (216) 522-2038

U.S. Small Business Administration District Office
2 Nationwide Plaza
Columbus, OH 43215 2592
Tel: (614) 469-6860; Fax: (614) 469-2391

U.S. Small Business Administration Branch Office
525 Vine St., Suite 870
Cincinnati, OH 45202
Tel: (513) 684-2814; Fax: (513) 684-3251

Small Business Development Center
Ohio Dept. of Development
77 South High Street, 28th Floor
Columbus, OH 43216-6108
Tel: (614) 466-2711; Fax: (614) 466-0829

Ohio Department of Development
International Trade Division
P.O. Box 1001
Columbus, OH 43216-1001
Tel: (614) 466-5017; Fax: (614) 463-1540
Email: itd@odod.ohio.gov
Web site: www.ohiotrade.tpusa.com
Overseas offices: Brussels, Belgium; Tokyo, Japan; Toronto, Canada; Hong Kong; Ramatgan, Israel; Mexico City, Mexico

Ohio Department of Agriculture
8995 East Main St.
Reynoldsburg, OH 43068
Tel: (614) 728-6200
Email: wwwagri@ohio.gov
Web site: www.state.oh.us/agr

Port of Cleveland-Cuyahoga County Port Authority
101 Erieside Avenue
Cleveland, OH 44114
Tel: (216) 241-8004; Fax: (216) 241-8016

Cleveland World Trade Center
200 Tower City Center
50 Public Square
Cleveland, OH 44039
Tel: (216) 592-2242; Fax: (216) 687-6788
Email: wtcc@clevegrowth.com
Web site: www.wtccleveland.org

World Trade Center Columbus
37 North High Street
Columbus, OH 43215
Tel: (614) 225-6907; Fax: (614) 469-8250

Greater Cincinnati Chamber of Commerce
300 Carew Tower
441 Vine Street
Cincinnati, OH 45202
Tel: (513) 579-3100; Fax: (513) 579-3101
Email: info@gccc.com
Web site: www.gccc.com

Toledo Area International Trade Association
Enterprise Suite 200
300 Madison Avenue
Toledo, OH 43604-1575
Tel: (419) 243-8191; Fax: (419) 241-8302
Email: kim.danes@toledochamber.com
Web site: www.joinusattoledochamber.com

Oklahoma

U.S. Department of Commerce
Export Assistance Center
301 Northwest 63rd Street, Suite 330
Oklahoma City, OK 73116
Tel: (405) 231-5302; Fax: (405) 231-4211
Email: OOklahom@doc.gov

U.S. Department of Commerce
Export Assistance Center
700 N. Greenwood Avenue, Suite 1400
Tulsa, OK 74106
Tel: (918) 581-7650; Fax: (918) 594-8413
Email: OTulsa@doc.gov

U.S. Small Business Administration District Office
210 Park Avenue, Suite 1300
Oklahoma City, OK 73102
Tel: (405) 231-5521; Fax: (405) 231-4876

Small Business Development Center
Southeastern Oklahoma State University
517 University
Station A, Box 2584
Durant, OK 74701
Tel: (580) 924-0277; Fax: (580) 920-7471
Email: gpennington@sosu.edu

Oklahoma Department of Commerce
International Trade and Investment Division
301 N.W. 63rd Street, Suite 300
Oklahoma City, OK 73116
Tel: (405) 231-5302; Fax: (405) 231-4211
Overseas offices: Antwerp, Belgium; Seoul, South Korea; Mexico City, Mexico; Singapore

Oklahoma Department of Commerce
International Trade and Investment Division
700 N. Greenwood Avenue, Suite 1400
Tulsa, OK 74106
Tel: (918) 594-8116; Fax: (918) 594-8413

Oklahoma Department of Agriculture
International Marketing
2800 North Lincoln
Oklahoma City, OK 73105
Tel: (405) 521-3864; Fax: (405) 521-4912
Web site: www.state.ok.us/~okag/aghome.html

Oklahoma Department of Commerce
Export Finance Program
P.O. Box 26980
Oklahoma City, OK 73126-0980
Tel: (800) TRY-OKLA, (405) 815-6552
Fax: (405) 815-5142
Web site: www.odoc.state.ok.us

Center for International Trade Development
Oklahoma State University
204 CITD
Stillwater, OK 74078-8084
Tel: (405) 744-7693; Fax: (405) 744-8973

Oregon

U.S. Department of Commerce
Export Assistance Center
One World Trade Center
121 SW Salmon Street, Suite 242
Portland, OR 97204
Tel: (503) 326-3001; Fax: (503) 326-6351
Email: OPortlan@doc.gov

U.S. Small Business Administration District Office
1515 SW Fifth Ave.
Portland, OR 97201-5494
Tel: (503) 326-2682; Fax: (503) 326-2808

Small Business Development Center
Lane Community College
44 West Broadway, Suite 501
Eugene, OR 97401-3021
Tel: (541) 726-2250; Fax: (541) 345-6006
Email: cutlers@lanecc.edu

Oregon Economic Development Department
International Trade Division
One World Trade Center
121 SW Salmon Street
Portland, OR 97204
Tel: (503) 229-5625; Fax: (503) 222-5050
Web site: www.econ.state.or.us
Overseas offices: Tokyo, Japan; Seoul, South Korea; Taipei, Taiwan

Oregon Department of Agriculture
Agriculture Development & Marketing Division
1207 N.W. Naito Parkway, Suite 104
Portland, OR 97209
Tel: (503) 872-6600; Fax: (503) 872-6601

World Trade Center Portland
One World Trade Center
121 SW Salmon Street, Suite 250
Portland, OR 97204
Tel: (503) 471-1409; Fax: (503) 471-1401
Email: wtcpd@pgn.com
Web site: www.wtcpd.com

Pacific Northwest International Trade Association
One World Trade Center
121 SW Salmon Street, Suite 1100
Portland, OR 97204
Tel: (503) 471-1399; Fax: (503) 675-9068

Pennsylvania

U.S. Department of Commerce
Export Assistance Center
615 Chestnut Street, Suite 1501
Philadelphia, PA 19106
Tel: (215) 597-6101; Fax: (215) 597-6123
Email: OPhilade@doc.gov

U.S. Department of Commerce
Export Assistance Center
2002 Federal Building
1000 Liberty Avenue
Pittsburgh, PA 15222-4194
Tel: (412) 395-5050; Fax: (412) 395-4875
Email: OPittsbu@doc.gov

U.S. Department of Commerce
Export Assistance Center
One Commerce Square
228 Walnut St., Room 850
Harrisburg, PA 17101
Tel: (717) 221-4510; Fax: (717) 221-4505
Email: OHarrisb@doc.gov

U.S. Small Business Administration District Office
1000 Liberty Avenue
Federal Bldg., Suite 1128
Pittsburgh, PA 15222-4004
Tel: (412) 395-6560; Fax: (412) 395-6562

U.S. Small Business Administration District Office
900 Market Street, 5th Floor
Philadelphia, PA 19107
Tel: (215) 580-2722; Fax: (215) 580-2762

U.S. Small Business Administration Branch Office
100 Chestnut St.
Harrisburg, PA 17101
Tel: (717) 782-3840; Fax: (717) 782-4839

U.S. Small Business Administration Branch Office
20 N. Pennsylvania Ave.
Wilkes-Barre, PA 18701-3589
Tel: (717) 826-6497; Fax: (717) 826-6287

Small Business Development Center
University of Pennsylvania
The Wharton School
Vance Hall, 4th Floor
3733 Spruce St.
Philadelphia, PA 19104-6374
Tel: (215) 898-1219; Fax: (215) 573-2135
Email: pasbdc@wharton.upenn.edu
Web site: www.libertynet.org/pasbdc

Minority Business Development Center
William Green Federal Building
6th and Arch Streets, Room 10128
Philadelphia, PA 19106
Tel: (215) 861-3597; Fax: (215) 861-3595

Pennsylvania Office of International Business Development
308 Forum Building, 3rd Floor
Harrisburg, PA 17120
Tel: (717) 787-7190; Fax: (717) 234-4560
Web site: www.dced.state.pa.us
Overseas offices: Brussels, Belgium; Toronto, Canada; Frankfurt, Germany; Tokyo, Japan; Mexico City, Mexico

Pennsylvania Department of Agriculture
Bureau of Market Development
2301 N. Cameron Street
Harrisburg, PA 17110-9408
Tel: (717) 783-3181; Fax: (717) 787-1858
Web site: www.pda.state.pa.us

Philadelphia Industrial Development Corporation (PIDC)
2600 Centre Square West
1500 Market Street
Philadelphia, PA 19102-2126
Tel: (215) 496-8020; Fax: (215) 977-9618

Greater Pittsburgh World Trade Center
436 7th Avenue
Pittsburgh, PA 15219
Tel: (412) 227-3180; Fax: (412) 227-3188
Email: wtcpt@pitt.edu
Web site: www.wtcpa.org

Southern Alleghenies Planning and Development Commission
Export Center
541 - 58th Street
Altoona, PA 16602
Tel: (814) 949-6525; Fax: (814) 949-6505
Web site: www.sapdc.org

Wharton Export Network
Wharton School, U. of Pennsylvania
3733 Spruce St.
433 Vance Hall
Philadelphia, PA 19104-6357
Tel: (215) 898-4189; Fax: (215) 898-1299

Puerto Rico and the U.S. Virgin Islands

U.S. Department of Commerce
Export Assistance Center
525 F.D. Roosevelt Avenue, Suite 905
San Juan, PR 00918
Tel: (787) 766-5555; Fax: (787) 766-5692
Email: OSanJuan@doc.gov

U.S. Small Business Administration District Office
City Bank Tower, Suite 201
252 Ponce De Leon Avenue
Hato Rey, PR 00918
Tel: (809) 766-5572; Fax: (809) 766-5309

U.S. Small Business Administration District Office
3013 Golden Rock, Suite 165
Christianstead
St. Croix, VI 00820-4355
Tel: (809) 778-5380; Fax: (809) 778-1102

U.S. Small Business Administration District Office
3800 Crown Bay
Virgin Islands Maritime Building
St. Thomas, VI 00802
Tel: (809) 774-8530; Fax: (809) 776-2312

Puerto Rico Small Business Development Center
Edificio Union Plaza, Suite 701
416 Ponce De Leon Avenue
Hato Rey, PR 00918
Tel: (787) 763-6811; Fax: (787) 763-4629
Email: cmarti@ns.inter.edu

Small Business Development Center
University of the Virgin Islands
8000 Nisky Center, Suite 202
Charlotte Amalie
St. Thomas, VI 00802-5804
Tel: (809) 776-3206; Fax: (809) 775-3756

Promoexport
P.O. Box 195009
San Juan, PR 00919-5009
Tel: (787) 765-2727; Fax: (787) 765-4260

Puerto Rico Department of Agriculture
P.O. Box 10163
San Juan, PR 00908
Tel: (787) 722-0871; Fax: (787) 723-8512

Puerto Rico Economic Development Administration
P.O. Box 362350
San Juan, PR 00936-2350
Tel: (787) 758-4747; Fax: (787) 764-1415
Web site: www.predco.com

Virgin Islands Government Development Bank
Bureau of Economic Research
1050 Norre Gade #5, Suite 301
Charlotte Amalie
St. Thomas, VI 00802
Tel: (340) 714-1700; Fax: (340) 774-8106

Rhode Island

U.S. Department of Commerce
Export Assistance Center
One West Exchange Street
Providence, RI 02903
Tel: (401) 528-5104; Fax: (401) 528-5067
Email: OProvide@doc.gov

U.S. Small Business Administration District Office
380 Westminster Mall
Providence, RI 02903
Tel: (401) 528-4562; Fax: (401) 528-4539

Small Business Development Center
Rhode Island Export Assistance Center
Bryant College
1150 Douglas Pike
Smithfield, RI 02917-1284
Tel: (401) 232-6111; Fax: (401) 232-6933

Rhode Island Economic Development Corporation
International Trade Division
One West Exchange Street
Providence, RI 02903
Tel: (401) 222-2601; Fax: (401) 222-2102
Email: ried@riedc.com
Web site: www.riedc.com

Rhode Island Division of Agriculture
235 Promenade Street
Providence, RI 02908
Tel: (401) 222-2781; Fax: (401) 222-6047
Web: www.state.ri.us/dem

World Trade Center Rhode Island
Center for International Buisness
1150 Douglas Pike
Smithfield, RI 02917
Tel: (401) 351-2701; Fax: (401) 421-8510
Email: ebarr@akka.com
Web site: www.rieac.org

South Carolina

U.S. Department of Commerce
Export Assistance Center
555 N. Pleasantburg Dr.
Building 1, Suite 109
Greenville, SC 29607
Tel: (864) 271-1976; Fax: (864) 271-4171
Email: Office.Greenville@mail.doc.gov

U.S. Department of Commerce
Export Assistance Center
P.O. Box 975
Charleston, SC 29402
Tel: (843) 727-4051; Fax: (843) 727-4052
Email: Office.CharlestonSC@mail.doc.gov

U.S. Department of Commerce District Office
1835 Assembly Street, Suite 172
Columbia, SC 29201
Tel: (803) 765-5345; Fax: (803) 253-3614
Email: Office.Columbia@mail.doc.gov

U.S. Small Business Administration District Office
1835 Assembly Street, Room 358
Columbia, SC 29201
Tel: (803) 765-5377; Fax: (803) 765-5962

Small Business Development Center
University of South Carolina
College of Business Administration
1710 College Street
Columbia, SC 29208
Tel: (803) 777-4907; Fax: (803) 777-4403

South Carolina Department of Commerce
International Trade Development
P.O. Box 927
Columbia, SC 29202
Tel: (803) 737-0400; Fax: (803) 737-0418
Web site: www.callsouthcarolina.com
Overseas offices: London, England; Frankfurt, Germany; Tokyo, Japan

South Carolina Department of Agriculture
Wade Hampton State Office Building
P.O. Box 11280
Columbia, SC 29211
Tel: (803) 734-2210; Fax: (803) 734-2192
Web site: www.state.sc.us/scda

South Carolina Ports Authority
P.O. Box 22287
Charleston, SC 29413
Tel: (843) 723-8651; Fax: (843) 577-8127
Web site: www.port-of-charleston.com

World Trade Center - Charleston
385 Meeting Street, Suite 102
Charleston, SC 29403
Tel: (843) 577-4080; Fax: (843) 577-6003
Email: info@scwtc.org
Web site: www.scwtc.org

South Dakota

U.S. Department of Commerce
Export Assistance Center
Augustana College
2001 S. Summit Avenue
Room SS-44
Sioux Falls, SD 57197
Tel: (605) 330-4264; Fax: (605) 330-4266
Email: OSiouxFa@doc.gov

U.S. Small Business Administration District Office
110 South Phillips, Suite 200
Sioux Falls, SD 57102
Tel: (605) 330-4231; Fax: (605) 330-4215

Small Business Development Center
University of South Dakota
School of Business
414 East Clark
Vermillion, SD 57069-2390
Tel: (605) 677-5287; Fax: (605) 677-5427
Email: stracy@usd.edu

International Business Institute
1200 S. Jay Street
Aberdeen, SD 57401
Tel: (605) 626-3098; Fax: (605) 626-3004

South Dakota Department of Agriculture
523 East Capitol Ave.
Pierre, SD 57501-3182
Tel: (605) 773-3375; Fax: (605) 773-3481
Web site: www.state.sd.us/doa

Tennessee

U.S. Department of Commerce
Export Assistance Center
Old Historic City Hall
601 West Summit Hill Drive, Suite 300
Knoxville, TN 37902-2011
Tel: (423) 545-4637; Fax: (423) 545-4435
Email: OKnoxvil@doc.gov

U.S. Department of Commerce
Export Assistance Center
Parkway Tower, Suite 114
404 James Robertson Parkway
Nashville, TN 37219-1505
Tel: (615) 736-5161; Fax: (615) 736-2454
Email: ONashvil@doc.gov

U.S. Department of Commerce
Export Assistance Center
Buckman Hall
650 East Parkway South, Suite 348
Memphis, TN 38104
Tel: (901) 323-1543; Fax: (901) 320-9128
Email: OMemphis@doc.gov

U.S. Small Business Administration District Office
50 Vantage Way, Suite 201
Nashville, TN 37228-1500
Tel: (615) 736-5881; Fax: (615) 736-7232

Small Business Development Center
International Trade Center
University of Memphis
Building 1, South Campus
Memphis, TN 38152
Tel: (901) 678-2500; Fax: (901) 678-4072
Web site: www.tsbdc.memphis.edu

Tennessee Department of Economic and Community Development
Tennessee Export Office
320 6th Avenue North
8th Floor, Rachel Jackson Bldg.
Nashville, TN 37243
Tel: (615) 741-5870; Fax: (615) 741-7306
Web site: www.state.tn.us

Tennessee Department of Agriculture
P.O. Box 40627
Melrose Station
Nashville, TN 37204
Tel: (615) 837-5117; Fax: (615) 837-5333
Web site: www.state.tn.us/agriculture

World Trade Center Chattanooga
535 Chestnut St., Suite 210
Chattanooga, TN 37402
Tel: (423) 752-4316; Fax: (423) 265-9751
Email: infor@twtc.org
Web site: www.twtc.org

Texas

U.S. Department of Commerce
Export Assistance Center
P.O. Box 420069
Dallas, TX 75342-0069
Tel: (214) 767-0542; Fax: (214) 767-8240
Email: ODallas@doc.gov

U.S. Department of Commerce
Export Assistance Center
One Allen Center
500 Dallas, Suite 1160
Houston, TX 77002
Tel: (713) 718-3062; Fax: (713) 718-3060
Email: OHouston@doc.gov

U.S. Department of Commerce
Export Assistance Center
c/o City of San Antonion IAD
P.O. Box 839966
San Antonio, TX 78283
Tel: (210) 228-9878; Fax: (210) 228-9874
Email: OSanAnto@doc.gov

U.S. Department of Commerce
Export Assistance Center
P.O. Box 12728
Austin, TX 78711
Tel: (512) 916-5939; Fax: (512) 916-5940

U.S. Small Business Administration Branch Office
606 North Carancahua Ave., Suite 1200
Corpus Christi, TX 78476
Tel: (512) 888-3331; Fax: (512) 888-3418

U.S. Small Business Administration District Office
10737 Gateway West, Suite 320
El Paso, TX 79935
Tel: (915) 633-7001; Fax: (915) 633-7005

U.S. Small Business Administration District Office
4300 Amon Carter Blvd., Suite 114
Ft. Worth, TX 76155
Tel: (817) 885-6581; Fax: (817) 885-6588

U.S. Small Business Administration District Office
222 East Van Buren Street, Suite 500
Harlingen, TX 78550
Tel: (956) 427-8625; Fax: (956) 427-8537

U.S. Small Business Administration District Office
9301 Southwest Freeway, Suite 550
Houston, TX 77074-1591
Tel: (713) 773-6500; Fax: (713) 773-6550

U.S. Small Business Administration District Office
1205 Texas Avenue, Suite 408
Lubbock, TX 79401-2693
Tel: (806) 743-7462; Fax: (806) 743-7487

U.S. Small Business Administration District Office
727 E. Durango, Room A527
San Antonio, TX 78206
Tel: (210) 472-5900; Fax: (210) 472-5935

Small Business Development Center
Regional Network Office
1402 Corinth Street
Dallas, TX 75215
Tel: (214) 860-5835; Fax: (214) 860-5813

Small Business Development Center
Regional Network Office
University of Houston
1100 Louisiana, Suite 500
Houston, TX 77002
Tel: (713) 752-8425; Fax: (713) 756-1500
Email: fyoung@uh.edu

Small Business Development Center
Regional Network Office
Texas Tech University
2579 South Loop 289, Suite 114
Lubbock, TX 79423-1637
Tel: (806) 745-3973; Fax: (806) 745-6207
Email: odbea@ttacs.ttu.edu

Small Business Development Center
Regional Network Office
University of Texas at San Antonio
Cypress Tower, Suite 450
1222 North Main Street
San Antonio, TX 78212
Tel: (210) 558-2470; Fax: (210) 458-2464

Minority Business Development Center
3505 Boca Chica Tower, Suite 174
Brownsville, TX 78521
Tel: (956) 546-3400; Fax: (956) 546-3400
Email: orella98@hotmail.com

Minority Business Development Center
5959 Gateway West, Suite 425
El Paso, TX 79925
Tel: (915) 774-0626; Fax: (915) 774-0680
Email: elpasombdc@ibm.net

Ex-Im Bank Southwest Regional Office
1880 South Dairy Ashford II, Suite 585
Houston, TX 77077
Tel: (281) 721-0465; Fax: (281) 679-0156
Web site: www.exim.gov

Texas Department of Economic Development
Office of Trade & International Relations
P.O. Box 12728
Austin, TX 78711-2728
Tel: (512) 936-0249; Fax: (512) 936-0445
Overseas offices: Mexico City, Mexico

Texas Department of Economic Development
Export Finance
P. O. Box 12728
Austin, TX 78711-2728
Tel: (512) 936-0281; Fax: 512) 936-0520

Texas Department of Agriculture
Marketing Division
P.O. Box 12847
Austin, TX 78711
Tel: (512) 463-7624; Fax: (512) 463-9968
Web site: www.agr.state.tx.us

Houston World Trade Association
1200 Smith St., Suite 700
Houston, TX 77002
Tel: (713) 844-3637; Fax: (713) 844-0200
Email: pfoley@houston.org
Web site: www.houston.org

San Antonio World Trade Center
118 Broadway, Suite 324
San Antonio, TX 78216
Tel: (210) 978 7600; Fax: (210) 978-7610
Email: wtcsa@newpro.net
Web site: www.newpro.net/~wtcsa

World Trade Center El Paso/Juarez
123 Pioneer Plaza
Suite 118, Centre Building
El Paso, TX 79901
Tel: (915) 544-0022; Fax: (915) 544-0030
Email: wtcepj@wtcepj.org
Web site: www.wtcepj.org

World Trade Center Rio Grande Valley at McAllen
Neuhaus Tower, Suite 401
200 South Tenth Street
McAllen, TX 78501-4850
Tel: (956) 686-1982; Fax: (956) 618-1982
Email: info@main.rgv.net
Web site: www.rgv.net

Greater Dallas Chamber
International Trade Department
World Trade Center
2050 Stemmons Freeway, Suite 150
P.O. Box 420829
Dallas, TX 75342-0829
Tel: (214) 712-1930; Fax: (214) 748-5774
Web site: www.dallaschamber.org

Greater Austin Chamber of Commerce
International Committee
P.O. Box 1967
Austin, TX 78767
Tel: (512) 322-5695; Fax: (512) 478-6389
Web site: www.austinchamber.org

Brownsville Economic Development Council
1205 North Expressway
Brownsville, TX 78520
Tel: (956) 541-1183; Fax: (956) 546-3938
Web site: www.bedc.com

Free Trade Alliance of San Antonio
203 S. St. Marys, Suite 130
San Antonio, TX 78205
Tel: (210) 229-9036; Fax: (210) 229-9724
Email: ftasa@stic.nut

Utah

U.S. Department of Commerce
Export Assistance Center
324 S. State Street, Suite 221
Salt Lake City, UT 84111
Tel: (801) 524-5116; Fax: (801) 524-5886
Email: OSaltLak@doc.gov

U.S. Small Business Administration District Office
Federal Building, Room 2237
125 South State Street
Salt Lake City, UT 84138
Tel: (801) 524-5800; Fax: (801) 524-4160

Small Business Development Center
Salt Lake Community College
1623 South State St.
Salt Lake City, UT 84115
Tel: (801) 957-3480; Fax: (801) 957-3489
Email: FinnerMi@slcc.edu

Utah International Business Development Office
324 S. State Street, Suite 500
Salt Lake City, UT 84111
Tel: (801) 538-8737; Fax: (801) 538-8889
Web site: www.ce.ex.state.ut.us/internat/welcome.htm
Overseas offices: Brussels, Belgium; Tokyo, Japan; Mexico City, Mexico; Seoul, South Korea; Taipei, Taiwan

Utah Technology Finance Corporation
177 East 100 South
Salt Lake City, UT 84111
Tel: (801) 364-4346; Fax: (801) 741-4249
Web site: www.utfc.org

World Trade Association of Utah
324 S. State Street, Suite 221
Salt Lake City, UT 84111
Tel: (801) 524-5116; Fax: (801) 524-5886

Vermont

U.S. Department of Commerce
Export Assistance Center
National Lilfe BUilding, Drawer 20
Montpelier, VT 05609-0501
Tel: (802) 828-4508; Fax: (802) 828-3258
Email: OMontpel@doc.gov

U.S. Small Business Administration District Office
87 State Street
Montpelier, VT 05602
Tel: (802) 828-4422, Fax: (802) 828-4485

Small Business Development Center
Vermont Technical College
P.O. Box 422
Randolph, VT 05060-0422
Tel: (800) 464-SBDC, (802) 728-9101
Fax: (802) 728-3026
Email: dkelpins@vtc.vsc.edu

Vermont Department of Economic Development
National Life Building, 6th Floor
Montpelier, VT 05620-0501
Tel: (802) 828-3211; Fax: (802) 828-3258
Web site: www.state.vt.us/dca/economic/developm.htm

Vermont Department of Agriculture
116 State Street
Drawer 20
Montpelier, VT 05602-2901
Tel: (802) 828-2416; Fax: (802) 828-3831
Web site: www.cit.state.vt.us/agric

Vermont World Trade Office
60 Main Street, Suite 102
Burlington, VT 05401
Tel: (802) 865-0493; Fax: (802) 860-0091
Email: vwto@together.net
Web site: www.vermontworldtrade.org

Virginia

U.S. Department of Commerce
Export Assistance Center
P.O. Box 10026
Richmond, VA 23240-0026
Tel: (804) 771-2246; Fax: (804) 771-2390
Email: ORichmon@doc.gov

U.S. Department of Commerce
Export Assistance Center
1616 N. Ft. Myer Drive, Suite 1300
Arlington, VA 22209
Tel: (703) 524-2885; Fax: (703) 524-2649

U.S. Small Business Administration District Office
Federal Bldg., Suite 1150
400 North 8th Street, Box 10126
Richmond, VA 23240-0126
Tel: (804) 771-2400; Fax: (804) 771-8018

Small Business Development Center
Department of Economic Development
707 East Main Street, Suite 300
Richmond, VA 23219
Tel: (804) 371-8253; Fax: (804) 225-3384
Email: rwilburn@dba.state.va.us

Virginia Economic Development Partnership
Division of International Trade and Investment
Riverfront Plaza, West Tower, 19th Fl.
P.O. Box 798
Richmond, VA 23218-0798
Tel: (804) 371-8123; Fax: (804) 371-8860
Email: exportva@vedp.state.va.us
Web site: www.exportvirginia.org
Overseas offices: Frankfurt am Main, Germany; Budapest, Hungary; Tokyo, Japan

Virginia Economic Development Partnership
Division of International Trade and Investment
CIT Building, Suite 602
2214 Rock Hill Road
Herndon, VA 20170
Tel: (703) 689-3059; Fax: (703) 689-3056

Virginia Economic Development Partnership
Division of International Trade and Investment
212 South Jefferson Street
Roanoke, VA 24011-1938
Tel: (540) 857-6029; Fax: (540) 857-6161

Virginia Department of Agriculture and Consumer Services
International Marketing Division
1100 Bank Street, Suite 915
Richmond, VA 23219
Tel: (804) 786-3953; Fax: (804) 225-4434
Web site: www.state.va.us/~vdacs/divmkt/oim.htm

World Trade Center Norfolk
Virginia Port Authority
600 World Trade Center
Norfolk, VA 23510
Tel: (757) 683-8000; Fax: (757) 683-2897

Washington

U.S. Department of Commerce
Export Assistance Center
2001 Sixth Avenue, Suite 650
Seattle, WA 98121
Tel: (206) 553-5615; Fax: (206) 553-7253
Email: Seattle.Office.Box@mail.doc.gov

U.S. Department of Commerce
Export Assistance Center
c/o Greater Spokane Chamber of Commerce
801 W. Riverside Avenue, Suite 400
Spokane, WA 99201
Tel: (509) 353-2625; Fax: (509) 353-2449

U.S. Department of Commerce
Export Assistance Center
950 Pacific Avenue, Suite 410
Takoma, WA 98402
Tel: (253) 593-6736; Fax: (253) 383-4676

U.S. Small Business Administration District Office
1200 6th Ave. Suite 1700
Seattle, WA 98101-1128
Tel: (206) 553-7310; Fax: (206) 553-7099

U.S. Small Business Administration District Office
801 W. Riverside Ave. #200
Spokane, WA 99201-0901
Tel: (509) 353-2800; Fax: (509) 353-2829

Small Business Development Center
501 Johnson Tower
P.O. Box 644851
Pullman, WA 99164-4851
Tel: (509) 335-1576; Fax: (509) 335-0949

U.S. National Marine Fisheries Trade and Industry Services Division
7600 Sand Point Way, N.E.
Bin C15700, Building 1
Seattle, WA 98115
Tel: (206) 526-6117; Fax: (206) 526-6544

Washington State Department of Trade and Economic Development
2001 Sixth Avenue, 26th Floor
Seattle, WA 98121-2545
Tel: (206) 464-7143; Fax: (206) 956-3151
Web site: www.wa.gov/cted/
Overseas offices: Paris, France; Tokyo, Japan; Vladivostok, Russia; Taipei, Taiwan

Washington State Department of Agriculture
Market Development Division
P.O. Box 42560
Olympia, WA 98504-2560
Tel: (360) 902-1915; Fax: (360) 902-2089

Export Finance Assistance Center of Washington
2001 6th Avenue, Suite 650
Seattle, WA 98121
Tel: (206) 464-7150; Fax: (206) 464-7230

Washington Public Ports Association
P.O. Box 1518
Olympia, WA 98507-1518
Tel: (360) 943-0760; Fax: (360) 753-6176

World Trade Center Seattle
2200 Alaskan Way, Suite 410
Seattle, WA 98121
Tel. (206) 441-5144; Fax: (206) 374-0410
Email: info@wtcse.com
Web site: www.wtcseattle.com

World Trade Center of Tacoma
3600 Port of Tacoma Road, Suite 309
Tacoma, WA 98424
Tel: (253) 383-9474; Fax: (253) 926-0384
Email: info@wtcta.org
Web site: www.wtcta.org

IMPACT (Agricultural Marketing)
Washington State University
P.O. Box 646214
Pullman, WA 99164-6214
Tel: (509) 335-6653; Fax: (509) 335-3958
Web site: impact.wsu.edu

Washington Council on International Trade
2200 Alaskan Way, Suite 430
Seattle, WA 98121-1684
Tel: (206) 443-3826; Fax: (206) 443-3828
Email: wcitinfo@wcit.org
Web site: www.wcit.org

Washington State International Trade Fair
2200 Alaskan Way, Suite 480
Seattle, WA 98121
Tel: (206) 728-9393; Fax: (206) 728-9399
Email: wsitf@wsitf.org
Web site: www.wsitf.org

West Virginia

U.S. Department of Commerce
Export Assistance Center
c/o Wheeling Jesuit University/NTTC
316 Washington Avenue
Wheeling, WV 26003
Tel: (304) 243-5493; Fax: (304) 2243-5494
Email: OWheelin@doc.gov

U.S. Department of Commerce
Export Assistance Center
405 Capitol Street, Suite 807
Charleston, WV 25301
Tel: (304) 347-5123; Fax: (304) 347-5408
Email: OCharles@doc.gov

U.S. Small Business Administration Branch Office
405 Capitol Street, Suite 412
Charleston, WV 25301
Tel: (304) 347-5220; Fax: (304) 347-5350

U.S. Small Business Administration District Office
168 W. Main St.
Clarksburg, WV 26301
Tel: (304) 623-5631; Fax: (304) 623-0023

Small Business Development Center
West Virginia Development Office
950 Kanawha Blvd., 32nd Floor
Charleston, WV 25301
Tel: (304) 558-2960; Fax: (304) 558-0127
Email: palmeh@mail.wvnet.edu

West Virginia Department of Development
Office of International Development
Capitol Complex
Building 6, Room B517
Charleston, WV 25305-0311
Tel: (304) 558-2234; Fax: (304) 558 1957
Web site: www.wvdo.org
Overseas offices: Nagoya, Japan

West Virginia Department of Agriculture
Marketing and Development Division
1900 Kanawha Blvd. East
Charleston, WV 25305
Tel: (304) 558-2210; Fax: (304) 558-2270
Web site: www.wvlc.wvnet.edu/agric/wvda.html

Wisconsin

U.S. Department of Commerce
Export Assistance Center
517 E. Wisconsin Avenue, Room 596
Milwaukee, WI 53202
Tel: (414) 297-3473; Fax: (414) 297-3470
Email: OMilwauk@doc.gov

U.S. Small Business Administration District Office
212 E. Washington Ave., Suite 213
Madison, WI 53703
Tel: (608) 264-5261; Fax: (608) 264-5541

U.S. Small Business Administration Branch Office
310 West Wisconsin Avenue, Suite 400
Milwaukee, WI 53203
Tel: (414) 297-3941; Fax: (414) 297-1377

Small Business Development Center
University of Wisconsin
432 North Lake Street, Room 423
Madison, WI 53706
Tel: (608) 263-7794; Fax: (608) 262-3878
Email: Kauten@admin.uwex.edu

Wisconsin Department of Commerce
Division of International Development
P.O. Box 7970
201 W. Washington Avenue
Madison, WI 53707
Tel: (608) 266-1767; Fax: (608) 266-5551
Web site: badger.state.wi.us/agencies/commerce
Overseas offices: Frankfurt, Germany; Hong Kong; Tokyo, Japan; Seoul, South Korea; Mexico City, Mexico

Port of Milwaukee
2323 S. Lincoln Memorial Drive
Milwaukee, WI 53207
Tel: (414) 286-3511; Fax: (414) 286-8506
Web site: www.port.mil.wi.us

Port of Green Bay
2561 S. Broadway
Green Bay, WI 54304
Tel: (920) 448-4290; Fax: (920) 492-4957

International Agribusiness Center
2811 Agriculture Drive
Madison, WI 53704-6777
Tel: (608) 224-5117; Fax: (608) 224-5111
Web site: http://badger.state.wi.us/agencies/datcp

Milwaukee World Trade Center
424 E. Wisconsin Avenuett
Milwaukee, WI 53202
Tel: (414) 274-3840; Fax: (414) 274-3846
Email: wistrade@wistrade.org
Web site: www.wistrade.org

Wyoming

U.S. Department of Commerce
Wyoming is served by the Denver office:

U.S. Department of Commerce
Export Assistance Center
1625 Broadway, Suite 680
Denver, CO 68020
Tel: (303) 844-6623; Fax: (303) 844-5651
Email: Odenver@doc.gov

U.S. Small Business Administration District Office
100 East B Street, Room 4001
Box 2839
Casper, WY 82602-2839
Tel: (307) 261-6500; Fax: (307) 261-6535

Small Business Development Center
University of Wyoming
P.O. Box 3922
Laramie, WY 82071
Tel: (307) 766-3505; Fax: (307) 766-3406
Web site: www.uwyo.edu/sbdc

Wyoming Department of Commerce
Division of Economic & Community Development
214 W. 15th Street
Cheyenne, WY 82002
Tel: (307) 777-2800; Fax: (307) 777-2837
Web site: www.wyomingbusiness.org

Appendix IV
U.S. and Overseas Contacts for Major Foreign Markets

Organization

This appendix contains major contacts for information on specific countries. U.S. embassies, consulates, and trade centers located in foreign countries are given first in each listing. The United States maintains a diplomatic presence in most, but not all, of these countries. Many of these offices provide commercial services through the U.S. & Foreign Commercial Service or through State Department commercial representatives.

Addresses of U.S. government representatives overseas are followed by foreign embassies in the United States. Many of these countries also maintain consulates in major U.S. cities. The embassies will not assist you with exporting into their country, but may be a good source for directories, import regulations, travel information, and general information on business practices.

American Chamber of Commerce, or AmCham, offices in foreign countries are also included here. Their services are primarily for their members, but they often sell directories and other publications of interest to U.S. exporters.

Note on U.S. Mailing Addresses

Many of the U.S. embassies and consulates listed here have U.S. mailing addresses given in addition to their local address. If you are writing to a diplomatic mission which has a U.S. mailing address, you should use that address. The mail will not go through foreign postal services, which means the cost is lower and service often faster. Mexican and Canadian posts often use P.O. Boxes in U.S. border cities. Here are some examples of accepted forms for addressing mail to APO or FPO addresses or to State Department

Posts with APO/FPO Numbers

Name
Organization
PSC or Unit number, Box number
APO AE 09080 or APO AA 34038 or PO AP 96337

Posts without APO/FPO Numbers

Diplomatic Pouch Address
Name of Person/Section
Name of Post
Department of State
Washington, D.C. 20521-four digit add-on (see 9-digit ZIP Code explanation and listing)

If a post has only an international address given, use that. Be sure to include the name of the country, any postal codes given, and the proper postage.

Note: Do not combine any of the above forms (e.g., international plus APO/FPO addresses). This will only result in confusion and possible delays in delivery. Mail sent to the Department for delivery through its pouch system for posts with APO/FPO addresses cannot be accepted and will be returned to the sender.

Contacts

Afghanistan

Afghanistan
Embassy of the Republic of Afghanistan
(Embassy ceased operations August 28, 1997)

Albania

U.S. Embassy, Consular Section
Tirana (E), Tirana Rruga E. Labinoti 103, Albania

Tel: [355] (42) 32875
Fax: [355] (42) 32222
US Mailing Address: PSC 59, Box 100 (A), APO AE 09624

Embassy of the Republic of Albania
2100 S Street NW
Washington, DC 20008
Tel: (202) 223-4942; Fax: (202) 628-7342

Algeria

U.S. Embassy, Consular Section
4 Chemin Cheikh Bachir El-Ibrahimi
B.P. Box 549 (Alger-Gare)
16000 Algiers, Algeria
Tel: [213] (2) 601-425, 601-255, (2) 693-973 (FCS)
Fax: [213] (2) 603-979, (2) 691-863 (FCS)
US Mailing Address: c/o Dept. of State, Washington, DC 20521-6030

Embassy of the Democratic and Popular Rep. of Algeria
2118 Kaloroma Road NW
Washington, DC 20008
Tel: (202) 265-2800; Fax: (202) 667-2174

Andorra

Embassy of Andorra
Two United Nations Plaza, 25th Floor
New York, NY 10017
Tel: (212) 750-8064; Fax: (212) 750-6630

Angola

Embassy of the Republic of Angola
1615 M Street NW, Suite 900
Washington, DC 20036
Tel: (202) 785-1156; Fax: (202) 785-1258
Web site: www.angola.org/angola/

Diplomatic representation for the US embassy
No. 32 Rua Houari Boumedienne
Miramar, Luanda, Angola
Tel: [244] (2) 345-481, 346-418 Fax: [244] (2) 346-924
US mailing address: C.P. 6484, Luanda; American Embassy, Department of State, Washington, DC20521-2550 (pouch)

Antigua & Barbuda

Embassy of Antigua and Barbuda
3216 New Mexico Avenue NW
Washington, DC 20026
Tel: (202) 362-5122; Fax: (202) 362-5225

Argentina

Embassy of the U.S., Buenos Aires, Argentina
4300 Colombia
1425 Buenos Aires, Argentina
Tel: [54] (1) 777-4533, 777-4534, (1) 772-1041 (FCS)
Fax: [54] (1) 777-3530, (1) 777-0673 (FCS)
US Mailing Address: Unit 4334, APO AA 34034

Embassy of the Argentine Republic
1600 New Hampshire Avenue NW
Washington, DC 20009
Tel: (202) 939-6400; Fax: (202) 332-3171
Web site: www.ar/cwash

American Chamber of Commerce in Argentina
Viamonte 1133, Piso 8
1053 Buenos Aires, Argentina
Tel: [54] (1) 371-4500; Fax: [54] (1) 371-8400

Armenia

United States Embassy
18 Marshall Baghramyan St.
Yerevan 375019, Armenia
Tel: [374] (2) 524-661, 04 151-551; Fax: [374] (2) 151-550
Email: usinfo@arminco.com

Embassy of the Republic of Armenia
2225 R Street NW
Washington DC 20008
Tel: (202) 319-1976; Fax: (202) 319-2982

Australia

U.S. Embassy
Moonah Pl.
Canberra, ACT 2600, Australia
Tel: [61] (2) 6214-5600; Fax: [61] (2) 6214-5970
US Mailing Address: APO AP 96549
Email: usfcs@australia.net.au

U.S. Consulate General
553 St. Kilda Rd.
P.O. Box 6722
Melbourne, VIC 3004, Australia
Tel: [61] (3) 9526-5900, (3) 9526-5923 (FCS)
Fax: [61] (3) 9510-4646, (3) 9510-4660 (FCS)
US Mailing Address: Unit 11011, APO AP 96551-0002

U.S. Consulate General
16 St. Georges Terr., 13th Fl.
Perth, WA 6000, Australia
Tel: [61] (8) 9231-9400, (9) 231-9400 (FCS)
Fax: [61] (9) 231-9444, (9) 231-9444 (FCS)
US Mailing Address: Unit 11021, APO AP 96553-0002

U.S. Consulate General
MLC Centre
19-29 Martin Place, 59th Fl.
Sydney NSW 2000, Australia
Tel: [61] (2) 9373-9200, (2) 9221-0573 (FCS)
US Mailing Address: Unit 11026 APO AP 96554-5000

Embassy of Australia
1601 Massachusetts Avenue NW
Washington, DC 20036
Tel: (202) 797-3000; Fax: (202) 797-3168
Web site: www.aust.emb.nw.dc.us

American Chamber of Commerce in Australia
88 Cumberland St. #4; Gloucester Walk
Sydney, NSW 2000, Australia
Tel: [61] (2) 9241-1907; Fax: [61] (2) 9251-5220
Email: nsw@amcham.com.au

Austria

American Embassy
Boltzmanngasse 16
1090 Vienna, Austria

U.S. Embassy, Consular Section
Gartenbaupromenade 2, 4th Floor
A-1010 Vienna, Austria
Tel: [43] (1) 313-39, (1) 313-39 (FCS)
Fax: [43] (1) 513-4351, (1) 310-6917 (FCS)
US Mailing Address: c/o Dept. of State, Washington, DC 20521-9900

Embassy of Austria
3524 International Court NW
Washington, DC 20008
Tel: (202) 895-6700; Fax: (202) 895-6750
Web site: www.austria.org/

American Chamber of Commerce in Austria
Porzellangasse 35
A-1090 Vienna, Austria
Tel: [43] (1) 319-5751; Fax: [43] (1) 319-5151
Email: Office@amcham.or.at

Azerbaijan

U.S. Embassy
Prospect Azadlig 83
Baku, Azerbaijan
Tel: [994] (12) 98-03-35, 98-03-36
US Mailing Address: c/o Dept. of State, Washington DC 20521-7050

Embassy of the Republic of Azerbaijan
927 - 15th St. NW, Suite 700
Washington, DC 20005
Tel: (202) 842-0001; Fax: (202) 842-0004

Bahamas

U.S. Embassy, Consular Section
P.O. Box N-8197
Nassau, Bahamas
Tel: (242) 322-1181, 328-2206; Fax: (242) 328-7838
US Mailing Address: c/o Dept. of State, Washington, DC 20521-3370

Embassy of the Commonwealth of the Bahamas
2220 Massachusetts Avenue NW
Washington, DC 20008
Tel: (202) 319-2660; Fax: (202) 319-2668

Bahrain

U.S. Embassy, Consular Section
Bldg. No. 979, Road 3119
Zinj District; P.O. Box 26431
Manama, Bahrain
Tel: [973] 273-300, ext. 1102; Fax: [973] 256-242
US Mailing Address: FPO AE 09834-5100

Embassy of the State of Bahrain
3502 International Drive NW
Washington, DC 20008
Tel: (202) 342-0741; Fax: (202) 362-2192

Bangladesh

U.S. Embassy, Consular Section
Diplomatic Enclave
Madani Ave.
Baridhara
G.P.O. Box 323
Dhaka 1212, Bangladesh
Tel: [880] (2) 884-700, 884-722; Fax: [880] (2) 883-744
Email: dhaka@usia.gov
US Mailing Address: Dept. of State, Washington, DC 20521-6120

Embassy of the People's Republic of Bangladesh
2201 Wisconsin Avenue NW
Washington, DC 20007
Tel: (202) 342-8372; Fax: (202) 333-4971

Barbados

U.S. Embassy, Consular Section
Canadian Imperial Bank of Commerce Bldg.
Broad Street; P.O. Box 302
Bridgetown, Barbados W.I.
Tel: (246) 436-4950; Fax: (246) 431-0179
US Mailing Address: FPO AA 34055

Embassy of Barbados
2144 Wyoming Avenue NW
Washington, DC 20008
Tel: (202) 939-9200; Fax: (202) 332-7467

Belarus

U.S. Embassy
46 Starovilenskaya St.
Minsk 220002 Belarus
Tel: [375] (172) 34-77-61, 31-50-00; Fax: [375](172)34-78-53
US Mailing Address: c/o Dept. of State, Washington DC 20521-7010

Embassy of the Republic of Belarus
1619 New Hampshire Avenue NW
Washington, DC 20009
Tel: (202) 986-1606; Fax: (202) 986-11805

Belgium

Embassy of the United States
27 Boulevard du Regent
B-1000 Brussels, Belgium
Tel: [32] (2) 512-2210; Fax: [32] (2) 511-9652
US Mailing Address: PSC 82 Box 002, APO AE 09724-1015

Embassy of Belgium
3330 Garfield Street NW
Washington, DC 20008
Tel: (202) 333-6900; Fax: (202) 333-3079
Email: usa@belgium-emb.org
Web site: www.belgium-emb.org/usa/

American Chamber of Commerce in Belgium
Avenue des Arts 50, Boite 50
1000 Brussels, Belgium
Tel: [32] (2) 513-6770; Fax: [32] (2) 513-3590
Email: gch@post1.amcham.be

Belize

Embassy of the United States
29 Gabourel Lane; P.O. Box. 286
Belize City, Belize
Tel: [501] (2) 77161; Fax: [501] (2) 30802
US Mailing Address: Unit 7401, APO AA 34025

Embassy of Belize
2535 Massachusetts Avenue NW
Washington, DC 20008
Tel: (202) 332-9636; Fax: (202) 332-6888

Benin

U.S. Embassy, Consular Section
Rue Caporal Bernard Anani; B.P. 2012
Cotonou, Benin
Tel: [229] 30-06-50, 30-05-13; Fax: [229] 30-14-39, 30-19-74
US Mailing Address: c/o Dept. of State, Washington DC 20521-2120

Embassy of the Republic of Benin
2737 Cathedral Avenue NW
Washington, DC 20008
Tel: (202) 232-6656; Fax: (202) 265-1996

Bermuda

U.S. Consulate General
P.O. Box HM325
Hamilton HMBX, Bermuda
Tel: (441) 295-1342; Fax: (441) 295-1592
US Mailing Address: PSC 1002, FPO AE 09727-1002

Bolivia

U.S. Embassy, Consular Section
P.O. Box 425
La Paz, Bolivia
Tel: [591] (2) 430251; Fax: [591] (2) 433900
US Mailing Address: APO AA 34032

Embassy of the Republic of Bolivia
3014 Massachusetts Avenue NW
Washington, DC 20008
Tel: (202) 483-4410; Fax: (202) 328-3712

American Chamber of Commerce of Bolivia
Casilla 8268
La Paz, Bolivia
Tel: [591] (2) 432-573; Fax: [591] (2) 432-472
Email: amgalin@caoba.entelnet.bo

Bosnia & Herzegovina

U.S. Embassy
Djure Djakovica 43
Sarajevo, Bosnia-Herzegovina
Tel: [387] (71) 445-700, 667-391, 667-389, 667-743, 667-390, 659-969, 659-992
Fax: [387] (71) 659-722

Embassy of Bosnia and Herzegovina
2109 E Street NW
Washington, DC 20037
Tel: (202) 337-1500; Fax: (202) 337-1502

Botswana

U.S. Embassy
P.O. Box 90
Gaborone, Botswana
Tel: [267] 353-982; Fax: [267] 356-947
US Mailing Address: c/o Dept. of State, Washington DC 25201-2170

Embassy of the Republic of Botswana
1531-1533 New Hampshire Avenue NW
Washington, DC 20036
Tel: (202) 244-4990; Fax: (202) 244-4164

Brazil

U.S. Embassy, Consular Section
Avenida das Nacoes
Lote 3, Brasilia, Brazil
Tel: [55] (61) 321-7272
Fax: [55] (61) 225-9136, 61-225-9136 (FCS)
US Mailing Address: Unit 3500, APO AA 34030

U.S. Consular Agency
Travessa Padre
Eutiquio 1309
Belem, Brazil
Tel: [55] (91) 223-0800, (91) 223-0413 (FCS), (91) 223-0413 (FCS)
US Mailing Address: Unit 3500, APO AA 34030

U.S. Consulate General
Avenida Presidente Wilson, 147
Rio de Janeiro, Brazil
Tel: [55] (21) 292-7117, (21) 292-7117 (FCS)
Fax: [55] (21) 220-0439, (21) 240-9738 (FCS)
US Mailing Address: APO AA 34030

U.S. Consulate General
Rua Padre Joao Manoel, 933
Sao Paulo 01411
P.O. Box 8063
Sao Paulo, Brazil
Tel: [55] (11) 881-6511, (11) 853-2011 (FCS)
Fax: [55] (11) 852-5154, (11) 853-2744 (FCS)
US Mailing Address: Unit 3502, APO AA 34030

Brazilian Embassy
3006 Massachusetts Avenue NW
Washington, DC 20008
Tel: (202) 238-2700; Fax: (202) 238-2827
Web site: www.brasil.emb.nw.dc.us

American Chamber of Commerce for Brazil - Rio de Janiero
C.P. 916
Praca Pio X-15, 5th Fl.
Rio de Janiero, RJ 20040, Brazil
Tel: [55] (21) 203-2477; Fax: [55] (21) 263-4477

American Chamber of Commerce for Brazil - Sao Paulo
Rua da Paz 1431
CEP 04713-001 Sao Paulo Brazil
Tel: [55] (11) 5180-3804; Fax: [55] (11) 5180-3777

Brunei Darussalam

U.S. Embassy, Consular Section
Third Floor, Teck Guan Plaza
Jalan Sultan
Bandar Seri Begawan, Brunei Darussalam
Tel: [673] (2) 229-670; Fax: [673] (2) 225-293
US Mailing Address: Box B, APO AP 96440

Embassy of the State of Brunei Darussalam
Watergate, Suite 300
2600 Virginia Avenue NW
Washington, DC 20037
Tel: (202) 342-0159
Fax: (202) 342-0158

Bulgaria

U.S. Embassy, Consular Section
1 Saborna St.
Sofia, Bulgaria
Tel: [359] (2) 980-5241/8, (2) 988-4801 (FCS)
Fax: [359] (2) 981-8977, (2) 980-3850 (FCS)
US Mailing Address: Unit 1335, APO AE 09213-1335

Embassy of the Republic of Bulgaria
1621 - 22nd St. NW
Washington, DC 20008
Tel: (202) 387-7969; Fax: (202) 234-7973
Email: bulgaria@access.digex.net

American Chamber of Commerce in Bulgaria
19 Patriarch Evtimii Blvd., Floor 5, Apt. 10
1000 Sofia, Bulgaria
Tel: [359] (9) 81-5950
Fax: [359] (9) 80-4206
Email:amcham@lnd.internet-bg.bg

Burkina Faso

U.S. Embassy
01 B.P. 35
Ouagadougou, Burkina Faso
Tel: [226] 30-67-23/5; Fax: [226] 30-38-90
US Mailing Address: c/o Dept. of State, Washington DC 25201-2440

Embassy of Burkina Faso
2340 Massachusetts Avenue NW
Washington, DC 20008
Tel: (202) 332-5577; Fax: (202) 667-1882

Burma (Myanmar)

U.S. Embassy, Consular Section
581 Merchant St.
GPO 521
Rangoon, Myanmar
Tel: [95] (1) 282055, 282182; Fax: [95] (1) 280409
US Mailing Address: Box B, APO AP 96546

Embassy of the Union of Myanmar
2300 S Street NW
Washington, DC 20008
Tel: (202) 332-9044; Fax: (202) 332-9046

Burundi

U.S. Embassy, Consular Section
B.P. 1720, Avenue des Etats-Unis
Bujumbura, Burundi
Tel: [257] 223-454; Fax: [257] 222-926
US Mailing Address: c/o Dept. of State, Washington DC 25201-2100

Embassy of the Republic of Burundi
2233 Wisconsin Avenue NW, Suite 212
Washington, DC 20007
Tel: (202) 342-2574; Fax: (202) 342-2578

Cambodia (Kampuchea)

U.S. Embassy
27, EO Street 240
Phnom Penh, Cambodia
Tel: [855] (23) 426436, 426438; Fax: [855] (23) 426437
US Mailing Address: Box P, APO AP 96546

Royal Embassy of Cambodia
4500 - 16th Street NW
Washington, DC 20011
Tel: (202) 726-7742; Fax: (202) 726-8381
Email: Cambodia@embassy.org
Web site: www.embassy.org/cambodia/

Cameroon

U.S. Embassy, Consular Section
Rue Nachtigal, B.P. 817
Yaounde, Cameroon
Tel: [237] 23-40-14; Fax: [237] 23-07-53
US Mailing Address: c/o Dept. of State, Washington DC 25201-2520

Embassy of the Republic of Cameroon
2349 Massachusetts Avenue NW
Washington, DC 20008
Tel: (202) 265-8790; Fax: (202) 387-3826

Canada

U.S. Embassy, Consular Section
100 Wellington St.
Ottawa, ON K1P 5T1, Canada
Tel: (613) 238-5335, 238-4470, (613) 238-5335 (FCS)
Fax: (613) 238-5720, (613) 233-8511 (FCS)
Web site: www.usis-canada.usia.gov/index.html (USIS)
US Mailing Address: P.O. Box 5000, Ogdensburg, NY 13669-0430

U.S. Consulate General
Suite 1050, 615 Macleod Trail SE
Calgary, AB T2G 4T8, Canada
Tel: (403) 266-8962, (403) 265-2116 (FCS)
Fax: (403) 264-6630, (403) 266-4743 (FCS)

U.S. Consulate General
Suite 910, Cogswell Tower
Scotia Sq.
Halifax, NS B3J 3K1, Canada
Tel: (902) 429-2480, (902) 429-2482 (FCS)
Fax: (902) 423-6861, (902) 423-6861 (FCS)

U.S. Consulate General
P.O. Box 65
Postal Station Desjardins
Montreal, PQ H5B 1G1, Canada
Tel: (514) 398-9695, 514-398-9695 (FCS)
Fax: (514) 398-0973, 514-398-0711 (FCS)
US Mailing Address: P.O. Box 847, Champlain, NY 12019-0847

U.S. Consulate General
360 University Avenue
Toronto, ON M5G 1S4, Canada
Tel: (416) 595-1700, (416) 595-5413 (FCS)
Fax: (416) 595-0051, (416) 595-5419 (FCS)
US Mailing Address: P.O. Box 135, Lewiston, NY 14092-0135

U.S. Consulate General
1095 West Pender St.
Vancouver, BC V6E 2M6, Canada
Tel: (604) 685-4311, 604-685-3382 (FCS)
Fax: (604) 685-5285, 604-687-6095 (FCS)
US Mailing Address: P.O. Box 5002, Point Roberts, WA 98281-5002

Embassy of Canada
501 Pennsylvania Avenue NW
Washington, DC 20001
Tel: (202) 682-1740; Fax: (202) 682-7726
Web site: www.cdnemb-washdc.org

Cape Verde

U.S. Embassy, Consular Section
Rua Abilio Macedo 81
C.P. 201
Praia, Cape Verde
Tel: [238] 61-56-16; Fax: [238] 61-13-55
US Mailing Address: Dept. of State, Washington DC 25201-2460

Embassy of the Republic of Cape Verde
3415 Massachusetts Avenue NW
Washington, DC 20007
Tel: (202) 965-6820; Fax: (202) 965-1207
Web site: www.capeverdeusembassy.org/

Central African Republic

U.S. Embassy, Consular Section
Avenue David Dacko
B.P. 924
Bangui, Central African Republic
Tel: [236] 61-02-00, 61-62-10; Fax: [236] 61-44-94
US Mailing Address: Dept. of State, Washington DC 25201-2060

Embassy of Central African Republic
1618 - 22nd Street NW
Washington, DC 20008
Tel: (202) 483-7800; Fax: (202) 332-9893

Chad

U.S. Embassy, Consular Section
B.P. 413
N'Djamena, Chad
Tel: [235] 51-70-09, 51-90-52, 51-92-33
Fax: [235] 51-56-54
US Mailing Address: Dept. of State, Washington DC 25201-2410

Embassy of the Republic of Chad
2002 R Street NW
Washington, DC 20009
Tel: (202) 462-4009; Fax: (202) 265-1937

Chile

U.S. Embassy, Consular Section
Av. Andres Bello 2800
Santiago, Chile
Tel: [56] (2) 232-2600; Fax: [56] (2)330-3710
US Mailing Address: Unit 4127, APO AA 34033

Embassy of Chile
1732 Massachusetts Avenue NW
Washington, DC 20036
Tel: (202) 785-1746; Fax: (202) 887-5579

Chilean-American Chamber of Commerce
Av. Americo Vespucio sur 80-9 Piso
Las Condes Chile
Tel: [56] (2) 290-9700; Fax: [56] (2) 206-0911
Email: amcham@amchamchile.cl

China (People's Republic of)

U.S. Embassy, Consular Section
Xiu Shui Bei Jie 3
Beijing 100600, P.R. of China
Tel: [86] (10) 6532-3831, (10) 6532-3831 (FCS)
Fax: [86] (10) 6532-3178, (10) 6532-3297 (FCS)
US Mailing Address: PSC 461, Box 50, FPO AP 96521-0002
Tel: [86] (10) 6532-3831

U.S. Consulate General
52, 14th Wei Road
Heping District
Shenyang 110003, P.R. of China
Tel: [86] (24) 282-0038, (24) 220-0057 (FCS)
Fax: [86] (24) 282-0074, (24) 220-0074 (FCS)
US Mailing Address: PSC 461, Box 45, FPO AP 96521-0002

U.S. Consulate General
No. 1 South Shamian Street
Shamian Island 20031
Guangzhou 510133, P.R. of China
Tel: [86] (20) 886-2418, 886-2402, (20) 67-8742 (FCS)
Fax: [86] (20) 886-2341, (20) 666-409 (FCS)
US Mailing Address: PSC 461, Box 100, FPO AP 96521-0002

U.S. Consulate General
1469 Huai Hai Zhong Lu
Shanghai, P.R. of China
Tel: [86] (21) 6433-6880, (21) 6433-2492 (FCS)
Fax: [86] (21) 6433-4122, (21) 6433-1576 (FCS)
US Mailing Address: PSC 461, Box 200, FPO AP 96521-0002

Embassy of the People's Republic of China
2300 Connecticut Avenue NW
Washington, DC 20008
Tel: (202) 328-2500; Fax: (202) 588-0032
Web site: www.china-embassy.org/

American Chamber of Commerce in Beijing
Great Wall Sheraton Hotel, Room 318
North Donghuan Ave.
Beijing 100026, P.R. China
Tel: [86] (10) 6590-5566 x2378
Fax: [86] (10) 6590-5273

American Chamber of Commerce in Shanghai
Shanghai Centre, Room 435
1376 Nanjing Xi Lu
Shanghai 200040, P.R. China
Tel: [86] (21) 6279-7119; Fax: [86] (21) 6279-8802

Colombia

U.S. Embassy, Consular Section
Calle 22-D Bis, No. 47-51
Apartado Aereo 3831
Bogota, Colombia
Tel: [57] (1) 315-0811; Fax: [57] (1) 315-2197
US Mailing Address: Unit 5120, APO AA 34038

Embassy of Colombia
2118 Leroy Place NW
Washington, DC 20008
Tel: (202) 387-8338; Fax: (202) 232-8643
Web site: www.colombiaemb.org

Colombia-American Chamber of Commerce
Apdo. Aereo 8008
Bogota, Colombia
Tel: [57] (1) 621-5042; Fax: [57] (1) 621-6838
Email: amchamcolombia@compuserve.com

Comoros

Embassy of the Federal and Islamic Republic of the Comoros
c/o Permanent Mission of the Federal and Islamic Republic of the Comoros
336 East 45th Street, Second Floor
New York, NY 10017
Tel: (212) 349-2030

Congo

U.S. Embassy, Consular Section
Avenue Amilcar Cabral
B.P. 1015
Brazzaville, Congo
Tel: [242] 83-20-70; Fax: [242] 83-63-38
US Mailing Address: Box C, APO AE 09828

Embassy of the Republic of the Congo
4891 Colorado Avenue NW
Washington, DC 20011
Tel: (202) 726-5500; Fax: (202) 726-1860

Costa Rica

U.S. Embassy, Consular Post
Pavas
San Jose, Costa Rica
Tel: [506] 220-3939
Fax: [506] 220-2305, 231-4783 (FCS)
US Mailing Address: APO AA 34020

Embassy of Costa Rica
2114 S Street NW
Washington, DC 20008
Tel: (202) 234-2945; Fax: (202) 265-4795

Costa Rican-American Chamber of Commerce
P.O. Box 4946
1000 San Jose, Costa Rica
Tel: [506] 220-2200; Fax: [506] 220-2300

Cote d'Ivoire

U.S. Embassy, Consular Section
5 Rue Jesse Owens
01 B.P. 1712
Abidjan, Côte d'Ivoire
Tel: [225] 21-09-79; Fax: [225] 22-32-50,
US Mailing Address: Dept. of State, Washington, DC 20521-2010

Embassy of the Republic of Côte d'Ivoire
2424 Massachusetts Avenue NW
Washington, DC 20008
Tel: (202) 797-0300

American Chamber of Commerce in Côte d'Ivoire
01 B.P. 3394
Abidjan, Côte d'Ivoire
Tel: [225] 214-616; Fax: [225] 222-437

Croatia

U.S. Embassy, Consular Section
Andrije Hebranga 2
Zagreb, Croatia
Tel: [385] (1) 455-5500
Fax: [385] (41) 455-8585, (41) 440-235 (FCS)
US Mailing Address: Unit 25402, APO AE 09213-5080

Embassy of the Republic of Croatia
2343 Massachusetts Avenue NW
Washington, DC 20008
Tel: (202) 588-5899; Fax: (202) 588-8936
Email: webmaster@croatiaemb.org
Web site: www.croatiaemb.org

Cyprus

U.S. Embassy, Consular Section
Metochiou St. and Ploutarchou St.
Engomi
Nicosia, Cyprus
Tel: [357] (2) 476-100; Fax: [357] (2) 465-944
Web site: www2.spidernet.net/web/~amcenter/www1.htm
US Mailing Address: P.O. Box 4536, FPO AE 09836

Embassy of the Republic of Cyprus
2211 R Street NW
Washington, DC 20008
Tel: (202) 462-5772; Fax: (202) 483-6710

Czech Republic

U.S. Embassy, Consular Section
Trziste 15
11801 Prague 1, Czech Republic
Tel: [420] (2) 5732-0663; Fax: [42] (2) 5732-0614
US Mailing Address: Unit 1330, APO AE 09213-1330

Embassy of the Czech Republic
3900 Spring of Freedom Street NW
Washington, DC 20008
Tel: (202) 274-9100; Fax: (202) 966-8540
Email: 72360.544@compuserve.com
Web site: www.czech.cz/washington/

American Chamber of Commerce in the Czech Republic
Karlovo namesti 24
110 00 Prague 1, Czech Republic
Tel: [42] (2) 299-887; Fax: [42] (2) 291-481

Denmark

U.S. Embassy, Consular Section
Dag Hammarskjolds Alle 24
2100 Copenhagen O, Denmark
Tel: [45] (35) 55-01 44; Fax: [45] (35) 43-02-23
Web site: www.usis.dk/usis/amb.html (USIS)
US Mailing Address: APO AE 09716

Royal Danish Embassy
3200 Whitehaven Street NW
Washington, DC 20008
Tel: (202) 234-4300; Fax: (202) 328-1470
Email: ambadane@erols.com
Web site: www.denmarkemb.org

Djibouti

Embassy of the Republic of Dijibouti
1156 - 15th Street NW, Suite 515
Washington, DC 20005
Tel: (202) 331-0270; Fax: (202) 331-0302

U.S. Embassy, Consular Section
Plateaudu Serpent Blvd. Marechal Joffre
B.P. 185
Djibouti, Djibouti
Tel: [253] 35-39-95; Fax: [253] 35-39-40
US Mailing Address: Dept. of State, Washington, DC 20521-2150

Dominica

Embassy of the Commonwealth of Dominica
3216 New Mexico Avenue NW
Washington, DC 20016
Tel: (202) 364-6781; Fax: (202) 364-6791

Dominican Republic

U.S. Embassy, Consular Section
Corner of Calle Cesar Nicolas Penson & Calle Leopoldo Navarro
Santo Domingo, Dominican Republic
Tel: (809) 221-2171; Fax: (809) 686-7437
US Mailing Address: Unit 5500, APO AA 34041

Embassy of the Dominican Republic
1715 - 22nd Street NW
Washington, DC 20008
Tel: (202) 332-6280; Fax: (202) 265-8057
Web site: www.domrep.org

American Chamber of Commerce of the Dominican Republic
P.O. Box 95-2
Santo Domingo, Dominican Rep.
Tel: (809) 544-2222; Fax: (809) 544-0502

Ecuador

U.S. Embassy, Consular Section
Avenida 12 de Octubre y Avenida Patria
P.O. Box 538
Quito, Ecuador
Tel: [593] (2) 562-890, (2) 561-404 (FCS)
Fax: [593] (2) 502-052, (2) 504-550 (FCS)
US Mailing Address: Unit 5309, APO AA 34039-3420

Embassy of Ecuador
2535 - 15th Street NW
Washington, DC 20009
Tel: (202) 234-7200; Fax: (202) 667-3482
Email: mecuawaa@pop.erols.com
Web site: www.ecuador.org/

Ecuadorian-American Chamber of Commerce
Edif. Multicentra 4P
La Nina y Avda. 6 de Diciembre
Casilla 17-07-8823
Quito, Ecuador
Tel: [593] (2) 507-450; Fax: [593] (2) 504-571
Email: ccea@ecamcham.com

Egypt

U.S. Embassy, Consular Section
8, Kamal El-Din Salah St.
Garden City
Cairo, Arab Republic of Egypt
Tel: [20] (2) 355-7371, 357-2201, (2) 357-2330 (FCS)
Fax: [20] (2) 357-2472, (2) 355-8368 (FCS)
US Mailing Address: APO AE 09839-4900

Embassy of the Arab Republic of Egypt
3521 International Court NW
Washington, DC 20008
Tel: (202) 895-5400; Fax: (202) 244-4319

American Chamber of Commerce in Egypt
Cairo Marriott Hotel #1541
Zamalek, Cairo, Egypt
Tel: [20] (2) 340-8888, x1541; Fax: [20] (2) 340-9482
Email: info@amcham.org.eg

El Salvador

U.S. Embassy, Consular Section
Final Blvd. Santa Elena
Antiguo Cuscatlan
San Salvador, El Salvador
Tel: [503] 278-4444; Fax: [503] 278-6011
US Mailing Address: Unit 3116, APO AA 34023

Embassy of El Salvador
2308 California Street NW
Washington, DC 20008
Tel: (202) 265-9671

American Chamber of Commerce of El Salvador
87 Av. Norte #720, Apt. A
Col. Escalon
San Salvador, El Salvador
Tel: [503] 223-3292, 224-3646; Fax: [503] 224-6856

Equatorial Guinea

Embassy of the Republic of Equatorial Guinea
1511 K Street NW, Suite 405
Washington, DC 20005
Tel: (202) 393-0525; Fax: (202) 393-0348

Eritrea

U.S. Embassy
Franklin D. Roosevelt St..
P. O. Box 211
Asmara, Eritrea
Tel: [291] (1) 12-00-04; Fax: [291] (1) 12-75-84

Embassy of the State of Eritrea
1708 New Hampshire Ave. NW
Washington, DC 20009
Tel: (202) 319-1991; Fax: (202) 319-1304

Estonia

U.S. Embassy
Kentmanni 20
EE 0001
Tallinn, Estonia
Tel: [372] (6) 312-021; Fax: [372] (6) 312-025
US Mailing Address: Dept. of State, Washington, DC 20521-4530

Embassy of Estonia
2131 Massachusetts Avenue NW
Washington, DC 20008
Tel: (202) 588-0101; Fax: (202) 588-0108
Web site: www.estemb.org/

American Chamber of Commerce Estonia
Tallinn Business Center
Harju 6-234A
10130 Tallinn Estonia
Tel: [372] (6) 310-522; Fax: [372] (6) 310-521
Email: acce@datanet.ee

Ethiopia

U.S. Embassy, Consular Section
Entoto Street
P.O. Box 1014
Addis Ababa, Ethiopia
Tel: [251] (1) 550-666; Fax: [251] (1) 552-191
US Mailing Address: Dept. of State, Washington, DC 20521-2030

Embassy of Ethiopia
2134 Kalorama Road NW
Washington, DC 20008
Tel: (202) 234-2281; Fax: (202) 328-7950

European Commission

Delegation of the European Commission
2300 M Street NW
Washington, DC 200037
Tel: (202) 862-9500; Fax: (202) 429-1766

Fiji

U.S. Embassy, Consular Section
31 Loftus St.
P.O. Box 218
Suva, Fiji
Tel: [679] 314-466; Fax: [679] 300-081
US Mailing Address: Dept. of State, Washington, DC 20521-4290

Embassy of the Republic of Fiji
2233 Wisconsin Avenue NW, Suite 240
Washington, DC 20007
Tel: (202) 337-8320; Fax: (202) 337-1996
Email: fijiemb@earthlink.net

Finland

U.S. Embassy, Consular Section
Itainen Puistotie 14A
FIN-00140 Helsinki, Finland
Tel: [358] (9) 171931; Fax: [358] (0) 174681
US Mailing Address: APO AE 09723

Embassy of Finland
3301 Massachusetts Avenue NW
Washington, DC 20008
Tel: (202) 298-5800; Fax: (202) 298-6030
Web site: www.finland.org/

France

U.S. Embassy, Consular Section
2 Avenue Gabriel
75382 Paris Cedex 08, France
Tel: [33] (1) 43-12-22-22; Fax: [33] (1) 42-66-97-83
US Mailing Address: PSC 116, APO AE 09777

U.S. Consulate General
12 Avenue d'Alsace
Strasbourg, France
Tel: [33] 88-35-31-04, 88-35-31-04 (FCS)
Fax: [33] 88-24-06-95, 88-24-06-95 (FCS)
US Mailing Address: APO AE 09777

U.S. Consulate General
12 Blvd. Paul Peytral
13286 Marseille Cedex, France
Tel: [33] 91-54-92-00, 91-54-92-00 (FCS)
Fax: [33] 91-55-09-47, 91-55-09-47 (FCS)
US Mailing Address: Unit 21551, APO AE 09777

U.S. Commercial Office
31 Rue du Marechal Joffre
Nice, France
Tel: [33] 93-88-89-55, 93-88-89-55 (FCS)
Fax: [33] 93-87-07-38, 93-87-07-38 (FCS)
US Mailing Address: APO AE 09777

Embassy of France
4101 Reservoir Road NW
Washington, DC 20007
Tel: (202) 944-6000; Fax: (202) 944-6072
Web site: www.info-france-usa.org

American Chamber of Commerce in France
21 Avenue George V
75008 Paris, France
Tel: [33] 1-40-73-89-90; Fax: [33] 1-47-20-18-62
Email: amchamfr@amchamfr.com

Gabon

U.S. Embassy, Consular Section
Blvd. de la Mer
B.P. 4000
Libreville, Gabon
Tel: [241] 762-003/4, 743-492; Fax: [241] 745-507
US Mailing Address. Dept. of State, Washington, DC 20521-2270

Embassy of the Gabonese Republic
2034 - 20th Street NW, Suite 200
Washington, DC 20009
Tel: (202) 797 1000; Fax: (202) 332-0668

The Gambia

U.S. Embassy, Consular Section
P.M.B. No. 19
Banjul, The Gambia
Tel: [220] 392-856, 392-858; Fax: [220] 392-475
US Mailing Address: Dept. of State, Washington, DC 20521-2070

Embassy of The Gambia
1155 - 15th Street NW, Suite 1000
Washington, DC 20005
Tel: (202) 785-1399; Fax: (202) 785-1430

Georgia

U.S. Embassy, Consular Section
25 Antoneli Str.
380026 Tbilisi, Georgia
Tel: [995] (32) 98-99-67; Fax: [995] (32) 93-37-59
US Mailing Address: Dept. of State, Washington, DC 20521-7060

Embassy of the Republic of Georgia
1511 K Street NW, Suite 400
Washington, DC 20005
Tel: (202) 393-5959; Fax: (202) 393-6060

Germany

U.S. Embassy, Consular Section
Deichmanns Aue 29
53170 Bonn Germany
Tel: [49] (228) 339-1; Fax: [49] (228) 339-2663
Web site: www.usia.gov/posts/bonn.html (USIS)
US Mailing Address: PSC 117, APO AE 09080

U.S. Embassy Branch Office, Consular Section
Clayallee 170
Berlin, Germany
Tel: [49] (30) 832-9233, (30) 251-2061 (FCS)
Fax: [49] (30) 831-4926, (30) 238-6296 (FCS)
US Mailing Address: Unit 26738, APO AE 09235-5500

U.S. Commercial Office
Kennedydamm 15-17
Duesseldorf, Germany
Tel: [49] (211) 75350, (211) 431-744 (FCS), (211) 431-431 (FCS)
US Mailing Address: PSC 117, Box 220, APO AE 09080

U.S. Consulate General
Alsterufer 27/28
20354 Hamburg, Germany
Tel: [49] (40) 41171-351, 40-41171-304 (FCS)
Fax: [49] (40) 443-004, 40-410-6598 (FCS)
US Mailing Address: Unit 22550, APO AE 09215-0002

U.S. Consulate General
Koeniginstrasse 5
80539 Munich, Germany
Tel: [49] (89) 2888-722, 89-2888-748 (FCS), 89-285-261 (FCS)
US Mailing Address: Unit 24718, APO AE 09108

Embassy of the Federal Republic of Germany
4645 Reservoir Road NW
Washington, DC 20007-1998
Tel: (202) 298-4000; Fax: (202) 298-4249
Web site: www.germany-info.org

American Chamber of Commerce in Germany
Rossmarkt 12
60311 Frankfurt am Main, Germany
Tel: [49] (69) 929-104-0; Fax: [49] (69) 929-104-11

Ghana

U.S. Embassy, Consular Section
Ring Road East
P.O. Box 194
Accra, Ghana
Tel: [233] (21) 77-53-48; Fax: [233] (21) 77-60-08
US Mailing Address: Dept. of State, Washington, DC 20521-2070

Embassy of Ghana
3512 International Drive NW
Washington, DC 20008
Tel: (202) 686-4520; Fax: (202) 686-4527

Greece

U.S. Embassy, Consular Section
91 Vasilissis Sophias Blvd.
10160 Athens, Greece
Tel: [30] (1) 721-2951; Fax: [30] (1) 645-6282
US Mailing Address: PSC 108, APO AE 09842-0108

Embassy of Greece
2221 Massachusetts Avenue NW
Washington, DC 20008
Tel: (202) 939-5800; Fax: (202) 939-5824
Web site: www.embassy.org/greece

American-Hellenic Chamber of Commerce
16 Kansari St., 3rd Fl.
10674 Athens, Greece
Tel: [30] (1) 361-8385, 363-6407; Fax: [30] (1) 361-0170

Grenada

U.S. Embassy
P.O. Box 54
St. George's, Grenada, W.I.,
Tel: (809) 444-1173/8; Fax: (809) 444-4820

Embassy of Grenada
1701 New Hampshire Avenue NW
Washington, DC 20009
Tel: (202) 265-2561

Guatemala

U.S. Embassy, Consular Section
7-01 Avenida de la Reforma
Zone 10
Guatemala City, Guatemala
Tel: [502] (2) 31-15-41; Fax: [502] 31-88-85
US Mailing Address: APO AA 34024

Embassy of Guatemala
2220 R Street NW
Washington, DC 20008
Tel: (202) 745-4952; Fax: (202) 745-1908

American Chamber of Commerce in Guatemala
6a Avenida 14-77
Zona 10
01010 Guatemala City, Guatemala
Tel: [502] (2) 664-822; Fax: [502] (2) 683-106

Guinea

U.S. Embassy, Consular Section
Rue KA 038
B.P. 603
Conakry, Guinea
Tel: [224] 41-15-20, 41-15-21; Fax: [224] 41-31-57
US Mailing Address: Dept. of State, Washington, DC 20521-2110

Embassy of the Republic of Guinea
2112 Leroy Place NW
Washington, DC 20008
Tel: (202) 483-9420; Fax: (202) 483-8688

Guinea-Bissau

U.S. Embassy, Consular Section
1 Rua Ulysses S. Grant
Bairro de Penha Bissau
C.P. 297
1067 Codex
Bissau, Guinea-Bissau
Tel: [245] 25-2273/6; Fax: [245] 25-2282
US Mailing Address: Dept. of State, Washington, DC 20521-2080

Embassy of the Republic of Guinea-Bissau
918 - 16th Street NW, Mezzanine Suite
Washington, DC 20006
Tel. (202) 872-4222; Fax: (202) 872-4226

Guyana

U.S. Embassy, Consular Section
99-100 Young and Duke Sts.
Kingston
Georgetown, Guyana
Tel: [592] (2) 54-900; Fax: [592] (2) 58-497
US Mailing Address: Dept. of State, Washington, DC 20521-3170

Embassy of Guyana
2490 Tracy Place NW
Washington, DC 20008
Tel: (202) 265-6900
Email: guyanaem@erols.com

Haiti

U.S. Embassy, Consular Section
5 Harry Truman Blvd.
P.O. Box 1761
Port-au-Prince, Haiti
Tel: [509] 22-0354; Fax: [509] 23-1641
US Mailing Address: Dept. of State, Washington, DC 20521-3400

Embassy of the Republic of Haiti
2311 Massachusetts Avenue NW
Washington, DC 20008
Tel: (202) 332-4090; Fax: (202) 745-7215
Email: embassy@haiti.org
Web site: www.haiti.org/embassy

Haitian-American Chamber of Commerce & Industry
Complexe 384, Apt. 8
Delmas, Haiti
Tel: [509] 460-143; Fax: [509] 460-143

Honduras

U.S. Embassy, Consular Section
Avenida La Paz
Apartado Postal No. 3453
Tegucigalpa, Honduras
Tel: [504] 36-9320; Fax: [504] 36-9037
US Mailing Address: APO AA 34022

Embassy of Honduras
3007 Tilden Street NW
Washington, DC 20008
Tel: (202) 966-7702; Fax: (202) 966-9751

Honduran-American Chamber of Commerce
Apdo. Postal 1838
Tegucigalpa, Honduras
Tel: [504] 327-043; Fax: [504] 322-031

Hong Kong

U.S. Consulate General
26 Garden Rd., Hong Kong
Tel: [852] 2523-9011
Fax: [852] 2845-4845, 2845-9800 (FCS)
US Mailing Address: Box 30, FPO AP 96522-0002

American Chamber of Commerce in Hong Kong
1904 American Tower
12 Harcourt Road
Central, Hong Kong
Tel: [852] 2526-0165; Fax: [852] 2810-1289
Email: amcham@amcham.org.hk

Hungary

U.S. Embassy, Consular Section
V. 1054 Szabadsag Ter 12
Budapest, Hungary
Tel: [36] (1) 267-4400; Fax: [36] (1) 269-9326
US Mailing Address: American Embassy Budapest, Department of State, Washington, DC 20521-5270

Embassy of the Republic of Hungary
3910 Shoemaker Street NW
Washington, DC 20008
Tel: (202) 362-6730; Fax: (202) 966-8135

American Chamber of Commerce in Hungary
Deak Ferenc u. 10, Room 403
1052 Budapest, Hungary
Tel: [36] (1) 266-9880; Fax: [36] (1) 266-9888
amcham@hungary.com

Iceland

U.S. Embassy, Consular Section
Laufasvegur 21
Reykjavik, Iceland
Tel: [354] (1) 562-9100; Fax: [354] (1) 562-9118
US Mailing Address: PSC 1003, Box 40, FPO AE 09728-0340

Embassy of Iceland
1156 - 15th Street NW, Suite 1200
Washington, DC 20005
Tel: (202) 265-6653; Fax: (202) 265-6656
Email: icemb.wash@utn.stjr.is
Web site: www.iceland.org/

India

U.S. Embassy, Consular Section
Shanti Path
Chanakyapuri 110021
New Delhi, India
Tel: [91] (11) 611-3033, 688-9033; Fax: [91] (11) 6419-0017
US Mailing Address: Dept. of State, Washington, DC 20521-9000

U.S. Consulate General
5/1 Ho Chi Minh Sarani
Calcutta 700071, India
Tel: [91] (33) 22-3611, (33) 242-3611 (FCS)
Fax: [91] (33) 225-994, (33) 242-2335 (FCS)
US Mailing Address: Dept. of State, Washington, DC 20521-6250

U.S. Consulate General
220 Mount Rd.
Madras 600006, India
Tel: [91] (44) 827-3040, (44) 827-3040 (FCS)
Fax: [91] (44) 825-0240, (44) 825-0240 (FCS)
US Mailing Address: Dept. of State, Washington, DC 20521-6260

Embassy of India
2536 Massachusetts Avenue NW
Washington, DC 20008
Tel: (202) 939-7000

American Business Council - India
c/o General Electric International Operations
AIFACS Building
1 Rati marq
New Delhi 110 001, India
Tel: [91] (11) 688-8714; Fax: [91] (11) 688-8714

Indonesia

U.S. Embassy, Consular Section
Medan Merdeka Selatan 5
Jakarta, Indonesia
Tel: [62] (21) 344-2211; Fax: [62] (21) 386-2259
US Mailing Address: Box 1, APO AP 96520

U.S. Consulate General
Jalan Raya Dr. Sutomo 33
Surabaya, Indonesia
Tel: [62] (31) 568-2287/8; Fax: [62] (31) 567-4492
US Mailing Address: Box 18131, APO AP 96520-0002

Embassy of the Republic of Indonesia
2020 Massachusetts Avenue NW
Washington, DC 20036
Tel: (202) 775-5200; Fax: (202) 775-5365

American Chamber of Commerce in Indonesia
World Trade Center, 11th Fl.
Jalan Sudirman Kav. 29-31
12920 Jakarta, Indonesia
Tel: [62] (21) 526-2860; Fax: [62] (21) 526-2861

Ireland

U.S. Embassy, Consular Section
42 Elgin Rd.
Ballsbridge
Dublin, Ireland
Tel: [353] (1) 668-8777; Fax: [353] (1) 668-9946
US Mailing Address: Dept. of State, Washington, DC 20521-5290

Embassy of Ireland
2234 Massachusetts Avenue NW
Washington, DC 20008
Tel: (202) 462-3939

United States Chamber of Commerce in Ireland
20 College Green
Dublin 2, Ireland
Tel: [353] (1) 679-3733; Fax: [353] (1) 679-3402

Israel

U.S. Embassy, Consular Section
71 Hayarkon St.
Tel Aviv, Israel
Tel: [972] (3) 519-7575; Fax: [972] (3) 517-3227
Email: acs.amcit-telaviv@dos.us-state.gov
US Mailing Address: PSC 98, Box 100, APO AE 09830

Embassy of the State of Israel
3514 International Drive NW
Washington, DC 20008
Tel: (202) 364-5500; Fax: (202) 364-5610
Web site: www.israelemb.org/

Israel-America Chamber of Commerce & Industry
America House
35 Shaul Hamelech Blvd.
Tel Aviv 64927, Israel
Tel: [972] (3) 695-2341; Fax: [972] (3) 695-1272
Email: amcham@amcham.co.il

Italy

U.S. Embassy, Consular Section
Via Veneto 119/A
00187 Rome, Italy
Tel: [39] (6) 4674-1; Fax: [39] (6) 4882-672
US Mailing Address: PSC 59, Box 100, APO AE 09624

U.S. Consulate General
Lungarno Amerigo Vespucci 38
50123 Florence, Italy
Tel: [39] (55) 239-8276, (55) 211-676 (FCS)
Fax: [39] (55) 284-088, (55) 283-780 (FCS)
US Mailing Address: PSC 59 Box F, APO AE 09613

U.S. Consulate General
Via Principe Amedeo, 2/10
20121 Milan, Italy
Tel: [39] (2) 290-351, (2) 498-2241 (FCS)
Fax: [39] (2) 290-01165, (2) 481-4161 (FCS)
US Mailing Address: Box M, PSC 59, APO AE 09624

U.S. Consulate General
Piazza della Repubblica
80122 Naples, Italy
Tel: [39] (81) 583-8111, (81) 761-1592 (FCS)
Fax: [39] (81) 761-1869, (81) 761-1869 (FCS)
US Mailing Address: Box 18, PSC 810, FPO AE 09619-0002

Embassy of Italy
1601 Fuller Street NW
Washington, DC 20009
Tel: (202) 328-5500; Fax: (202) 483-2187
Web site: www.italyemb.nw.dc.us/italy.index.html

American Chamber of Commerce in Italy
Via Cantu 1
20123 Milan, Italy
Tel: [39] (2) 869-0661; Fax: [39] (2) 805-7737

Jamaica

U.S. Embassy, Consular Section
Jamaica Mutual Life Center
2 Oxford Rd., 3rd Floor
Kingston, Jamaica
Tel: (809) 929-4850/9; Fax: (809) 926-6743
US Mailing Address: Dept. of State, Washington, DC 20521-3210

Embassy of Jamaica
1520 New Hampshire Avenue NW
Washington, DC 20036
Tel: (202) 452-0660; Fax: (202) 452-0081
Email: emjam@sysnet.net

American Chamber of Commerce of Jamaica
77 Knutsford Blvd.
Kingston 5, Jamaica
Tel: (809) 929-7866, 929-7867; Fax: (809) 929-8597

Japan

U.S. Embassy, Consular Section
10-5, Akasaka 1-chome
Minato-ku
Tokyo 107, Japan
Tel: [81] (3) 3224-5000; Fax: [81] (3) 3505-1862)
Web site: www.senri-i.or.jp/amcon/usa_01.htm (Osaka Consulate)
US Mailing Address: Unit 45004, Box 258, APO AP 96337-0001

U.S. Consulate
Nishiki SIS Building, 6F
10-33 Nishiki 3-chome
Naka-ku
Nagoya 460, Japan
Tel: [81] (52) 203-4011, (52) 203-4011 (FCS)
Fax: [81] (52) 201-4612, (52) 201-4612 (FCS)
US Mailing Address: c/o U.S. Embassy Tokyo
Unit 45004, Box 280
APO AP 96337-0001

U.S. Consulate
5-26 Ohori 2-chome
Chuo-ku
Fukuoka 810, Japan
Tel. [81] (92) 751-9331/4, (92) 751-9331/4 (FCS)
Fax: [81] (92) 713-9222, (92) 713-9222 (FCS)
US Mailing Address: Unit 45004, Box 242, APO AP 96337-0001

U.S. Consulate General
Kita 1-Jo Nishi 28-chome, Chuo-ku
Sapporo 064, Japan
Tel: [81] (11) 641-1115, (11) 641-1115 (FCS)
Fax: [81] (11) 643-1283, 11-643-0911 (FCS)
US Mailing Address: Unit 45004, Box 276, APO AP 96337-0003

Embassy of Japan
2520 Massachusetts Avenue NW
Washington, DC 20008
Tel: (202) 939-6700; Fax: (202) 328-2187
Web site: www.embjapan.org

American Chamber of Commerce of Japan
Bridgestone Toranomon Bldg. 5F
3-25-2 Toranomon
Minato-ku
Tokyo 105, Japan
Tel: [81] (3) 3433-5381; Fax: [81] (3) 3436-1446
Email: info@accj.or.jp

Jordan

U.S. Embassy, Consular Section
Jabel Amman
P.O. Box 354
Amman 11118 Jordan
Tel: [962] (6) 820-101, 866-121; Fax: [962] (6) 820-159
US Mailing Address: APO AE 09892-0200

Embassy of the Hashemite Kingdom of Jordan
3504 International Drive NW
Washington, DC 20008
Tel: (202) 966-2664; Fax: (202) 966-3110

Kazakhstan

U.S. Embassy
99/97 Furmanova St.
Almaty, Kazakhstan 480012
Tel: [7] (3272) 633-905
US Mailing Address: U.S. Dept. of State, Washington, DC 20521-7030

Embassy of the Republic of Kazakhstan
1401 16th Street NW
Washington, DC 20036
Tel: (202) 232-5488; Fax: (202) 232-5845
Email: kazak@intr.net

Kenya

U.S. Embassy, Consular Section
Moi/Haile Selassie Ave.
Nairobi, Kenya
Tel: [254] (2) 334141
Fax: [254] (2) 340838
US Mailing Address: P.O. Box 30137, Unit 64100, APO AE 09831

Embassy of the Republic of Kenya
2249 R Street NW
Washington, DC 20008
Tel: (202) 387-6101; Fax: (202) 462-3829
Web site: www.cybertech-mall.com/kenya.html

Korea (South)

U.S. Embassy, Consular Section
82 Sejong-Ro, Chongro-ku
Seoul, Rep. of Korea
Tel: [82] (2) 397-4114; Fax: [82] (2) 738-8845
US Mailing Address: Unit 15550, APO AP 96205-0001

Embassy of the Republic of Korea
2450 Massachusetts Avenue NW
Washington, DC 20008
Tel: (202) 939-5600; Fax: (202) 387-0205
Web site: www.koreaemb.org

American Chamber of Commerce in Korea
Westin Chosun Hotel, 2nd Fl.
87 Sokong-dong Chung-ku
Seoul 100-070 Rep. of Korea
Tel: [82] (2) 753-6471; Fax: [82] (2) 755-6577
Email: info@amchamkorea.org

Kuwait

U.S. Embassy, Consular Section
P.O. Box 77
Safat 13001
Kuwait City, Kuwait
Tel: [965] 539-5307, 539-5308; Fax: [965] 538-0282
US Mailing Address: Unit 69000 APO AE 09880-9000

Embassy of the State of Kuwait
2940 Tilden Street NW
Washington, DC 20008
Tel: (202) 966-0702; Fax: (202) 966-0517

Kyrgyzstan

U.S. Embassy, Consular Section
Erkindik Prospekt No. 66
720002 Bishkek, Kyrgyzstan
Tel: [7] (3312) 22-26-9, 22-32-89
US Mailing Address: Dept. of State, Washington DC 20521-7040

Embassy of the Kyrgyz Republic
1511 K Street NW, Suite 706
Washington, DC 20005
Tel: (202) 347-3732; Fax: (202) 347-3718

Laos

U.S. Embassy, Consular Section
Rue Bartholonie
B.P. 114
Vientiane, Laos
Tel: [856] (21) 212581, 212582; Fax: [856] (21) 212584
US Mailing Address: Box V, APO AP 96546

Embassy of the Lao People's Democratic Republic
2222 S Street NW
Washington, DC 20008
Tel: (202) 332-6416; Fax: (202) 332-4923
Web site: www.laoembassy.com

Latvia

U.S. Embassy, Consular Section
Raina Boulevard 7
LV-1510 Riga, Latvia
Tel: [371] (2) 721-0005
US Mailing Address:PSC 78, Box R, APO AE 09723

Embassy of Latvia
4325 - 17th Street NW
Washington, DC 20011
Tel: (202) 726-8213; Fax: (202) 726-6785

American Chamber of Commerce in Latvia
Jauniela 24, Room 205
Riga, Latvia
Tel: [371] (2) 721-5205; Fax: [371] (2) 882-0090

Lebanon

Embassy of Lebanon
2560 - 28th Street NW
Washington, DC 20008
Tel: (202) 939-6300; Fax: (202) 939-6324
Email: EmbLebanon@AOL.com
Web site: www.embofleb.org

Lesotho

U.S. Embassy, Consular Section
P.O. Box 333
Maseru 100, Lesotho
Tel: [266] 312-666; Fax: [266] 310-116
US Mailing Address: Dept. of State, Washington DC 20521-2340

Embassy of the Kingdom of Lesotho
2511 Massachusetts Avenue NW
Washington, DC 20008
Tel: (202) 797-5533; Fax: (202) 234-6815

Liberia

U.S. Embassy, Consular Section
P.O. Box 10-0098
Mamba Point
Monrovia, Liberia
Tel: [231] 226370; Fax: [231] 226148
US Mailing Address: APO AE 09813

Embassy of the Republic of Liberia
5303 Colorado Ave. NW
Washington, DC 20011
Tel: (202) 723-0437; Fax: (202) 723-0436
Email: Liberia-Embassy@msn.com.
Web site: www.liberiaemb.org.

Lithuania

U.S. Embassy, Consular Section
Akmenu 6
2600 Vilnius, Lithuania
Tel: [370] (2) 223-031; Fax: [370] (2) 670-6084
US Mailing Address: PSC 78, Box V, APO AE 09723

Embassy of the Republic of Lithuania
2622 - 16th Street NW
Washington, DC 20009
Tel: (202) 234-5860; Fax: (202) 328-0466

American Chamber of Commerce in Lithuania
P.O. Box 78
2000 Vilnius, Lithuania
Tel: [370] (2) 611-181; Fax: [370] (2) 226-128
Email: acc@post.omnitel.net

Luxembourg

American Embassy
22 Blvd. Emmanuel-Servais
2535 Luxembourg City, Luxembourg
Tel: [352] 460-123; Fax: [352] 461-401
US Mailing Address: Unit 1410, APO AE 09126-1410

Embassy of the Grand Duchy of Luxembourg
2200 Massachusetts Avenue NW
Washington, DC 20008
Tel: (202) 265-4171; Fax: (202) 328-8270

American Chamber of Commerce in Luxembourg
7 rue Alcide de Gasperi
Luxembourg-Kirchberg
L-2981 Luxembourg
Tel: [352] 43-17-56; Fax: [352] 43-17-56
Email: info@amcham.lu

Macedonia (Former Yugoslav Republic of)

U.S. Embassy
Bul. Ilinden bb
91000 Skopje, FYR of Macedonia
Tel: [389] (91) 116-180; Fax: [389] (91) 117-103
US Mailing Address: Embassy Skopje, Department of State, Washington, DC 20521-7120

Embassy of the Former Yugoslav Republic of Macedonia
3050 K St. NW, Suite 210
Washington, DC 20007
Tel: (202) 337-3063; Fax: (202) 337-3093
Email: RMACEDONIA@AOL.COM
Web site: www.gov.mk

Madagascar

U.S. Embassy
14 16 Rue Rainitovo
B.P. 620
Antsahavola
Antananarivo, Madagascar
Tel: [261] (2) 21257, 20089; Fax: [261] (2) 34539
US Mailing Address: Dept. of State, Washington DC 20521-2040

Malawi

U.S. Embassy
P.O. Box 30016
Lilongwe 3, Malawi
Tel: [265] 783-166; Fax: [265] 780-471
US Mailing Address: Dept. of State, Washington DC 20521-2280

Malaysia

U.S. Embassy, Consular Section
P.O. Box 10035
50700 Kuala Lumpur, Malaysia
Tel: [60] (3) 248-9011; Fax: [60] (3) 242-2207
US Mailing Address: P.O. Box 10035, 50700 Kuala Lumpur, APO AP 96535-8152

Embassy of Malaysia
2401 Massachusetts Avenue NW
Washington, DC 20008
Tel: (202) 328-2700; Fax: (202) 483-7661

American Malaysian Chamber of Commerce
11-03, Level 11, AMODA
22 Jalan Imbi
55100 Kuala Lumpur, Malaysia
Tel: [60] (3) 248-2407; Fax: [60] (3) 242-8540
Email: exedir@amcham.po.my

Mali

U.S. Embassy, Consular Section
Rue Rochester NY and Rue Mohamed V
B.P. 34
Bamako, Mali
Tel: [223] 22-54-70; Fax: [223] 22-37-12
US Mailing Address: Dept. of State, Washington DC 20521-4210

Embassy of the Republic of Mali
2130 R Street NW
Washington, DC 20008
Tel: (202) 332-2249; Fax: (202) 332-6603
Email: info@mali.emb.nw.dc.us

Malta

U.S. Embassy, Consular Section
P.O. Box 535
Valletta, Malta
Tel: [356] 235960; Fax: [356] 223-322

Embassy of Malta
2017 Connecticut Avenue NW
Washington, DC 20008
Tel: (202) 462-3611; Fax: (202) 387-5470
Web site: www.magnet.mt

Marshall Islands

U.S. Embassy, Consular Section
P.O. Box 1379
Majuro, MH 96960-1379, Republic of the Marshall Islands
Tel: [692] 247-4011; Fax: [692] 247-4012
US Mailing Address: P.O. Box 1379, Majuro, MH 96960-1379

Embassy of the Republic of the Marshall Islands
2433 Massachusetts Avenue NW
Washington, DC 20008
Tel: (202) 234-5414; Fax: (202) 232-3236

Mauritania

U.S. Embassy, Consular Section
B.P. 222
Nouakchott, Mauritania
Tel: [222] (2) 526-60; Fax: [222] (2) 515-92

Embassy of the Islamic Republic of Mauritania
2129 Leroy Place NW
Washington, DC 20008
Tel: (202) 232-5700; Fax: (202) 319-2623

Mauritius

U.S. Embassy, Consular Section
Rogers House, 4th Fl.
John Kennedy St.
Port Louis, Mauritius
Tel: [230] 208-2347; Fax: [230] 208-9534
US Mailing Address: Am. Emb. Port Louis, Dept. of State, Washington DC 20521-2450

Embassy of the Republic of Mauritius
4301 Connecticut Avenue NW, Suite 441
Washington, DC 20008
Tel: (202) 244-1491; Fax: (202) 966-0983
Email: embassy.mauritius@mcione.com

Mexico

U.S. Embassy, Consular Section
Paseo de la Reforma 305
Col. Cuauhtemoc
06500 Mexico D.F., Mexico
Tel: [52] (5) 211-0042; Fax: [52] (5) 208-3373
US Mailing Address: P.O. Box 3087, Laredo TX 78044-3087

U.S. Consulate General
Avenue Lopez Mateos 924N
Ciudad Juarez, Mexico
Tel: [52] (16) 13-4048; Fax: [52] (16) 16-9056
US Mailing Address: P.O. Box 10545, El Paso, TX 79995-0545

U.S. Consulate General
Progreso 175
Guadalajara, Mexico
Tel: [52] (3) 625-2998, (3) 625-0321 (FCS)
Fax: [52] (3) 626-6549, (3) 626-3576 (FCS)
US Mailing Address: Box 3088, Laredo, TX 78044-3088

U.S. Consulate General
Avenida Constitucion 411
Poniente
64000 Monterrey, NL, Mexico
Tel: [52] (83) 45-2120, (83) 45-2120 (FCS)
Fax: [52] (83) 45-7748, (83) 42-5172 (FCS)
US Mailing Address: Box 3098, Laredo, TX 78044-3098

Embassy of Mexico
1911 Pennsylvania Avenue NW
Washington, DC 20006
Tel: (202) 728-1600
Web site: quicklink.com/mexico (Consulate General in NY)

American Chamber of Commerce of Mexico
4405 NW 73rd Ave. #048-185
Miami, FL 33166-6400
Tel: [52] (5) 724-3800; Fax: [52] (5) 703-3908

Micronesia

U.S. Embassy, Consular Section
P.O. Box 1286
Pohnpei 96941, Federated States of Micronesia
Tel: [691] 320-2187; Fax: [691] 320-2186

Embassy of the Federal States of Micronesia
1725 N Street NW
Washington, DC 20036
Tel: (202) 223-4383; Fax: (202) 223-4391

Moldova

U.S. Embassy, Consular Section
Strada Alexei Mateevici 103
Chisinau 277014, Moldova
Tel: [373] (2) 23-37-72; Fax: [373] (2) 23-30-44
US Mailing Address: Dept. of State, Washington DC 20521-7080

Embassy of the Republic of Moldova
1511 K Street NW
Washington, DC 20005
Tel: (202) 783-3012; Fax: (202) 783-3342
Email: 103714.2137@compuserve.com

Mongolia

U.S. Embassy, Consular Section
Micro Region 11
Big Ring Road
Ulaanbaatar, Mongolia
Tel: [976] (1) 329095, 329606; Fax: [976] (1) 320-776
US Mailing Address: PSC 461, Box 300, FPO AP 96521-0002

Embassy of Mongolia
2833 M Street NW
Washington, DC 20007
Tel: (202) 333-7117; Fax: (202) 298-9227

Morocco

U.S. Embassy, Consular Section
2 Ave. de Marrakech
Rabat, Morocco
Tel: [212] (7) 76-22-65; Fax: [212] (7) 76-56-61
US Mailing Address: PSC 74, Box 003, APO AE 09718

U.S. Consulate General
8 Blvd. Moulay Youssef
Casablanca, Morocco
Tel: [212] (2) 26-45-50, (2) 26-45-50 (FCS)
Fax: [212] (2) 20-41-27, 22-02-59 (FCS)
US Mailing Address: PSC 74 Box 024, APO AE 09718(CAS)

Embassy of the Kingdom of Morocco
1601 - 21st Street NW
Washington, DC 20009
Tel: (202) 462-7979; Fax: (202) 265-0161

American Chamber of Commerce in Morocco
Holiday Inn, Suite 201
Casablanca 01, Morocco
Tel: [212] (2) 293-028; Fax: [212] (2) 491-880

Mozambique

U.S. Embassy, Consular Section
Avenida Kaunda 193
P.O. Box 783
Maputo, Mozambique
Tel: [258] (1) 49-27-97; Fax: [258] (1) 49-01-14
US Mailing Address: Dept. of State, Washington DC 20521-2330

Embassy of the Republic of Mozambique
1990 M Street NW, Suite 570
Washington, DC 20036
Tel: (202) 293-7146; Fax: (202) 835-0245

Namibia

U.S. Embassy, Consular Section
Ausplan Building
14 Lossen St.
Private Bag 12029
Ausspannplatz, Windhoek, Namibia
Tel: [264] (61) 221-601; Fax: [264] (61) 229-792
US Mailing Address: Dept. of State, Washington DC 20521-2540

Embassy of the Republic of Namibia
1605 New Hampshire Avenue NW
Washington, DC 20009
Tel: (202) 986-0540; Fax: (202) 986-0443

Nepal

U.S. Embassy, Consular Section
Pani Pokhari
Kathmandu, Nepal
Tel: [977] (1) 411179; Fax: [977] (1) 419963
US Mailing Address: Dept. of State, Washington DC 20521-6190

Netherlands

U.S. Embassy
Lange Voorhout 102
2514EJ The Hague, The Netherlands
Tel: [31] (70) 310-9209; Fax: [31] (70) 361-4688
US Mailing Address: PSC 71, Box 1000, APO AE 09715
Web site: www.xxlink.nl/amemb/

U.S. Consulate General
Museumplein 19
Amsterdam, The Netherlands
Tel: [31] (20) 664-5661, 575-5309, 20-575-5351 (FCS)
Fax: [31] (20) 575-5310, 20-575-5350 (FCS)
US Mailing Address: PSC 71, Box 1000, APO AE 09715

Royal Netherlands Embassy
4200 Wisconsin Avenue NW
Washington, DC 20016
Tel: (202) 244-5300; Fax: (202) 362-3430

American Chamber of Commerce in the Netherlands
Van Karnebeeklaan 14
The Hague 2585 BB, Netherlands
Tel: [31] (70) 365-9808; Fax: [31] (70) 364-6992
Email: amchamnl@worldaccess.nl

New Zealand

U.S. Embassy, Consular Section
29 Fitzherbert Ter.
P.O. Box 1190
Thorndon
Wellington, New Zealand
Tel: [64] (4) 472-2068; Fax: [64] (4) 471-2380
US Mailing Address: PSC 467, Box 1, FPO AP 96531-1001

U.S. Consulate General
4th Fl., Yorkshire General Building
Cnr. Shortland and O'Connell Sts.
Auckland, New Zealand
Tel: [64] (9) 303-2038, (9) 303-2038 (FCS)
Fax: [64] (9) 366-0870, (9) 366-0870 (FCS)
US Mailing Address: PSC 467, Box 99, FPO AP 96531-1099

Embassy of New Zealand
37 Observatory Circle NW
Washington, DC 20008
Tel: (202) 328-4800; Fax: (202) 667-5227
Email: paddynz@dc.infi.net
Web site: www.emb.com/nzemb/

American Chamber of Commerce in New Zealand
P.O. Box 106-002
Downtown
Auckland 1001, New Zealand
Tel: [64] (9) 309-9140; Fax: [64] (9) 309-1090

Nicaragua

U.S. Embassy, Consular Section
Km. 4-1/2 Carretera Sur
Managua, Nicaragua
Tel: [505] (2) 666010; Fax: [505] (2) 666074
US Mailing Address: APO AA 34021

Embassy of Nicaragua
1627 New Hampshire Avenue NW
Washington, DC 20009
Tel: (202) 939-6570; Fax: (202) 939-6545

American Chamber of Commerce of Nicaragua
Apdo. Postal 2720
Managua, Nicaragua
Tel: [505] (2) 673-099; Fax: [505] (2) 673-098

Niger

U.S. Embassy, Consular Section
Rue des Ambassades
B.P. 11201
Niamey, Niger
Tel: [227] 72-26-61/4; Fax: [227] 73-31-67
US Mailing Address: Dept. of State, Washington DC 20521-2420

Embassy of the Republic of Niger
2204 R Street NW
Washington, DC 20008
Tel: (202) 483-4224; Fax: (202) 483-3169

Nigeria

U.S. Embassy, Consular Section
2 Eleke Crescent
P.O. Box 554
Lagos, Nigeria
Tel: [234] (1) 261-0097; Fax: [234] (1) 261-0257
US Mailing Address: Dept. of State, Washington DC 20521-8300

Embassy of the Federal Republic of Nigeria
1333 - 16th Street NW
Washington, DC 20036
Tel: (202) 986-8400

Norway

U.S. Embassy, Consular Section
Drammensveien 18
0244 Oslo 2, Norway
Tel: [47] 22-44-85-50; Fax: [47] 22-44-33-63
US Mailing Address: PSC 69, Box 1000, APO AE 09707

Royal Norwegian Embassy
2720 - 34th Street NW
Washington, DC 20008
Tel: (202) 333-6000; Fax: (202) 337-0870
Web site: www.norway.org/

American Club in Oslo - AmCham Norway
Drammensveien 20C
N-0255 Oslo, Norway
Tel: [47] 22-54-60-40; Fax: [47] 22-54-67-20
Email: amchamno@online.no

Oman

U.S. Embassy, Consular Section
P.O. Box 202, Code 115
Muscat, Oman
Tel: [968] 698-989, 699-049; Fax: [968] 699-779

Embassy of the Sultanate of Oman
2535 Belmont Road NW
Washington, DC 20008
Tel: (202) 387-1980; Fax: (202) 745-4933

Pakistan

U.S. Consulate General
Diplomatic Enclave
Ramna 5
Islamabad, Pakistan
Tel: [92] (51) 826-161 through 79; Fax: [92] (51) 214-222
US Mailing Address: P.O. Box 1048,Unit 62200, APO AE 09812-2200

U.S. Consulate General
8 Abdullah Haroon Rd.
Karachi, Pakistan
Tel: [92] (21) 568-5170, 21-568-5170 (FCS)
Fax: [92] (21) 568-3089, 21-568-1381 (FCS)
US Mailing Address: PSC 1241, Box 2000,Unit 6220, APO AE 09814-2400

U.S. Consulate General
50 Empress Rd.
New Simla Hills
P.O.Box 1048, Gulberg 5
Lahore, Pakistan
Tel: [92] (42) 636-5530; Fax: [92] (42) 636-5177
US Mailing Address: Unit 62216, APO AE 09812-2216

Embassy of Pakistan
2315 Massachusetts Avenue NW
Washington, DC 20008
Tel: (202) 939-6200; Fax: (202) 387-0484
Web site: www.imran.com/Pakistan/Pakistan_Embassy.html

American Business Council of Pakistan
GPO Box 1322
74000 Karachi, Pakistan
Tel: [92] (21) 526436; Fax: [92] (21) 568-3935

Panama

U.S. Embassy, Consular Section
Apartado 6959
Panama 5, Rep. de Panama
Tel: [507] 227-1777; Fax: [507] 227-1964
US Mailing Address: Unit 0945, APO AA 34002

Embassy of the Republic of Panama
2862 McGill Terrace NW
Washington, DC 20008
Tel: (202) 483-1407; Fax: (202) 483-8413

American Chamber of Commerce & Industry of Panama
P.O. Box 168
Balboa, Anacon
Panama City, Rep. of Panama
Tel: [507] 269-3881; Fax: [507] 223-3508

Papua New Guinea

U.S. Embassy, Consular Section
P.O. Box 1492
Port Moresby, Papua New Guinea
Tel: [675] 321-1455; Fax: [675] 321-3423
US Mailing Address: APO AE 96553

Embassy of Papua New Guinea
1615 New Hampshire Avenue NW, 3rd Floor
Washington, DC 20009
Tel: (202) 745-3680; Fax: (202) 745-3679
Email: Kundu Wash@AOL.com

Paraguay

U.S. Embassy, Consular Section
1776 Mariscal Lopez Ave.
Casilla Postal 402
Asuncion, Paraguay
Tel: [595] (21) 213-715; Fax: [595] (21) 213-728
US Mailing Address: Unit 4711, APO AA 34036-0001

Embassy of Paraguay
2400 Massachusetts Avenue NW
Washington, DC 20008
Tel: (202) 483-6960; Fax: (202) 234-4508

Paraguayan-American Chamber of Commerce
General Diaz 521
Edif. Internacional El Faro, Piso 4
Asuncion, Paraguay
Tel: [595] (21) 442-135; Fax: [595] (21) 442-135
Email: pamchamb@infonet.com.py

Peru

U.S. Embassy, Consular Section
Avenida la Encalada
Block 17, Monterrico
Lima, Peru
Tel: [51] (1) 434-3000; Fax: [51] (1) 433-303
US Mailing Address: APO AA 34031-5000

Embassy of Peru
1700 Massachusetts Avenue NW
Washington, DC 20036
Tel: (202) 833-9860; Fax: (202) 659-8124

American Chamber of Commerce of Peru
Av. Ricardo Palma 836
Miraflores
Lima 18, Peru
Tel: [51] (1) 241-0708; Fax: [51] (1) 241-0709
Email: amcham@amcham.org.pe

Philippines

U.S. Embassy, Consular Section
1201 Roxas Blvd.
Manila 1000, The Philippines
Tel: [63] (2) 523-1001; Fax: [63] (2) 522-4361
US Mailing Address: APO AP 96440

Embassy of the Philippines
1600 Massachusetts Avenue NW
Washington, DC 20036
Tel: (202) 467-9300; Fax: (202) 328-7614

American Chamber of Commerce of the Philippines
P.O. Box 2562, MCC
Manila, The Philippines
Tel: [63] (2) 818-7911; Fax: [63] (2) 816-6359

Poland

U.S. Embassy, Consular Section
Aleje Ujazdowskie 29/31
00-054 Warsaw, Poland
Tel: [48] (22) 628-3041; Fax: [48] (22) 628-8298
US Mailing Address:Am. Emb. Warsaw, Dept. of State,
Washington, DC 20521-5010

Embassy of the Republic of Poland
2640 - 16th Street NW
Washington, DC 20009
Tel: (202) 234-3800; Fax: (202) 328-6271
Email: embpol@dgs.dgsys.com
Web site: www.wtinet.com/wti/pe.htm

American Chamber of Commerce in Poland
Swietorkrzyska 36/m.6
00-116 Warsaw, Poland
Tel: [48] (22) 622-5525; Fax: [48] (22) 620-2698

Portugal

U.S. Embassy, Consular Section
Avenida das Forcas Armadas
1600 Lisbon, Portugal
Tel: [351] (1) 727-3300; Fax: [351] (1) 726-9721
US Mailing Address: PSC 83, APO AE 09726

Embassy of Portugal
2125 Kalorama Road NW
Washington, DC 20008
Tel: (202) 328-8610; Fax: (202) 462-3726

American Chamber of Commerce in Portugal
Rua De D. Estefania, 155, 5 Esq.
1000 Lisbon, Portugal
Tel: [351] (1) 357-2561; Fax: [351] (1) 357-2580

Qatar

U.S. Embassy
149 Armed Bin Ali St.
Fariq Bin Omran
P.O. Box 2399
Doha, Qatar
Tel: [974] 864-701, 864-702; Fax: [974] 877-499
US Mailing Address: Dept. of State, Washington DC 20521-6130

Embassy of the State of Qatar
4200 Wisconsin Avenue NW
Washington, DC 20016
Tel: (202) 274-1600

Romania

U.S. Embassy, Consular Section
Strada Tudor Arghezi 7-9
Bucharest, Romania
Tel: [40] (1) 210-4042; Fax: [40] (1) 210-0395
US Mailing Address: American Embassy Bucharest,
Department of State, Washington, DC 20521-5260

Embassy of Romania
1607 - 23rd Street NW
Washington, DC 20008
Tel: (202) 332-4846; Fax: (202) 232-4748

American Chamber of Commerce in Romania
Str. M. Eminescu nr. 105-107, Ap. 1
Sector 2
Bucharest, Romania
Tel: [40] (1) 210-9399; Fax: [40] (1) 210-9399

Russia

U.S. Embassy, Consular Section
Novinskiy Bulvar 19/23
Moscow, Russia
Tel: [7] (095) 252-2451; Fax: [7] (095) 956-4261
US Mailing Address: APO AE 09721

U.S. Consulate General
Ulitsa Furshtatskaya 15
St. Petersburg, Russia
Tel: [7] (812) 275-2701, (812) 850-1902 (FCS)
Fax: [7] (812) 110-7022, (812) 850-1903 (FCS)
US Mailing Address: St. Petersburg 191028, PSC 78, Box L, APO AE 09723

U.S. Consulate General
Ulitsa Pushkin 32
Vladivostok, Russia
Tel: [7] (4232) 268-458, (4232) 268-458 (FCS)
Fax: [7] (4232) 268-445, (4232) 268-445 (FCS)
US Mailing Address: Dept. of State, Washington DC 20521-5880

Embassy of the Russian Federation
2650 Wisconsin Avenue NW
Washington, DC 20007
Tel: (202) 298-5700; Fax: (202) 298-5735
Web site: www.seanet.com/RussianPage/RConsulate/RConsulate.html (Consulate in Seattle)

American Chamber of Commerce in Russia
Kosmodamianskaya Nab., 52 Str. 1, 8th Floor
113054 Moscow, Russia
Tel: [7] (095) 961-2141; Fax: [7] (095) 961-2142
Email:amchamru@amcham.ru

Rwanda

U.S. Embassy, Consular Section
Blvd. de la Revolution
B.P. 28
Kigali, Rwanda
Tel: [250] 75601, 75602; Fax: [250] 72128
US Mailing Address: Dept. of State, Washington DC 20521-2210

Embassy of the Republic of Rwanda
1714 New Hampshire Avenue NW
Washington, DC 20009
Tel: (202) 232-2882; Fax: (202) 232-4544
Email: rwandemb@rwandemb.org

St. Kitts & Nevis

Embassy of St. Kitts and Nevis
3216 New Mexico Avenue NW
Washington, DC 20016
Tel: (202) 686-2636; Fax: (202) 686-5740

St. Lucia

Embassy of St. Lucia
3216 New Mexico Avenue NW
Washington, DC 20016
Tel: (202) 364-6792; Fax: (202) 364-6728

St. Vincent & The Grenadines

Embassy of St. Vincent & the Grenadines
3216 New Mexico Avenue NW
Washington, DC 20016
Tel: (202) 364-6730; Fax: (202) 364-6736

Saudi Arabia

U.S. Embassy, Consular Section
P.O. Box 94309
Riyadh 11693, Saudi Arabia
Tel: [966] (1) 488-3800; Fax: [966] (1) 488-7360
US Mailing Address: Unit 61307, APO AE 09803-1307

U.S. Consulate General
P.O. Box 81
Dhahran Airport 31932, Saudi Arabia
Tel: [966] (3) 891-3200, (3) 891-3200 (FCS)
Fax: [966] (3) 891-6816, (3) 891-8332 (FCS)
US Mailing Address: Unit 66803, APO AE 09858-6803

U.S. Consulate General
P.O. Box 149
Jeddah 21411, Saudi Arabia
Tel: [966] (2) 667-0080, (2) 667-0040 (FCS)
Fax: [966] (2) 667-3078, (2) 665-8106 (FCS)
US Mailing Address: Unit 62112, APO AE 09811-2112

American Business Association
P.O. Box 88
Dharan Airport
31932 Dharan, Saudi Arabia
Tel: [966] (3) 857-6464; Fax: [966] (3) 857-8883

Royal Embassy of Saudi Arabia
601 New Hampshire Avenue NW
Washington, DC 20037
Tel: (202) 337-4088; Fax: (202) 342-0271
Web site:www.saudiembassy.net

Senegal

U.S. Embassy
B.P. 49
Avenue Jean XXIII
Dakar, Senegal
Tel: [221] 23-42-96; Fax: [221] 22-29-91
US Mailing Address: Dept. of State, Washington DC 20521-2130

Embassy of the Republic of Senegal
2112 Wyoming Avenue NW
Washington, DC 20008
Tel: (202) 234-0540; Fax: (202) 332-6315

The Seychelles

U.S. Embassy, Consular Section
Victoria House
Box 251
Victoria, Mahe, Seychelles
Tel: [248] 225-256; Fax: [248] 225-189
US Mailing Address: Unit 62501, Box 148, APO AE 09815

Embassy of the Republic of Seychelles
c/o Permanent Mission of Seychelles to the United Nations
820 Second Avenue
New York, NY 10017
Tel: (212) 687-9766; Fax: (212) 972-1786

Sierra Leone

U.S. Embassy, Consular Section
Corner Walpole and Siaka Stevens St.
Freetown, Sierra Leone
Tel: [232] (22) 226-481; Fax: [232] (22) 225-471
US Mailing Address: Dept. of State, Washington DC 20521-2160

Embassy of Sierra Leone
1701 - 19th Street NW
Washington, DC 20009
Tel: (202) 939-9261; Fax: (202) 483-1793

Singapore

U.S. Embassy, Consular Section
30 Hill St.
Singapore 0617
Tel: [65] 338-0251; Fax: [65] 338-4550
US Mailing Address: FPO AP 96534

Embassy of the Republic of Singapore
3501 International Place NW
Washington, DC 20008
Tel: (202) 537-3100; Fax: (202) 537-0876
Email: singemb@bellatlantic.net

American Chamber of Commerce in Singapore
#16-07 Shaw Centre, Scotts Rd.
Singapore 228208
Tel: [65] 235-0077; Fax: [65] 732-5917
Email: info@amcham.org.sg

Slovak Republic

U.S. Embassy
Hviezdoslavovo Namestie 4
81102 Bratislava, Slovak Rep.
Tel: [421] (7) 533-3338; Fax: [421] (7) 533-5439
US Mailing Address: Box 5630, Unit 25402, APO AE 09213-5630

American Chamber of Commerce in the Slovak Republic
Hotel Danube, Rybne nam 1
813 38 Bratislava, Slovak Rep.
Tel: [421] (7) 5340-508; Fax: [421] (7) 5340-556

Embassy of the Slovak Republic
2201 Wisconsin Avenue NW, Suite 250
Washington, DC 20007
Tel: (202) 965-5160; Fax: (202) 965-5166
Email: svkemb@concentric.net.

Slovenia

U.S. Embassy
Box 254
Prazakova 4
1000 Ljubljana, Slovenia
Tel: [386] (61) 301-427; Fax: [386] (61) 301-401
US Mailing Address: AmEmbassy Ljubljana, Department of State, Washington DC 20521-7140

Embassy of the Republic of Slovenia
1525 New Hampshire Avenue NW
Washington, DC 20036
Tel: (202) 667-5363; Fax: (202) 667-4563

South Africa

U.S. Consulate General
Broadway Industries Center
Heerengracht, Foreshore
Cape Town, South Africa
Tel: [27] (21) 214-280, (21) 214-280 (FCS)
Fax: [27] (21) 254-151, (21) 254-151 (FCS)
Web site: africa.com/pages/uscons/page1.htm
US Mailing Address: Dept. of State, Washington DC 20521-2480

U.S. Consulate General
11th Fl., Kline Center
141 Commissioner St.
P.O. Box 2155
Johannesburg, South Africa
Tel: [27] (11) 331-1681, (11) 331-3937 (FCS)
Fax: [27] (11) 331-1327, (11) 331-6178 (FCS)
US Mailing Address: Dept. of State, Washington DC 20521-2500

Embassy of the Republic of South Africa
3051 Massachusetts Avenue NW
Washington, DC 20008
Tel: (202) 232-4400; Fax: (202) 265-1607
Web site: www.southafrica.net/

American Chamber of Commerce in South Africa
P.O. Box 1132
Houghton 2041
Johannesburg, South Africa
Tel: [27] (11) 880-1630; Fax: [27] (11) 880-1632

Spain

U.S. Embassy, Consular Section
Serrano 75
28006 Madrid, Spain
Tel: [34] (1) 587-2200
Fax: [34] (1) 577-5735, (1) 575-8655 (FCS)
US Mailing Address: APO AE 09642

U.S. Consulate General
Paseo Reina Elisenda 23-25
Barcelona, Spain
Tel: [34] (3) 280-2227, (3) 280-2227 (FCS), (3) 205-7705 (FCS)
US Mailing Address: PSC 64, APO AE 09642

Embassy of Spain
2375 Pennsylvania Avenue NW
Washington, DC 20037
Tel: (202) 452-0100; Fax: (202) 833-5670

American Chamber of Commerce in Spain
Avda. Diagonal 477
08036 Barcelona, Spain
Tel: [34] (3) 405-1266; Fax: [34] (3) 405-3124

Sri Lanka

U.S. Embassy, Consular Section
P.O. Box 106
210 Galle Rd.
Colombo 3, Sri Lanka
Tel: [94] (1) 448-007; Fax: [94] (1) 437-345
US Mailing Address: Dept. of State, Washington DC 20521-6100

Embassy of the Democratic Socialist Republic of Sri Lanka
2148 Wyoming Avenue NW
Washington, DC 20008
Tel: (202) 483-4025; Fax: (202) 232-7181
Email: slembasy@clark.net
Web site: www.slembassy.org

American Chamber of Commerce of Sri Lanka
Colombo Hilton, 3rd Fl.
P.O. Box 1000
Colombo 1, Sri Lanka
Tel: [94] (1) 336-074; Fax: [94] (1) 336-072

Sudan

U.S. Embassy
P.O. Box 699
Khartoum, Sudan
Tel: [249] (11) 774-700, 774-611, Fax: [249] (11) 774-137
US Mailing Address: APO AE 09829

Embassy of the Republic of the Sudan
2210 Massachusetts Avenue NW
Washington, DC 20008
Tel: (202) 338-8565; Fax: (202) 667-2406

Suriname

U.S. Embassy, Consular Section
Dr. Sophie Redmondstraat 129
P.O. Box 1821
Paramaribo, Suriname
Tel: [597] 472-900; Fax: [597] 479-829
US Mailing Address: AmEmbassy Paramaribo, Dept. of State, Washington DC 20521-3390

Embassy of the Republic of Suriname
4301 Connecticut Avenue NW, Suite 108
Washington, DC 20008
Tel: (202) 244-7488; Fax: (202) 338-7142
Email: embsur@erols.com

Swaziland

U.S. Embassy
Central Bank Bldg., Warner Street
P.O. Box 100
Mbabane, Swaziland
Tel: [268] 46441; Fax: [268] 45959
US Mailing Address: Dept. of State, Washington DC 20521-2350

Embassy of the Kingdom of Swaziland
3400 International Drive NW, Suite 3M
Washington, DC 20008
Tel: (202) 362-6683; Fax: (202) 244-8059

Sweden

U.S. Embassy, Consular Section
Strandvagen 101
S-11589 Stockholm, Sweden
Tel: [46] (8) 783-5300, (8) 783-5346 (FCS)
Fax: [46] (8) 661-1964, (8) 660-9181 (FCS)
Web site: www.usis/usemb.se/mission.html (USIS)
US Mailing Address: Dept. of State, Washington DC 20521-5750

Embassy of Sweden
1501 M Street NW
Washington, DC 20005
Tel: (202) 467-2600; Fax: (202) 467-2656
Web site: www.sweden.nw.dc.us/Sweden/

American Chamber of Commerce in Sweden
P.O. Box 16050
SE-103 21 Stockholm, Sweden
Tel: [46] (8) 506-126-10; Fax: [46] (8) 506-129-10
Email: amcham@chamber.se

Switzerland

U.S. Embassy, Consular Section
Jubilaeumstrasse 93
3005 Bern, Switzerland
Tel: [41] (31) 357-7011; Fax: [41] (31) 357-7344
Web site: www3.itu.ch/EMBASSY/US-embassy/
US Mailing Address: Dept. of State, Washington DC 20521-5110

U.S. Mission to the World Trade Organization
America Center of Geneva
World Trade Center II
Geneva Airport
Route de Pre-Bois 29
Geneva, Switzerland
Tel: [41] (22) 798-1605, 798-1615, 22-749-5281 (FCS), 22-749-5308 (FCS)
US Mailing Address: U.S. Dept. of State (Geneva), Washington, D.C. 20521-5120

Embassy of Switzerland
2900 Cathedral Avenue NW
Washington, DC 20008
Tel: (202) 745-7900; Fax: (202) 387-2564
Web site: www.swissemb.org

Swiss-American Chamber of Commerce
Talacker 41
8001 Zurich, Switzerland
Tel: [41] (1) 211-2454; Fax: [41] (1) 211-9572
Email: info@amcham.ch
Web site: http://www.amcham.ch

Syria

U.S. Embassy
Abou Roumaneh
Al-Mansur St., No. 2
P.O. Box 29
Damascus, Syria
Tel: [963] (11) 333-2814; Fax: [963] (11) 224-7938
US Mailing Address: Dept. of State, Washington DC 20521-6110

Embassy of the Syrian Arab Republic
2215 Wyoming Avenue NW
Washington, DC 20008
Tel: (202) 232-6313; Fax: (202) 234-9548

Taiwan (Republic of China)

Although the United States does not maintain official relations with Taiwan (Republic of China), unofficial commercial relations are maintained through the American Institute in Taiwan and the Coordination Council for North American Affairs.

American Institute in Taiwan
7 Lane 134
Hsin Yi Road, Section 3
Taipei 106, Taiwan, R.O.C.
Tel: [886] (2) 709-2000; Fax: [886] (2) 709-2013
Web site: ait.org.tw/

American Institute in Taiwan, Trade Center
Room 3207, International Trade Building
Taipei World Trade Center
333 Keelung Road Section 1
Taipei 10548, Taiwan
Tel: [886] (2) 720-1550; Fax: [886] (2) 757-7162
Email: aitcomm@arc.org.tw

American Institute in Taiwan, Washington DC
1700 North Moore Street, Suite 1700
Arlington, VA 22209-1996
Tel: (703) 525-8474; Fax: (703) 841-1385

American Chamber of Commerce in Taipei
Suite 1012, Chia Hsin Bldg. Annex
86 Chung Shan N Road, Sec. 2
Taipei 104 Taiwan, R.O.C.
Tel: [886] (2) 581-7089; Fax: [886] (2) 542-3376
Email: amcham@amcham.com.tw

Tajikistan

U.S. Embassy
c/o Hotel October
105A Prospekt Rudaki
Dushanbe, Tajikistan
Tel: [7] (3772) 21-03-56

Tanzania

U.S. Embassy, Consular Section
P.O. Box 9123
Dar es Salaam, Tanzania
Tel: [255] (51) 666010; Fax: [255] (51) 666701
US Mailing Address: Dept. of State, Washington DC 20521-2140

Embassy of the United Republic of Tanzania
2139 R Street NW
Washington, DC 20008
Tel: (202) 939-6125; Fax: (202) 797-7408
Email: tanz-us@clark.net

Thailand

U.S. Embassy, Consular Section
125 Wireless Rd.
Bangkok, Thailand
Tel: [66] (2) 205-4000; Fax: [66] (2) 254-2990
US Mailing Address: APO AP 96546

Royal Thai Embassy
1024 Wisconsin Avenue NW, Suite 401
Washington, DC 20007
Tel: (202) 944-3600; Fax: (202) 944-3611
Email : thai.wsn@thaiembdc.orgx
Web site: http://www.thaiembdc.org

Asia-Pacific Council of American Chambers of Commerce
c/o Citibank N.A.
20th Fl., 82 N. Sathorn Rd.
Bangkok 10500, Thailand
Tel: [66] (2) 232-3020; Fax: [66] (2) 639-2571

American Chamber of Commerce in Thailand
140 Wireless Road, 7th Fl.
10330 Bangkok, Thailand
Tel: [66] (2) 251-9266; Fax: [66] (2) 651-4472

Togo

U.S. Embassy, Consular Section
Rue Pelletier Caventou and Rue Vauban
B.P. 852
Lome, Togo
Tel: [228] 21-77-17; Fax: [228] 21-79-52

Embassy of the Republic of Togo
2208 Massachusetts Avenue NW
Washington, DC 20008
Tel: (202) 234-4212; Fax: (202) 232-3190
Email: info@republicoftogo.com

Trinidad & Tobago

Embassy of the Republic of Trinidad & Tobago
1708 Massachusetts Avenue NW
Washington, DC 20036
Tel: (202) 467-6490; Fax: (202) 785-3130

U.S. Embassy, Consular Section
15 Queen's Park West
P.O. Box 752
Port of Spain, Trinidad & Tobago
Tel: [11] (809) 622-6372; Fax: [11] (809) 628-5462
US Mailing Address: Dept. of State, Washington DC 20521-3410

American Chamber of Commerce of Trinidad & Tobago
Trinidad Hilton, Upper Arcade
Lady Young Rd.
Port of Spain, Trinidad & Tobago
Tel: (809) 627-8570; Fax: (809) 627-7405

Tunisia

U.S. Embassy, Consular Section
144 Ave. de la Liberte
1002 Tunis-Belvedere, Tunisia
Tel: [216] (1) 782-566; Fax: [216] (1) 789-719
US Mailing Address: Dept. of State, Washington DC 20521-6360

Embassy of Tunisia
1515 Massachusetts Avenue NW
Washington, DC 20005
Tel: (202) 862-1850; Fax: (202) 862-1858

Turkey

U.S. Embassy, Consular Section
110 Ataturk Blvd.
Ankara, Turkey
Tel: [90] (312) 468-6110; Fax: [90] (312) 467-0019
US Mailing Address: PSC 93, Box 5000, APO AE 09823

U.S. Consulate General
104-108 Mesrutiyet Caddesi
Tepebasi
Istanbul, Turkey
Tel: [90] (212) 251-3602, (212) 293-9146 (FCS)
Fax: [90] (212) 251-2554, (212) 252-2417 (FCS)
US Mailing Address: PSC 97, Box 0002, APO AE 09827-0002

U.S. Commercial Office
Turkish American Association
Sehit Nevres Blvd.
Izmir, Turkey
Tel: [90] (232) 421-3643, 421-3644, 232-441-2446 (FCS), 232-489-0267 (FCS)
US Mailing Address: APO AE 09827

Embassy of the Republic of Turkey
1714 Massachusetts Avenue NW
Washington, DC 20036
Tel: (202) 659-8200
Email: embassy@turkey@org
Web site: www.turkey.org

Turkish-American Businessmen's Association
Barbados Bulvari
Esr. Apr. #48, K.5 D.16
80700 Balmumcu
Istanbul, Turkey
Tel: [90] (212) 274-2824; Fax: [90] (212) 275-9316

Turkmenistan

U.S. Embassy
Pushkin St., No. 9
Ashgabat, Turkmenistan
Tel: [9] (9312) 35-00-45, 35-00-46; Fax: [9] (9312) 51-12-05

Embassy of Turkmenistan
2207 Massachusetts Ave. NW
Washington, DC 20008
Tel: (202) 588-1500; Fax: (202) 588-0697
Web site: www.infi.net/~embassy/

Uganda

U.S. Embassy, Consular Section
10 12 Parliament Avenue
P.O. Box 7007
Kampala, Uganda
Tel: [256] (41) 259-792/5; Fax: [256] (41) 241-863
US Mailing Address: Dept. of State, Washington DC 20521-2190

Embassy of the Republic of Uganda
5911 - 16th Street NW
Washington, DC 20011
Tel: (202) 726-7100; Fax: (202) 726-1727
Email: ugaembassy@rocketmail.com

Ukraine

U.S. Embassy, Consular Section
ul. Yuria Kotsubyinskoho 10
254053 Kiev 53, Ukraine
Tel: [380] (44) 244-7345; Fax: [380] (44) 244-7350
US Mailing Address: Dept. of State, Washington DC 20521-5850

Embassy of Ukraine
3350 M Street NW
Washington, DC 20007
Tel: (202) 333-7507; Fax: (202) 333-7510
Email: infolook@aol.com

American Chamber of Commerce in Ukraine
42-44 Shovkovyehna vul., LL2
252004 Kyiv, Ukraine
Tel: [380] (44) 490-5800; Fax: [380] (44) 490-5801
Email: acc@chamber.ru.kiev.ua

United Arab Emirates

U.S. Embassy, Consular Post
Al-Sudan St.
P.O. Box 4009
Abu Dhabi, United Arab Emirates
Tel: [971] (2) 436-691; Fax: [971] (2) 434-771
US Mailing Address: AmEmbassy Abu Dhabi, Dept. of State, Washington DC 20521-6010

U.S. Consulate General
Dubai International Trade Center, 21st Fl.
P.O. Box 9343
Dubai, United Arab Emirates
Tel: [971] (4) 313-115, (4) 378-584 (FCS)
Fax: [971] (4) 314-043, (4) 313-121 (FCS)
US Mailing Address: Dept. of State, Washington DC 20521-6020

Embassy of the United Arab Emirates
3000 K Street NW, Suite 600
Washington, DC 20007
Tel: (202) 338-6500; Fax: (202) 337-7029

American Business Council of Dubai
P.O. Box 9281
Dubai, United Arab Emirates
Tel: [971] (4) 314-735; Fax: [971] (4) 314-227

United Kingdom

U.S. Embassy, Consular Section
24/31 Grosvenor Sq.
London W1A 1AE , England
Tel: [44] (171) 499-9000; Fax: [44] (171) 409-1637
US Mailing Address: PSC 801, Box 40, FPO AE 09498-4040

U.S. Consulate General
Queen's House
14 Queen Street
Belfast BT1 6EQ, Northern Ireland
Tel: [44] (1232) 328-239; Fax: [44] (1232) 248-482
US Mailing Address: PSC 180, Box 40, APO AE 09498-4040

British Embassy
3100 Massachusetts Avenue NW
Washington, DC 20008
Tel: (202) 462-1340; Fax: (202) 898-4255
Web site: britain.nyc.ny.us/

American Chamber of Commerce of the United Kingdom
75 Brook St.
London W1Y 2EB, England
Tel: [44] (171) 493-0381; Fax: [44] (171) 493-2394

Uruguay

U.S. Embassy, Consular Section
Lauro Muller 1776
Montevideo, Uruguay
Tel: [598] (2) 23-60-61; Fax: [598] (2) 48-86-11
US Mailing Address: APO AA 34035

Embassy of Uruguay
1918 F Street NW
Washington, DC 20006
Tel: (202) 331-1313; Fax: (202) 331-8142
Email: uruguay embassy.org
Web site: www.embassy.org/uruguay/

Chamber of Commerce Uruguay-USA
Plaza Independencia 831 Of. 209
Casilla de Correo 809
C.P. 11100
Montevideo, Uruguay
Tel: [598] (2) 908-91-86; Fax: [598] (2) 908-91-87
Email: amcham@zfm.com

Uzbekistan

U.S. Embassy, Consular Section
ul. Chilanzarskaya 82
Tashkent, Uzbekistan
Tel: [7] (3712) 77-14-07; Fax: [7] (3712) 40-63-35
US Mailing Address: Dept. of State, Washington DC 20521-7110

Embassy of the Republic of Uzbekistan
1511 K Street NW, Suite 619
Washington, DC 20005
Tel: (202) 887-5300

Venezuela

U.S. Embassy, Consular Section
Calle Suapure y Calle F
Colinas de Valle Arriba
P.O. Box 62291
Caracas 1060-A, Venezuela
Tel: [58] (2) 977-2011; Fax: [58] (2) 977-0843
US Mailing Address: APO AA 34037

Embassy of the Republic of Venezuela
1099 - 30th Street NW
Washington, DC 20007
Tel: (202) 342-2214; Fax: (202) 342-6820
Email: embavene@dgsys.com
Web site: http://www.embavenez-us.org

Venezuelan-American Chamber of Commerce & Industry
2 da. Av. de Campo Alegre
Apdo. 5181
1010-A Caracas, Venezuela
Tel: [58] (2) 263-0833; Fax: [58] (2) 263-0586

Vietnam

U.S. Embassy
7 Lang Ha
Ba Dinh District
Hanoi, Socialist Republic of Vietnam
Tel: [84] (4) 843-1500; Fax: [84] (4) 835-0484
US Mailing Address: PSC 461, Box 400, FPO AP 96521-0002

Embassy of the Socialist Republic of Vietnam
1233 - 20th Street NW, Suite 400
Washington, DC 20036
Tel: (202) 861-0737; Fax: (202) 861-0917
Email: vietnamembassy@msn.com

American Chamber of Commerce in Vietnam
17 Ngo Quyen, Unit #01
Hanoi, Vietnam
Tel: [84] (4) 825-1950; Fax: [84] (4) 824-3960

American Chamber of Commerce in Vietnam
30 Le Thanh Ton; Dist. 1
Ho Chi Minh City, Vietnam
Tel: [84] (8) 829-5892; Fax: [84] (8) 829-6078

Western Samoa

U.S. Embassy, Consular Section
5th Fl. Beach Road; P.O. Box 3430
Apia, Western Samoa
Tel: [685] 21631; Fax: [685] 22030
US Mailing Address: Dept. of State, Washington DC 20521-4400

Embassy of Western Samoa
c/o Western Samoan Mission to the U.N.
820 Second Avenue, Suite 800D
New York, NY 10017
Tel: (212) 599-6196; Fax: (212) 599-0797

Yemen

U.S. Embassy Consular Section
Dhahr Himyar Zone, Sheraton Hotel District
P.O. Box 22347
Sanaa, Republic of Yemen
Tel: [967] (1) 238-843/52; Fax: [967] (1) 251-563
US Mailing Address: Dept. of State, Washington DC 20521-6330

Embassy of the Republic of Yemen
2600 Virginia Avenue NW, Suite 705
Washington, DC 20037
Tel: (202) 965-4760; Fax: (202) 337-2017

Yugoslavia

U.S. Embassy
Kneza Milosa 50
Belgrade, Serbia, Yugoslavia
Tel: [381] (11) 645-655; Fax: [381] (11) 645-221
US Mailing Address: Unit 25402, APO AE 09213-5070

Embassy of the Federal Republic of Yugoslavia
2410 California Street NW
Washington, DC 20008
Tel: (202) 462-6566

Zaire

U.S. Embassy
310 Avenue de Aviateurs
Kinshasa, Zaire
Tel: [243] (12) 21532, (88) 43608; Fax: [243] (12) 21232, (88) 00228
US Mailing Address: Unit 31550, APO AE 09828

Embassy of the Republic of Zaire
1800 New Hampshire Avenue NW
Washington, DC 20009
Tel: (202) 234-7690; Fax: (202) 686-3631

Zambia

U.S. Embassy
P.O. Box 31617
Lusaka, Zambia
Tel: [260] (1) 250-955; Fax: [260] (1) 252-225
US Mailing Address: Dept. of State, Washington DC 20521-2310

Embassy of the Republic of Zambia
2419 Massachusetts Avenue NW
Washington, DC 20008
Tel: (202) 265-9717; Fax: (202) 332-0826

Zimbabwe

U.S. Embassy
P.O. Box 3340
Harare, Zimbabwe
Tel: [263] (4) 794-521; Fax: [263] (4) 796-488
US Mailing Address: Dept. of State, Washington DC 20521-2180

Embassy of the Republic of Zimbabwe
1608 New Hampshire Avenue NW
Washington, DC 20009
Tel: (202) 332-7100; Fax: (202) 483-9326

Appendix V

Selected Bibliography

AgExporter. Monthly magazine published by U.S. Department of Agriculture's Foreign Agricultural Service. For businesses selling farm products overseas; provides tips on exporting, descriptions of markets with the greatest sales potential, and information on export assistance available from the U.S. Department of Agriculture. The audience is U.S. agricultural producers, exporters, trade organizations, state departments of agriculture and any other export-oriented organization. Cost: $59, Domestic; $68, International. Order from NTIS, 5285 Port Royal Road, Springfield, VA 22161; Tel: (703) 605-6060; Fax: (703) 605-6900; Email: info@ntis.fedworld.gov; Web site: www.fedworld.gov.

Agricultural Trade Highlights. This monthly report has been discontinued.

AID Procurement Information Bulletin. Advertises notices of intended procurement of Agency for International Development-financed commodities. Available from USAID's Office of Small and Disadvantaged Business Utilization/Minority Resource Center, Washington, DC 20523-1414; Tel: (202) 712-1500; Fax: (202) 216-3056. The *Bulletin* is also posted on AID's web site. Go to www.info.usaid.gov/ and look under "Business & Procurement." Subscription cost: free.

American Export Register. This two-volume directory of nearly 50,000 U.S. exporters and the materials, products, or services they sell internationally is published annually. Advertising is accepted. The cost is $100 for print,; $125 for cd rom. Contact Thomas Publishing Company, Inc., Five Penn Plaza, New York, NY 10001; Tel: (212) 290-7355; Fax: (212) 290-8878; Email: info@aernet.com.

Blunders in International Business. By David Ricks. Full of anecdotes covering mistakes and blunders from all aspects of international business including marketing, management, production, translation, and strategy. Cost: $20.95. Available from Blackwell Publishers, 238 Main St., Cambridge, MA 02142; Tel: (617) 876-7000, (800) 903-1181; Web site: www.blackwellpublishers.co.uk.

Breaking Into the Trade Game: A Small Business Guide to Exporting. Both a comprehensive how-to manual and a reference book providing the reader with the contacts and resources to ease entry into markets around the world. Highlights export success stories of small businesses. Cost: free. Available from the Small Business Administration district offices or from the main office at 409 Third St. SW, Washington, DC 20416; Tel: (800) 8-ASK-SBA, (202) 205-6720; Web site: www.sbaonline.sba.gov.

Bureau of the Census Foreign Trade Report: Annual U.S. Exports, Harmonized Schedule B Commodity by Country, FT 447 and ***Bureau of the Census Foreign Trade Report: Monthly Exports and Imports***, SITC Commodity by Country, FT 925. Available on CD-ROM, $1,200 for an annual subscription, $150 for one month. Available from the Bureau of the Census, Tel: (301) 457-4100; Fax: (301) 457-4714 (General info), (301) 457-3842 (Orders only); Web site: www.census.gov

Business America: The Magazine of International Trade. Monthly publication of the Department of Commerce contains country-by-country marketing reports, incisive economic analyses, worldwide trade leads, advance notice of planned exhibitions of U.S. products worldwide, and success stories of export marketing. Annual subscriptions cost $47. (S/N 703-011-00000-4). Contact Superintendent of Documents, U.S. Government Printing Office, Washington, DC 20402; Tel: (202) 512-1800; Web site: www.access.gpo.gov/su_docs.

Commerce Business Daily (CBD). Published daily, Monday through Friday (except holidays), by the Department of Commerce, CBD lists government procurement invitations, contract awards, subcontracting leads, sales of surplus property, and foreign business opportunities as well as certain foreign government procurements. A first-class mail subscription is $324 per year or $162 for six months; second-class, $275 per year or $137.50 for six months (GPO S/N 703-013-00000-7.) Contact Superintendent of Documents, U.S. Government Printing Office, Washington, DC 20402; Tel: (202) 512-1800; Web site: www.access.gpo.gov/su_docs. It is also available through the Internet for $95 to $195 per year. Contact Loren Data Corp., 4640 Admiralty Way, Suite 430, Marina del Rey, CA 90292; Tel: (310) 827-7400; Email: info@ld.com.; Web site: www.ld.com.

Country Commercial Guides. Prepared overseas by the Commerce Department and the State Department and other agencies of the U.S. Trade Promotion Coordinating Committee. Each Guide presents information on one country's commercial environment including market conditions, economic situations, political environment, best export sectors, trade regulations, investment incentives, finance techniques, upcoming trade events, marketing strategies, services for exporters, business travel tips, listings of contacts, and more. More than 100 CCGs are now available. They can be accessed through the NTDB, the EBB, or the State Department's web site at http://www.state.gov/. To purchase separate CCGs, contact NTIS; Tel: (703) 605-6060; Fax: (703) 605-6900; Email: infor@ntis.fedworld.gov; Web site: http://www.fedworld.gov.

Dictionary of International Trade, 3rd Edition. By Edward G. Hinkelman. More than 4,000 international trade, economic, banking, legal, and shipping terms, plus trade organizations, addresses, maps and tables. Cost: $32.00. Available from World Trade Press, 1450 Grant Avenue, Suite 204, Novato, CA 94945; Tel: (415) 898-1124; Fax: (415) 898-1080; Email: WorldPress@aol.com.; Web site: www.worldtradepress.com.

Directory of United States Exporters. Annual publication listing U.S. export firms, export executives, and products exported. Cost: $450.00. Available from the Journal of Commerce, Two World Trade Center, 27th Fl., New York, NY 10048; Tel: (212) 837-7000.

Do's and Taboos ... A series of paperback books with tips on international business and etiquette. Titles include *Do's and Taboos Around the World, Do's and Taboos of Hosting International Visitors, Do's and Taboos of International Trade, Do's and Taboos of Preparing for your Trip Abroad,* and *Do's and Taboos of Using English Around the World.* All are by Roger E. Axtell and are published by John Wiley & Sons, 605 Third Ave., New York, NY 10158-0012; Tel: (212) 850-6000, (800) 225-5945 (orders); Fax: (212) 850-6008.

Economic Bulletin Board (EBB). The PC-based EBB is an on-line source for trade leads as well as the latest statistical releases from the Bureau of the Census, the Bureau of Economic Analysis, the Bureau of Labor Statistics, the Federal Reserve Board, the Department of the Treasury, and other federal agencies. It has been divided into two separate components: *State of the Nation* and *GLOBUS.* Internet Connection charges are $50 per quarter or $150 per year for unlimited access to the STAT-USA site. For more information, or to order, contact Stat-USA at Tel: (800) STAT-USA or (202) 482-1986; Fax: (202) 482-2164; Web site: www.stat-usa.gov.

The Economist. Weekly publication on current affairs and business. Includes reports, analysis, and comments on key events in business, finance, science, and technology. Special editorial surveys focus on specific countries, industries, or markets. Cost: $125 for one year. Available in the U.S. from The Economist, P.O. Box 58524, Boulder, CO 80322-8524; Tel: (800) 456-6086; Fax: (800) 666-0079.

Economist Intelligence Unit. A publishing company which sells research reports, country profiles, newsletters, and online information to help companies operate and expand abroad. Also sells individual country studies, quarterly country reports, and forecasts. For more information, contact the Economist Intelligence Unit, 111 W. 57th St., 11th Fl., New York, NY 10019; Tel: (212) 554-0600; Fax: (212) 586-1181; Web site: www.eiu.com.

Europa World Year Book. Annual. Provides analytical, statistical, and directory information on each country's economic, social, and political structure. Often available at public libraries. Two volumes. Cost: $815.00. Order in the U.S. from: Gale Group, P.O. Box 95501, Chicago, IL 60694-5501; Tel: (800) 877-GALE; Fax: (800) 414-5043; Email: galeord@gale.com; Web site: www.gale.com/gale.html.

Export Administration Regulations. Annual subscription provides the basic manual and supplemental updates for about a year. The EAR were recently restructured to clarify the regulatory language, simplify their use, and to generally make the export control regulations more user-friendly. These changes were published in an interim rule on March 25, 1996, in the Federal Register. The EAR are found in 15 Code of Federal Regulations (CFR), chapter VII, subchapter C. The National Technical Information Service (NTIS) will provide the EAR in electronic or paper formats with three update bulletins (to the those subscribing to the paper version) per cycle. The annual subscription fee is $89.00 for the paper format, $252.00 for the electronic version, and $100 for cd rom. For additional information on the EAR and their availability, contact NTIS, 5285 Port Royal Road, Springfield, VA 22161; Tel: (703) 605-6060; Fax: (703) 3605-6900; Email: info@ntis.fedworld.gov; Web site: www.fedworld.gov.

Export Documentation. By Donald E. Ewert and Richard Brown. Contains hundreds of samples of documents, such as quotation analyses, letters of credit, draft collection letters, purchase orders, shipper's letters of instructions, export license applications, and more. Available from: International Trade Institute, 5055 N. Main Street, Dayton, OH 45415; Tel: (937) 276-5995; Fax: (513) 276-5920. Cost: $67.50 each

The Exporter. Monthly magazine on the business of exporting. Available from Trade Data Reports, 90 John Street, Suite 505, New York, NY 10038; Tel: (212) 587-1340; Fax: (212) 587-1344. Annual subscription cost: $218.

Exporters' Encyclopedia. Annual handbook covering more than 220 world markets. Annual cost: $565.00. Available from Dun's Information Services, Business Reference Solutions Dept., 3 Sylvan Way, Parsippany, NJ 07054-3896; Tel: (973) 605-6000, (800) 526-0651.

Export-Import Financing. By Harry M. Venedikian and Gerald Warfield. Cost: $69.95. Available from John Wiley & Sons, 605 Third Ave., New York, NY 10158-0012; Tel: (212) 850-6000, (800) 225-5945 (orders).

Export-Import Procedures & Documentation. By Thomas E. Johnson. Cost: $75.00. Available from AMACOM, P.O. Box 1026, Saranac Lake, NY 12983-1026; Tel: (800) 262-9699 (orders).

Export Reference Manual. Published annually and updated weekly, the manual is a two-volume looseleaf reference service containing up-to-date, country-by-country shipping and market research information. Social, political, economic, and commercial conditions of each country are profiled. Detail is given to policies, regulations, issues, development, and laws pertaining to commerce, especially foreign trade. Contact Bureau of National Affairs, Inc., 9435 Key West Ave., Rockville, MD 20850; Tel: (800) 372-1033; Fax: (800) 253-0332.

Export Today. The "how to" international business magazine for U.S. exporters. Export Today, 733 15th Street, N.W., Suite 1100, Washington, D.C. 20005; Tel: (202) 737-1060, Fax: (202) 783-5966. 8 issues/year, Cost: $49.00.

Foreign Agricultural Service Attache Country Reports. FAS overseas offices regularly prepare food and agricultural market and trade reports on more than 150 products. These reports include such topics as: production, supply and distribution situation; trade trends and forecasts; foreign government legislation and regulations; and trade policies affecting U.S. trade. Reports for the current month, current year and select reports for the previous year are available on the FAS Home Page (www.fas.usda.gov). Some reports can also be accessed through the Department of Commerce's EBB or the NTDB.

Financing and Insuring Exports: A User's Guide to Ex-Im Bank and FCIA Programs. A reference guide to Ex-Im Bank and FCIA programs for commercial bankers, other private lenders, and exporters. Cost: $75.00. Contact Ex-Im Bank, 811 Vermont Avenue, NW, Washington, DC 20571; Tel: (800) 565-EXIM, (202) 565-3946; Web site: www.exim.gov

FINDEX: The Worldwide Directory of Market Research Reports, Studies and Surveys. This reference guide to commercially available market and business research, including international market research, contains listings of thousands of reports, studies, and surveys. Prices vary depending on whether customers order print, CD-ROM, or online versions. Contact Kalorama Information, 7200 Wisconsin Avenue,

Bethesda, MD 20814; Tel: (800) 298-5699; Email: order@findexonline.com; Web site: www.marketresearch.com.

The Global Marketing Imperative: Positioning Your Company for the New World of Business. By Michael Czinkota, et. al. Cost: $27.95. Available from NTC Contemporary Publishing, 4255 W. Touhy Ave., Lincolnwood, IL 60646-1975; Tel: (847) 679-5500, (800) 323-4900 (orders); Fax: (847) 679-2494.

The Global Road Warrior. An ultra-pragmatic reference resource for the international business traveler and communicator. For each country, sections on: Country At-a-Glance, Business Travel, Essential Terms, Communications, Business Services, Electrical Requirements, Hardware and Software Technical Support, Internet Connection, Business Culture, Business Ceneters, World Rankings. Print Version: 85 countries, 665 pages, US$29.95. CD-ROM (Cross-platform PC Windows and Mac): 106 countries, approximately 1,400 print pages, US$39.95. Available from World Trade Press, 1450 Grant Avenue, Suite 204, Novato, CA 94945; Tel: (415) 898-1124; Fax: (415) 898-1080; Email: WorldPress@aol.com.; Web site: www.worldtradepress.com.

ICC Guide to Documentary Credit Operations. International Chamber of Commerce, Publication 515. Cost: $39.95. Order from: ICC Publishing Inc., 156 Fifth Avenue, New York, NY 10010; Tel: (212) 206-1150; Fax: (212) 633-6025; Web site: www.icc-ibcc.org/.

Incoterms 1990 and ***Guide to Incoterms 1990.*** International Chamber of Commerce Publications 460 and 461/90. Order from: ICC Publishing Inc., 156 Fifth Avenue, New York, NY 10010; Tel: (212) 206-1150; Fax: (212) 633-6025; Web site: www.icc-ibcc.org/.

Industry Sector Analyses (ISAs). Prepared annually by the commercial sections of American embassies for the U.S. Department of Commerce's US&FCS. Available on the National Trade Data Bank (NTDB). For more information contact Stat-USA at Tel: (800) STAT-USA or (202) 482-1986; Fax: (202) 482-2164; Web site: www.stat-usa.gov.

Inside Washington: Government Resources for International Business and ***Power Money: The International Executive's Guide to Government Resources.*** These publications are complete source books on government assistance programs and services. The cost for *Inside Washington* is $49.95. The cost for *Power Money* is $35.00. For more information, contact Delphos International, 1101 30th St. NW, Suite 200, Washington, DC 20007; Tel: (202) 337-6300; Fax: (202) 333-1158.

Intercultural Interacting. By V. Lynn Tyler. Explains the elements of interacting with people from other cultures; includes learning exercises. Available from David M. Kennedy Center for International Studies, Publication Services, Brigham Young University, P.O. Box 24538, Provo, UT 84602-4538; Tel: (801) 378-6528, (800) 528-6279.

The International Economic Review (IER). Monthly staff publication of the U.S. International Trade Commision Office of Economics. The IER reports are intended to keep the Commission informed about significant developments in international economics and trade and to provide technical information and advice on international trade matters to policy makers. It can be viewed on the Internet for free on the USITC's web site at www.usitc.gov/.

International Financial Statistics (IFS). Published monthly by the International Monetary Fund, IFS presents statistics on exchange rates, money and banking, production, government finance, interest rates, and other subjects. It is available by annual subscription for $246, which includes 12 issues plus the yearbook. Single copies are $30, or $65 for the yearbook only. Contact the International Monetary Fund, Publication Services, 700 19th Street NW, Washington, DC 20431; Tel: (202) 623-7430; Fax: (202) 623-7201; Email: publications@imf.org; Web site: www.imf.org.

International Trade Reporter: Current Reports. Weekly newsletter. Cost: $1,159 per year. Contact Bureau of National Affairs, Inc., 9435 Key West Ave., Rockville, MD 20850; Tel: (800) 372-1033; Fax: (800) 253-0332; Email: icustrel@bna.com.

Journal of Commerce. Daily newspaper. Information on domestic and foreign economic developments plus export opportunities, shipyards, agricultural trade leads, and trade information. Feature articles on tariff and non-tariff barriers, licensing controls, joint ventures, and trade legislation in foreign countries. Order from Journal of Commerce, Two World Trade Center, 27th Fl., New York, NY 10048; Tel: (800) 221-3777, (212) 837-7000.

National Trade Data Bank (NTDB). The NTDB contains export promotion and international trade data collected by 15 U.S. government agencies. Updated each month and released on two CD-ROM discs, the data bank enables access to more than 200,000 documents. The NTDB contains the latest Census data on U.S. imports and exports by commodity and country; the complete set of Country Commercial Guides; current market research reports compiled by the Commercial Service; the complete Commercial Service International Contacts (CSIS), which contains over 80,000 names and addresses of individuals and firms abroad interested in importing U.S. products; State Department country reports on economic policy and trade practices; the publications *Export Yellow Pages* and the *National Trade Estimates Report on Foreign Trade Barriers*; the *Export Promotion Calendar*; and many other data series.

The NTDB can be purchased in the form of CD-ROM discs for $59 per monthly issue or $575 for a 12-month subscription. Non-U.S. shipments will be charged $75 monthly or $775 for an annual subscription. It is also available on the Internet through Stat-USA. The NTDB is also available at over 1,100 federal depository libraries nationwide. Call the Trade Information Center at (800) USA-TRADE for a list of these libraries.

For more information, or to order, contact Stat-USA at Tel: (800) STAT-USA or (202) 482-1986; Fax: (202) 482-2164; Email: stat-usa@doc.gov; Web site: www.stat-usa.gov.

National Trade Estimate Report on Foreign Trade Barriers. Annual report that surveys significant foreign barriers to U.S. exports, based upon information compiled within USTR, the U.S. Departments of Commerce and Agriculture, and other U.S. government agencies. Discusses more than 40 of the largest export markets for the United States. Available from the U.S. Trade Representative (USTR), 600 17th Street NW, Washington, DC 20508; Tel: (202) 395-3230. Cost: free.

OAG Air Cargo Guide. A basic reference publication for shipping freight by air. Contains current domestic and international cargo flight schedules, information on air carriers' special services, labeling, airline, and aircraft decodings, air carrier and freight forwarders directory, cargo charter information, small package service, and more. Cost: $239 per year. Available from Official Airline Guides, Inc., Transportation Guides Division, P.O. Box 56717, Boulder, CO 80322; Tel: (800) 323-3537.

Official Export Guide. Edited by Tery Moran-Lever. Gives comprehensive export information from source to market for shippers, freight forwarders, and transportation companies. Features marketing, shipping, and documentation information. Includes nearly 200 country profiles with trade data to find new markets, surveys of major world ports, and Export Administration Regulations. Cost: $369.00. Available from the North American Publishing Company, 401 N. Broad St., Philadelphia PA 19108; Tel: (215) 238-5300.

Organization for Economic Cooperation and Development (OECD) Economic Surveys. These economic development surveys produced by OECD cover each of the 27-member OECD countries individually. Each survey presents a detailed analysis of recent developments in market demand, production, employment, and prices and wages. Short-term forecasts and analyses of medium-term problems relevant to economic policies are provided. An annual subscription costs $395; a single copy, $26. Contact OECD Washington Center, 2001 L Street NW, Suite 650, Washington, DC 20036; Tel: (202) 785-6323; Fax: (202) 785-0350; Web site: www.oecdwash.org.

Passport to the World series. A series of books on business cultures in more than 25 different countries. Cost: $6.95 each. Available from World Trade Press, 1450 Grant Avenue, Suite 204, Novato, CA 94945; Tel: (415) 898-1124; Fax: (415) 898-1080; Email: WorldPress@aol.com; Web site. www.worldtradepress.com.

Price Waterhouse Doing Business in ... series. Each book covers investment climate, accounting, taxation, business law, and other information on doing business in an individual country. Available free from Price Waterhouse offices around the U.S. or from the national office. Price Waterhouse, 1251 Ave. of the Americas, New York, NY 10020; Tel: (800) 579-1646; Fax: (212) 259-1706. Cost: $650 for the complete set, including a one year subscription.

Short Course in International Trade Series
Twelve stand-alone training and reference books that teach the key skills of international trade.

A Short Course in International Negotiating
A Short Course in International Marketing
A Short Course in International Payments
A Short Course in International Contracts
A Short Course in International Economics
A Short Course in International Business Culture
A Short Course in International Entrepreneurial Trade
A Short Course in International Marketing Blunders
A Short Course in International Trade Documentation
A Short Course in International Licensing
A Short Course in International Marketing Plans
A Short Course in International Trade Finance

Cost: $19.95 each. Available from World Trade Press, 1450 Grant Avenue, Suite 204, Novato, CA 94945; Tel: (415) 898-1124; Fax: (415) 898-1080; Email: WorldPress@aol.com.; Web site: www.worldtradepress.com.

Thomson Polk World Directory. Annual publication. Lists banks located around the world with addresses of banks and other information. Cost: $309.00 for the annual edition, $345.00 for a one time purchase. Available from: Thomson Financial Publishing, 4709 W. Golf Road, 6th Floor, Skokie, IL 60076; Tel: (800) 321-3373.

Trade Shows Worldwide. Annual publication. Martin Conners and Charity Anne Dorgan, editors. Details of more than 6,800 conventions, conferences, trade shows, and expositions, plus convention centers, exhibit builders, transportation firms, and industry suppliers. Five-year date and location information provided. Covers U.S., Canada, and 60 other countries. Arranged by subject category, location, and name. Cost: $277.00. Available from Gale Group, P.O. Box 95501, Chicago, IL 60694-5501; Tel: (313) 961-2242, (800) 877-GALE; Fax: (800) 414-5043; Email: galeord@gale.com; Web site: www.gale.com.

UN Statistical Yearbook. Published by the United Nations (UN), this yearbook contains data for 220 countries and territories on economic and social subjects including population, agriculture, manufacturing, commodity, export-import trade, and many other areas. Contact United Nations Publications, Room DC2-0853, New York, NY 10017; Tel: (212) 963-8302; Fax: (212) 963-3489; Web site: www.un.org/publications. Updated annually. Cost: $120.

U.S. Global Outlook, 1995-2000 Focuses on seven export growth sectors, including medical equipment, computer software and information services, whose exports are projected to grow at double digit rates between 1995 and 2000. The Global Outlook also assesses U.S. export prospects in 18 key markets among the industrialized nations; the Big Emerging Markets of Asia, Africa and Latin America; and the Economies in Transition of Russia and Eastern Europe. Stock number: 003-009-00050-0. Cost: $20. To order, contact the U.S. Government Printing Office, PO Box 371954, Pittsburgh, PA 15250-7954; Tel: (202) 512-1800; Fax: (202) 512-2250; Web site: www.access.gpo.gov/su_docs.

Wall Street Journal. Daily weekdays. Covers general national and international news, with a focus on finance and business. Also publishes European and Asian editions. Order from WSJ, 200 Burnett Rd., Chicopee, MA; Tel: (800) JOURNAL; Fax: (413) 592-4782; Email: wsj.service@cor.dowjones.com; Web site: www.wsj. com.

World Factbook. Produced annually in July by the CIA, this publication provides country-by-country data on demographics, economy, communications, and defense. To order, contact U.S. Government Printing Office, PO Box 371954, Pittsburgh, PA 15250-7954; Tel: (202) 512-1800; Fax: (202) 512-2250; Web site: www.access.gpo.gov/su_docs. Cost: $59.

World Trade. Monthly magazine. Provides information to help exporters increase global sales. Available from World Trade, 17702 Cowan, Suite 100, Irvine, CA 92714; Tel: (714) 798-3500, Fax: (714) 790-0501.

World Trade Almanac. A reference work with economic, marketing, trade, cultural, legal, and travel surveys for the world's top 100 economies. Available as a book or CD-ROM from World Trade Press, 1450 Grant Avenue, Suite 204, Novato, CA 94945; Tel: (415)898-1124; Fax: (415) 898-1080; Email: WorldPress@aol.com; Web site: www.worldtradepress.com. Cost: $87.00 (print), $89.00 (CD-ROM).